Building Optimism

Building Optimism

Why Our World Looks the Way it Does, and How to Make it Better

Coby Lefkowitz

First published in 2024
Copyright © Coby Lefkowitz 2024
The moral right of the author has been asserted.

ALL RIGHTS RESERVED.

Without limiting the rights under copyright restricted above, no part of this publication may be reproduced, stored in or introduced into a retrieval system, or transmitted, in any form or by any means (electronic, mechanical, photocopying, recording or otherwise), without the prior written permission of the copyright owner of this book. The views of the author belong solely to the author and are not necessarily those of the publisher or the publishing service provider.

ISBN: 978-8-218-52482-1 (paperback)
ISBN: 979-8-218-54977-0 (ebook)

Cover design by Stephen Vosloo
Text design and typesetting by Typography Studio

Table of Contents

Introduction ... 1

PART ONE: FOUNDATIONS OF OPTIMISM

1. On Building Optimism ... 21
2. The Need for Optimism ... 63
3. The Pendulum of Development ... 91
4. Theory Has to Meet Reality—A Common Sense Way of Building ... 117
5. Why Does Everywhere Look the Same? ... 179
6. An Optimistic Foundation ... 215

PART TWO: OPTIMISM IN ACTION

7. How to Create Better Communities ... 249
8. What Better Communities Look Like (And What They Do Not Look Like) ... 275
9. Why Are Some Places More Optimistic Than Others? ... 299
   - *Charleston* ... 301
   - *Santa Barbara* ... 337
   - *Portland* ... 367

10.	The Optimism of Universities	399
11.	Moving Beyond Utilitarianism: In Defense of Beautiful, Aspirational Places	417
12.	On Stewardship	443
13.	A Call to All Who Occupy the Built Environment	469
	Acknowledgements	481
	Image Credits	485
	References	495

For Mom and Dad,
who instilled the optimism within me.

Introduction

Few things impact our lives more than where we live and the world that surrounds us. You might be thinking to yourself that this is obvious, so obvious it can't really be what I've decided to go with for the beginning of this book. *Of course we're impacted by our surroundings.* We often think of the places people live in terms of proximity to activities: If you live near the coast, you can go to the beach all the time. If you live near the mountains, you can ski all winter long. And if you live in a rural area, you can live in pastoral tranquility with cows and big trucks. Or personalities get ascribed to particular places: New Yorkers are brash and tough. Angelenos are laidback and health-conscious. Texans love freedom and barbecue. Canadians are polite and like the cold. Whether these things are true or not matters little in our perceptions of what it might be like to live in one of these places.

But rarely do we think of the day-to-day lives these people lead, or how the places they live in actually operate. How do commuters get to work? Where do they go to the grocery store? What does their block look like? Such mundanities are overlooked. When asked to recall specifics of places beyond broad geographic features or cultural personalities, it's difficult to know where to start. Sure, we might picture a specific building, bit of infrastructure, or restaurant we've seen online. If we've been to a city or town, we might even be able to get a little more granular and explain what that place feels like. But there's little popular understanding of how those cities and towns work, or their impact on us.

The truth is, we spend very little time considering these questions, and even less on their consequences, but where we live is crucial in shaping so many aspects of our lives. It informs how we view the world, and who we're friends with. It impacts our health (both mental and physical), and can either open opportunities up to us, or close them off. It plays a role in what we do, how we spend our time, and how we interact with the world generally. It can either be the greatest form of liberation, or a functional and damning imprisonment. Besides one's genetics and the lessons we learn from our parents and teachers, there is nothing more determinative in the creation of what makes us *us* than where we live.

With this understanding, we come to a paradox. Where we live is one of the most important components of our lives—it's where we spend a great majority of our waking hours—and yet, we spend very little time thinking about where we live. This isn't to say that people don't consider what school district they want their kids to go to, or how they want their homes to look, but that the decision process usually ends there for those fortunate enough to be able to make such choices. For those who have less of a say, they take what housing they can get, so long as they're able to pay their rent or their mortgage (no small tasks). If they live close enough to where they need to go, that's a bonus. Everything else falls into line. What results is a transactional and utilitarian relationship with a community. This is no way to live. Not truly, at least.

Think, for a moment, about some of your favorite places you've been to. I don't mean this rhetorically—*actually* take a moment to think about them. What are some of the elements that come to mind? A bench underneath a shaded tree overlooking a charming square? An old winding road paved with cobbles? Or perhaps a coffee shop or bakery you can walk to from your hotel room or short-term rental? How narrow are the streets? Are there colorful, ornate, or beautiful buildings around you? What's on the ground floors of those buildings? Are these operators local, or some multinational chain? Perhaps there's a chorus of delightful sounds that join together in a grand ensemble: the hum of people talking over food and children laughing as they play, set in perfect harmony to a mélange of street musicians and speaker systems blaring regional hits. Or maybe your favorite places conjure an indescribable form of bliss. A feeling you get when you're transported back to this setting whose essential qualities escape description from your tongue or your mind, but are warmly felt by your heart. You don't know what it is about this place, but life feels better here. Calmer. More joyful. Graceful. And perhaps even more humane.

What's different about your favorite place and where you live? For some lucky few, these may be the same place. But for the rest of us, our favorite town or city is likely very different from where we live. Why is this? These two places probably share a lot of the same core features. They both have shops, homes, offices, restaurants, hospitals, day care centers, and parks. Maybe there are even bike trails, bodies of water, and other natural settings and amenities worthy of tourist exploration nearby. If there are, and in all likelihood this is the case, why should two places that have very similar components feel so different?

You might again be thinking to yourself, well, this is obvious. *In my favorite place, the buildings are charming. I can walk everywhere. There are lovely shops, and there are no shortage of places to sit and take in life as it passes by. There are many things to do, and people to see. There's great freedom in how I can structure my day, and where I can go. At home, I have to drive everywhere, all of the buildings look the same, and all of the stores are the same too. It's not great, but it gets the job done. It's just the way it is.*

But does this have to be the way it is? In North America, prior to the ubiquity of the interstate highway system, Euclidean zoning codes, a rigid bureaucratic state, and domination of life by cars, we had many places that were very similar to those we'd recall as our favorites today. In fact, some of our most popular domestic tourist destinations are vestiges from this era: New York, Boston, Washington, D.C., Philadelphia, Montreal, Charleston, Quebec City, San Francisco, New Orleans, Chicago, and Savannah, to name a few, in addition to countless neighborhoods that retain their core historic bones but enjoy less notoriety. Since we've created places of exceptional quality once before, we know it's not as though there's some law of the universe or immutable cultural trait that inhibits us North Americans from building well.

Why, then, does it feel like so many contemporary places are sad, soulless, ugly, dangerous, banal, and ... just plain bad? The long answer can be found throughout the pages that follow, specifically in Part One, which details our status quo and the barriers that prevent us from building the kinds of beautiful, walkable, and foundationally good communities that are the gold standard of societal life. The short answer is that the built environment is little more than a series of embodied decisions that have been made over time, which compound on top of one another to deliver the world we live in today. Lines can be drawn, of varying degrees of straightness, from every built place in the world to a single decision that informed the creation of that place—either in part or in whole.

Historically, these decisions were made organically according to the needs of the people in a given community. While this might not always have delivered good or safe outcomes, builders were free to iterate on designs, plans, and ways of knowledge, such that centuries of wisdom in how to build became imbued in the structures of a particular time. When married with thoughtful regulations, such as adequate provision for light and air, modern water and sewer infrastructure, integrity of building materials, and restrictions on overcrowding, to name but a few critical safeguards, our communities were capable of reaching extraordinary heights of quality.

This trajectory should have continued through today, with our communities progressing incrementally in the fields of architecture, urban design, landscape architecture, urban planning, and construction technology to aggregate into overall improved quality of life, perhaps nearing the sublime. But curiously, that hasn't happened.

There can be no doubt that individual quality of life has improved significantly during this time period. Average living standards from a century ago would feel barbaric by modern accounting. On-demand running water, electricity, air conditioning, and heat were unattainable for most of the world's population, to say nothing of television, mobile phones, or high-speed internet, which would have seemed unthinkable, bordering on magical, if they were to be described to the average person in 1924. Yet we take them for granted as the most basic facilities that the average household in North America in 2024 has today. The spiritual and intangible qualities of our communities have, however, regressed dramatically. Instead of the soulful and prideful ways of building that resulted in places like Paris, Venice, Kyoto, Jerusalem, Amsterdam, Havana—I'll stop here and save the reader several hundred more cities—our world has devolved into barren, segregated, boring, and dangerous realms of car dependency and mono-use, along with a host of other not-so-nice things.

For much of the last century, layers of bureaucratic complexity have compounded, hindering progress and mandating an uncompromising adherence to codes and rules. While building codes and regulations have governed the development of society for many centuries, the level of prescription they've reached is unique to our time. So much so that it wouldn't be inaccurate to say our places are shaped more by the hands of technocrats and codes than by architects, designers, and artists. The overthrow of our traditional ways has been so complete that we now often spend more time applying and waiting for approval to do something than actually doing it:

builders a century ago would have completed the job in this time and would not have even thought to ask permission to do so. Shoehorning a few square feet of space where people can exist free of cars or congestion in the hearts of our largest cities has become about as difficult as running for elected office. And more contentious. Distressingly, the smallest interventions come with great trouble. For much of civilized history, this difficulty in improving where one lives would have been impossible to comprehend. *Cities only exist because of people*, our ancestors might think if presented with this claim. *How could they be built for anything else?*

As a society, our collective decisions have pushed us towards a vapid, pseudo-scientific, homogeneously zoned culture dependent on cars—and a dogged determination to uphold it. They have supplanted soulfulness, beauty, and common sense as the heart of how we build our communities. Policies impacting our built environment can be partially or wholly blamed for crises in housing costs, inequality, obesity, mental health, environmental degradation, climate change, artistic expression, and loss of community, to name just a few consequences. No matter how nonsensical some of our more infamous modern institutions may seem, like the all-too-familiar rows of power centers, strip malls, gas stations, and big box stores lining six-lane highways, they're actually highly organized and structured areas. Ugly and unloved? Yes. Dangerous and expensive? Also yes. But they're not chaotic and spontaneously occurring. We've done this to ourselves.

While some might find the decisions made by prior generations of planners and civic officials depressing and entirely without reason—which is not a difficult conclusion to arrive at—the knowledge that much of what we loathe in the built environment was the result of considered labor makes me hopeful. Not because I'm glad for the wanton destruction of communities and the environment, and the grave repercussions that have resulted because of it. I'm hopeful because it means we don't need to move mountains or boil the ocean in order to build the types of places that so many of us love and would love to live in. People may indeed be more stubborn than the mountains or the oceans at times, but we don't have to play God in order to realize places of comparable beauty in the built environment. All we have to do is change a few decisions and ways of building, *et voilà*! Our new communities can rival the best ones of history.

What's more, the places of our dreams are also the most sustainable, salubrious, environmentally friendly, fiscally sound, and equitable types that we can build. In short, the best places to live in are also the most common sense ones to build.

* * *

It's very easy to look out at our world and see only what is wrong with it. It's also easy to find the types of places we would rather live in. Geographically, they're all over the place, just in short supply. What's less clear, however, is how we go from the woeful status quo of today to a better, more handsome, and common sense world for tomorrow. That's what this book is all about.

In an anecdotal survey barraging unsuspecting people in my day-to-day life, few could answer just how buildings are actually created. This is consistent with broader perspectives I've seen online. One day there's a vacant lot, a large field, or a smaller building, and the next, seemingly, there's a new community of homes, an office complex, or a fast-food drive-through. People understand construction quite well, as it's something they can see. It's less obvious what allowed that building to rise. The underlying zoning, building codes, lot regulations, financing, investor relations, pre-development work, design, engineering, insurance, and dozens of other steps that must take place before a structure can ever rise out of the ground. It's in these unseen steps that the battle between common sense and depravity, or beauty and banality, is lost before any dirt is moved.

If we want to change our development patterns to create a superior world, then we must understand the intersection between this desire and the pragmatism of actually getting places built. While there are many tangible steps to take in service of realizing this, which are explained in greater detail in the chapters within this book, one of the most important things that must happen isn't tangible: it's about what we believe.

In America, there is now a widespread belief that we are no longer capable of doing good things (despite the significant evidence to the contrary). This worldview assumes that our best days are behind us. The belief extends down through the built environment. Loud are the cries that tell us we can't improve the world, lobbed at a favored scapegoat of choice. Not only are these beliefs wrong, but they're damaging. A prevailing cynicism about the world is a self-fulfilling prophecy. If one doesn't believe positive change is possible—or worse, they scoff at the idea—they won't do the requisite work to effectuate change that would make the world a better place ... so nothing happens. Why would you do something you don't believe in? In very simple terms, then, the first step towards realizing a finer world is believing that one is possible. This is an inherently optimistic philosophy, as only optimism can move us forward. Cynicism or contentment are not motivators of change.

Key to changing beliefs is showing what a superior world would look like. If a person has no notion of what something might be like, it's very hard for them to believe in the future prospect of it. Things become rather abstract. But show them what's possible, and a whole new world opens up. Though this might seem simple, it is remarkably powerful, especially for rather impenetrable industries like real estate development and architecture. High barriers to entry at one end of the spectrum and navel-gazing, gatekeeping, and snobbery on the other already do enough to discourage would-be practitioners from getting involved in these fields. The genesis of change is really as simple as someone noting, *I like that building, I want to build something like that!* Once this person is sufficiently invested in the industry, the nuances and intricacies of the built environment can be discussed in greater detail. Cynicism at the top of this funnel, however, is corrupting, resulting in the well-supported belief that many new dreadful buildings are created by people who dread what they do.

On its own, though, reference isn't enough. It's one thing to show someone a picture of a medieval Italian hill town as inspiration for what an optimal future might look like, but it's quite another to show something in their own backyard, which removes questions of cultural and regional viability, even if the example is historic. In order to remove all shadows of doubt, however, it's best to show contemporary projects close to where one lives (or within a few hours drive) as a one-to-one comparison. At this point, there can be no denying that great things are still possible!

We have some work cut out for us on this front in North America. Over much of the last century, many of the places we've built have been insipid, and as a matter of fact, abhorrent. The despair wrought by mid-century and contemporary development can feel overwhelming, and near ubiquitous. The key word, though, is "near". Most only see the banal, soulless, and ugly structures immediately surrounding them, so they think it's not possible to do good. In relative terms, this is understandable, as the percentage of quality new places is indeed rather small. But in absolute terms, there's no shortage of people who are working towards realizing a better built environment.

Projects of exceptional quality have risen around North America over the last 20 or so years, indiscriminate of context. Great places have been realized in large cities, small towns, rural plains, mountain ledges, and everywhere in between. It's been a great joy to see these types of projects increase with frequency in recent years, but it hasn't been surprising. That's because the great developments of today exist at the tail end of a virtuous cycle that's been gaining momentum for decades. From a few projects built in the late '80s and early '90s (notably Seaside, Florida, the first New Urbanist community), North America gained tangible evidence that exceptional buildings can still be created here. This was the kernel that made believing in a better future possible.

In concrete terms, when the creation of one new high-quality place (which can be defined as a project that is thoughtful, responds to its surrounding context, and is built on good foundations of attractive design and sound urbanism) is realized, it serves as precedent for future projects to jump off of. The first project sets a stake in the ground, which enables a second to become incrementally easier to build, as officials, neighbors, and contractors know what to expect for the next time. Soon enough, two good projects lead to five, which might grow to ten. These projects could continue multiplying until entire neighborhoods are transformed as demand for high-quality places rises, while opposition to them wanes. Indeed, this is how our cities and towns historically developed. As places became more prosperous, investments were made back into the built environment, spurred on by a competition of pride and desire to improve one's world. Soon enough, quality became the expectation, not the exception. Though we've gotten away from this expectation, it's my hope that it will return.

* * *

It's in this spirit of the possibility of creating great new places that the inspiration for this book began. Beyond the default skepticism of the real world, many corners of the internet likewise exist with cynicism as the modus operandi. Online culture privileges snarkiness, criticism, and meanness, while it spurns positivity, optimism, and progress. Everywhere one looks, people can readily be mobilized to oppose anything, but rarely do they come together to fight for something. This is also true of the built environment. It's very easy to oppose new housing, criticize development patterns, or lament the devastation of a city or the loss of a building. A post decrying the utter dreariness of a poorly executed Brutalist office building, or the destruction of a vibrant neighborhood in order to accommodate an urban highway might gain several hundred thousand engagements. (Most) people intuitively understand that these are not great things, and so it's easy to join a chorus critiquing them. We also intuitively know what places feel good. At least historically speaking. An image or video of an old plaza in Europe has no trouble garnering much support online.

This book isn't about the past, though. It's not meant to be an accounting of all grievances of Modernity, or exclusive praise of traditional ways of building. It's too easy to focus on these things, especially as they enjoy much attention already. This is a book about making our contemporary world better—something I rarely see positive advocacy for. Part of the reason for this lack of advocacy is because there's less certainty involved with it. Will someone accept a new idea? The creation of a new idea is an intellectual leap of faith, which is scary. The action of creating a belief, which is required for positive advocacy, is inherently an untested and subjective practice. Because of this novelty, there's a big risk that others will oppose what the advocate believes in. As this action is inextricably linked to the person who conceived it, there's no small amount of emotional connection associated with the idea. This is tricky, as it doesn't feel good when others reject our ideas. But even worse, it feels downright awful to have them criticize our most cherished beliefs. This is quite the presumptive stumbling block to advocate for positive change. Better to protect one's feelings, and sacred ideas, from the debilitating criticisms of the masses by never exposing them.

This is an entirely rational position, but we have to move beyond this fear. There aren't very many people who are predisposed to taking the risk of effectuating such a change. If someone so inclined towards this reform allows the negativity of others to stop them from believing in it, the movement is mortally wounded—the cynics have won! Well, we can't have that, can we?

How do we move beyond this fear towards the creation of a better world? Well, for me, it started with a tweet. Yes, I realize how this reads, but hear me out! As a longtime user of Twitter (now X), I had seen my fair share of tweets leaning into the tired tropes of criticism, cynicism, and partisan debates go viral. Instead of open discussion and a dissemination of hopeful ideas on the platform, I was bombarded with not-so "breaking news", depraved arguments between incorrigible avatars, and garrulous chat from officious actors. There was very little optimism or positivity.

Without much intention at first, I started tweeting pictures of new developments that I believed were pretty good. As these posts started to gain some traction organically, I felt there might be an opportunity to expand these sporadic tweets into something more structured. After all, people seemed to be enjoying these attractive projects that adhered to common sense development patterns. Instead of sprawling, car-dependent subdivisions, or large, anonymous, and imposing new apartment buildings (colloquially referred to as five-over-ones), the places I shared tended to all have some charm, idiosyncrasies, and unique vernaculars, in relatively walkable contexts. Whether they were large apartment buildings, lecture halls, townhomes, parking garages, or entire neighborhoods, the places I shared all had some soul and personality to them. Though this is arguably subjective (we'll dive into these arguments in Chapter 4), one could say that all of these projects were beautiful. While others were posting articles about new developments or general observations about what constitutes a good place, few (at least as far as I could see at the time) were advocating for the specific belief that many of the challenges that North America faced could be solved by building more beautiful communities, and a lot of them.

With some (small) traction, I decided to lay down a few ground rules to guide my fledgling project:

1. Post one new high-quality development every day, for one year straight.
2. Select only developments in America and Canada, as it's the world I live in and know the most about (and because of the extent of the hopelessness of our development patterns).
3. Include as many pictures as possible to show people what these places look like. The visual medium is much better at inspiring optimism than the written or spoken ones. People can't understand what makes a place good or bad if they can't see it.
4. Feature the architect, developer, or other prominent stakeholders in each post to celebrate their work. As many of the projects I profiled bucked the status quo, and went against what many contemporary architecture and design publications would choose to feature, it was important to highlight the work of those who might not have otherwise been heralded despite the significance of their contributions, and to encourage on the creation of more new work!
5. Ensure that projects do not adhere to a specific style, typology, or region, in order to show that great projects of all purposes, styles, and sizes could be realized around the continent, not just in a select few wealthy or design-forward places.
6. Use only projects that have been built in the last twenty years, with a focus on those built in the last ten. Anything older feels as though it's a vestige of a prior era, which diminishes the cause.

I called this project "A Year of Building Optimism", and I began posting developments daily towards the end of December 2021. The goal—both of this project, and now of this book that I've expanded it into—is to spread an optimistic belief that we can still create great places in America. As a direct contradiction to the cynicism of most commentary on the built environment, as well as the unholy state of most contemporary development, this project aims to expose people to new buildings and plans with the mission of establishing a virtuous cycle of optimism, where creating finer places restores belief in our ability do good things. This is hopefully the first step towards realizing better communities, where people can be armed with the requisite information on how to create the types of places that everyone might be able to enjoy, not just the wealthy or the well-connected.

I must confess, I had some doubts at the beginning of this project. There had to be a reason why there wasn't a strong emphasis on high-quality, humane new development (outside of the bounds of luxury single family homes and five-star resorts) on social media and popular publications. Sure, there were some voices, and select articles, but they were often confined to a specific architectural school or ideology. While there were many who advocated for the creation of more housing generally, it was largely in the pursuit of the utilitarian (and essential) goal of providing shelter for all who need it. There was not, however, any romantic, qualitative, or aspirational component to their advocacy. Did people really care for the strain of beautiful architecture, sound urbanism, and common sense city building I was espousing? Moreover, could I actually post every day? Were there even 365 places of subjective quality high enough to share, or would I have to dilute the project of its more aspirational goals in service of completing it, at the risk of potentially diminishing the overall advocacy?

Since I'm writing this now, you might have guessed that these challenges were ultimately overcome. Throughout the project, I was overjoyed by the support for the sort of world I was dreaming could one day become the new status quo. I've met many optimists, friends, and kindred spirits along this journey, and have learned much from all of them. There is a significant grassroots movement that has spread around the world—far beyond the confines of North America—demanding a different way. It's not that these folks weren't always there, but that the community for such advocacy was either nonexistent or fragmented in disparate corners. While social media platforms can bring people together in cruel opposition to those they disagree with, they also have great power in bringing people together over something fundamentally good.

Throughout this project, it was not uncommon to have people tell me that they hadn't thought building such places was possible in North America, but after seeing some of the projects featured they were inspired to go out and create wonderful projects of their own. Though I can hardly claim any credit for this, as it's the architects, developers, builders, engineers, contractors, enlightened city officials, and tradespeople who did all the work—I merely posted pretty pictures of their efforts—it has been deeply gratifying to play a small part of this movement.

But it's time to move beyond the domain of social media and specific articles on various platforms, to solidify this movement into something less ephemeral. Though optimism is the first step required in building the world of our dreams, there's quite a long journey ahead of us from here to there. The good news is that it's possible.

Unless you're reading these words in untouched nature, everything around you is the result of human intervention: the good, the bad, the ugly, and the sublime. If we're going to shape the built environment regardless of what we do, our touch ought to be as magnificent as possible. This might seem bold, but really, why should it be? We built with such aspirations for centuries. Armed with modern technology, we can make our modern cities and towns even better than the places we revere from the past. Tourists spend tens of billions of dollars a year visiting lovely, walkable places. Is this not a sign of their perceived worth? Instead of saving for years just to get a glimpse of Paris, would it not be better to live in a place that might one day evoke the same feelings?

If we want a world that's more sustainable, walkable, affordable, equitable, dynamic, and beautiful, these outcomes are only a few choices—and a few sections of code—away. Yes, much skill and dedicated training was required to create the iconic structures of the past. But we can relearn these ways. Our first step, and the solution to the problems we face today, is to adopt a philosophy based on optimism and abundance. Once we achieve our dreams in select places, it's imperative that we scale this solution up to the greatest extent possible. An Optimism that limits itself to select neighborhoods or towns can never have the impact that's required to meaningfully render societal change.

And so, in these pages it's my intention to weave a hopeful narrative, to prove our best days aren't behind us. I promise this is not some naive optimism that's blind to the challenges of our world, or the practicalities of what it takes to actually create the sorts of places I'm advocating for. In the pages that follow, there will be a unity of romanticism and pragmatism, such that I hope the reader will find this work to be less of an abstract call to do something (anything!), and more of a practical guide delineating what cities, towns, and people can do.

In the pursuit of this mission, I must ask for the reader's occasional patience as we wade through some rather technical concepts and dense histories which require an exploration of the minutiae of our byzantine regulatory environment. I also ask for your understanding that the world in which I write these words will inevitably change in many unpredictable ways in the months, years, and decades after the publication of this book, such that parts of it will not seem relevant—or even conceivable—to yours. I hope that my inability to foresee the changes that come to pass does not harm the overall message of this labor, as it's my ultimate goal for you to apply the lessons herein to your own community, in your own context and your own time. This book is not meant to be an accounting of the end of history, but merely one entry in the continuum of humanity's collective knowledge. I hope in future years that if you find yourself reading this, you might remark how unbelievable it was to be preoccupied with issues of supply, demand, beauty, sustainability, and walkability, just as we look back on issues of basic sanitation, overcrowding, segregation, and clean water with horror in the cities of yesterday. There is nothing that could be more heartening to me, because if you do it means that the beliefs espoused in this book will have become truths, at least in some small ways, in some small circles, if not more widely adopted.

More than anything, I hope for an Optimism that inspires people of all walks of life to go out and create a better world, a world capable of being loved and potentially dreamed about. I hope that the icons of modern society aren't relegated to antiquity, but are instead a continuously replenished resource. That we're not content with London, Rome, Paris, Kyoto, Venice, or some other favored historic city. That we can carry on the tradition of attraction, desirability, and common sense, to create new Romes, new Parises, and new Kyotos that far surpass their ancestors—with the qualification that they be inclusive of all who wish to live within their borders.

A better world is possible. Once we come to believe this, we must be relentless in our pursuit of it. Though this change won't occur without some friction, don't be discouraged. The world is in desperate need of your Optimism!

Coby Lefkowitz, September 2024

Part One
Foundations of Optimism

1.

On Building Optimism: A Brief History of How We Got Here

Most new places in North America aren't very good. From sprawling tracts of homogenous homes and strip malls full of chain stores, to anonymous five-over-one apartment buildings and offices located in the most grotesque usage of the word "park" in the English language. For nearly a century, we've extracted beauty and joy from our towns and cities, only to replace them with boxes of varying sizes along ever-widening roads, damning the environment, our cities, and ourselves in the process.

When looking at the landscape of recent development, it's easy to lose faith in our ability to do good things. It feels as though we've forgotten how to do it, or moved past a time where creating such places was desirable. As profit imperatives weigh ever more heavily on the development process from both large institutional groups and smaller speculators—who care little for lasting quality—value engineering and spreadsheet architecture have proliferated, pushing the dream of a better world ever further from our grasp.

Somewhere along the way, we've accepted this as the status quo, acquiescing to a world with many serious challenges, deficiencies, and high levels of undesirability. In order to cope with it, it seems, many of us have simply become numb to the world around us. Instead of enjoying a walkable, dynamic, salubrious, sustainable, and lovable community as the place where we live full time, those fortunate enough to travel internationally have settled for a few days in some city halfway across the world, at considerable expense, to satisfy these conditions. Those less fortunate are left with little to do but accept the fate cast unto them, sometimes questioning, but rarely being provided for.

We've come up with all manner of excuses for why we live this way, from the cost it takes to develop good places and our inability to create them, to a favored scapegoat or conspiracy that places blame on some faceless evil actor as a further coping mechanism. These excuses do little more than shirk the responsibility and render many to believe ours is a world incapable of reform.

I know what you might be thinking. *North Americans want a big yard, picket fence, and highways to ferry them everywhere seamlessly. This is just how we do things here. We don't build walkable, beautiful communities here. And even if we did want to create more of these places, nothing will ever change, because that's not how our societies are structured. This is the world we've been given, might as well accept it.*

Not the most positive start for a book about optimism, admittedly. But hear me out! If we're to embark on a mission to create a better world for tomorrow, we have to know what we're up against, and accept some foundational truths. Except to illustrate what a more optimistic, common sense foundation might look like, negativity will be minimized in these pages. Promise. It'd be far too easy to criticize the state of contemporary development patterns, or lament the decisions that have put us in this position, without offering an antidote to them. That's just complaining.

Moreover, the prevailing cynicism of how many view our world is not acceptable. Not when the built environment has such a profound impact on us. Not when much of this cynicism is unfounded. And certainly not when we're in a position to do something about it.

We spend the vast majority of our lives in places shaped by other people—what urbanists and architects call the built environment, a term I'll be using so much you'll either find a familiar comfort in it or never want to come across again. Be forewarned. This goes well beyond skyscrapers and highways; except for those fleeting moments in untouched wilderness, virtually all of the interactions we have with the world are in the built environment.

As humans, we have a funny habit of not being able to leave any patch of Earth we come across untouched. These interventions might be as subtle as a path stamped down in an overgrown forest, or stone walls meant to delineate boundaries—so masterfully done that they feel as though nature put them there herself. Even fields that seem as pure as the highest mountain peaks are often the result of land intentionally cleared of trees, where nothing has grown in their stead.

There are other places we might not traditionally associate with "the built environment" that have been nursed by people and whose natural beauty has been augmented as a result of it, such as gardens, hiking trails, or parks. So even when one thinks they're outside the grasp of human reach, chances are they're still well within it.

Why does this matter? It matters because where we spend our time significantly impacts our mental and physical health, and cognitive function. Economies hinge on good or bad development patterns. Communities rise or disintegrate based on the spaces they're provided. Natural and built environments are either destroyed or rendered more prosperous through the result of our actions. While I could draw dichotomies ad infinitum, simply put, every aspect of one's life is influenced by the quality of the places they're surrounded by. If we're surrounded almost exclusively by settings of our own making, few things could be more important than making these places right.

The cynic might despair reading this information, as it seems that for much of the last century we've only been capable of creating places that are extractive, utilitarian, and destructive. *Why create anything,* they might ask, *if it's just going to be bad? What's the use in surrounding our bad places with even more bad places? We'd be better off doing nothing.*

This way of thinking might make sense at surface level, but when we dig a bit deeper it doesn't pass muster. There are countless examples of extraordinary places created by people around the world. Rome famously wasn't built in a day, but took centuries of incremental growth to form itself into the city so many of us admire today. The same is true for thousands of other villages, towns, and cities we dream of visiting or living in. If these settings were created once, there's no reason why we can't create them again. It's not as though some immutable laws of the universe prohibit us from doing this. Every place you interact with in the built environment is the result of a series of decisions—the dreamy, the dreadful, and everything in between. A line can be drawn from everything you see in the built world to a single decision made in a planning meeting, a back office, a section of zoning / building code, a construction document, or the sporadic choices individual people make outside the bounds of formal municipal approvals.

It's true that we've made many bad decisions in the recent past. But that doesn't mean we can't reverse our course and draw new lines to chart a better future. Our inaction is the only limiting force preventing us from redirection. It may be difficult, but history shows us a better way is possible.

* * *

The only reason we have a framework for knowing which places are lovely, and which places are less so, is because there are both exceptional and poor examples all around us. If we didn't have good references, we'd have no basis for understanding the bad, and no ability to compare the two. So, at the very least, we know that we've created some lovely places in the past. Point to the good guys! While this may seem trivial, it's not only worth noting, but deserves celebration. So strong is our fatalism that we forget how much good there is around us, especially in our own backyards.

While even the most ardent pessimist would have to concede that the world has many wonderful places that are worthy of our dreams and praise (who can dispute the magnificence of Florence, Amsterdam, Havana, or Marrakech?), they might counter that in North America, we just don't have that heritage. This isn't true.

We have in our close reach an abundance of extraordinary cities and towns. From Old Quebec, to pockets of Philadelphia, Manhattan, Brooklyn, Charleston, D.C., New Orleans, Montreal, Chicago, and Santa Barbara, hundreds of such locations exist. It must be true, then, that at one point we possessed the skills for creating great cities and towns. We are no cultural exception to the creation of great built environments.

This doesn't mean that everything we built in the past was inherently good. We may well suffer from a survivorship bias that overrates prior ages of building because only the best homes, warehouses, offices, and monuments made it through to the present day. Many structures of the past, if not most, were not of sufficient quality to last. Conditions of the industrialized powerhouses of Great Britain and America in the 19th and early 20th centuries were infamously bad. In the wake of Chicago's devastating 1871 fire, wooden tenements were hastily erected to house all those affected by the disaster. These slums soon became overcrowded as the city struggled to house its rapidly growing population. From 1870 to 1880, Chicago grew by nearly 70%, from just under 300,000 people to just over 500,000. By 1930, nearly 3 million more people would move to the city in the hopes of securing economic and personal liberation that was largely unattainable on the surrounding farms and in the distant lands they arrived from. If overcrowding was an issue in 1871, it was an epidemic just a few decades later. People crushed together in quantities that would be inconceivable today. Quite a bit tighter than splitting a bed with your brother and sister on a family road trip. Families were much bigger than they are today, and several families might live in the same apartment, with five, six, or seven or more people sharing one small room. Very little light got into these homes as the buildings covered almost 100% of the lot area.[1] Air quality was abhorrent. Homes crowded around factories that belched soot and God-knows-what-else into the precious little circulating air within them. These places couldn't be described as habitable, not by industrial standards, and certainly not by modern judgements, barely rising to even a utilitarian level.

"Penury and poverty are wedded everywhere to dirt and disease," wrote Jacob Riis in his pioneering 1890 work, which documented the conditions of slums in New York City in the 1880s.[2] Continuing, Riis noted, "Neatness, order, cleanliness, were never dreamed of in connection with the tenant-house system ... while reckless slovenliness, discontent, privation, and ignorance were left to work out their invariable results, until the entire premises reached the level of tenant-house dilapidation, containing, but sheltering not, the miserable hordes that crowded beneath smouldering, water-rotted roofs or burrowed among the rats of clammy cellars."

Elsewhere in New York, shacks and shanties that bore some resemblance to pre-industrialized logging camps were widespread. Where just a quarter century later these sites were occupied by grand pre-war apartment buildings that have since come to be revered around the globe, in the 1890s they hardly rose to the title of informal settlement.

How did the penury and poverty that Riis observed give way to distinguished structures and enviable addresses? In order to answer this, we must take a quick diversion across the Atlantic. Though this book is (primarily) focused on North America, it's worth taking a look at London, as many American projects took inspiration from the progress made in the British capital.

The first "Model Dwelling" schemes arose in London in the 1840s, uniting the need for higher-quality housing for the working poor with subjective moral imperatives. These interventions aimed to improve the overall station of life for the most impoverished, not just where they lived.[3] Model Dwellings were erected for all different types of people—single men, single women, families, the elderly, and the infirm. Their scope ranged from small dorms consisting of individual rooms with shared common bathrooms and lounging spaces, up to several-room apartments that families could comfortably occupy. Philanthropists and activists who wanted to move beyond simply campaigning for improved living conditions to putting their principles into practice were the progenitors of these schemes. Social reformers, as they became known since their work sought to reform society, refused to accept the intolerable conditions faced by the many vulnerable who were subjected to them.

Octavia Hill was one of the key figures of this movement, and among its most prodigious. At the peak of her work, she cared for the homes and lives of 4,000 East Londoners, relying on strict rules to uphold order.[4] In working with the Kyrle Society, whose slogan was "Bring Beauty Home", she focused on delivering high-quality housing with access to open space, fresh air, and constructive entertainment like literature, art, and music.[5] For Hill, simply providing better living conditions wasn't enough. She sought to offer an example of what a more honorable, robust, and enlightened life might look like. She believed in the importance of cultivating communities that transcended the utilitarian mode of charity that prevailed at the time, with a maternalism that demanded her residents mold themselves into upstanding members of society.

These themes were consistent with the work of other reformers in the London scene, though redevelopment through slum clearance was often favored to Hill's insistence of renovation in place. Sir Sydney H. Waterlow founded the Improved Industrial Dwellings Co. in 1863, which aimed to instill pride in the lives of the 30,000 residents who lived in one of his more than 6,000 buildings.[6] Plans for IIDC's Langbourne Buildings in Finsbury Square noted that it was "advisable to give to each dwelling an individu-ality of appearance; and also dissipate the feeling, unfortunately but too general, that the occupants of the 'model dwellings' are the recipients of charity", lamenting that it was "unquestionable that in most of the buildings of this class the long rows of windows have a dreary monotonous effect, and impress on the mind the idea of a workhouse or of a penitentiary."[7] Matthew Allen, who authored the Langbourne plan on behalf of Waterlow, continued, "I am not alone in believing that the homes of workmen cannot by any pos-sibility be rendered too attractive, complete, and comfortable; and that while they will often meet with stolid indifference anything of a 'missionising' tendency, the working classes gladly welcome and warmly appreciate the efforts made to obviate the evils and improve the condition of their dwellings."

The Boundary Estate, perhaps the most successful social housing scheme of the time, was a redevelopment of the Old Nichol, one of London's most infamous slums and inspiration for pop-ular books of the time depicting the squalor of industrial life, like the polemical *A Child of the Jago*. Unlike other projects that were carried out by social reformers, charitable trusts or reli-gious institutions, the Boundary Estate was spearheaded by a local government agency, the London County Council. It was one of the earliest government-led social housing schemes in the world. Homes for 5,500 were planned. Although officials desired everyone who had lived in the Old Nichol to have a home in the Boundary Estate, many were not rehoused due to the dfficulty in tracking down those who had lived there previously. Others who could be found but were not rehoused had secured accommodation somewhere else during construction and didn't want to go through the trouble of moving again. Unlike many Public Housing projects that have been built since, the Boundary Estate was mixed use, functioning as a proper community, with 18 shops, 77 workshops (to encourage entrepreneurship and more socially acceptable hobbies than gambling, drinking, and general debauchery), and two schools.[8]

Not only did the Boundary Estate dramatically improve the conditions of the old slum notorious for crime and insalubrity—and provide opportunities for jobs and more respectable leisure—it did so in style. Architect Owen Flemming's plan, with aid from his colleague Rowland Plumbe, saw 1,069 dwellings of extraordinary aesthetic value erected across 23 blocks. The redevelopment was of such high-quality that many of the original buildings have been preserved under Grade II listing status, signifying their importance as cultural landmarks.

Fall at The Boundary Estate (left). Rochelle School at The Boundary Estate (right).

Back on this side of the Atlantic, social reformers like Jane Addams and Ellen Gates Starr of Chicago's Hull House, and Stanton Coit and Jacob Riis in New York, drew inspiration from the British to cure the destitution faced by residents in America's worst slums.[9] The ills of neighborhoods like New York's Five Points and the Lower East Side (including modern-day Little Italy, NoLiTa, and Chinatown), Chicago's Near North Side and Old Town, and Philadelphia's Society Hill and Queen Village were confronted head on. Hannah Fox and Helen Parrish of the Octavia Hill Association of Philadelphia (which, as you may have guessed, took direct inspiration from Octavia Hill's work in London), were noteworthy for the incrementalism of their transformations.[10] Workman Place along South Front Street in Queen Village endures as a proud, and attractive reminder of the possibility of positive reform. The homes remain among the highest-quality stock in the neighborhood, with ample outdoor space, much greenery, and considered detailing. Few would recognize them as the deeply affordable housing of their day.

At the larger scale of the intervention spectrum was Alfred Tredway White. A 19th-century engineer, White was also a devoted philanthropist, educator, and social reformer. He abhorred the conditions the working classes were forced to live in, believing that the quality of where one lived directly impacted who they became. He wrote: "The badly constructed, unventilated, dark and foul tenement houses of New York, in which our laboring classes are forced to live, are the nurseries of the epidemics which spread with certain destructiveness into the fairest homes; they are the hiding-places of the local banditti ... in fact they produce these noxious and unhappy elements of society as surely as the harvest follows the sowing, and by these, punish the carelessness of those who own no responsibility as keepers of their brethren."[11]

Convinced that salubrious housing was critical to improve the quality of life of the immigrants he taught and interacted with in his native Brooklyn, White traveled to England to learn from figures like Waterlow. The influence this had is easy to see. The IIDC's emphasis on providing handsome dwellings for the working class is masterfully reflected in White's Home, Tower, and Riverside Buildings, all designed by William Field & Son. Located in Cobble Hill and Brooklyn Heights, these 6 story blocks featured outdoor staircases (reminiscent of many of Waterlow's structures), wrought iron balconies, large common courtyards, and richly detailed facades. They were cross ventilated, which was transformative in an era where few buildings inhabited by the working class enjoyed any fresh air. Units were spacious, brightly lit, had running water, and were tailored for the needs of families. White's buildings never occupied much more than half of the lot, leaving ample space for playgrounds, gardens, and common amenities in the courtyards.

He experimented with other forms of housing as well, believing people at different stations of life required different living accommodations. At Warren Place Mews, 34 small row houses were built for working class families at low incomes. They rented for just $18 a month when they were completed in 1878, the equivalent of around $600 today.[12] Spanning just 11 and a half feet wide, 32 feet deep, and little more than 1,000 square feet in total, the Romanesque Revival style Workingman's Cottages are modest but proud structures. Red-orange brick adorns the masonry structures, tactically used in select locations to draw one's eyes upwards to window lines, pilasters, and entrances framing doorways. A lush and expertly manicured garden runs down the narrow lane which separates the two rows of homes. Each cottage has a dedicated yard in the back. Walking through the mews on its slate pathways, it's easy to see how living in such a dignified, beautiful place would draw the best out of someone. Lush, intimate, and bountifully adorned, these homes would be a feat most luxury developers today would dream of achieving. Indeed, they regularly sell for well over a million dollars, no small feat for such humble dwellings.

In an 1885 publication for the National Conference on Charities and Correction, White detailed how he was able to deliver the cottages for just $1,150 per home ($35,000 in today's dollars), or rent out units in his apartment buildings (5th floor walk ups with two rooms and scullery), for as low as $1.60 a week.[13] Diligently accounting for every expense, he economized on space, bought materials in bulk, and most importantly, employed a "philanthropy and five percent" strategy. Five per cent philanthropists offered their investors an annual dividend capped at 5%, putting a ceiling on profit margins, and by extension, rent. This strategy accomplished a few things. First, it allowed White to keep home prices affordable to the lowest earning members of society, the simple laborers, home cleaners, seamstresses, artisans, and boatmen who made up the majority of his tenants, but who couldn't pay more than $2 per week in rent. This strategy departed considerably from the speculators of the time who would throw homes up as cheaply as they could in order to chase annualized returns upwards of 40%. It mattered little to these investors when their properties inevitably began to deteriorate just a few years later—they were already long gone. Second, it allowed White to dramatically expand his impact. Real estate was and remains a highly capital intensive industry. As funds for public housing were non-existent at the time, capital had to come from somewhere else. Without investors, no low-income housing would be built, and 5% was a reasonable return on investment for those enlightened benefactors.

After returning ~5% in distributions to investors, all excess cash was either reinvested into the property, spent on events (a six-piece brass band performed every two weeks throughout the summer at his properties), or was given back to the tenants themselves. Surveying his corporation's financial performance for 1885, $1,177 out of $34,500 in gross revenue (3.4%) was paid back to the tenants in the spirit of "practical co-operation".[14] These distributions were a "visible recompense to those who by promptness, nearness, and good order contribute the most to the success of the enterprise. These dividends form a great incentive to the tenants to cultivate habits of neatness and promptness." Aligning incentives in such a way is a win-win. The benefits to real estate managers were obvious. And for tenants, if they treated their properties with respect, they would in turn have better living conditions and receive a portion of the returns (nearly comparable to what private investors received).

Reading through White's essays and papers, it's easy to understand how he was able to improve the lives of so many: he cared deeply for the cause. This would not have been possible if he wasn't fastidious in his management, nor worked hard enough to understand all of the intricacies of how buildings are actually created and maintained.

White's efforts earned praise from all corners, but perhaps his greatest champion was Jacob Riis, who frequently wrote glowingly of these buildings and their positive impact on the many working families they housed.[15] So inspired was Riis by White's work that he attributed the philanthropist as his inspiration for *How The Other Half Lives*.

Through a goal of building "the most advanced tenement houses in the world", White not only improved the lives of his neighbors, but also inspired builders nationwide to construct a higher standard of housing for the poor.[16] Though he only built homes for a few thousand families, White's influence extended to many millions, both directly via the creation of *The New York State Tenement House Act of 1901* (in which he was instrumental in crafting), and indirectly from those who took influence from his projects and speeches. He is but one cog—albeit a very important one—in a virtuous cycle of profound implications for our built environment.

Remarkably, we now vie to live in areas that were once the most odious slums. Countless buildings developed by social housing organizations are now quite fashionable to live in. That's sustained

Warren Place Mews in Cobble Hill, designed by William Field & Son.

Optimism in action. This history is not meant, however, to imply that the neighborhoods where these activists plied their trade have not known struggle since, nor that development via social reform is an entirely desirable form of building. The paternalism (and in some cases materialism) exhibited by these organizations would not only seem antiquated by today's standards, but ruthlessly controlling. Many social reformers attached strong doses of subjective morality to their projects, whether via religion, temperance, or strict living standards where tenants had to earn the right to access certain privileges.

However, just because some of the practices the reformers employed may not be directly relevant to us today doesn't mean we should disregard the lessons their work has for us. Most notably, we suffer from a lack of the sort of comprehensive vision that can both solve the issues of our times, and propel us forward into collective prosperity. Though there have been some worthy interventions in the last several decades, most of all, there's been indifference. Instead of a nation driven forward by a distinct "American Dream" for a better world (whether that dream was ever real is a different story for another time), we exist rudderless, paralyzed by the challenges we face. Somewhere along the way, we lost our way.

* * *

In the years between America's involvement in World War II and now (though some cracks began to show in the 1920s), the standard of our built environment has regressed considerably. This isn't to say that the aggregate state of society was better before this regression (it wasn't) or that things are all bad now (they're not), but that there's been an undeniable shift in the state of our cities, towns, and communities generally.

I've selected pre-World War II as the general time period for this diversion for a few reasons. Though it's not a perfect marker, rarely is there ever a single moment in a single place that can be pointed to definitively as the start of something, especially something as nebulous as the quality of community. The key qualification for this inflection point, in my mind, is that before World War II there was a general belief that we could build great things—that our cities could be the envy of the world. Even in the depths of the Great Depression, some of the continent's most famous structures were completed: New York's Empire State Building (1931), Nevada's Hoover Dam (1936), San Francisco's Golden Gate Bridge (1937), and Vancouver's Lion's Gate Bridge (1938). Across every building and infrastructural typology, in the depths of a moment where hope was in short supply, places of exceptional quality were designed to inspire just that. They were created not only to facilitate their utilitarian raisons d'etre, like allowing cars to drive from one place to another where they previously couldn't, but to elevate people while they did these tasks. Rockefeller Center, effectively an office park, has no business being as elegant as it is. And yet that is precisely the business it's in, where magnificence functions as its calling card and has made the development one of the world's most iconic locations. The same goes for the Chrysler Building.

Regrettably, this hope largely gave way to codified individualism, prejudice, and hyper rationality. Gracelessly, we moved from an age of building grand projects meant to evoke pride, wonder and ambition in the general populace, to a tedious planning and regulation of society for which we cared little for the broader consequences of, and understood even less.

Zoning codes were first crafted in the U.S. in the beginning of the 20th century in an attempt to manage the exponential growth of cities due to mass immigration and the maturation of industrialization. "Manage" is the key word. Los Angeles adopted Ordinance 9774 in 1904, codifying one of the country's first land use restrictions into law, before expanding on it to form the nation's first formal zoning codes in 1908.[17] At surface level, the ordinance was aimed at establishing residential districts where industrial uses wouldn't be allowed. Makes sense; living next to the noxious fumes and loud noises that belched out of factories, with who knows whatever else was released, doesn' seem desirable. Below surface level, however, the regulation was designed to manage a different, more insidious outcome: racial segregation. Ordinance 9774 was a thinly veiled provision to separate Chinese families and the laundry facilities they ran from their White neighbors. This veil was pretty easy to see through as most of the intensive industrial development in Los Angeles at the time was confined to Downtown, San Pedro, and some other outlying neighborhoods, away from the speculative tract housing developments that were in their first stages of an ultimately successful conquest over the region. If the city had really cared about protecting residential areas from deleterious impact, it would have restricted the extraction of oil, which was far more pervasive than other industrial uses, and in some ways more damaging. Yet drilling continued within neighborhoods without municipal intervention. In some cases, it was encouraged as a form of civic boosterism to flout the economic prosperity of the region. Miraculously, this practice remained for more than a century. If one wanted to, a homeowner could still construct an oil well in their residential neighborhood in the city of Los Angeles as recently as 2021. The county was even later to the game, banning the construction of new wells in 2023, with plans to phase out existing drilling over 20 years.[18]

Other early codes didn't attempt to mask their intentions at all. In Baltimore, the City Council adopted block-by-block segregation in 1910 prohibiting Blacks from living next to Whites. Inspiration quickly spread throughout the South. Atlanta copied Baltimore's provision nearly word for word (a precedent we'll see with other zoning codes).[19] Richmond enacted racial segregation via zoning in 1911. Louisville, St. Louis, New Orleans and hundreds of other smaller cities and towns adopted similar laws in the following years.

Opposition to these codes was strong, with formal protests and judicial challenges. In the 1917 case of *Buchanan v. Warley*, the Supreme Court ruled against racial segregation of residential areas, unanimously holding that prohibiting the sale of real property from one party to another based on race was unconstitutional.

But this didn't stop land use regulations from being wielded towards exclusionary ends. The racial segregationists of the South found common cause with Berkeley's 1916 zoning code—the first to regulate residential neighborhoods by their intensity of use. Or, said another way, the first to designate that only single family homes could be built on certain plots of land. While this was not explicitly race based zoning, it effectively was, as only wealthier families (who were nearly exclusively White for other historic reasons) could afford single family homes. Supporters of the ordinance bragged that this would keep neighborhoods reliably free of "Asiatics or Negroes".[20] When combined with private mechanisms like restrictive covenants on the sale of private property that forbade the transfer of deeds to predefined groups, a dark era of segregation in North America was codified, propped up by theoretically pragmatic regulations like Ordinance 9774.

As these seeds germinated, one of the most significant precedents for the next century of development patterns was sowed via the Supreme Court case of *Village of Euclid v. Ambler Realty Co.* in 1926. In response to industry moving south from Cleveland, Euclid, which borders the city to the Northeast, adopted a zoning ordinance to prevent industrial uses within its borders. Ambler Realty wasn't happy about this, as they bought land within the village with the explicit intent of developing factories. Euclid's ordinance, they claimed, amounted to an unconstitutional taking and violation of due process. The Supreme Court did not agree. The majority ruled that using zoning (a relatively new concept) to prohibit certain uses was a valid exercise of a municipality's police power.

Though presumably more innocuous than other laws that preceded it, the precedent of *Euclid v Ambler* allowed municipalities to arbitrarily regulate their land to a degree of prescriptiveness without any historic equivalent. Up until the decision, nearly every locale in the world had the right to situate different uses next to, on top of, or below each other. A cafe could comfortably (and legally) exist underneath an office, which might itself be underneath a third-floor apartment. Nothing prohibited a school or a grocer from being located next to any of these uses. If people really wanted to get crazy, they could throw all of these things into the same building, or series of buildings neighboring one another, in any combination they liked. After Euclidean zoning, it became possible to segregate all of these uses away from one another, turning the historic city inside out. And segregate we did.

As satisfying as it might be to lay blame at the feet of one decision, the devolvement of our built environment can't solely be attributed to Euclidean zoning. While it shaped our society in some meaningful(ly bad) ways, its impact has been dramatically augmented by the scaling up of our communities facilitated by cars and highways. A qualifier before we delve into this topic: in some circles, it's become popular to view cars as inherently bad for our cities, but this isn't really true. Motor vehicles only go where roads lead them. They can be phenomenally useful tools if managed correctly. if someone can't walk well, or needs to urgently see a doctor, quick and efficient door-to-door access is important. Being able to get groceries in the middle of a snowstorm in winter, or visit far-flung family members many hundreds of miles away, are extraordinary benefits.

Cities like Amsterdam and Copenhagen have (in many ways) figured out how different forms of transport can peaceably coexist by balancing allocations of road space to ensure one mode doesn't overpower the others. Driving a car is just one of several options someone has at their disposal for how to get around (it's usually not the most efficient or affordable way), so cars can still be used where needed without dominating a city. Not so in North America, where we've reoriented our entire infrastructure to become "car dependent" where many of us can't go anywhere without a car. It didn't start this way, though.

Prior to World War II, American cities looked much the same as their European and Asian counterparts, just with more grids and a few hundred years less of history. Looking at pictures of Cincinnati or Baltimore, one would be excused for confusing them with Manchester or Liverpool. When first introduced, the advent of cars didn't really change the fabric of cities all that much. This was evident in Manheim, the German gridded city where the gas-powered automobile was invented by Karl Benz (eponymously of Mercedes-Benz fame). Compositionally, these first cars were little different from the carriages which preceded them, where horses were swapped out for engines. Private cars quickly made their way to the United States, with the first vehicles produced before the turn of the century. But they didn't truly take off until Henry Ford introduced the Model T in 1908. Prices started around $850 ($29,000 in 2024 dollars) before dropping to the equivalent of $4,600 by 1924 thanks to the efficiencies of the assembly line.[21] Sales skyrocketed. Where prior models only had production runs of a few thousand cars, 15 million Model Ts were sold from 1908 to 1927. In 1906, there were only 100,000 cars on American streets. By 1927, there were more than 20 million.[22]

Model Ts, and other cars, needed roads to drive on. Champions of this new technology in federal and local government were only too happy to accommodate this need. Beginning in 1916 with the *Federal Aid Road Act*, and continuing through the 1920s with the *Federal Aid Highway Act of 1921*, the foundation for a network of roads crisscrossing the country was laid down. Over the next two decades, spurred on by generous federal funding, roads were paved around the country, including the famous Route 66. Rural communities, previously difficult to traverse, or completely inaccessible, gained new connections. Uneven, dusty (and when it rained, impossibly muddy) streets in cities and towns were paved over. While this made getting around easier for people bicycling and walking, it also made doing so more dangerous. Bumpily moving along a road at the pace of a horse's trot requires some degree of concentration. But when streets are easier to drive on, people drive faster, and lose their focus. This leads to deaths. In 1913, the first year of recorded data, motor-vehicle deaths occurred at a rate of 4.4 per 100,000 people, or 4,200 total casualties. In 1937, this peaked at a rate of 30.8, nearly 40,000 people in total.[23]

Many of these deaths can be attributed to putting too much power in the hands of those ill-equipped to wield it. With no driver's education, or even established norms of how one should drive, streets were chaotic. Stop signs, lane lines, and driver's licenses didn't exist. Practically anyone could try their hand behind the wheel, with little oversight. Cars had no brake lights, so if drivers stopped short (which happens every minute on the roads), there was no way of anticipating it. For some, this wasn't an issue, as they breezed through all intersections without a moment's hesitation, seldom slowing down to see if traffic might be coming from the other direction. There was no reason why they should've been so confident—there weren't even traffic signals to let them know they could go through a green light. Left turns were treated like right turns, with offenders earning the name "corner cutters" for making quick movements against the flow of traffic, hitting unsuspecting pedestrians crossing the other side of the street.[24] Pileups were common. Drunk driving, pervasive.

Driving got safer after its Great Depression depths. Things we hardly spend a moment thinking about, like seat belts or reliable brakes, were introduced. Roads began to resemble those we drive on today. Just like zoning, public thoroughfares began to be divided strictly by use. Most frequently, they were dedicated exclusively to cars. Trams, pedestrians, and bicyclists had to find other ways around. This had its benefits, however. Kids were barred from literally playing in traffic. Trains became separated by grade so they didn't have to compete for road space with other modes of transportation, and railroad crossing signals were implemented. Where streets once faintly resembled the imagined glories of toddlers, with trucks, trains, and unsuspecting action figures smashing together (with attendant whooshing and crashing sound effects), they became more rational, and safer. Thankfully, these scenes now rarely make it past playroom reenactments.

Aside from donning new paved surfaces, the streets themselves were little different than in the pre-automobile era. Gradually, that began to change. Detroit completed the first urban highway, Davison Freeway, in 1942.[25] Dozens of homes and businesses were demolished (or picked up and moved) to make way for the road. Davison Avenue was transformed from a tree-lined boulevard to an open-air sewer for cars, splitting the Highland Park neighborhood into two. Subsequent expansions (it currently spans 8 lanes wide) have ensured Highland Park hasn't recovered since.

Compared to what was to come, the engineers responsible for constructing the first highways were little more than raptors testing the fences, perhaps aware of their power, but not empowered to see it to its conclusion. This changed in 1956, where America's infatuation with cars and roads was blown open. The creation of the Interstate Highway System unleashed a scale of infrastructure development that was historically unprecedented up to that point, paradigmatically shifting development patterns towards private car ownership. Conceived as a project for national defense by President Eisenhower (the full name of the law was the *National Interstate and Defense Highways Act*), the bill authorized 47,000 miles of highways that were constructed at a cost of more than $500 billion (inflation adjusted). It took 35 years to complete.[26] Conquering farm lands, complex natural ecosystems, and dense urban communities with equal parts deftness and indifference (sometimes bordering on hostility), the Act expanded the previous interstate system by more than 20 times its pre-1956 mile count.[27]

Though this system was, and continues to be, lauded by supporters as essential to the mid century growth that launched America into superpower status, it was also successful in a different, less celebrated way. The interstate highway system and the broader network of 1,000,000 miles of federally supported roads (out of 4.2 million road miles nationally) ushered America into an era of unique individualism and expanded segregation.[28]

Yes, the development of a national network of roads allowed for increased logistical interconnectivity and economic productivity, which are both good things as far as I'm concerned. But this prosperity wasn't shared equally. It was a kind of scattered adventure: connectivity for some, and severance for others. What Eisenhower's highway system most uniformly accomplished was to stretch us out and pull us apart. These were, after all, key components of the program's stated goals. As much as the Interstate Highway System was an infrastructure initiative, it was equally a de-densification project to diffuse potential targets in the Cold War, where dense cities could be attacked for concentrated destructive impact.

This stretching and pulling had many adverse impacts. Strong communities were destroyed to facilitate the movement of private vehicles to new communities segregated by class, use, and almost always at the beginning, race. More than 13,500 miles tore through cities, displacing hundreds of thousands and damning those who remained to grim conditions. Enabled by the highways, millions across the country moved out of cities. Most of these emigres were middle class white families, earning the movement the name "White Flight". They drove along elevated highways, never quite interacting with the city they lived closest to, merely using it transactionally as a place to work from 9:00 in the morning to 5:00 in the evening, before driving back home, ignorant of the destruction that enabled them to live in separate communities many miles outside of the city's limits. Could there be anything more individualistic than this?

Hardly, but such was the zeitgeist. This was the cultural peak of Modernism, a philosophy that viewed itself as fundamentally scientific, espousing hyper rationalism, individualism, and an embrace of technology to further human progress. You may know some of its exports, like the Scandinavian mid-century furniture favored by anointed tastemakers (and maybe by you as well!), to abstract art that no one really understands when looking at on their own, but are convinced it must be good because those same tastemakers told them so. But Modernism was, and is, so much more influential than this.

By the time World War II ended, Modernism was no longer the avant-garde movement it had once been at the beginning of the 20th century, pushing art, design, and thought to places previously inconceivable. It was now mainstream. Modernism was a philosophy that explicitly rejected the past in an embrace of the future, seductive at a time where much of the world was rebuilding after two devastating wars and a crippling depression. The past had wrought such profound destruction and iniquity on a scale so vast, it was enough to think "pre-Modern" humanity was beyond redemption. One could understand the motivation to move beyond all that was associated with those times. For our cities and towns, this worldview demanded that any traditional place, structure, or way of building become *verboten*, at least to any sufficiently modern, thoughtful person of the day.

Modern urban planning practices and the private automobile were the perfect tools to rebuild this broken world. They embodied a scientific, rational, and hopeful future predicated on technology, which would allow the world to rise triumphantly beyond its darkest moments. Where the human condition was untenable and messy in the pre-Modern period, a cure for its effective management had seemingly been found.

Modernism penetrated all realms of thinking and creation. In architecture and city building, there was perhaps no figure of greater consequence than Charles-Édouard Jeanneret, the Swiss-French architect and theorist better known by the name he selected for himself, Le Corbusier. Modernism's abstractions were made tangible in the built environment through his plans. In denigrating pre-Modern communities as laid out along the "Pack-Donkey's way", Le Corbusier viewed the traditional city as anachronistic, an overcrowded vestige of habitation from the time before reason and industrial capability prevailed. In this way, Corbu set himself directly against one of the most prominent architectural theorists of the prior generation, Camillo Sitte. Sitte lamented the development of industrialized cities for stripping beauty and the arts out of everyday life. He heralded traditional cities for their intimate plazas, perpendicular streets that met to form terminating vistas that provided enclosure where one's sight line down the street was drawn towards a building or monument, and irregularly curv-ing lanes, which he considered vital to successful city-building.[29] Le Corbusier did not.

Writing in his 1929 manifesto, *The City of To-Morrow and Its Planning*, Le Corbusier criticized Sitte's *City Planning According to Artistic Principles* as "a most wilful piece of work" describing its advocacy for artistic and organic cities as "an appalling paradoxical misconception in an age of motor-cars".[30] He felt that "a modern city lives by the straight line, inevitably for the construction of buildings, sewers and tunnels, highways, pavements. The circulation of traffic demands the straight line; it is the proper thing for the heart of a city."

These ideas materialized in Ville Contemporaine, a 1922 plan for a hypothetical city of three million people. Le Corbusier took heavy inspiration from machines, famously stating "A house is a machine for living in" and that, "Machines will lead to a new order both of work and of leisure".[31] Revering the mechanized processes of mass production for its hyper-efficient creation of goods, Le Corbusier set about designing his city much in the way a refrigerator or a truck might be produced. If these products could be churned out with precision, consistency, and good taste, he observed, why should a city be any different?

With a rigid orthogonality, he envisioned the city as a collection of strictly segregated zones, where long and wide highways dedicated to private automobiles were the principal arteries of moving from one zone to the next. Corbu worshiped the car and oriented his entire plan around it, similar to the way a church unfolds around a nave. As far as the buildings were concerned, there could be no detailing. Citing the architect Adolph Loos' seminal *Ornament and Crime:* "The more a people are cultivated, the more decor disappears."[32] As Modernism was the height of humanity's intellectual journey, its adherents reasoned, they were too sophisticated to be fooled by the simple tricks of cheap ornamentation, favoring the intellectually honest structures whose form followed their functions. Minimalism would rule the day. When combined with machine processes, Ville Contemporaine's buildings took the form of stark identically reproduced skyscrapers situated in parks, gradually tapering off in height from the central district outwards to a shorter, but still identical, composition. These buildings were to be evenly distributed around the city as pews to witness the car driving down the aisles of the church of Modernity.

By providing everything with a clearly defined space, separating all uses cured the chaotic competition over scarce land that historic cities struggled with. Building things on top of one another, without so much as a few square feet of relief from the screaming salesman or rabid preacher, was barbaric. Looking down from a bird's eye view onto the city—a view only possible thanks to the technological progress of the airplane—everything would be perceived as perfectly symmetrical, and entirely rational, befitting the triumph of the Modern man.

Ville Contemporaine was a totalitarian masterpiece. There was to be no derivation from the exacting lines. Everything succumbed to the plan—and by extension, the car. People included. This was the only way to overcome the conditions of the past. Humanity had to be put in place, and internalize that fact.

Despite his self-perceived brilliance, Le Corbusier saw little traction at first. He needed something bolder to bring attention to his ideas. What better way to show the superiority of the Modern world over the traditional one than by planning a direct claim

Le Corbusier's Plan Voisin for Paris.

over it? Then people would understand. Fed up with the squalor, overcrowding, and perceived anachronistic nature of his adopted city, Paris, Le Corbusier proposed the Plan Voisin. It would cover around one square mile of land in the center of the city, demolishing relics of the past for marvels of the future. Building off of the principles of Ville Contemporaine, Plan Voisin would have provided homes for 78,000 people, in identical four-winged towers. 90% of the land would have been preserved for open space and circulation. Naturally, the proposal was sponsored by a car company (Avions Voisin).

This was a very different kind of vision for the future than previous optimists had espoused, and it marked a turning point in the history of our built environment. Instead of improving the slums or building new cities with the daily routines and emotions of people in mind, as the social reformers and Sitte valued, Le Corbusier's Modernist plans rejected human experience for technocratic optimization. He put ideology, technology, and rationalism above humans—though admittedly, we aren't known to be the most rational beings. Of course, Modernism wasn't an incontrovertible science (no science is), but rather an aesthetic movement that expressed itself through a very particular vision of the future, prone to the fallibilities and shortsightedness of any ideology that condescends to know all, as philosopher Alain de Botton convincingly argues in his riveting *The Architecture of Happiness*.[33] Aesthetic or scientific, for the first time in history, cities were no longer planned around the needs of people, but rather, the demands of the car. The consequences would be profound.

Paris was saved from destruction, but other cities were not so lucky. Le Corbusier's plans were exported around the world. For our purposes, we'll focus on their landfall on the American side of the Atlantic from the French capital.

American cities had been tinkering with piecemeal elements of Modernist planning for decades, like ordered Euclidean zoning, the mass production of cars, and the creation of highways and modern towers. But it wasn't until a general philosophy that encompassed all of these elements was put together that their ultimate impact on society would be felt. While there wasn't ample opportunity to implement this philosophy during the Great Depression or World War II, due to a lack of resources and focus being directed on other fronts, as soon as stability was reached in the postwar period, Modernism presented something of an easy roadmap to guide cities and towns into the future of the 20th century.

This materialized in two distinct ways, which I call the twin swords: one to cut down, the other to cut through. The first sword cleaved highways through dense thickets. Following Le Corbusier's dictat that normative traffic circulation must take the form of a straight line through the heart of a city, entire neighborhoods were demolished to make way for urban freeways, subsidized generously from the federal government. Gashes often discriminately severed neighborhoods whose land was the cheapest and held little political power such that they couldn't put up much of a fight. Not only were homes destroyed, but for those that remained, connections to those on the other side became unsupportable. Where two families might have gotten together every Sunday for dinner before the highways were built, afterwards they now had to go around, which could be a significant detour. Without these connections, beloved local businesses closed, community centers emptied, and economic productivity declined meaningfully. Scars from these decisions still exist in many neighborhoods today, segregating and subjugating.

Much like a machete, this first sword hacked vertically through neighborhoods for roads and highways. The second cut horizontally, in service of demolishing blighted slums. Broadly, these were not slums that the 19th-century social reformers would recognize. While it's true that conditions were quite bad in some of these areas, many were simply gritty working-class neighborhoods, far from the supposed squalor that inflicted them. With caprice and discrimination against minority racial and religious groups, entire neighborhoods were cleared, leveraging federal subsidies from Title I of the 1949 *Housing Act*, better known as Urban Renewal. Neighborhoods that may have otherwise been perfectly fine if, in the minds of certain planners, not for the color of their residents' skin or their religious beliefs, were designated as "blighted" and in need of reform.

Wrecking balls crashed through urban fabric, replacing finely networked communities with austere towers that turned their backs on the streets and offered little in the way of geniality. Greenery and open space were abundant, but it was superficial, and not really usable. Patches of grass without programming, seats, or enclosure did not welcome people to spend time in them. They were dead spaces. At night, without lights or protection from security, these became dangerous areas that were best to be avoided. Sadly, those who lived there could not. While good in theory, without effective management or an understanding of

The Wendell O. Pruitt Homes and William Igoe Apartments complex in St Louis. Completed in 1955. Demolished in 1972.

the intimacies of what makes for successful design (which none of these developments benefited from), they fell on hard times, and were ultimately neglected by those who erected them Infamous examples include New York's Public Housing developments (NYCHA projects) and St. Louis' Pruitt-Igoe complex, which was so poorly executed that it was demolished before it could even turn 20. Pruitt-Igoe remains a vacant, overgrown lot 50 years later, hardly a 10-minute bike ride from the city's iconic Arch. Other neighborhoods that were cleared for redevelopment as in Norfolk were never built in the first place, displacing former residents and ultimately eviscerating civic life for no reason.

These policies cut beyond our cities, with highways moving outwards from core areas to raze our countryside and form new suburbs. The cause for this may look similar to the challenges we face today; A housing crisis gripped the country following the war. Very few homes were built in the 15 years from the beginning of the Great Depression to V-J Day. This problem was compounded by the fact that GIs returning from Europe and the Pacific were eager to start families but there weren't enough family appropriate homes. Furthermore, despite strict quotas on who could enter the country (through legislation like the *Emergency Quota Act of 1921* and the *Johnson-Reed Act of 1924*), nearly a million immigrants entered the U.S. between 1930 and 1945.[34] And this number only includes those who were officially recorded.[35] Homes were needed, desperately. The National Housing Agency, a temporary wartime entity, estimated in 1944 that the U.S. would need 12,600,000 new dwelling units during the first decade after the war to meet demand.[36]

The federal government recognized the dramatic need and got to work. Prohibitive mortgage terms, like high down payments and one year interest payback periods, were revised to allow prospective home buyers to put as little as 5% of the purchase price down, and spread interest payments over 30 years. Lenders might not have done this on their own, given how risky debt could be, so the loans became federally insured, meaning the government would protect against losses from borrowers who didn't pay back their loans. This gave banks far more confidence in extending mortgages which by extension, enabled developers to secure financing to build the housing the country desperately needed.

Inspiration for these new suburbs was provided, if indirectly, by Le Corbusier. Though they didn't look like Ville Contemporaine at first glance, compositionally, they were nearly identical. Accessed via straight, orthogonal road systems, these new suburbs were hyper rational. Everything had its place, and nothing could be outside of its own place. Houses here. Strip malls there. Apartments nowhere (less Corbuserian, admittedly). Under the guise of individualism, and abiding to a structure that would make Corbu proud, the unadorned homes were homogeneously mass produced like washing machines or sheet metal, sat in the middle of their own parks surrounded by ample green space, and were subservient to fleets of equally mass produced cars.

With funding at the ready, and a plan cemented for idealized communities, all that was needed was a system that could adequately scale upwards to satisfy the demand. Building 12 million homes requires some level of coordination, after all. Re-enter zoning.

Euclidean zoning is similar to a coloring book. The lines are already there, you just need to fill them in. I should mention it's not a very good coloring book, as most of the areas are all the same color, which makes for a rather drab artistic exercise and commensurately insipid communities, but I digress. In the post-war period, a page in the Euclidean book would mostly be the color of single family homes (let's say green), with some pockets of red and blue for retail and office strips. Though boring, this coloring book was very useful for communities who wanted to plan for a future of growth but didn't have the internal capabilities to do so.

There are nearly 20,000 incorporated places in the United States. For clarity, an incorporated place is defined by the census as "any governmental unit incorporated under state law as a city, town, borough, or village legally prescribed limits, powers, and functions".[37] The vast majority of these units are home to fewer than 10,000 people, making it infeasible for each one to support a planning department. There are only so many planners to go around, and that's before the churn which sees many trained experts leave the profession in search of more inspired or lucrative disciplines. After the war, most towns didn't (and still don't) have the time nor the resources to develop their own plans and codes. It was simply easier to copy what neighboring towns did. And so, standard codes were transcribed from one municipality to the next, straight across the country. No town wanted to be left behind the march of Modernity. For unincorporated areas that had no pretensions about progress, they needed mechanisms to manage the rapid growth which was consuming farmland, and similarly adopted the codes of incorporated areas. This is the genesis of why everywhere in the U.S. now looks the same. Whether you're in Boise, Tampa,

Omaha, or anywhere in between, the coloring book (and the people who color in those lines) is very similar, if not the same. More on this later in Chapter 5.

These new suburban homes weren't built for all who needed them. Programs were selectively subsidized for populations that public officials deemed worthy. The Underwriting Manual of the Federal Housing Administration (FHA), the framework which laid out who would be insured by federally backed loans and who would not, explicitly excluded certain groups. As Richard Rothstein detailed in his influential, *Color of Law*, the FHA and the Home Owners Loan Corporation (HOLC) created maps that designated a gradient of "safe" to "hazardous" neighborhoods where mortgages could be insured.[38] If a neighborhood was deemed safe, a mortgage could be issued with minimal concern. But if a neighborhood were labeled hazardous, no loans were to be issued. No loan, no home. No ability to build equity and wealth. This process became known as redlining, because "hazardous" neighborhoods were colored red on the maps, and all who lived in them were deemed too risky to extend a mortgage to.

With the Federal Government's commitment to building a network of highways crisscrossing the country (de-densifying cities in the process) and the backstopping of loans to support mass construction to solve the housing crisis, funds were near limitless for those who were able to build at scale according to FHA standards. Levittown, Long Island, is the early case study for this pattern of growth. Originally planned for 2,000 homes, so abundant were the funds, so generous were the subsidies, and so strong was the demand, that by 1951 the Levitt family had constructed more than 17,000. Home models varied slightly in later phases, but at the outset they were functionally identical in order to economize costs through efficient production of component materials to deliver as much housing as possible. Through a mass production process not unlike Ford's assembly line, 26 specialized teams

Aerial of one of the early phases of Levittown, Long Island.

of contractors could build one of Levitt's 750 square foot cottages in under a day, with each of the 26 steps of the process optimized for maximum efficiency. To further reduce costs, workers were not paid by the hour, but by the number of homes they completed, incentivizing speed. Attics that had room for two extra bedrooms were left unfinished. For those who were allowed to buy a home in Levittown, the deal was almost too good to be believed by today's standards. GIs returning from war could buy a home for just $7,000, with no money down, and $65 monthly payments.[40] Purchasers of the homes signed clauses which forbade "the premises to be used or occupied by any other persons than members of the Caucasian race".[41]

Suburban Modernism guided American development patterns as a philosophy throughout the mid-century period. So powerful was this vision, and so strong the belief in it, that hundreds of billions of public dollars were leveraged in service of it. Some still believe in the promises of this post-war paradigm today, which have become embodied in the idealized American dream of a generously sized single family home, several car garage, and large lawn separated from all other uses by long and straight roadways. This, many reason, is what rational individualism looks like, the highest state any sufficiently modern person can aspire to be. That it's effectively a socialized housing and highway program seems to matter little, because people believe so strongly in the original promises of the program and the orthodoxy of individualism.

But gradually the direct connection to this philosophy receded. Divorced from the earliest theorists who were deeply concerned about solving the most pressing challenges of their day, we've been left with the vestiges of realized plans that never quite succeeded in translating the enlightened values of Modern theory into place. The result has been an overwhelmingly disorienting, segregated, inefficient, and unsustainable built environment. One that, while temporarily addressing a housing shortage, sowed the seeds for a future one. It is my belief, as we'll explore in the next chapter, that the negative outcomes this way of building have delivered far outweigh the positives.

It's been some time since the results of this philosophy were rejected, but there hasn't quite been another worldview to replace it. We're simply copying and pasting simulacra of the earliest postwar suburban developments (and institutional urban derivatives like blocky apartment buildings) without thinking about why we're doing it. Though the earliest subdivisions are no better than the new ones today (they're probably, on balance, worse), there was an excitement around their creation because they represented a belief in the possibility of a better world that was fresh, innovative, and upwardly mobile. Difficult though it may be to see today, these subdivisions were, in many essential ways, remarkable improvements over the conditions of the past. We haven't, however, continued the upwards trajectory of our built environment in recent decades. We are copying and pasting the results of policies that are no longer relevant, without questioning the outcomes. Few viable alternatives to bring us into a new era have materialized.

I don't mean to be dismissive of the work attempted to rectify mid-century development patterns or their vestiges. Groups like the Postmodernists tried to offer another path. Few ideologies, however, can achieve sustained success if they orient themselves around the opposition to something else. Once their opponent vanishes, so too, will they. PoMo rejected the severity, austerity, and rigid formality of Modernism, but did so in such a playful way that arguably it didn't take itself seriously enough. So how could the rest of the country adopt such a philosophy? While this is a gross underaccounting of the labors of this period, it's not unfair to say—and indeed it has proven true— that this philosophy was not sufficient to chart a sustained course of progress in the built environment.

After decades lacking a general direction following the dissolution of Modernism, we've become untethered from place and untethered from meaning of place as no substantive worldview has taken its position. Modernism, for all its flaws, at least offered some structure for building. We've become numb to a world where there is no operating guide for moving forward. The scale of our planning and infrastructure apparatus is so vast and incomprehensible, and our needs so extraordinary, that it seems like we can't do anything. So instead of believing in something, we find ourselves agnostic towards just about anything. Instead of working tirelessly to solve our problems as earlier reformers did, or dreaming of a better world as the Modernists did, we've become prisoners to the codes that have damned us. It is a national Stockholm syndrome. We've fallen for our oppressors because we don't know where else to turn. We feel as though we no longer have any agency.

But we do. It just starts with a bit of belief.

Le Corbusier espoused his Modern belief set for the world in a 1923 collection of essays entitled *Toward a New Architecture*. A century later, we find ourselves in need of a new general philosophy on how to structure and interact with our built environment. Our surroundings impact us too much to acquiesce to our unacceptable status quo.

And so, on the pages that follow, I propose a new general philosophy for our world. It's one predicated on a unity of the pragmatic and romantic. There are very many serious challenges facing North America: climate change, lack of affordability, economic stagnation, segregation, prejudice, structural fragility, declining physical and mental health. The list goes on. None of these challenges, however, are insurmountable. There are no immutable laws of the universe which say we cannot address them head on. To let these challenges continue out of some laziness or cynicism towards embracing change is deeply harmful. Optimism is the required course of action to take.

In our pursuit of Optimism through pragmatism, we must take caution that the achievement of our goals does not come at the expense of the people they're meant to serve. We could theoretically solve our housing crisis by building 10 million concrete cottages measuring 500 square feet at a distance no closer than 60 miles to the core of a dozen major cities, but many other challenges, perhaps more severe, would accompany this proposed solution. The places that are the most utilitarian, in their courtship of lowest common denominator answers, often find themselves the most poorly equipped in the march towards longevity, privileging myopic solutions such as they do. That the most marginalized must accept a cruel spartanism is an iniquity not often discussed. We must seek to do more.

We must create a better world. One that is beautiful, aspirational, dynamic, diverse, sustainable, walkable, affordable, opportune—but not utopian, as utopias have no place in reality. They're purely fictional. The definition of utopia is "no place". We very much want to build real places. And what's more, we know what these real places could look like. All of the listed Optimistic elements have been made manifest in our world before to great effect. A select few places have been able to harness these elements together at the same time. Even fewer have made these conditions last, at scale, for the many. Ours is a mission of abundance such that these kinds of places may become available to as much of the population as possible, without subsidy (familial or governmental, as these are subject to the caprices of varying administrations, or the winds of time), tradeoff, or coercion. Leveraging an Optimistic mentality, we can solve the problems plaguing our world today effectively and wonderfully.

Optimism is inherently a positive force. But lose it, or adopt a worldview that rejects humanity in favor of something else, and we quickly regress. Where the East End of London was, for a time, one of the worst patches of land one could stumble across in the world, it's now one of the most desirable. In and around the areas redeveloped by social reformers, and sometimes in the buildings created by the reformers themselves, rents are among the most expensive in the United Kingdom. These places, optimistic though their genesis was, have arguably become too successful. Alfred Tredway White's Workman's cottages now sell for millions of dollars, on the rare occasions they do come up for sale.

It would be wrong to forget the context of why the remnants from this era were created in the first place, and disregard the conditions that have (mercifully) been left to the past. It would be equally wrong, however to ignore the triumph of these interventions, and the lessons their creation has for us. Regretfully, we are guilty of this transgression. Caught in between an ardent preservation that's content to maintain the past, and a lapse in the collective memory of the conditions that led to the creation of the places we so revere today, we are lost. Untethered from our history, we cling frantically at those few shreds of good that we enjoy lest they meet the same fate as their perished siblings. If we love these places so much, pragmatism would demand we simply create more of them. It's inconceivable that housing once developed for the most marginalized is now out of grasp for all but the wealthiest simply because we stopped creating these sorts of places. An artificial scarcity has divorced context and common sense, and the least advantaged groups pay the cost. We cannot look back at a job well done and rest on those laurels forever. Without sufficient watering and replenishment, those laurels will die.

If architecture is an honest reflection of a society's values—and what could be more telling than the structures we erect that we labor our whole lives to acquire and then reside among—what does it say about ours? Are we a people devoid of ambition, morality, and meaning? If we don't respect the project of building cities, or societies, that's one thing, but I don't believe that to be true. So the question becomes: what do we want our buildings to say about us? What do we value? Do we worship at the feet of Gods, or commerce? Do we withdraw into ourselves, or do we hold sacred communion with our neighbors? Do we seek a higher plane of living, or are we content with whatever scraps we're provided? Our values can be read in wood and stone, and the stories they tell are incorruptible. What tales will we tell?

Working towards crafting new stories about who we are will doubtless be challenging. Much of the last century has proven how difficult the right sort of storytelling is. And yet, I'm hopeful. I'm hopeful because we know how to create places that are fundamentally good for our well being, physical health, mental disposition, economy, safety, social structure, and a host of other metrics. We know how to create joyous realms that are worthy of our affections. We've done it before. Ambition alone, or clutching to an idealized past, is not enough, however. We cannot simply want to do good. We have to acknowledge, and then respond, to the operating realities that we're constrained by today. Even the smallest of projects requires buy-in from many dozens of people, from public officials, bankers, and neighborhood groups, to architects, graphic designers, code enforcers, and construction trades. Getting all of these people to believe they're on the same team is no simple thing.

So, how do we go about doing this? How do we progress the built environment forward in the next century when it has regressed so far in the last? It starts with the belief that we can create great places anew—a belief that a better world is not only possible, but essential to cultivate. We can accomplish this by looking at examples of great places that have been built recently and within our context, not 200 years ago in a place opposite the world from us. Inspiration then leads to realization. When people see that something can be done, they'll be more inclined to do more things like it in the future. When they think it's impossible—or don't see anything like it at all—there's little hope of creating something better. One cannot very well move forward with something they have no knowledge of, or do not think has any reasonable chance of success. How could you think about doing something if you've never seen it done before? Creating something without a reference to existing precedents is very hard. Thankfully, we have references.

The first precedents for this contemporary strain of Optimism can be traced back to the pioneering work of the first New Urbanists. Driven by a desire to rectify the ills of midcentury planning and sprawling development patterns, a small group of architects and planners (Andrés Duany, Elizabeth Plater-Zyberk, Elizabeth Moule, Stefanos Polyzoides, Peter Calthorpe, Hank Dittmar, and Daniel Solomon, among others) formed the Congress for the New Urbanism in 1993. According to the founding charter, "The Congress for the New Urbanism views disinvestment in central cities, the spread of placeless sprawl, increasing separation by race and income, environmental deterioration, loss of agricultural lands and wilderness, and the erosion of society's built heritage as one interrelated community-building challenge".[41]

These principles have informed a generation of practitioners of the built environment, both directly and indirectly. They form part of an Optimistic philosophy, but more is needed. Where the Modernist planners espoused hyper rationality, individualism, an embrace of technology, minimalism, and orthogonality, the Optimist privileges the pursuit of walkable, sustainable, organic (spontaneously occurring), affordable, beautiful, malleable, contextual, stylistically agnostic, diverse, and common sense communities that adhere to the needs of people first. Optimism is a perspective that welcomes technology and innovation, but only when they complement humanity, not usurp it. Importantly, the Optimist embraces an abundance agenda that advocates for building as many high-quality places as possible that adhere to these underlying principles such that as many as possible may access fundamentally good communities, without scarcity, bad faith regulation, or hostility inhibiting them. Optimism may prefer the construction of infill projects on lots in existing urban areas, but it also provides the framework for town extensions in greenfields such as they may be required.

Much is wrong with our current built environment and the underlying regulations, incentives, and imperatives that drive our development patterns. There's much to be indignant about, and righteously oppose. There's a lot to shake our fists at, grimly mock, or blink absently at. It's so easy to fall prey to fatalism for all of these reasons. But we must triumph over this cynicism. There's so much worth celebrating. Let me modify that: there's so much that *needs* celebrating.

Optimism is a movement that provides application-free membership to all. Without people who embody the ideals of this movement, there would be no cities, towns, neighborhoods, nor communities worth spending time in. Doing away with unapproachable, high-brow rhetoric that presumes to tell others what they ought to do and what they ought to like, we must emphasize that ours is a welcoming, joyous mission, that encourages many different voices and perspectives. That we're working on creating a better future where all of us get to enjoy the benefits of our collective work. That we're not afraid to be excited about the future we're building and have a little fun! If we don't derive joy from the things we surround our lives with, what's the point? For too long, our communities have been greatly deprived because of their rejection of these very ideas.

You may not be sympathetic to the need for this new philosophy. It may sound utopian, superfluous, and perhaps not even that desirable. As the next chapter attempts to argue, however, nothing could be further from the truth. The many challenges our modern society presents require a vigilant and urgent response. Optimism is both the most pragmatic solution, and the most aspirational.

2.
The Need for Optimism

Many of our communities are boring, and some are expensive, but what's so bad about that? Well, if only they were boring and sort of expensive, there would certainly be room for improvement, but there wouldn't be a need for a defiant call to action of the sort I'm proposing.

The problems that afflict our communities, of course, go far beyond tediousness and high sticker prices. Prevailing development patterns in North America, and increasingly in other parts of the world that have followed our lead, guarantee negative outcomes. In orienting our world around cars, codifying zones that prohibit economic mobility and enshrine segregation, and mandating standards that lead directly to the destruction of our natural and social environments, we have lost unimaginable sums in economic output (one study estimates that sprawl and its discontents cost the U.S. more than $1 trillion annually), to say nothing of the unquantifiable tears in our social fabric.[1]

What's worse, these problems threaten to further devolve if we don't do anything about them.

The scale of our challenges is too large to go unaddressed.

I want to pause a moment before diving into this section, and caution that the grievances described herein are not meant as empty complaints. This book wasn't written with the intention to rile a few people up for sport. Every issue discussed in this chapter is one that we can take action to solve. I urge you not to read these next few pages with anger, remorse, or dismissiveness, but with a resolve that anything can be rectified, in time, with sufficient thoughtfulness, and with appropriate policy. Creativity and humility will be required to overcome some of these challenges, to be sure. And though we've been desperately short of both of these virtues over the last several decades, the great thing is that there are many talented people dedicating themselves to solving these very issues, with these very traits, today. We've gotten ourselves into this situation, and it's well within our power to get ourselves out of it. Okay, now to the bad stuff.

Environmental Degradation and Human Suffering

The prevailing North American development pattern since the end of World War II has been that of decentralized, car-dependent, low-density, and segregated urban (then suburban, then exurban) expansion. Or, colloquially, sprawl. This has been tantamount to total war on natural and agricultural environments. A back-of-the-envelope analysis demonstrates the scale of these losses.

From 1982 to 2017, 68,334 square miles of natural and agricultural lands were cleared for development.[2] The vast plurality of this was dedicated exclusively to single family zoned neighborhoods. A smaller portion was razed for rural transportation (new roads and highways). To put these numbers in perspective, we cleared an amount of land larger than the total area of Florida in the last 35 years (with Florida itself doing its fair share). But this was just a continuation of a trend that began a few decades earlier. From 1958 through 1981, it's estimated that 39 million acres were demolished, bringing the total land lost to development from 1958 to 2017 to 129,000 square miles.[3] If the area we razed were its own state, it would be the fifth-largest in the country, just behind Montana. Though the proliferation of what we now recognize as car-dependent suburban development began in the latter half of the 1940s, we don't have enough data from this time period to add it to the tally. Those eager to have a comprehensive number will have to be satisfied with assuming that another 5,000 to 10,000 square miles were developed from ~1945 to 1958.

Of course, not all of the building during this period should be looked down upon. Humans need places to live. That takes up land and that's alright. But what's the ideal amount of land we should dedicate for our settlements? Well, this is mostly subjective. Places can be wonderful to live in at a variety of densities, from just a few people per square mile in rural communities to many tens of thousands, like in Paris' beloved core arrondissements. Density doesn't automatically make a place good or bad. It's the form that matters. So how can we say how much land cleared for development constitutes inefficient sprawl?

Prescribing the right density for all places to adhere to isn't my intention. But for the purposes of understanding how much land we could have saved had we opted for some other development pattern, we'll have to use something for a base case of comparison. I suggest we look to streetcar suburbs, those communities that developed around streetcar lines from roughly 1888 through 1930, in areas that were then suburban, but by today's public perception are unmistakably urban. Through a gentle density of less intense development, streetcar suburbs offered more open space and greenery than the cores of the cities they extended from, while still supporting a high enough base of people to allow the lines to run profitably. Lest you think these were merely some dreamy, yet ultimately novel mode of transportation as they exist today, streetcar lines were remarkably expansive. By 1907, 34,404 miles of tracks had been laid down, a significant amount when one considers the *Interstate Highway Act* leveraged 47,000 in this form in total.[4]

A streetcar along St. Charles Avenue in New Orleans (left), and Clark Park in Philadelphia (right).

Streetcar suburbs are a good base reference for a few reasons. First, they're downright lovely. These early suburbs were lined with trees, had charming architecture in a variety of typologies and styles, and sprinkled mixed uses throughout, making it easy to live one's life without ever needing a car. Indeed, these neighborhoods immediately preceded the era of car-dependent suburbs, so they offer us an alternative trajectory that we might have followed had we not embraced that technology so forcefully, especially for the first ring of suburbs closest to the hearts of major cities.

While each one has its own idiosyncrasies, the basic form of all streetcar suburbs is much the same. Some of your favorite neighborhoods began their lives From Boston to Seattle, and Huntington, West Virginia, to Pasadena, California, these suburbs dominated development patterns just as sprawling subdivisions do today. Some of my personal favorites, which we'll use for this analysis, are in Philadelphia and New Orleans.

Clark Park is the platonic ideal of a neighborhood public space. Generously shaded by London Planes, Red Oaks, and Dogwoods, there are many tables to eat lunch at or play chess on with friends, benches to rest while watching kids or dogs play in the open fields, and paths to stroll along. What really makes it shine, though, is the symbiotic relationship it enjoys with the streets that surround it. Each gives the other life. When the first streetcars began to run at the end of the 19th century along Baltimore Avenue, which borders the park to the north, they brought with them the speculative development of proud brick apartment buildings, and stately Victorian and Queen Anne row homes. Today, these structures are home to graduate students, young families, blue collar workers, emigres from East Africa, and artists who populate the park in between trips to the co-op, the nearby Ethiopian restaurants, or one of the neighborhood's countless quaint cafes. When the sun is shining, and the people are out, there are few better examples of tranquil urban life than this.

Clark Park sits on the border of University City to the east (home to the campuses of the University of Pennsylvania and Drexel University) and West Philadelphia proper, fittingly, to the west. University City (19104 zip code) had a population density of 18,048 per square mile in 2019, while West Philadelphia proper (19143) stood at 19,726. Down in New Orleans, Uptown enjoys many of the same qualities as West Philly, only the university is called Tulane, the park (Audubon) is much larger, and the trees are Willows. In 2021, it had a population density of 9,012 people per square mile, 1,000 people less than before Hurricane Katrina.[5] If we take the average population density of these neighborhoods, we arrive at the figure 15,595. This is fairly consistent with other streetcar suburbs around the country, notably in Boston, where Brighton, Dorchester, and the nearby suburb of Somerville all hover around 17,000 per square mile.[6]

To preempt the reader's concern, I understand these amounts might not mean much in the abstract. For most (normal) people, thinking of neighborhoods in terms of population density is like guessing how many jelly beans are in a given jar. Who can be sure, and who really cares so long as they're delicious? Well, it matters a little more than the number of beans in a glass container, as will soon be shown. Let's look to other cities for reference.

If we compare the average density of a pre-war streetcar suburb to that of a typical postwar neighborhood in say, Phoenix, a significant variance becomes readily apparent. Across three zip codes a short drive from downtown (85016, 85020, 85040), the average density is 3,847 people per square mile. The story is much the same in other sunbelt cities that have adopted car-dependent development patterns. San Bernardino, CA (3,474), Irving, TX (3,580), San Antonio, TX (2,876), Jacksonville, FL (1,271), and Henderson, NV (2,984), all have roughly similar densities.[7] The list goes on, but I'll spare you.

This isn't a perfect comparison, but that's sort of the point. The developers of streetcar suburbs were rarely large-scale entities capable of building thousands of homes at once, but rather were often smaller builders who completed modest rows ranging anywhere from a few homes to a few dozen. Many such builders would come together to create a neighborhood, each offering their own little flair in their selected corner. This form of development pattern allowed for a level of malleability that's explicitly prohibited in the subdivisions we know today. Qualifiers considered, we can confidently say there exists a 10,000 to 12,000 person variance in the density between streetcar suburbs and postwar subdivisions— and sometimes far greater than this.

If we were able to go back to 1950 and alter the trajectory of our development patterns, what would our built environment look like? 151 million people lived in the U.S. in 1950. By 2020, the population had grown to just over 330 million. If we accommodated these nearly 180 million new Americans in streetcar suburbs (at our average population density between West Philly and New Orleans), this would have only required approximately 11,500 square miles of land, as opposed to the 129,000 square miles we did develop. The amount of area we would have saved—more than 117,000 square miles—is larger than Italy.

Perniciously, our destruction of the environment has not been contained to the land we've razed. We export negative externalities (consequences in normal parlance) that travel far beyond the boundaries of the land we touch. Among the many, a few include disrupting ecosystems with native fauna forced to move in search of new places to survive (which leads to further knock-on effects), increasing the surface area and propagation of stormwater runoff, deforestation, water and air pollution, and increasing local temperatures.

Let's look a bit closer at air pollution, which comes from many different sources. There are your usual suspects, like particulate matter that escapes from mining and fracking operations, nitrous oxide belched out by heavy industrial and waste management processes, and discharges from agricultural and livestock cultivation. Methane accounts for around 11% of America's total greenhouse gas emissions, much of which can be blamed on the national obsession with beef.[8] The reader might want to skip that trip to the In-N-Out or McDonald's drive-through later today, for more reasons than one.

That's because the largest contributor to air pollution is, by far, transportation, which accounts for 28% of total U.S. greenhouse gas emissions. Nearly three-quarters of this number comes from cars and trucks, with airplanes (8%), boats/ships (3%), and rail (2%) contributing significantly less.[9]

The more we drive, the more we pollute. And because most of the places we live require us to drive everywhere to carry out our basic daily activities, we're polluting at an extraordinarily high rate, every single day. By design.

We can see this impact on the environment. In Christopher Jones and Daniel Kammen's landmark 2013 study on the spatial distribution of U.S. carbon footprints, household emissions across 31,000 zip codes in all 50 states were analyzed.[10] Jones and Kammen found that households living in population-dense areas had significantly lower greenhouse-gas emissions than their suburban and exurban counterparts, which could be up to 3 times as high. This can be seen on maps of emissions broken down by households, where dark red areas represent suburban and exurban communities, and deep greens are either the cores of major metropolitan areas or sparsely populated rural lands. Red is bad. Car-dependent areas are very, very red.

Household emissions vary by kind and degree. From food and dry goods consumption, to energy usage, housing type, and, of course, transportation. While all of these sources tend to be higher in wealthier suburban areas due to greater consumption capacity, transportation is significantly higher because of the requisite further miles that one must travel in order to go from one place to another. Though the heart of Manhattan might not seem like it's particularly green—the city's reputation as the concrete jungle does it no favors on this account—it is one of the most environmentally friendly places on Earth. Seriously. This is because of how easy it is for nearly everyone to walk, bike, or take public transportation to accomplish much of what they need to do, and how efficiently the city's resources are distributed. Same goes for the hearts of other major cities that are highly walkable, bikeable, and well serviced by public transportation.

Counterintuitively, verdant suburban communities where homes have many trees and enjoy large patches of grass are among the least sustainable forms of living, despite all of their greenery. Driving offsets any marginal increase in carbon absorption that a few plants might confer. If these areas were built at the same level of intensity as streetcar suburbs, households would emit 50% fewer metric tons of carbon every year, with the potential for further reductions depending on how car independent they became.

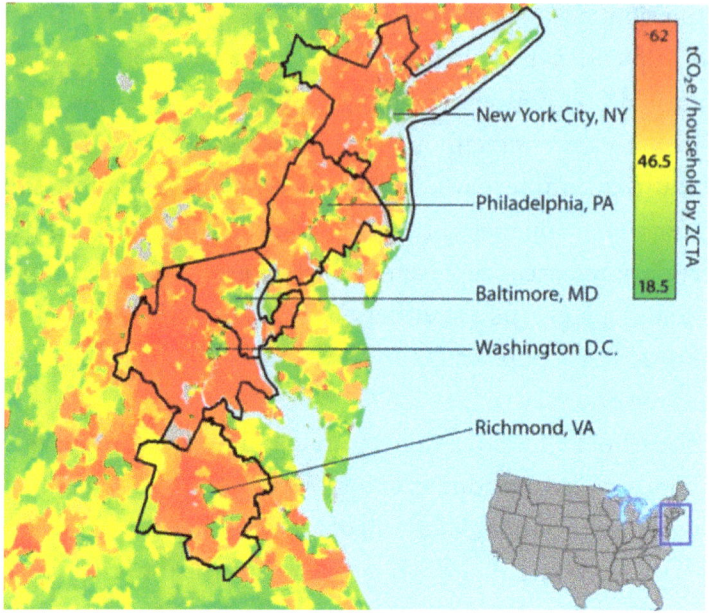

Maps showing carbon dioxide emissions per household, where suburban and exurban communities (red) produce far more emissions per capita than urban (and rural) communities (green).

Shifting the emissions maps from deep red to light green across tens of millions of households would have extraordinary societal benefits.

In a 2020 paper published by the American Chemical Society, a team of researchers found that out of the 100,000 Americans who die every year from air pollution related conditions, more than 30,000 deaths were due to diesel and gasoline fuel combustion emissions.[11] When combined with the 39,000 people killed in traffic accidents in 2020 (a number that increased to 43,000 in 2021), our car-dependent development patterns are responsible for at least 70,000 excess deaths per year.[12] Cars are often lauded for the freedom that they confer, which is true to an extent, but there cannot be complete liberation if tens of thousands a year die as a result. What freedom exists in spending nearly $11,000 a year, the national average expense of owning and operating a car, just to be able to get from point A to point B?[13] Not only is this an inherently limiting way of moving about our world, but it's killing and bankrupting us—two things that I don't personally find very good.

Getting rid of internal combustion engines and embracing electric vehicles would cure all of our problems then right? Not exactly. 40,000 people a year would still be killed pollution, as accidents occur regardless of how the vehicle is powered. We would still have to drive on roads and park in lots, paying exorbitant prices for the privilege. There are a few additional problems here worth diving into. Parking garages are built with concrete, a major contributor to global carbon dioxide emissions in its own right, accounting for about 8% of global emissions.[14] The creation of cement, a key component of concrete, is mainly to blame here. Through firing limestone, clay, and other materials in a kiln, .93 pounds of carbon dioxide is released into the air for every pound of concrete that's produced with regular cement. Spaces in parking garages don't discriminate against internal combustion or electric vehicles (except for those with charging stations, but I digress). And as cars grow larger, more concrete will be needed to support their added heft. From 1990 to 2021, average new vehicle weight increased by 25%.[15]

So, parking garages are bad for the environment. But what about roads? Unfortunately, they're not great either. We build roads in America using asphalt, a distilled crude petroleum product. And we build a lot of them. In some municipalities, it's not uncommon for more than 30% of the land to be dedicated to asphalt-covered roads and parking lots. Certain car-dependent cities punch well above this number. As recently as 2011, more than 64% of downtown Houston was paved for surface parking lots, roads, and garages.[16] When cars drive over asphalt, fine particulate matter is kicked up that slowly finds its way into the atmosphere, and into our lungs. It's little wonder that people living within 100 meters of highways have significantly higher symptoms of asthma than those who live further away.[17] On warm and sunny days when the asphalt expands, this effect is augmented with emissions increasing by up to 300%, according to a 2020 paper published in the academic journal *Science Advances*.[18] Residents in heavily paved desert metropolises like Phoenix and Las Vegas thus are barraged with disproportionately high

As you might have expected, that's not the only problem with asphalt. Because it has a black or dark gray color depending on the mix, it absorbs heat during the day and retains it at night. Acting as much like an oven as it does a smooth driving surface, asphalt is primarily responsible for what's known as the Urban Heat Island effect, a phenomenon where temperatures in built-up areas are markedly higher than their non built-up counterparts. This difference can be as high as 20°F between two areas that are just a dozen miles apart. Less extreme, but no less notable, are the variances that can exist between neighborhoods separated by only a few blocks, where one has ample trees, while the other is covered in asphalt and bereft of a protective canopy. If you've ever walked along a busy road in the summer, you know how intense this effect can be, and how relieving it is to find some shade.

Higher temperatures also lead to an increase in the rate of heat-related deaths and illnesses. For homes that don't have air conditioning, dangerous circumstances arise for vulnerable groups when nighttime temperatures fail to fall below 80°F.[19] Due to the ubiquity of roads and parking lots, and the popularity of asphalt as a roofing material, this is a threshold that's becoming increasingly difficult to dip below in the hotter areas of the country. On average, there are more than 700 heat-related deaths a year in the U.S.[20] As our planet warms, expect this number to rise if we don't reduce the amount of paved surfaces.

More roads leads to an increase in the rate of water pollution, in addition to air pollution. When it rains under normal, non-paved conditions, stormwater is absorbed into the ground or by plants, and eventually finds its way into lakes, streams, rivers, oceans, and other bodies of water. It does so relatively unimpeded, except where it runs through agricultural areas, picking up pesticides and agricultural waste along the way. Impervious conditions in a paved world impede this natural process. Instead of being absorbed into the ground, water runs off of smooth and slick surfaces. Similar to agricultural runoff, asphalt runoff gathers all manner of things you wouldn't want to be collected together, and puts them in places you wouldn't want them to go. It pollutes our water supplies, natural ecosystems, and potentially even agricultural products.

It doesn't matter how "green" the cars driving on top of our roads or parking in garages are—even if they're topped by solar panels or are adorned by hanging plants. The underlying system will never be beneficial to the natural environment.

Of course, anything that impacts the natural world affects us humans as well, being as we are of nature. Increases in pollution-related deaths are a testament to this, as are the asphalt lists which pit us against one another in modern jousting contests at every intersection, leading not just to more traffic-related deaths, but heat-related ones as well. And this is just the tip of the iceberg.

Car-dependent development patterns often lead to sedentary lifestyles. When a car is required to go nearly anywhere, there isn't much opportunity for natural exercise. Walking is a form of active transport which, like bicycling, can satisfy our daily minimum exercise needs. Where someone living in a city may walk 10,000 steps in a day without thinking much about it simply because it's the easiest way to get around, another whose built environment doesn't privilege this walkability may struggle to get 3,000 steps in, even if they make a conscious effort to exercise. All the worse for those who don't.

In a study that began in 1985 and ended in 2007, researchers from the University of Illinois found a 98% correlation between higher car usage and obesity.[21] This doesn't mean those who drive are fated to become obese, but that if someone isn't making a concerted effort to exercise—which is very difficult with the exhaustion of work, raising kids, going to school, and other binding constraints our modern lives generally require of us—it is far more likely that they will become obese. This is a society-wide problem. As of 2020, 42% of Americans were clinically obese, requiring them to spend upwards of $173 billion (2019 dollars) in additional medical expenses.[22] The further one has to commute, or the more spread out the things one has to do are, the worse these effects become. With increased rates of obesity comes the added risks of strokes, heart disease, diabetes, and all manner of negative health outcomes. This is a health crisis of our own making.

Higher rates of stress, as measured by cortisol levels, accompany increased time in cars, especially in congested areas.[23] This not only leads to detrimental physical health outcomes, but negative social and mental health outcomes as well. Indeed, mental illness has even been attributed to the increases in stress and depersonalization in a world where we're less connected to others. If one rarely gets the chance to interact with people because they're always in cars and have little room for serendipitous interactions, they will naturally have less of a social life. The societal rise of disorders like depression may also be linked to a lack of active transport in a world dependent on cars. By foregoing activities that increase the flow of oxygen to the brain, one may find themselves with a lack of clarity, concentration, and focus.[24]

Think about someone who commutes a lot. The more time they spend in the car, the less time they get to spend with family, friends, or mindlessly scrolling their phones. Or whatever the equivalent to that is when the reader comes across this passage. If the hours they're spending in the car are leading to higher rates of stress because of traffic and other drivers whose only purpose on the road seems to be to ruin our commuters' day, those precious few hours they do get with family and friends can become precarious. Our commuter might say things they don't mean and act in ways they wouldn't under normal levels of stress. Not only did the jerk who cut them off on their way back from work cause our commuter to spill their soda, but that jerk is living in her head as she eats with family, seething that her favorite pants got ruined. With less time spent with those we care for, and more disagreeable behavior towards them when we do get time together, our social and familial relations can become strained, sometimes fracturing entirely.

It is all too easy to fall prey to the negative effects of social exclusion in low-density, car-dependent neighborhoods. That's not because loneliness is endemic to the suburbs or exurbs, and cities are inherently convivial places. That's certainly not the case. Many people living in cities can feel deep sadness due to a lack of connection with their neighbors; it's just easier to be less social when it's more difficult to see people. After a long day of work, how often are you excited to go to the gym? Especially when the siren calls from the couch in the living room are too sweet to resist. It's easy to make an excuse for how tired we are, after looking at the couch, and think we'll go when we feel better. Weeks can pass before we grace the gym with our presence. The same sort of thing applies to going out to see friends or family. If the only way to see the ones we love is to get back in the car and drive another 15 minutes after already coming home from work, a communal watch of Monday night football can always wait until next week. Over time, these decisions compound, and the stakes get even higher.

In a 2016 study from the University of York, "perceived loneliness" was found to be associated with a 32% increased risk of stroke, and a 29% increased risk of heart disease.[25] The good news is that these findings cut the other way, too. In a meta-analysis of 148 studies, which included more than 308,000 participants, people with stronger social relationships had a 50% increased likelihood of survival. Not having close friends is comparable to excessive smoking and overconsumption of alcohol.[26] Survival of the fittest?

Maybe when we were hunting on the savannas, existing in the state of nature. In the modern world, though, it seems the friendliest survive. If someone who is 80 years old can no longer operate a car but must drive quite a distance to see the people they know, sustaining those relationships will be very hard. If only they lived somewhere where they could walk to see their friends and family. Their life would be richer, and likely longer, too. We must build places that are more capable of fostering social interaction. It's a matter of public health.

The Housing Challenge

Unless you've been living under a rock or in a $25-million home—and who can tell the difference these days—America has been engulfed in a housing crisis over the last decade. Some areas of the country have known these pressures for far longer. This crisis has perhaps most acutely been felt in Superstar cities like New York and San Francisco (places of global significance with a lot of jobs and many cultural amenities where more people want to live than there is enough housing for), but no place has been immune, with suburban and rural communities also feeling the pain. Half of all renters in 2022, amounting to some 22.4 million households, were burdened by housing costs. This means they spent more than 30% of their gross income on housing, and an even higher percentage of net income after taxes. 12 million of these households were severely burdened, spending more than half their gross income on housing.[27] For many of these families and individuals, after rent is paid there may not be enough money left over for food, transportation, schooling, or work supplies, to say nothing of leisure activities. Immensely difficult decisions on what to prioritize must be made. That these choices need to be made in the first place is indicative of a deep societal failing.

The outlook is also bleak for prospective homeowners. In 2022, the national price-to-income ratio was 5.4, meaning the national median home sold for 5.4 times the national median income.[28] That's a gross income number, not a net, so even dual-income households would likely have to spend many more years saving. And the lucky ones are those who can save anything at all. Price-to-income ratios are dramatically higher in the most expensive metro areas. San Francisco, that bastion of unaffordability, had a price-to-income ratio of 9.9 in 2022, where median home values and incomes were $1,348,700, and $136,700, respectively.[29] A working-class family who makes half of this median salary would regard their prospects of affording a home in San Francisco after factoring in high state and city taxes, the expense of raising kids, and the general cost of living, as pure fantasy. I believe that $70,000 should be enough for a family to build a life, even a modest one.

With little hope of building a strong economic foundation, there has been an exodus of working- and middle-class families from the city in the last decade. While some have moved a few hours' drive away to attain more reasonably priced housing (in exchange for the debilitating effects of super-commuting), many others choose to leave the state entirely. The story is the same in the state's other Superstar city, Los Angeles, which had a higher price-to-income ratio: 10.8. In case the reader might be tempted to dismiss this number as being driven up by wealthy elites in Beverly Hills, Malibu, and West Hollywood, none of these places are actually in the City of Los Angeles, but Los Angeles County, which had a price-to-income ratio of 8.8. Still not cheap, of course. When people lose hope, they go somewhere they can find some. Since 1992, 5 million more Americans have moved out of California than have moved in, a process known in demographics as net domestic outflow.[30] Despite this, the state grew from just under 30 million people in 1990 to 39.5 million in 2020, sustained by robust immigration and natural increases through higher fertility rates.[31] But these bolstering agents have begun to diminish. Fertility rates dropped from 63.4 births per 1,000 women in 2011 to 52.8 in 2021, leading to 80,000 fewer children being born in the state each year.[32] Between 2010 and 2020, 310,000 people immigrated to California, far lower than the 1.2 million in the aughts, and 2.4 million in the 90s.[33] Without the backstop of immigrants and babies, California has shrunk by more than 550,000 people since 2020, marking the first time it has lost population since it became a state in 1850. With nowhere to live, there's no reason to come.[34]

How can we know that Californians are leaving because of housing costs and not for some other reason? Well, because that's what people who have left the state have consistently told surveyors when they've been asked.[35] In one survey conducted by the *Los Angeles Times*, 40% of Californians were considering leaving the state due to the high cost of living.[36] Up For Growth, a non-profit advocacy organization, found that California was 900,000 homes short of meeting demand in its 2023 Housing Underproduction report.[37] When there aren't enough homes to go around in the areas that need them the most, prices inevitably go up.

This isn't just an issue for Superstar coastal cities and states. Nationally, the U.S. is anywhere between 3.8 million to 5 million homes short of demand, though it's tough to pin a number down because housing preferences aren't uniform.[38] If one-bedroom apartments were more affordable, would 30% of all working-aged adults live with a (non-romantic) roommate, or choose to live by themselves?[39] If there were enough apartments generally, would 58% of people aged 18 to 29 be living with their parents?[40] How can we project the housing needs of immigrants and refugees who have yet to come to our country, or are living here without permission and without notice, but performing essential roles? And if there were more reasonably priced starter homes proximate to major employment and cultural centers, would married couples live in their own homes, as opposed to staying with family or being forced to move out of state or to far away exurbs?

One group who certainly has a claim to needing more housing is the more than 650,000 homeless people in America.[41] Around 140,000 of them are chronically homeless, meaning they have been continuously homeless for at least a year, or have been homeless four times in the last three years, for a cumulative amount of at least one year.[42] Chronically homeless individuals make up about a fifth of the total population, but because they disproportionately skew towards living on the streets, as opposed to sleeping in their cars or moving from place to place, they're the most common image of the crisis. Most people who are homeless, though, are only sporadically so, precariously moving between different kinds of housing. We rarely see the families who spend just a week at a shelter, or bounce between relatives' homes for some time, finding couches where they can. While we might see someone sleeping out of their car or their RV, this feels a lot different than a tent underneath a highway.

Regardless of how it manifests, the primary challenge faced by any homeless person, definitionally, is that they do not have a permanent home to live in. If a homeless person is provided permanent housing, by definition they are no longer homeless. The solution should be simple then: build more housing, provide more people homes, and there will be fewer homeless people. Definitionally. Of course, many of these homes and facilities will also need to have supportive services for those who require them, but that's easily accommodatable. Unfortunately, though, our zoning codes are not responsive to the needs of the most marginalized people, and our governments have not proven up to the task of managing the resources at their disposal today. Instead of the market being able to quickly respond to the demands of many millions who face housing precarity (and hundreds of thousands of unhoused who require critical urgency), we've inhibited the creation of new housing by adhering to codes designed several generations ago that no longer suit our needs.

Research has consistently found that the amount of available housing is the most determinative influence on rates of homelessness. In their 2022 book, *Homelessness Is a Housing Problem*, housing and policy researchers Gregg Colburn and Clayton Page Aldern found that the greatest predictors of homelessness are downstream of housing availability—rents and vacancy rates.[43] The higher rents are, and the lower vacancy rates are (anything lower than a 5% vacancy rate is considered an emergency level), the greater homelessness will be. Dozens of cities in America were below this emergency threshold at the end of 2022.[44] These findings stand in contrast to the popular narrative that homelessness is principally a result of individual circumstances, personal choice, mental health, substance abuse, or economic precarity in the abstract. Perhaps surprisingly, poverty doesn't seem to be the principal driver of homelessness. If poverty were directly correlated to homelessness, cities like Detroit and Cleveland, whose poverty rates in 2022 were the highest in the country at 31.5% and 31.2% respectively, would have the most severe crises.[45] Instead, they have among the lowest rates of homelessness because housing is both plentiful and cheap. Meanwhile, wealthy cities with higher rents and lower availability, like Los Angeles and Boston, have very high rates of homelessness.

When prices increase in an entire region beyond what an individual or family is able to pay, and they don't have the means or connections to move somewhere else, they may fall into homelessness. According to research from Zillow, "Communities where people spend more than 32% of their income on rent can expect a more rapid increase in homelessness."[46] Homelessness is directly tied to the cost of housing, which explains why expensive coastal areas have a disproportionate share of the homeless population.

Housing markets respond to the core economic principle of supply and demand. As there is great demand to live in prosperous

Median gross rent versus PIT count (per capita)

Dashed lines indicate a linear regression of per capita PIT counts onto median gross rent between 2007 and 2019 for a sample of U.S. regions.

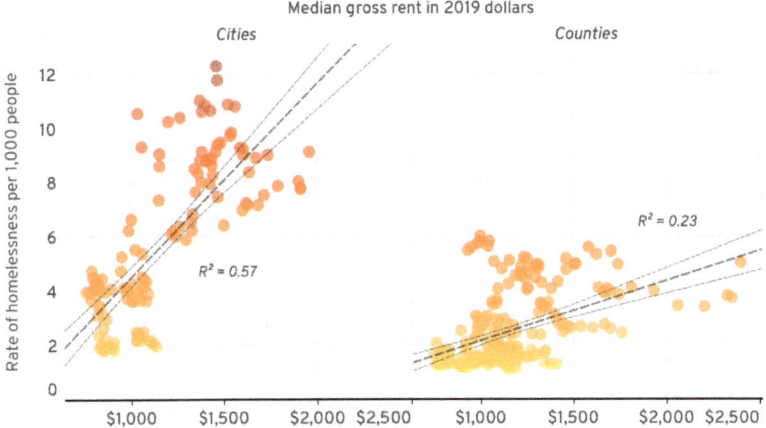

Bands indicate 95% confidence intervals for the slope of the regression line. Figure forthcoming in Colburn & Aldern (2022).

Rental vacancy rate versus PIT count (per capita)

Dashed lines indicate a linear regression of per capita PIT counts onto the natural log of rental vacancy rate between 2007 and 2019 for a sample of U.S. regions.

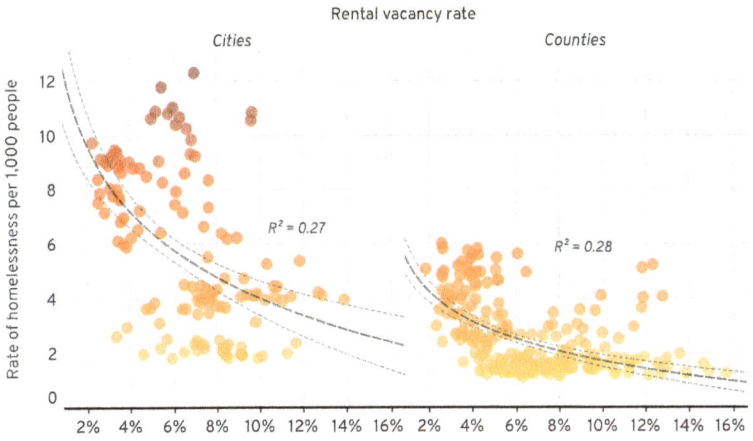

Bands indicate 95% confidence intervals for the slope of the regression line.

Median rent and median vacancy rates charted against rates of homelessness in American cities and counties.

cities, and very little availability of housing, those who have the means to secure somewhere to live push prices up, while those who don't have the resources either spend higher proportions of their income on rent, or are forced out of the market entirely. An unexpected medical bill, battle with addiction, failed relationship, or loss of family support (and in many cases, some combination of these factors), should not be a sentence to the streets. A properly functioning system would not allow for such a possibility. A status quo that is fine with forcing many thousands into inhumane conditions must be remediated.

One might be tempted to think *If we just throw enough money at the problem, eventually, we can solve it, right?* Well, not exactly. Our inability to solve the housing crisis isn't due to a lack of funding. Let's take one example, Los Angeles. From fiscal year 2013/14 to 2023/24, the City of Los Angeles and Los Angeles County allocated a collective $10 billion towards addressing homelessness.[47] Funds came from the city of Los Angeles, the county of Los Angeles, the state of California, and through ballot measures.[48] Measure H, a one-quarter cent sales tax on purchases made in L.A. County, was passed in March 2017. With a scheduled duration of 10 years beginning in July 2017, it is expected to leverage more than $3.5 billion throughout its life to address homelessness via the Los Angeles County Homeless Initiative. Annual funding has already exceeded expectations. In 2023-24, $609.7 million was allocated, rising from $466.75 million in 2022-23.[49] Has all of this money made a dent? No. The crisis has actually gotten worse. The homeless population of L.A. in 2015 was 44,359. In 2019, the year before the pandemic, this number rose to 66,436. After three years of the pandemic and several billion dollars in funding, there were more than 75,000 homeless people in L.A. This is simply unacceptable.

What's going on here? First, coordinating among various state, private, and local agencies in the county is very difficult. Who, exactly, is responsible for implementing solutions across 88 discrete incorporated cities across an area nearly the size of Connecticut? Second, challenges are compounded by homeowners who don't want any new housing near them (especially, regrettably, for formerly homeless individuals) and who have the ability to veto projects. Third, with so much money involved, and very little oversight, accountability runs low. Homelessness is a lucrative service. Managing it can be worth tens of millions of dollars. Twenty-seven staff members are listed on The County of Los Angeles Homeless Initiative directory as of the time of writing (March 2024).[50] This is just one of several agencies tasked with solving the crisis. For 2023–24, they received $16.8 million in funding for administrative costs, or more than $622,000 per employee. One would hope that the staff directory is wrong, or that these funds are being sent to other agencies, as this is more than three times what was spent per employee ($262,000) for the same work in 2022–23, when nineteen staff were listed on their directory, while homelessness increased by nearly 10%.[51] But it's difficult to know, because much of where the money is spent is obscured in budget line items. $40.2 million was spent on "Street-Based Outreach" in 2022–23, but what exactly does that mean? Are additional salaries being paid from there? Would a new Mercedes for a member of the executive staff constitute a legitimate expense? How else could outreach be conducted on Los Angeles' car-dependent streets, after all? We don't know. As for what we do know, administrative funding for the Los Angeles County's Homeless Initiative works out to around 2.75% of the total budget, a larger percentage than what many private equity firms charge to manage the money of the wealthiest people in the world.

Around the country, making money on the backs of the most marginalized is commonplace. From 2018 to 2023, the State of California spent $24 billion on homelessness, but didn't track any data, and existed with a near complete lack of accountability.[52] Billions of dollars were squandered (or pilfered, depending on how charitable one is feeling), while the homeless multiplied in number and in plight. Elsewhere, shelter operators have laundered progressive language to secure contracts worth hundreds of millions of dollars but deliver very little. One operator in New York, Childrens Community Services, secured $600 million to provide housing for 1,900 people (including children, as the name would suggest) struggling with homelessness.[53] That's $315,000 per person, or roughly the amount it would cost to build a market rate apartment at the time. By July 2017, the extent of the shelter's operations were 235 hotel rooms rented out across five hotels.[54] These funds had to have gone somewhere, but clearly they didn't go towards directly helping the people they were allocated for. Hotel rooms don't cost that much. $315,000 per person works out to $863 per night. If every beneficiary of Children's Community Services were put up in a five-star hotel for a year (like the Pierre or The Plaza), the average cost per night would only be $645, according to rates from Expedia.[55] This level of cartoonish corruption would be laughable if it weren't so deeply saddening for the families impacted.

Lest the reader think I'm cherry picking, this isn't an isolated problem. Many billions around the country are wasted on programs that don't deliver permanent housing and deepen the precarity felt by those seeking to escape their agonizing situations. Even when programs work as intended, shelters are a sort of semi-porous tape slapped on the holes of the bottom of a leaking bucket. They're not a permanent solution to this crisis, and yet few look beyond them. I don't mean to denigrate shelters. They are essential, but only as halfway stations, not final destinations. Unfortunately, they're shouldering far more of the burden than they were ever intended to. When temporary fixes are flexed to meet indefinite demands, there is little hope of permanent resolution. Policy has gotten complacent in assuming the free market would fill the void, while inhibiting the market from doing just that

Qualitatively, shelters can feel harsh, sterile, and jail-like. Some restrict genders from living among each other (which can separate people from the most important—or only—interpersonal relationships they have), outlaw the keeping of pets, and disallow possessions from being brought inside. These restrictions strip away the last fibers of humanity or social connection one may be holding on to. People—and we must remember their humanity—are forced to decide between a roof over their head or fundamental emotional support. It's a choice many reject. Indeed, Coalition on Homelessness, the nation's oldest advocacy and direct service organization dedicated to helping homeless individuals and families, has observed that a majority of the homeless participants in their surveys would prefer to live in a legal camp with amenities than an existing shelter.[56]

But camping isn't a realistic solution either as urban land is limited, and it presents material safety risks for those who set up camp. Allowing for a number of tents in a parking lot is no way to deal with a homelessness crisis. And yet, Los Angeles attempted just this, setting up a licensed tent city in 2023 at a cost of $44,000 per tent.[57] I could be wrong, but a $23 tent from Amazon seems more cost-effective to me. If the city really wanted to spring for a nice tent, REI sells a very well regarded one (based on user reviews) for less than $300. If only the absurdity ended here. But why would it? The campground cost $2,663 per participant, per month, to operate, significantly higher than if the city just paid market rates to lease proper apartments.[58] At the time of writing, the median one-bedroom in Los Angeles is $2,195, and the median studio is $1,700.[59] Los Angeles' homeless campground in East Hollywood is expected to be temporary until a formal Affordable Housing complex can be constructed. But even when it's built (if it's built), the construction cost for a studio or one-bedroom built via Affordable mechanisms regularly exceeds $1 million today.[60] These are small units. One can buy a mansion in many parts of the country for this amount, or three nice townhomes in Houston! This state of affairs would be bad enough if all the dollars L.A. has leveraged towards homelessness were going towards the construction of new housing. But as we've seen, they're not.

Optimism time: as previously mentioned, we know what to do to solve homelessness. First, start with housing. Or rather, Housing First. Developed in the early '90s by Dr. Sam Tsemberis in New York City, Housing First diverged from other homelessness programs by not making shelter conditional on some other issue being addressed. Said another way, if someone struggled with substance abuse, they didn't need to get clean before getting housing. It has proven extraordinarily successful. Studies conducted over the last 20 years in various regions have consistently found that 70–90% of Housing First participants remained stably housed two to three years after first receiving accommodation.[61] Not only does this program get people off the streets, but having a safe, warm, and private place to sleep at night seems to be a key factor in ameliorating other issues they may have struggled with. It's pretty hard to deal with your issues if you don't know where you're going to sleep at night. You can't build a stable base to get your life in order if you have no stability. Housing First provides that stability, and does so remarkably well.

For those who might need a little more help getting back on their feet, Permanent Supportive Housing initiatives, which marry housing development with social, mental, and physical support services, have also enjoyed much success. Even better, they've been shown to reduce the costs of homelessness at the municipal level as fewer resources need to be allocated to policing and hospital care.

In Denver, 80% of participants in a Permanent Supportive Housing program maintained their housing for six months after placement. The city ended up saving $31,500 per participant, as fewer civic and emergency services were expended.[62] Utah nearly solved its homelessness crisis, reducing the unhoused population by more than 90% through providing homes for nearly 2,000 people.[63]

Vancouver has proven that if building the needed housing will cost too much, or take too long at the outset, simply giving cash works too! In a pilot program, $7,500 was given to 50 people who had been homeless for more than six months.[64] Those who received the money found housing much more quickly than those who didn't (perhaps obviously). Contrary to what some might think, though, the money wasn't mismanaged; it helped get them back on track. When people are given money to participate in the market, more often than not they know what to do with it.

So, build more today, invest in Permanent Supportive Housing, be fine for tomorrow, right? Not exactly. Our housing needs aren't static, and they're not simply utilitarian. Once we build the four or five million homes we're currently short of, it's not like our housing needs will stop in perpetuity. We need a system that continuously improves the housing stock in a smooth, responsive process. Every year, there are more people either are born in, or move to the U.S., than those who die or migrate, leading to population increase. Others who already live in the country but progress onto different stages of their lives, require different spaces that might not exist. Whether someone is graduating from college, downsizing after their kids have moved out of the house, moving from another country, or just wanting a new space, there will always be a need for new homes in a growing society (and even in a shrinking one). Older units will need to be replaced by newer ones. This can be done in a thoughtful way where places of quality, designed to last well beyond our tenure in them, are built. In this way, there will be less fragility when the next crisis inevitably comes because we'll have adapted our culture to build more places of longer durability.

This is not happening today. Many suburban and exurban communities were not designed to last more than a few generations, and are running up against their usable lives. We can't afford to continue this ephemerality. Not only is it immensely wasteful to build a new generation of homes for each new generation, where mass amounts of embodied carbon are wasted on continuous construction and destruction, nearly all of these developments deepen car dependency and compound the negative externalities of generally unsustainable development patterns. We have to be mindful of not entrenching negative outcomes in the name of more beds.

These last pages were not meant to crush your spirit, but to motivate you. We can reverse (or mitigate) much of what we face, but we must be thoughtful in how we do it. The scale of our problems is so vast that the requisite solutions must be equally ambitious—nothing short of reshaping contemporary society. But before this revolution, we have to get down to brass tacks. The solutions proposed in this book are not based on blind naivety. In order for us to effectively solve our problems, we must have an understanding of what we're up against. Now that we do, the question becomes: how do we move forward?

3.
The Pendulum of Development

The problems of our day are too complex to deal with in an ad hoc manner. We need an operating framework in order to best manage them. This doesn't need to be overly prescriptive, a rigorous test of ideological purity, or a rubric where certain metrics score higher or lower based on an arbitrary scale of pseudo-scientific measures. But there does need to be some general guidance on how we should move forward, lest we devolve into chaos, or freeze into paralysis. This system should rely on empirical findings, but not rigidly so. There can be no dogma of data that denies human emotion. Certain intangible elements contribute deeply to our lived experience that we might not fully understand, like why certain streets are more enjoyable to walk along than others. Our lack of understanding of why they exist cannot be a reason for rejecting them. We should not tear down Chesterton's Fence. Moreover, as the Law of Holes states, "When you find yourself in a hole, stop digging." We're in a few holes right now. It's well past time that we stopped digging.

This may seem overly simplistic, but that's kind of the point. In order for us to progress forward, we have to stop doing the things that are holding us back. It shouldn't be difficult to implement, but unfortunately, whether through vested interest or ignorance, it has proven so. For too long, the disciplines of city building and planning have been pervaded by grand theories so rational to the point of rejecting human nature, or so protective that our cities have become ossified. Neither of these systems are suitable for the challenges we face, nor do they align with an Optimistic philosophy, as there's no small degree of rigid cynicism within each.

The Rightward Swing: Hyper Rationality and Top-Down Planning

Smashing through a city may well be the quickest way between two points. But that doesn't mean it's the optimal solution. If we believe that our cities and towns should be built around people (who else should they be built for, after all?) any policy that leads to the destruction of a community without commensurately replacing that which was erased is senseless. You can't very well build for people while annihilating their way of life.

Yet, as was discussed in the first chapter, this is precisely how mid-century planners treated urban communities—as places to be cut down and torn through in order to facilitate movement somewhere else. Sometimes, communities were demolished out of prejudice, never to be replaced. Other times, little more than caprice fueled decisions. So much for rationality. The drawers of straight lines on maps cared little for the neighborhoods their plans tore through, and in fact seemed to take a sort of pleasure from it, reveling in the accolades they received from fellow planners, mayors, and economic development agencies. Their urban highways were lauded as transformational infrastructure projects, signs of Modernity that liberated (certain) city dwellers, allowing them to claim their share of Arcadia. Little mattered more than *progress*. If some groups got the short end of the stick, well, that was just the cost of moving forward.

That's not entirely true, however. Upon closer inspection of the places where those who got the short end of the stick lived, attempts were likewise made to deliver Modernity to them. These neighborhoods were no good, planners reasoned. Destitute. Overcrowded. Dangerous. The language surrounding what was considered "dirty" or "blighted"—and who contributed to these conditions—was not difficult to decipher. Puerto Rican, Jewish, Black, and even Italian and Irish enclaves were all targeted for redevelopment.[1] Regardless of whether any of these neighborhoods were as bad as the technocrats imagined, the opportunity to wield the sword of progress was too tempting to be denied.

Here's how that progress worked. Under Title I of the *Housing Act of 1949*, commonly known as "Urban Renewal", the federal government authorized grants to municipalities for the purpose of clearing areas designated as slums. Allocations were generous. They subsidized up to two-thirds of the cost shouldered by cities for the acquisition and clearance of blighted properties.

In order to receive these grants, each city had to set up an agency explicitly tasked with undertaking Urban Renewal activities. These agencies were given the power of eminent domain to acquire properties they designated as substandard, and subsequently plan large-scale redevelopment. What actually constituted substandard in practice was fairly nebulous, and often according to one's own prejudice. After a neighborhood was razed, developers (either private actors or quasi-public entities) could tap into billions of dollars of state and federal aid earmarked for such projects. Cities, then as now, were in competition with one another to offer the best vision of the future. This competition was made more difficult because it also included heavily subsidized suburbs that had tacit governmental support to drain cities of people and resources. The phenomenon of White flight is one of the more prominent examples of this tacit support. Urban exodus was a double whammy, as the losses of cities directly aided the suburbs. Powerful figures were needed to chart a more prosperous course in the face of these challenges. In New York, that figure was Robert Moses, a czar of the built environment.

As Robert Caro detailed in his sprawling 1974 work *The Power Broker*, Moses was uniquely gifted at leveraging federal funds to realize the types of large-scale projects he believed would save the city from itself—ideology remarkably similar to the sort espoused by Le Corbusier regarding continental European cities.[3] Moses was doubtless influenced by Corbu's hyper rational proposals of redevelopment. As chairman of the Mayor's Committee on Slum Clearance, New York's Urban Renewal agency, he channeled more than $660 million (in 2023 dollars) in Title I funding from 1949 to 1960. Moses made sure that New York was the first—and, for a time, only—city receiving these funds, outpacing his competitors. 314 acres were cleared under this program and 28,400 apartments rose on these lands.[4] But that was only what he built through Title I. By the time Moses retired as an octogenarian in 1968, the total value of projects he had been responsible for was staggeringly more than $231 billion (in 2023 dollars). The scope of this work was vast. Beyond apartments, he oversaw the construction of 58 playgrounds; 2.5 million acres of parks; 416 miles of parkways, and 13 bridges. Straight lines ran everywhere. At one point, 25% of all federal construction dollars were being spent at Moses' discretion. A staff of 80,000 worked both directly and indirectly for him. His reign marked the height of top-down planning in the U.S., a system where control over large projects of great importance is presided over by very few. This scale was paralleled only by autocratic regimes in the pursuit of projects of national importance (or excessive pride, which is often indistinguishable).

Cities around the country took Moses' lead. Nationwide, more than 2,100 urban renewal projects were awarded federal aid between 1949 and 1974, with grants totalling more than $72 billion (in 2023 dollars). According to the National Commission on Urban

Problems 1969 *Building the American City* report, though 400,000 units had been demolished through Title I, only 106,961 new units had replaced them by 1967.[5] Of the residential areas that were cleared (some 57,000 total acres, or 90 square miles) only around 35% were proposed to be redeveloped for residential uses. Nearly as much land, 27%, was earmarked for highways and streets.[6] Less than 200,000 units were ultimately planned (though not all of them got built), meaning hundreds of thousands of families had their homes destroyed and didn't have a place to go after reconstruction.[7] Many of these families received little or no funds for moving assistance, forcing them to make deep concessions in what type of housing they would accept in the midst of a crisis, causing the very slum conditions planners set out to eradicate. New York's first Black Commissioner of the Department of Welfare, James R. Dumpson, noted that "Slum clearance has increased overcrowding among the lowest income groups; low-cost public housing has often created new ghettos".[8]

Various local and federal acts that funded the creation of urban highways displaced 330,000 more families. Moses' Cross Bronx Expressway is perhaps the most egregious example, where some 15,000 were directly displaced.[9] Well over 1 million people were estimated to have been displaced from urban renewal and urban highway schemes in total.[10] This included commercial redevelopment projects like New York's Lincoln Center, where 7,000 lower-class families and 800 businesses were displaced for the performing arts complex.[11] In Pittsburgh, The Hill neighborhood, which housed some 8,000 people, was demolished for a new arena, thousands of surface parking spaces, and highways.[12] Downtown Norfolk, Virginia, was nearly entirely demolished using urban renewal funds and to this day it's still a patchwork of parking and vacant lots.

These projects disproportionately impacted minority groups, who represented well over half of all the families displaced despite only comprising 11% or so of the population.[13] Urban renewal was commonly referred to as "Negro Removal" because black neighborhoods were disproportionately targeted for redevelopment. That these areas were often vibrant, strong communities comparable to other urban areas that weren't redeveloped was inconsequential to planners. The only way some of these neighborhoods could be perceived as slums was through the lens of prejudice. When combined with other policies that systematically excluded and oppressed marginalized populations, generations have been imperiled by the legacy of plans implemented in this era.

The Leftward Swing: Community Control

In the wake of the horrors borne of Modernist planning, activists came together to wrest control back from the agencies who exerted total power over their communities. Jane Jacobs was the leading figure of this movement, and exists as its patron saint today. In her seminal 1961 *Death and Life of Great American Cities*—a work of near Biblical importance in the world of urbanism—Jacobs formalized one of the first and loudest criticisms of the mid-century planning orthodoxy. Through keen observation, she was able to explain in plain English what made for good cities, streets, and neighborhoods, and how plans like Moses' were antithetical to them. Jacobs' advocacy rested on a few ideas that remain central to contemporary planning today. She believed that neighborhoods should be mixed-use so that people are constantly flowing through them, lending vibrancy and safety, something she called "eyes on the street", where the presence of people with stakes in the community deters crime. Who better to police the street than the restaurateur who wants to offer a welcoming environment for patrons, or a mother watching her daughter walk to the bus stop from her third-story window?

Jacobs advocated for fine-grained streets with many intersections, as long blocks can be isolating and imposing, and can discourage engagement. There should be a mixture of old and new buildings, she reasoned, such that wealthier tenants and residents can move into newer buildings, while small businesses and lower-income residents filter down to the older ones. Where sufficiently enabled, it's worth reiterating that, a mixture of old and new buildings also results in a mixture of the types of people who live in a neighborhood, giving space for the young, old, rich, poor, pious, and secular to rub shoulders and coexist. But none of this works without a lot of people living close together. Higher density ensures there will be enough customers for small businesses who rely on local traffic, provides more eyes on the street, and offers lower prices by spreading the cost of land across more people.

Manhattan's Greenwich Village was her case study and proving ground. It was the foil to the Le Corbusierian, car-dominated style of planning favored by Moses. Instead of wide roads and tall buildings sprouting from large patches of grass where the street level experience was ignored, the Village is an intimate network of short and narrow streets, with many old buildings in a diversity of styles at a human scale. Perhaps surprisingly given its supremely pleasant nature, the neighborhood is still very dense. Local businesses are the backbone of the community. At the time when Jacobs was writing, it had the added benefits of diversity and relative affordability. To this day, it remains one of the most sought out neighborhoods in North America. In short, the Village was something worth fighting for. And fight Jacobs did.

In the years immediately before and after America's involvement in World War II, several highway schemes were proposed for lower Manhattan. One such plan aimed to connect the Hudson and East River crossings by directing traffic from the Williamsburg and Manhattan bridges through SoHo and out to New Jersey via the Holland Tunnel. The creation of this Lower Manhattan Expressway, or Lomex, would have demolished 14 blocks and displaced 2,000 families along with more than 800 businesses.[14] Lomex would have destroyed an area, it must be noted, that is today one of the most beloved neighborhoods in the world.

Right around this time, Jacobs moved into a house on Hudson Street in the West Village, and began writing about cities. Working as a journalist for *Architectural Forum*, she explored the many ambitious urban redevelopment projects of the time aimed at removing perceived urban blight. Up and down the Eastern Seaboard, and across the Midwest, historic city centers were hollowed out, while rapidly growing western cities were developed almost exclusively around highways. These development patterns could not be more foreign to Jacobs' beloved Greenwich Village. There was a stunning disconnect between the places that planners deemed optimal and those that seemed to be the most felicitous for people.

Through her early criticism, Jacobs was becoming a prominent figure. She wasn't afraid of confronting those she disagreed with head on, which only augmented her stardom. Speaking to a group of leading architects, planners, mayors, and thought leaders at Harvard in 1956, she made waves when she implored that "the least we can do is to respect—in the deepest sense—strips of chaos that have a weird wisdom of their own not yet encompassed in our concept of urban order."[15] The rising arc of her fame coincided with Moses' most daring urban highway proposal yet—a depressed four-lane highway set to run through the middle of Washington Square, right under the park's famous Arch—a direct challenge to Jacobs' neighborhood. Sometimes leading protests, sometimes simply participating, she mobilized her community through collective activism, making phone calls, writing letters, and gathering signatures urging officials to abandon their plans. Eleanor Roosevelt even joined in. Ultimately, Jacobs was successful. Lomex, and its extension through Washington Square Park, were scrapped.

Jacobs triumphed because her advocacy was rooted in common sense. Without the heart of the community, there can be no community. When highways replace streets and parks, and intimate networks of human-scaled buildings give way to anonymous, imposing, and austere blocs, essential connections are severed. Humanity is subjugated to concrete tyranny. The plans and places Jacobs fought against were so flagrantly anti-democratic, and often inhumane, that her opposition quickly attracted much support. But her activism did far more than save Washington Square Park from the wrecking ball. It marked a turning point in how cities were developed.

From Top-Down to Bottom-Up: Finding the Middle Between Left and Right

Historically, much of urban development was carried out by small-scale builders in a relatively haphazard way. A shopkeeper might start with a modest stall and progressively expand into larger or more richly-adorned structures after finding success. Commutes were measured in steps. Merchants, artisans, and service providers lived above, or very near, the places they worked. While some societies had high levels of planning, even the most rigid allowed for buildings to color in between planned lines in relatively unrestricted ways. This sort of free-for-all created dynamic and compact communities, but it perhaps expectedly also delivered no small amount of chaos. Part of this was due to a lack of technology. One couldn't drive their car out to a suburban plot on the edge of town to find peace. Nor could they grow vertically, as the elevators that might raise them up from the disorder below had not yet been invented. And part of it was due to a lack of administrative organization.

Industrialization presented a scale of problems to urban management that traditional cities couldn't have comprehended. While

100 BUILDING OPTIMISM

A before and after comparison of the accumulated soot on the Athenaeum on Princess Street in Manchester, England.

cities had grown since antiquity (with ups and downs—the Black Death would certainly qualify as a "down" period for continental European cities), mass urbanization didn't truly begin until the 19th century with the rise of mechanized production. New factories promised profound increases in efficiency over traditional production processes, and by extension, more opportunity. Farmers and other rural workers were attracted to this opportunity, and moved en masse to cities, eager to secure passage away from lives that barely rose above subsistence. London's population increased from 1 million to over 6.2 million people between 1801 and 1901. Birmingham septupled in size. Paris grew to eight times its original population. Cities weren't equipped for this rapid growth. Slums of unimaginable horror became commonplace. Hundreds crowded together on blocks in complete destitution, where entire families (often six people or more) lived together in single rooms without light or fresh air. Manchester's infamous cellars beneath decrepit timber buildings sheltered the lowest rungs of society, whose homes were routinely flooded by improper drainage of human, industrial, and chemical waste. Many lived next to the factories they worked in, and pollution was in such abundance it was painted on the urban environment. Layers of soot covered the buildings and streets of industrial powerhouses, and coated the lungs of those who had no escape from the ubiquitous externalities of progress.

These challenges couldn't be solved through incrementalism or community organizing. State involvement was needed to save the desperate millions. Water and sewer systems were some of the first large-scale state interventions of the industrial city. The first modern sewer system was completed in Hamburg in 1843, before quickly spreading around the world. Though not sexy or publicly visible, these remain critical components of contemporary infrastructure. England's 19th-century cholera and typhoid outbreaks, which regularly claimed thousands of lives each year, were effectively eradicated by 1890. In the French capital, Haussmann's renovation (1853–1870) is better remembered today for its boulevards, parks, cafes, and streetlamps (Paris earned its 'City of Light' nickname thanks to his efforts), but at its core it was a public health project, which successfully rectified the terrors of the past, and accommodated the needs of the future. Paris was transformed from a chaotic and insalubrious maze of lanes into a paragon of urban cleanliness and efficiency. This didn't come without a cost, of course, as thousands of buildings were demolished to make way for the improvements. But it's very difficult to argue the city would have survived, much less become adored worldwide, without such top-down interventions. More on this in Chapter 6.

The legacy of top-down planning continued through to Moses, who fashioned himself the 20th-century Haussmann. He too cleared "slums", improved circulation, and provided more light, air, parks, and amenities to city residents. Haussmann ushered Paris into a more modern era. Moses believed he was doing the same for New York. Through top-down governance, Moses razed the city so that his vision could be built on top of it. Aware of the consequences of his actions, he was convinced his work was so essential that it overshadowed any concerns. In one speech, he (in)famously stated, "You can't make an omelet without breaking eggs ... when you operate in an overbuilt metropolis, you have to hack your way with a meat axe."[16] But where Haussmann had the backing of an emperor, Moses only had the imperiousness of one. Even though he was never elected, New York's supreme power broker ultimately had to respond to the will of the people, as his power rested on appointments from others who were elected. And the will of the people demanded that the pendulum of development shift, from absolute top-down planning to community-based bottom-up decision making, where Jane Jacobs resided, and where we've remained for much of the last 60 years.

At first blush, it appears we've reached the end of history; community-based decision making is a most noble way of shaping cities. Top-down planning, critics claim, was settled as having been a failure. How can any system that chooses winners and losers with such cruel unevenness be tolerated? And if we're building places for people, shouldn't the people have a say in how their community is built? Isn't that common sense?

Well, not exactly. Where top-down planning is carried out by just a few people who have the power to change everything, control by many thousands leads to a decentralized impotence that never changes anything. It's far easier for people to come together in opposition than to find something to positively mobilize towards. Too much feedback paralyzes the system completely. Not all of a community's opinions can be implemented, as many directly clash with one another. A thousand voices means at least a thousand opinions on what the future can or should look like. And those thousand voices are often not representative of the community writ large, just those who have the time, passion, and means to sacrifice what they might otherwise be doing to comment at a public hearing whose hours-long reviews are often held at inaccessible times (2 o'clock on Monday afternoons, 9 PM on Thursday nights). Those who can show up at 2 on a Monday afternoon tend to be older, better-capitalized people for whom the status quo serves just fine. And, moreover, those who perceive change to be a direct threat to their way of life and personal comfort, whether that change be something as small as a bike lane that requires more focus from a driver on the road, or as large as an apartment building that could threaten property values (and who knows what else, the logic follows). Thus, there exists a built-in constituency of "no" votes from a narrow demographic group, regardless of what a certain proposal may be, without would-be proponents having their say. Such a system is a vetocracy, not democracy.

Nearly every person who lives in a given neighborhood has either made a choice to live there or was born there. It's fair to say they probably have some level of emotional connection to that place and an appreciation for what already exists. Because of this connection, any change to how the neighborhood looks from the time when they first experienced it might make them sad, or unmoored. Perhaps not because of changes to the built environment in the abstract, but for the memories from another time which are no longer visible. We are nostalgic beings who don't deal with the inexorable march of time well. Where we live is a significant contributor to how we perceive ourselves. Any level of change thus represents a potential disruption to our identity, our lifestyle, or our notion of our own mortality. For some, this can prove an existential threat. For others, it might really be about the buildings. But my sense is that's a very small minority. It seems to be about preservation of self. Given the right tools, people will go to great lengths to preserve themselves.

Jerusalem Demsas, a staff writer for *The Atlantic*, captured these dynamics well in a 2022 article on community input: "Because participation in local politics, even at the ballot box, is extremely limited, elected officials are often swayed by just a handful of emails or phone calls in opposition to, for instance, a new apartment tower. But opponents aren't limited to petitioning their representatives directly. Anytime a developer seeks to build something outside the existing zoning code ... they have to get a 'variance' from the local zoning board. To receive that variance, developers have to present their projects at public meetings ... Even someone attempting to convert her garage into a mother-in-law suite might need the approval of her neighbors. It's like a homeowners' association from hell, backed by the force of the law."[17]

Though she would be deeply saddened to learn so, a thread can be tied between 'homeowners' associations from hell' and Jacobs' activism. Her victory in preserving the Greenwich Village of the 1960s was so robust that the neighborhood has hardly changed in more than half a century. Generations of Villagers haven't been able to agree on what a positive future might look like, but they've been empowered to oppose interventions they do not like. And so it hasn't evolved. Every proposed change is a Mosian bulldozer in hiding. To some, that's a good thing; the Village still retains much of the charm that it had in 1962. But decades of demand to live in this well-located and attractive area has meant that it's no longer the affordable, diverse, and bohemian haven it once was. The median rent for a one-bedroom in the West Village in December 2023 was $5,400.[18] Homes sold for a median price of $2 million, or more than $2,300 per square foot.[19]

As difficult as it may be to understand the context of the 1960s from our uber-expensive 2020s, there was a strong justification for preservation. At the same time Moses was running highways through the fabric of New York, some of the city's most prized individual treasures also met the wrecking ball. In what may be the greatest loss of American architectural heritage, McKim, Meade & White's original Pennsylvania Station was demolished in 1966, only to be replaced by a universally reviled structure. The "modern"

Penn Station, an underground warren of low-ceilinged passageways that traded soaring windows for strange scents, stained dated floors, and operating-room-white LED lights offers the intrepid commuter a constant sense of anxiety borne of overcrowding in frightfully improperly planned spaces. Penn Station's decline from masterpiece to rat maze is the design equivalent of a sequel to a Martin Scorsese movie being shot on a 2006 flip phone. Sure, they might technically both be movies, but the way we're made to feel while experiencing them could not be more different.

Hoping to save other structures from the fate of the original Penn Station, a broad movement helmed by notable figures like Jacqueline Kennedy and Lady Bird Johnson emerged to protect the country's most aesthetically and historically significant buildings. Organized preservation wasn't an entirely new thing. Charleston pioneered the country's first community-based historic preservation organization in 1920, however, its small size and parochial status ensured that the city wouldn't (or, with its unique context, couldn't) be a national model. But it wasn't until the tragic loss of Penn Station and scores of other significant structures around the country that a consciousness materialized surrounding remains the importance of saving parts of our collective built heritage.

The wrong lesson, I fear, was learned. Instead of honoring the legacy that made historic neighborhoods compelling in the first place, the movement focused almost entirely on aesthetic considerations, opting for a literal preservation via ossification as opposed to a living, dynamic tradition. Blocks became open-air museums replete with parking lots on the graves of their felled siblings for ease of access. Not very historic.

Gradually, adaptive reuse projects (where older structures are revived with new uses) shifted the paradigm of preservation. In drips beginning in the '70s, and rising to much greater frequency in the '90s, the first conversions were carried out in formerly industrial structures like SoHo's cast-iron beauties. Remarkably, buildings that used to host the worst ills of industrialization became fashionable places to live. This is not some sort of advertising sorcery, but a testament to the resilience of robust construction. If slaughterhouses and sweatshops can become vogue, imagine what purposeful design can accomplish? One would hope that this alternate reality would have been considered by preservationists, where the new accentuates the old. But sadly, it wasn't.

Co-Opted by Bad Faith and Vested Interest

Instead of creating architectural marvels that future generations might be able to enjoy, just as we've been able to enjoy the works of our ancestors, the preservation movement was at its creation, and still explicitly conservative, clinging with ferocity to the past. This has manifested in all manner of outlandish regulations, like not allowing shutters to be painted specific colors, prohibiting more energy-efficient windows that don't precisely match the style from hundreds of years ago (builders back then surely would have used more efficient windows if they could have!), or not allowing for adaptive reuse when the building would otherwise decay—a loss certainly greater than prohibiting a hair salon to take up shop in what was historically a residential structure.

This conservatism left the door open for bad faith actors to co-opt the movement under the guise of protecting built heritage. As exclusionary single family zoning had shown a prior generation of owners, artificially restricting the supply of housing not only preserved the character of a neighborhood, but it had the added benefit of increasing home values as it prohibited demand from being met. Under this system buildings could both be preserved and sound investments. The editors of *The Boston Globe* knew this well, writing in support for the designation of Beacon Hill as a historic district in 1955, "This is designed not to burden property-holders, but quite the opposite—to protect them from acts of architectural mayhem which could wreck their real estate values and spoil their pleasure and comfort."[20] There is some rationality to this, as historic structures require more money to maintain than newly developed buildings. But they're also worth more. If a buyer knows that a historic property will cost more to keep up, but that it will also be viewed as a scarce, irreplicable asset, then basic math points to preserving beloved structures, even without subsidy or generosity, both of which may run low from time to time. This math doesn't work for every historic building, as small towns without strong demand can't support such investment, but it does explain how homes in certain well-sited locations like Beacon Hill regularly sell for more than $5 million today, with some even eclipsing $10 million.

Not every neighborhood possesses the charms of Beacon Hill, of course. Located on a tidal estuary overlooking the Marin Headlands, San Francisco, enjoys one of the most beautiful urban settings in the world. With steep hills offering commanding views over some of the country's most culturally significant neighborhoods—when the fog lifts enough to permit one to see—them it is a city of profound romance. But there are also wide stretches of San Francisco that are perfectly unremarkable. Shabby looking, even. And I'm not talking about the city's iconic Victorian homes, which are little more than modest wooden boxes with cheap (yet eminently lovely!) ornamentation slapped on.

Despite being one of the most expensive cities in the country, much of San Francisco is shorter than three stories tall. And one of those levels is usually a garage dedicated to parking. This limits the amount of people who can live in San Francisco, and subsequently increases the cost of housing. Preservation in the city, which ranges from the absurd to the abusive, is a big reason why. Parking lots in the heart of downtown have received nominations for historic designation in order to preclude more housing, with contrived rationales of some cultural event or another of questionable significance.[21]

Ingleside Terraces, a detached single family neighborhood, is located within a 1-mile radius of both San Francisco State University (to the west), and the City College of San Francisco (to the east), institutions with a combined enrollment of more than 80,000 students. It enjoys preservation status, though many homes in the development are of dubious cultural or architectural value. That the Terraces was originally a whites-only neighborhood, where property deeds stated "That no person of African, Japanese, Chinese, or of any Mongolian descent shall be allowed to purchase, own, lease, or occupy said real property or any part thereof" seems not to have deterred the designation.[22] Indeed, preservation seems to have bolstered the neighborhood's original goals of excluding non–single family homes as a way of self-segregating. This legacy is inseparable from the case of Cecil F. Poole and his family, the first non-white residents who moved into the neighborhood in 1957 (45 years after its creation). As a move-in gift, the Poole's received a burning cross on their front lawn.[23]

To this day, in a city where 6% of the population is Black, less than 1% of the Ingleside Terraces census tract is.[24] This census tract includes portions of (historically designated) St. Francis Wood and Balboa Terrace, two similarly single family communities that were created with the explicit intention of excluding Black and Asian families. With home values of $1,638,500, 40% higher than the city's median home price, the preservation strategy seems to have worked.[25] Scott Wiener, one of the leading pro-housing voices in America, who represents San Francisco in the California State Senate, has noted that designations like St. Francis Wood and Ingleside Terraces create a template for other neighborhoods to evade their obligation to provide more housing. Indeed they have.

Using preservation of unremarkable places as a tool to deprive those who just happened to be born at an inopportune time, or were denied the chance originally, is not only anti-common sense, it's malicious and immoral. While I'm a great admirer of historic preservation generally, as I think protecting our most lovely and important structures creates an invaluable bond of shared heritage which makes our communities stronger, wielding it to the extent we see today has deprived us of building a future that can rival our past. What's more, preservation is almost completely arbitrary. Many historic districts have contributing structures from very different eras and schools of design. It strikes me as remarkably arrogant to presume some years down the road that a neighborhood should effectively be ossified at some random date. A date that usually has very little to do with character, and more to do with when the proponents for designation moved into the area.

Imagine if Barcelona had decided to stop building all new structures in the 15th century, content with what they had, and arrested growth altogether. We would know nothing of its famed superblocks, Guadi's magical creations, or Las Ramblas, one of the world's greatest streets. Even the city's historic medieval core, The Gothic Quarter, derives its name and much of its wonder from 19th-century interventions. Many of its medieval-looking buildings are in fact 19th- and 20th-century recreations, erected after the destruction levied from the War of Succession (1701–1714).[26] If Barcelona had never rebuilt after the war, and asked its residents to instead mourn the ruins in somber meditation each time they passed, how much cultural heritage and utility would the city have lost?

Modern preservation (and zoning codes) wielded by community groups puts a stop to the natural evolutionary process of neighborhoods, depriving them of the organic nature which made them great in the first place. Jacobs' victory over Moses emboldened communities around the country to fight against any level of change they perceived to be a threat. While these threats could be as severe as a highway running through a neighborhood, more often than not they were perfectly anodyne things, like shops or duplexes, or buildings of an architectural style or intensity that didn't exist when a given person moved in, which simply became pathologized. In this era of community control, people view anything that isn't allowed in their zone as something to be opposed, reasoning (illogically) that it must be bad if it is currently illegal, ignorant of the history and actors which have rendered it so. Buying a home or moving into a new neighborhood is an intensely emotional experience, but it is not a private action. It is necessarily shared with everyone one lives near. Ownership does not confer the rights of a fiefdom. It should start and end at one's property lines, not extend to every lot where one might conceivably take issue with what gets built. Who knows how far that might extend. Jacobs' activism has been co-opted by those who either didn't read her work, or didn't understand the context she was writing in. Deindustrialized, post-war New York was a very different place than the playground for the upwardly mobile and super-rich it has become today. It, along with cities around the country, must be allowed to break free of their 20th-century harnesses in order to become more responsive and grow to more felicitous forms.

The Optimistic Planning and Development System

Our cities are tapestries with stories woven into them from many different eras and cultures. They're at their best when they're at their most complex, brimming with the dynamism of storytellers trying to stake a claim that they, for a moment, were a part of that beautiful tale. We can't simply say "stop growth here", as that would defeat the promise of the city, which must necessarily evolve to fit the needs of its people if it wants to survive. When this evolution is inhibited, the system flashes red and careens towards destruction.

Policies that advantage the caprice of birth at the expense of those desirous of improving their lives by moving to a given place, can be described as nothing so much as un-American. We are a nation of immigrants. Of movers, and risk takers. A people who constantly strive for a better life. Arresting this process is treasonous to the virtues the country was established on. No amount of money, connections, or vested interest from powerful groups should be able to evade this simple truth.

The pendulum of development has swung too far in the direction of community control, and it must now move back towards some middle ground. This doesn't mean we should bulldoze neighborhoods, but it might take the form of state-level pre-emption, where neighborhoods and cities are prohibited from opting out of doing their fair share, shrugging responsibilities off to more marginalized communities—as is all too often the case today. If localities refuse to do their share of the greater good, they should not receive the benefits that accrue from the greater good. Self-determination can be attenuated commensurate with whatever is required of a municipality, and what it refuses to do. Police powers, for example, are delegated at the state level. If a town refuses to build its fair share of housing over a 5-year period, the state could restrict that town's ability to make land-use decisions, as they proved incapable of doing it on their own. For towns scared of new development, I would ask whether modifying zoning codes to allow for 500 homes in line with the character of the community is not better than 500 units in a few insipid towers, which would be allowed if zoning codes were repealed. California has recently legalized "Builder's Remedy", a tool that does just this. Whether Builder's Remedy is ultimately successful or not, the idea holds much promise.

As I understand it, the most Optimistic system is one that accommodates the need to satisfy public interest while still guaranteeing some level of self-determination and autonomy, such that people can craft neighborhoods in line with their collective visions without harming the greater public good. This last part is critical; Self interest can metastasize and shroud itself in the guise of good intentions gone awry, to the detriment of society.

An Optimistic development pattern would have a sort of "color in the lines" approach, where higher levels of government lay out the broad strokes of policies, plans, and infrastructure, and individuals do the rest. While this is theoretically how things work today, state capacity has been diminished to such a great extent, weighed down by bureaucracy, public review, and paternalistic acute-anticipation of development, that our system is in reality a cumbersome, paralyzed, and impotent husk. We must move towards a world that responds to the red flashing lights in our system, not ignores them in the name of protecting the interests of a well-connected or wealthy few.

Our proposed system, in which individual autonomy is truly encouraged by the higher levels of government, mandates action where it's required, by responding to signals like mass unaffordability, pollution, and high rates of obesity, as opposed to ignoring them. It is inherently proactive, not regressive, but not domineering either. Instead of community groups being empowered through vetocracy, they would be mobilized to shape the world in their vision.

In moving away from a vetocracy and towards a *drasocracy* (government by action), people will respond to the needs of their neighborhood through direct intervention, unburdened by a byzantine permitting apparatus, and not subjected to the extractions of out-of-town groups. Defensiveness will give way to pride. If something must be built, wouldn't it be far better for it to be representative of the people? And as good as it can possibly be? *Look what wonderful things we came together to build—this is who we are!* community residents might say. Just as preservationists ardently fight for historic buildings today, Optimists may come together and powerfully forge beautiful neighborhoods for the future. Optimism invites—no, demands—participation.

Optimism via drasocracy requires our communities to be shaped by many hands—an idea set forth by writer Daniel Herriges that I much like, and that is the hallmark of our greatest cities.[27] The places that an Afro-Caribbean community shapes will likely be very different to their Korean or Colombian counterparts, leading to many great unknown idiosyncrasies. And where these groups meet, extraordinary confluences might arise. Where would we as a people be without chicken tikka masala? Or pizza? Is the possibility of creating a BLT topped with mozzarella sticks and Sriracha, bookended by empanadas, not a bounty to all humanity? More seriously, participatory development could lead to an Afro-Anglo-Korean style of building that might be better able to alleviate concerns that these communities have with gentrification. Development wouldn't be done to them, but rather crafted by them. This would have the added benefit of mitigating displacement concerns, as housing would be unlocked for all who require it, ensuring people don't need to compete with each other for artificially scarce resources.

Importantly, this is a flexible system. Our challenges can't be accomplished by five-year plans or thousand-page documents that are equal parts banal and indecipherable. Though we might not know how, our world will change in unexpected ways that may require us to react expeditiously. If a local immigrant community suddenly becomes a safe harbor for refugees fleeing a civil war, it would be inhumane to turn these newcomers away in their time of greatest need, or force them into woeful conditions simply because of administrative incompetence. And yet, this exact scenario is happening in America every single day, with millions of people living out of the public eye, grateful to be here despite our lack of hospitality (to put it lightly). When we embrace these groups and make sufficient space for them (neither lack of room nor resources are problems we have in America, but rather improper allocation), our culture, economy, and society are greatly improved through this assimilation.

Optimism means pursuing the most common sense, elegant, and inclusive solution to a given problem at a given scale. The philosophy allows for large-scale planning in some cases, because there's no way individual stakeholders can facilitate significant infrastructure projects on their own. Nor should they be expected to subsume their own personal interest for the greater good. That's not realistic, as it takes a rare and selfless person to be able to accept change with total lack of bias. Optimism also acknowledges that at a more localized level, a backyard apartment or a pushcart operator selling fruit might not solve our biggest problems, but they might be the best step to take in the moment. One sole movement in a positive direction is better than inaction.

In truth, Moses wasn't the pure distillation of evil he's made out to be today, and Jacobs wasn't exclusively a force for good. Their legacies have both been distorted and valorized according to our modern lens of city building, and this may well evolve in the next phase. Large infrastructure projects in modern cities are a necessary evil in order to make them run. They're not sexy, and won't win many supporters, but as our largest places grow to include millions (and increasingly tens of millions) of people in their metropolitan areas, there have to be some concessions in support of the greater good rather than neighborhoods never seeing any change, in order to support the greater good. Our polarized culture demands we choose one side or the other, but we must reject this false choice.

The solution to our problems lies somewhere between Moses and Jacobs. We can take some of the tough, logistical work done by Moses and marry it with the enlightened ideals of Jacobs, creating cities that are fine-grained, diverse, and dynamic, but which still retain affordability, accessibility, and openness. This means rejecting the authoritarian, bird's-eye control favored by Moses and Le Corbusier that relegates people to secondary citizens, but also the processes that Jacobs' acolytes revere at the expense of reality and substance. We must be willing to compromise on certain things in order to achieve behind a greater common good for all, not just an improved life for some. When we're unwilling to compromise, or let ideology guide us in a fight that pits us versus them, everyone loses. There's no sense in moving down this path, and it's even worse when it's a path that flagrantly ignores the operating realities of our world. In the next chapter, we'll explore what goes wrong when we draw these dividing lines, and why reality must be the motivating force policy and intervention, not theory.

4.

Theory Has to Meet Reality—A Common Sense Way of Building

With the pendulum of development shifting towards a world where our communities are shaped by many hands in the service of broader ends, we must make sure that the threads we attempt to sew are viable. We cannot solve our problems without the solutions being grounded in some fundamental reality. Much as I admire utopian thinking, when it's divorced from on-the-ground realities or counteracts the goals we set out to achieve, it cannot reasonably be turned to as a solution for our challenges. Neither can mission statements, social media posts of righteousness, nor "reports" to be studied. But a little bit of utopianism married with pragmatism? Now that's something we can work with.

This unity begins with a little belief that the world can be better, and, indeed, that it must change. As you've made it this far, I expect you to hold a bit of this romanticism. But on its own, romance doesn't get us far. The recipe needs something more. A dash of common sense, a touch of empirical support, and a means of effectuating this change. When mixed together, we arrive at a proper balance of what I call romantic pragmatism. With this recipe, we can positively compound changes to the built environment in the same way that generations of negative decisions have brought us to the disagreeable state we are subjected to today. We don't need to contort our minds through dense theory to arrive at a new philosophy of the world that can only be understood through ascetic study or esoteric debate. We don't need to come up with convoluted rationales or subversive marketing as to why an Optimistic worldview should be implemented. All we need for these presumptive aspirational changes to take hold is to show that they are in fact the most practical ones to employ.

Importantly, romantic pragmatism has no tolerance for inertia nor obstinance getting in the way of our goals. If a given policy leads to results that directly contradict the stated goals of that policy, we cannot continue doing it out of an obdurate righteousness, or fear of shame, reprisal, or reputational damage, especially when so many people's lives are at stake.

Let's first look at housing and the natural environment to explore this dynamic. These two issues are dominated by passionate discourse and many theories about how we should most optimally be seeking to cure them. They're inextricably linked with emotion, which at times can be helpful. But if we're not careful, this emotion threatens to inform policy that can lead to great damage through a misunderstanding of fundamental operating realities.

A Better Theory of Housing

Housing affordability is one of the great challenges societies around the world face today. Finding a workable solution, however, is tricky, because every person has their own idea of what housing should be and are seldom willing to compromise on it. When vetocrats are given power, things get more difficult still. Each person has a different standard of housing that they require, and different housing options that they prefer. Some might want a small apartment in the heart of a city where they can spend most of their time away from home enjoying urban amenities, while others would prefer a large house in the countryside where they rarely have to leave. Between these two poles, there are countless other preferences. Our current system of exclusionary zoning denies these many preferences from being realized. It rests on a bed of illiberalism that presumes the default preference for most is a large single family home in a suburban setting, forcing the masses to accept this one option, while inhibiting access to other forms. Operationally, this is not unlike an ice cream parlor where vanilla is the only flavor available. Sure, some might like vanilla best, but it's not quite true to claim that everyone prefers it if there aren't any other options available. What system that purports to grant self-determination refuses the possibility of mint chocolate chip?

Unlike ice cream, however, the type of housing we allow and where we allow it has real consequences. Housing operates within a market structure. If there is more housing than there are people, housing will be cheaper. If there is less housing than there are people, housing will be more expensive. Cities deny it at their own peril. This basic fact cares little for theory. And because I must be hungry as I write this, by way of example, let's go to dinner.

At 8 o'clock on a Thursday night, 40 people arrive at The Milliner, an elegant restaurant located on the ground floor of a former hat factory. The kitchen has prepared 40 meals for those who made reservations. Most feature the chef's signature salmon dish. All of a sudden, a boom is heard. Through the window, patrons of The Milliner see the lights abruptly shut off in the neighboring building, a bar and grill that's a hotspot for young professionals looking to grab a quick bite before hitting the town for the night. *The generator must've gone bust*, a besuited man observes. Slowly, and slightly disorientedly, the yuppies amble their way over to the neighboring structure and begin queuing at the door. 10, then 20. Soon, upwards of 60 people are poking their heads through the windows, loitering by the maître d', and sowing disquiet for the respectable patrons inside. As the growing line of guests begins talking with one another, it soon becomes clear that the bar and grill wasn't alone in losing power. An entire section of the town's electrical grid went out. The Milliner is one of the only places open for miles, thanks to a fortuitous decision by its restaurateur to buy a back-up generator some months ago.

Mid-sear, the chef is pulled out of the kitchen to see what all the commotion is about and his eyes widen at the line out front. After a moment's pause, he jumps into action. *No trouble*, he thinks. The restaurant has a back room (unpermitted) that's currently used as storage, but can hold twice the restaurant's permitted capacity. Several apprentice cooks are fortunately in the kitchen as part of a monthly externship program, and can quickly be dispatched into action to serve the hungry crowd.

Not wanting to upset potential customers, the chef makes arrangements to do whatever he can to feed the erstwhile bar-goers. While he might have wanted to serve all his guests salmon, his supplier informed him earlier in the day they were running low going into the weekend. Chicken and tofu it'll have to be, as he had excess quantities of each in preparation for a large event over the weekend. Maybe even some fondant potatoes for those who thought they'd be eating fries next door.

But there's a problem. One of the original 40 patrons is on the city's planning board. Even worse, her husband is the president of the HOA of the gated community just down the street. Officiously, they both relish any opportunity they get to enforce rules. The couple begins shouting at the waitstaff—and anyone who will listen really—that it's just too bad for those who didn't make a reservation. They'll have to go somewhere else as there's no way they can be allowed to eat in the storage space—no matter how industrial chic or well-equipped for the task it may be. Unpermitted uses must not be permitted. The chef listens to the entitled couple, and decides against using the storage space for fear of earning a code violation which would force him to temporarily shut down the restaurant. Perhaps the private event space upstairs could be used, but there is only space for a few tables.

Hungry, agitated, and willing to spend more than a reasonable person would under normal circumstances, a bidding war erupts in the crowd outside to secure one of the 10 tables upstairs.

Naturally, the 10 wealthiest couples among the crowd, or those willing to spend the most, will pay what they have to in order to secure a meal. This leaves the other groups waiting (and who knows how many more might come from other parts of town in search of food) out in the cold, hungry.

To recap: due to a surge in demand, there were more people who wanted to eat than there were meals available. While the chef had enough space, food, and cooks to accommodate the surge, he wasn't able to do so because of occupancy and permitting restrictions. He was willing to compromise on certain preferences in order to provide meals for all, but was inhibited from doing so. And that, good reader, is how our housing system works in a nutshell.

In truth, it's a little more complicated than this. Instead of responding nimbly with more supply to accommodate all those who require it, our current set of solutions subsidize select consumers to consume more, often without expanding supply, thus exacerbating the problem for those who don't get subsidized. It might better be referred to as state-sponsored arson, providing fuel as cure for a raging fire rather than the proven method of water. Instead of reducing input costs (supply-oriented), the government subsidizes a few spots at the table for those of lesser means, regardless of the cost it takes to secure them (demand-oriented). Government arsons acquiesce to higher prices, resigned to the apocryphal belief they can do nothing to bring costs down, filling an ever-increasing gap between what a lower-income tenant can afford and what the property costs to run.

Returning to The Millinery, we find our besuited man sympathetic to the plight of those engaged in the manic bidding war to secure something to eat. He offers to pay half the check for people eating in the room upstairs, so long as they drove more than 10 miles to get there. It'd be a shame if they had to travel so far and then pay so much, he reasons. But not all the people upstairs came from more than 10 miles away. And so the cost of securing each additional meal increases incrementally, as those who drove more than 10 miles are able to consume more than they otherwise might be able to, and those who drove less have to pay more to compete for fewer meals. The besuited man's money doesn't ensure better quality or more nutritious food—to say nothing of the famous salmon—but just food, period. By the end of the night, there might not even be tofu available. What's more, in our parallel world, the system we've devised makes it very difficult, verging on impossible, to provide the additional meals demanded.

No matter how much the generous patron hands out, if the total meals don't increase from 40 to 100, there will still be 60 people who won't get any food. As the meals get more expensive, an increasing amount of those who are either not able to afford dinner, or are not being subsidized, will go hungry. This disproportionately impacts the working and middle classes, who either make too much, or are not lucky enough to be selected for subsidization (the pool of capital is finite), but also don't make enough money to comfortably secure a meal on their own.

Common sense would hold, then, that the solution isn't to continue playing a demand-side game where a scarce number of meals are up for grabs where prices rise as quality falls, but to allow the kitchen to create more meals, and perhaps a surplus of meals, such that everyone can get something good and nutritious to eat. Any focus on not providing more meals results in hunger. The solution isn't to go from 5 to 10 subsidized meals, but from 40 to 110 meals in total, while keeping the kitchen running so that when more people want to come for food, it can be provided easily.

Enabling more meals is a result of an outcome-based system: a structural fix to a structural problem, one that seeks to improve outcomes across the board. While there will always be people who need help getting to the table, which demand-side subsidies can certainly help with, these should not be the focus of our policies during a housing crisis, no matter how virtuous they seem on the surface. The government (or our besuited man sitting by the window) simply doesn't have enough funding to support this set of solutions. Private companies (or private chefs) do, however, if they're so allowed. Yet we limit them. When put in simplified, analogized terms, it's easier to understand and oppose the limitations of our current system. But as mentioned a few paragraphs ago, it's not so simple. A deeper dive of this most-important subject is merited. Dive, commencing.

In response to rising costs, it's become popular among certain groups to demand that housing production and management exclusively be met by schemes owned, subsidized, and incentivized by the government. Private actors, *verboten*. Profit imperatives in these scenarios are thus (theoretically) removed. We can call this "capital A" Affordable Housing. Researchers and policy experts generally agree that housing is considered affordable (note the lowercase "a" which means the government isn't necessarily involved) for a specific household when they spend less than 30% of their gross income on costs, including utilities. Currently, housing is unaffordable for half of all American renters by this 30% metric.[1] As Affordable Housing programs place caps on what tenants pay to keep costs below this threshold, nearly all of these unaffordable units are in privatized, market rate housing. At surface level, then, it's understandable why many are demanding a change from our mostly privatized system. As the government has no incentive to make a profit, the logic continues, if we dispense with profit-driven actors, costs will inevitably come down.

With such an easy solution available, devotees reason, anyone who chooses to operate market rate housing supports the impoverishment and subjugation of vulnerable people. This is immoral. To accept any level of compromise within this system is to bargain with oppression. Who would ever support that? Not the righteous. And so, according to this ideology, any level of privatization becomes pathologized, and justifiably so This is noble in theory, and doubtless well-intentioned, but does it match reality? In order to answer that, we must take a look at private versus Affordable Housing to find out.

The standard industry metric for valuing the returns of an investment property is known as a capitalization rate, or "cap rate" for short. It's a quick back-of-the-envelope calculation that shows how much an investor can expect to make at a given property in a given year. Valuations are constantly changing. Cap rates can rise (expand) or fall (compress) depending on a range of micro and macroeconomic factors. If cash flow is more certain (e.g. tenants with higher credit scores), the property is in a great location, the building is in a good condition, and the overall market is strong, rates tend to compress. If cash flow is precarious, the property isn't in the best area, it hasn't been well maintained, and the market is weak, rates will expand and valuations will fall. For example, if a newly constructed building in a great neighborhood makes $100,000 in annual net operating income (NOI), the property may be valued at a 4% cap rate, worth around $2,500,000. But if a shabbier building makes the same amount of NOI in a worse city and worse location, with a more insecure tenant situation, it may trade at a 10% cap rate, for a $1,000,000 valuation. There is an inverse relationship between returns and value. The higher the cap rate, the less the property is worth, and vice versa.

In the most expensive coastal markets with the most severe housing crises, cap rates have hovered between 3% and 5% in the late 2010s and early 2020s. These are pretty paltry returns, and that's before debt payments are factored in. Far lower returns than if investors had simply put their money in the S&P500, which on average yielded nearly 13% from January 2010 to December 2023 (factoring in reinvested dividends).[2] Rising interest rates in 2022 and 2023 have expanded cap rates somewhat, but not too much. Paltry returns mean, contrary to popular imaginations of landlording, that when there's a large unexpected repair, reassessment, or weather event (and there's no shortage of these things), it's not uncommon for many property owners to operate at zero or negative margins for prolonged periods of time. Far from lucrative, landlording can be an unprofitable venture— sometimes deeply so.

According to a leading commercial real estate database, LoopNet, as of January 2023, 370 of 481 apartment buildings listed for sale in Los Angeles were marketed with cap rates of less than 5%.[3] 55 of these listings were offered at cap rates of less than 3%. By March 2024, after more than a year of interest rate hikes, 303 of 531 properties were still listed with caps below 5%. 10 Year Treasury Bills—arguably the safest risk-adjusted investment one can make, as the U.S. is unlikely to default on its bonds— yielded more than 4% in the second half of 2023.[4] In plain English, this means that anyone who owned properties below a cap of 4% was making less money than the risk-free rate of return offered via Treasury Bills. Not exactly raking it in. After layering in interest payments, on an inflation-adjusted basis many owners would have lost money.

Counterintuitively, profits are higher in more affordable places like Cleveland, Memphis, or Little Rock, where cap rates may range between 5% and 8% in urban cores, and higher in outlying areas. With less demand to live in a neighborhood (be it a rural community, deindustrialized city, or tertiary market), cap rates rise and valuations fall. This means tax bills tend to drop as well. As taxes are often the largest component of operating expenses in a building, a lower purchase or assessment price can have a meaningful effect on profitability. The minimum threshold for investors to make their money back is thus greatly reduced. Beyond the iron law of supply and demand, taxes are a key reason why a new 1,200 square foot 2-bed, 2-bath apartment in the heart of downtown Memphis can rent for less than $1,500 a month, while an equivalent apartment in New York may be four to six times that price.

Over the last 20 years, multifamily apartments have become a more desirable asset class for investors, as they're willing to take lower returns for what they perceive to be a more stable, secure investment. "People always need somewhere to live" the modern real estate mogul can be heard musing in the distance, his echoes reverberating from location to location to location. Cap rates have compressed accordingly. In 2002, national cap rates for properties hovered north of 8%.[5] By 2022, they had dropped to 4.5%.[6]

Compression has been driven by the institutionalization of real estate. By institutionalization, I mean the process by which institutional investors have become a larger share of the market for multifamily assets. An institutional investor is a capital allocator who invests on behalf of large pools of people. These can be pension funds, sovereign wealth funds, insurance giants, endowments, or family offices, along with a few other groups. In short, they're the fuel that propels much of the investment world in order to generate sufficient returns for their beneficiaries. Asset managers like private equity and venture capital firms often raise money from institutional investors and allocate on their behalf. We'll explore this dynamic a bit more in depth in Chapter 5.

Avalon Bay, the fourth-largest owner of apartments in America (80,325 units as of 2023) and one of the ten most valuable publicly traded real estate companies in the world (with a market cap of $26.58 billion at year end 2023, down from ~$35 billion at the same time in 2021), is a good case study in the impact institutions have had on multifamily yield.[7] In 2021, Avalon acquired 1,932 units spread across seven properties for a combined $724.15 million. The average cap rate was 3.8%. Separately, they sold nine communities containing 2,404 apartments for $867.2 million, at a weighted average market cap rate of 3.7%.[8] The largest asset managers—whom opponents to market rate housing most forcefully direct their ire—are transacting deals at very thin margins.

With institutional capital entering the market, cap rates have been driven down, and valuations up. This has led to higher rents, a potential cause for concern when they accelerate significantly, but also higher quality apartments with professional management teams who have pushed out neglectful and malicious land(slum)lords. Cities that saw the highest median rent increases in the 2010s also tended to receive the highest allocation of institutional capital. Places like Denver (85% non-inflation adjusted increase in rents in the last decade), Phoenix (71%), and Atlanta (65%). Surprisingly, these cities remained relatively affordable to working- and middle-class households. Average rent in Denver ($1,660), Phoenix ($1,113) and Atlanta ($1,474) would be considered affordable, whereby households spend no more than 30% of their gross income on such housing costs, to those making $66,400, $44,520, and $58,960 respectively.[9] For dual-income households, which well over half of all Americans are a part of, these are fairly reasonable rents. That's not to say *job well done* and stop working for those for whom these prices aren't affordable, but it's an important reminder that high rates of rental growth don't necessarily mean housing has to be expensive. Increases in wages and productivity, along with a reduction in the prices of household goods and amenities, can outpace rent growth.

So, not only are returns low and being driven lower, and the quality of housing is increasing, but the bulk of the returns that are made are paid to the beneficiaries of institutional pension funds, insurance giants, endowments, and hedge funds; namely pensioners, scholarship students, middle-class families indexing into dividend-yielding real estate funds, and towards the rising cost of medical bills (a whole other issue that's best not discussed here). If your intuition is to blame Blackstone or some other color-plus-natural element amalgam for rising rents, don't. Institutional landlords control just 3% of America's single family rental supply (450,000 homes), or 0.3% of the total housing stock.[10] Hardly consequential. But if you must blame someone, Blackstone isn't the intellectually honest path to take. Rather, look to your public officials who have artificially constrained housing supply and allowed rent to become commodified. And if this isn't satisfactory, and the lust to blame corporate greed can't be quelled, perhaps direct your attention to the seventh grade science teacher in your school district, or the fireman who lives down the block, for whom our colored minerals invest on behalf of. When the veil of the system is pulled back, one instantly sees how absurd such accusations are. These are hardly the marauding forces of capitalism. Beneficiaries of institutional investment are honest folks whose livelihoods depend on the stable returns that an asset like real estate has historically yielded.

What's going on here? Why has the narrative persisted that developers are perniciously greedy, and that private markets are exclusively to blame for our current housing crisis, when the data doesn't seem to support these claims? Shouldn't developers be compared more often to farmers than speculators? Both provide existential goods for millions who aren't capable of creating them on their own. Margins are similarly tight, but not equally so. The average farm can expect to yield around 11% in profit, while the top-quartile operations can earn more than 20%—several multiples higher than housing.[11] Both housing development and farming are risky and unpredictable. The parallels run deeper still, to more enlightened notions of how each discipline should be practiced. Devotees of organic agriculture turn their nose up at conventional farming practices. Similarly, true believers of Affordable Housing shudder at the thought of something so important being left to the caprices of the market. But presently, neither noble solution is possible to achieve at scale, owing to costs and inadequate infrastructure (both physical and administrative). Just 1.5% of the world's agricultural land is farmed organically.[12] Instead of mandating that all food be organic—a vision whose immediate implementation would shepherd the deaths of hundreds of millions of people—we have to provide in the best way we can today, or face the prospect of an even greater crisis down the road. Sri Lanka's recent experiment in organic agriculture proved disastrous, leading to mass hunger, economic depravity, and a toppling of its own government.[13] Ideological purity cannot be trotted out as policy when so many lives are at stake and the proposed interventions cannot adequately provide for all those who require aid. Happily, this precept is broadly accepted.

But where farmers are valued for the services they provide, private developers seldom are. Most people understand that their food comes from a farmer. Few realize, however, that every building they have ever had occasion to occupy is the product of labor from a developer of some sort or another. A disproportionate amount of these structures have come from private developers. Developers have created your favorite places. And yes, your most loathed as well—but fear not, we're working on reducing those places through this book! Moreover, the practice of building employs millions all around the country, both directly and indirectly.[14] This is something that is worthy of celebration.

While anger is directed at caricatures of developers (rightly so in some cases), the origin of this angst—namely costs—is predominantly attributable to the trades. These are working-class, or upwardly mobile middle-class professionals like electricians, painters, plumbers, roofers, framers, etc., who tend to work for small businesses. Many of these small businesses provide employment opportunities to newly arrived immigrants or those who may have struggled to secure a job in another field. These men and women need to support their families as much as anyone else. Are they not deserving of just compensation?

This isn't to say that developers as a class are paupers. Hardly. But developers primarily make money through project-level fees that are funded from banks, or through selling their buildings to individual owners and investors. When multifamily owners sell to other investors, they're often the same sort of well-capitalized institutional groups who professionalize management and drive cap rates down.

Doubtless, there are some landlords who have owned housing for many years and whose margins far exceed the 3–8% national profit range. Others are little more than slumlords. There are still more who take to online forums in all manner of baseness, where they engage with other pernicious spirits about how to squeeze the last few dollars out of a unit while reducing costs as much as possible, sometimes forcing units to substandard habitability, where residents are viewed as nothing more than names on a rent roll—if even that favorably. Regrettably, I've seen some of these forums, which served primarily to conjure immense anger within me. It's the job of all of those who care about their communities, and the precariously housed, to take a strong stance against these actors, who can devastate entire lives through neglect and greed.

Unconvinced by these arguments as you may still be, perhaps the current state of Affordable Housing will persuade you that it's not the viable path forward many claim it to be.

"Capital A" Affordable Housing costs significantly more to construct than market rate housing. Outcomes are variable depending on the competence of the municipality and development team, and the complexity of the project, but it's not uncommon for the cost of an Affordable apartment to be two to four times higher than a market rate one. In Los Angeles, "luxury" units in non-high-rises can be delivered for around $300,000 to $400,000 per unit. Non-"luxury" market rate units can be completed for half of that, conditional on their size and location. Capital "A" Affordable units, on the other hand, can cost more than $850,000 for what is often a rather small and austere space.[15] In San Francisco, they routinely cost more than a million dollars.[16] In New York, where the Affordable construction apparatus is more robust and costs are subsequently more reasonable, some units can still run as high as $750,000. For the expense of a single apartment, you can buy a veritable palace in Pittsburgh. Again I ask: What's going on here?

Well, a lot of things. Let's start with the construction of the building itself. At surface level, if two identical structures are built next to each other at the same time, and using the same materials, it would be improbable to think the two structures would vary much in cost. They're the same building, in the same place, after all. And yet. Contracts for the construction of Affordable Housing using public funds often require the use of unionized labor with prevailing wage requirements (the rate paid based on a collective bargaining agreement), extensive environmental review, and years of community outreach. Affordable Housing thus becomes less about the construction of homes, and more of an omnibus to solve other objectives. Focus is diverted away from the primary task at hand. Regardless of the merits of job programs, environmental reviews, community input, or any other policy goal, using housing as the blunt object to ram through such initiatives has consequences, like guaranteeing that projects will be more expensive, leading to fewer overall homes. How much more expensive? A lot.

A 2021 report from the RAND Corporation found that project labor agreements (PLAs) added $43,000 in costs (14.5% increase) per unit of Affordable Housing compared to non-PLA projects.[17] The study focused on Proposition HHH, a bond measure that earmarked $1.2 billion for the creation of 10,000 Affordable units in Los Angeles. 5 years after its launch in 2016, only 1,000 homes were built, averaging $500,000 per unit. Costs have continued to inflate. By 2022, units were being built for nearly $840,000, more than 2.2 times higher than original estimates. These estimates, initially, were 15% higher than market rate costs at the time.[18]

The story is much the same across the country. In New York, a 2016 report from the city's Independent Budget Office found that prevailing wage requirements increased total project costs by 23%, and construction costs by 28%.[19] Through recent conversations with staff at the city's Housing Preservation and Development Office, I've learned prevailing wage requirements can add upwards of 40%, and sometimes 50%, in additional construction prices.

Arguing against subcontractors making more money can seem a rather parsimonious thing to do. In practice, however, it would be wrong to assume that prevailing wage agreements are some sort of Robin Hood program that claws back money from the wealthy for the benefit of the marginalized. Rafael E. Cestero, CEO of the non-profit Community Preservation Corporation, noted in a 2019 article that the "New York City mean wage, for full-time work in 2018, for bricklayers was approximately $82,000; under prevailing wage, that would jump to $114,600. A plumber made $78,000 in 2018; under prevailing wage, that would increase to $141,000."[20] Whether one believes that these wages should be higher or not is a matter that two reasonable people can disagree on. Inarguably, though, higher wages increase costs above an already expensive basis, manifesting in higher rents, and a reduction of desperately needed housing.

And it's getting worse. The multifamily construction price index rose by 6% in 2023, a slight drop from the year before.[21] But this is small comfort. 6% is still considerable, and 2022's price index growth of 8% was the highest rate in 40 years.[22] These costs aren't endemic to a given political economic system, nor are they driven by greed, but rather by material, labor, administrative, and regulatory imperatives.

Construction costs are just the tip of the iceberg for Affordable Housing. Even if—and it's a big if—a project's budget is reasonable, it's difficult to find enough competent people to execute on it. The public sector is woefully ill-equipped in this respect. Principally, the issue is that public agencies aren't designed to be developers.[23] The role of a real estate developer is complex, requiring specialized knowledge across many disciplines, from finance, design, zoning and entitlement programs, construction, property management, accounting, investor relations, and infrastructure among many others. There is a great deal of risk involved, faced even by the most experienced, capable developers. Forcing public officials to become developers would make an already confused system of 3,300 local public housing agencies even more disoriented, resulting in an even more inferior product.[24] As *The New York Times* has noted of Houston's struggles with homelessness, "As in other cities, dozens of local aid organizations, public and private, were operating in silos—competing for federal funds, duplicating services, not sharing information or goals, housing precious few people."[25]

Beyond this, there's no funding for public development. As the Urban Institute explained in a 2018 report, "Federal public housing construction has seen almost no new funding in nearly 40 years; current funding for public housing is primarily for maintenance and operations of existing properties, and even this is extremely inadequate."[26] Even if these non-developers wanted to try their hand at creating the spaces that matter more than anywhere else in someone's life (hint—this is not something one can, or should, try if they're not equipped), they don't have the people to do it. Staff are preciously short for the existing mandates of housing authorities, to say nothing of an expansive new endeavor. Calling for the creation of an entity that is set up to fail is senseless, profligate, and inefficient.

I don't want to come across as cynical, nor dismissive of the work being done by folks around the country who are desperately trying to alleviate our housing crisis. There's no shortage of programs, firms, and organizations laboring to deliver on the promise of a better tomorrow. But merely working on the problem means little if those efforts aren't properly directed. Writing in *Palladium Magazine*, Brian Balkus has observed that America struggles to build infrastructure efficiently and economically because public agencies have become reliant on consultants and middlemen in an attempt to make up for inadequate internal staffing.[27] Though he focused on infrastructure in his article, the piece just as readily applies to public and Affordable Housing agencies: "The expertise problem is compounded by the fact that agencies are often staffed with a workforce of people either just at the beginning of their careers or near the end of them. Those at the beginning tend to leave if they are ambitious, which leaves senior positions in the hands of agency lifers. Because of this dynamic, and the fact that it is not economically feasible to have the wide range of expertise needed in-house, public agencies employ consulting firms. These firms fill a valuable niche."

Rarely do these agencies or consulting firms have accountability to build their projects well, or under cost. They have no skin in the game. Consultants might actually benefit from cost overruns, change orders, and delays if their fees are tied to a percentage of job costs, as they often are. But this isn't just graft. Serious skill is required to navigate the byzantine apparatus that surrounds Affordable Housing development. In order to incentivize competent firms to work within such a chaotic system, Affordable developers earn fees upwards of 15–20% (and sometimes 25%) of a project's total costs, which is five to eight times higher than what's customarily charged in the private market. Who, I ask, should ire appropriately be directed at, if it need be directed at all?

As it's quite costly to replace consultants in the middle of a project, and difficult to attract, hire, and train new talent, it often makes sense to keep existing parties in place even when they are not performing well, guaranteeing substandard and costlier outcomes. These costs are a direct hit to project affordability. Necessarily, they must either be recouped via higher rent (which isn't possible in income-restricted units), or through cuts to annual budgets, which results in less assistance, fewer improvements to existing homes, fewer new homes, and severe declines in quality of life for those we're meant to be protecting. None of these are desirable outcomes, and yet we continue down this path littered with billboards advertising their eventuality, seemingly unbothered.

Every building requires a sufficient amount of funding for construction, and then a base of reserves once it's operating. This is true whether the structure is built by the government, a non-profit developer, or a for-profit one. Operating expenses like maintenance, insurance, property management, taxes, etc., cannot exceed the revenue a building brings in, or else it will operate at a loss. In the private sector, this means a building won't get built in the first place. In the public/Affordable sector, this means that more public funds, subsidies, or taxes will have to be used in order to prop up the operating loss. Perhaps subsidizing one property is manageable. Subsidizing millions of homes is not. We do not possess a limitless reserve of cash to cover up all shortfalls across all buildings.

As a rule, Affordable Housing projects face a financing gap in order to get built. Unlike market rate developments that can attract investments and financing from private individuals and institutions because of the returns they offer, Affordable projects offer no return. They must thus rely on federal subsidies, municipal coffers, and grants that have no expectation of yield, along with a select few tax credit investors who likewise expect no-to-low returns beyond reductions in tax liability, which is a very different sort of thing.

Funding being scarce, Affordable developers are forced to go hunting for many sources as it's highly unlikely a single foundation or agency will have enough money to backstop an entire project. For larger developments, it's not uncommon for a dozen funding sources to be involved. This number can easily grow to 20, or even 30.[28] Each of these entities adds additional costs to a project as they all have their own teams who need to process, review, and administer funds. Hundreds of additional people are thus added to a project who are often not on the same page, but must be managed as though they were. Attempting to coordinate all of these actors leads to delays, which, when combined with community review, can add several years and costs to a project. Factoring in all of these considerations, it's little wonder why Affordable projects are more expensive than market rate ones. And that's without even addressing the endemic misappropriation of funds in the industry.

If this reality doesn't comport with a given theory of how housing should work, one must only look at the numbers to understand why housing policy must be ideologically agnostic. To prove the point more finely, I've created a hypothetical comparative analysis of a market rate development versus an Affordable one. For both projects, we'll assume the same parameters: a 5,000 square foot lot located on a street zoned for multifamily housing. The site allows for a floor area ratio (FAR) of 2, meaning 10,000 square feet can be built (5,000 × 2 = 10,000). Apartments can only be constructed in a select few areas in our hypothetical city, which increases the land price in multifamily zones. With these parameters set, here are a few assumptions for the projects:

Price of the Land
- Market rate: $2 million
- Affordable: $2 million

Construction Costs
- Market rate: $400 per square foot
- Affordable: $600 per square foot

Apartment Count and Size
- Each: 16 apartments, 500 square feet. 20% of the building area will be lost to corridors, building systems, and common areas, 80% of the building will be rentable.

Rent
- Market rate: $3,000
- Affordable: $1,800 (affordable to a household making less than $65,000 per year)

Expenses:
- Each: 30% of annual rent
- What Affordable units gain from tax breaks is lost to higher overall operating expenses

Construction Loan
- Market rate: 60% loan-to-cost (LTC)
- Affordable: 50% loan-to-cost (LTC)
- Banks may not finance a higher proportion of Affordable projects due to perceived risk

Valuation of Property
- Market rate: 5% cap rate
- Affordable: 6.5% cap rate

Permanent Loan
- The size of the permanent loan will be dependent on a number of factors. Most traditional lenders rely on a ratio of a property's net operating income and its stabilized annual interest payments, known as the debt service coverage ratio (DSCR). As a general rule of thumb, stabilized market rate projects should have a DSCR of at least 1.25, meaning NOI is 25% higher than the interest payments. Once a project is completed, the construction loan (including closing costs) will ideally be fully paid off via this new mortgage. An Affordable project may find difficulty penciling on DSCR terms because the rent will be lower and the expenses will be higher than a market rate project, while the interest rate will be similar. Other financing options are available, but are not as broadly applicable. Regardless, a new permanent loan of some sort will be needed if the property is not sold after construction.

Stabilized Interest Rate

- Each: 8%
- Interest rates will be highly variable depending on when one reads this section. Refer only to this number within which the context and time this book was written in.

Market Rate v. Affordable Development Return Analysis		
	Market Rate Development	Affordable Development
Lot Size	5,000	5,000
Building Size	10,000	10,000
Net Liveable Square Feet	8,000	8,000
Apartments	16	16
Square Feet per Unit	500	500
Land Costs	$1,000,000	$1,000,000
Construction Costs	$4,000,000	6,000,000
Construction Costs Pdf	$400	$600
Soft Costs	$1,000,000	$2,000,000
Holding Costs	$300,000	$900,000
Total Costs	$6,300,000	$9,900,000
Per Unit Cost	$393,750	$618,750
Construction Loan	$3,780,000	$4,950,000
Equity Required	$2,520,000	$4,950,000
Monthly Rent	$3,000	$1,800
Annual Rent	$576,000	$345,600
Annual Expenses	$172,800	$172,800
Net Operating Income	$403,200	$172,800
Cap Rate	5.00%	6.50%
Valuation	$8,064,000	$2,658,462
Perm Loan	$4,032,000	$5,050,000
Interest Rate	8%	8%
Debt Payments	$322,560	$404,000
Debt Service Coverage Ratio	1.25	0.43
Net Income	$80,640	($231,200)
Equity Balance After Loan	$2,268,000	$5,050,000
Net Return on Income	3.56%	($4.58%)

As can be seen in the table on the preceding page the Affordable property would operate at a pretty significant loss of approximately $230,000 per year, whereas the market rate building would return just over 3.5%. This illustration shows two important things. First, most Affordable units require deep subsidies to be completed. Second, market rate developers don't make big margins on projects. In fact, they're meager even when rent is $3,000 a month for a small unit.

This analysis only tells part of the story, however. Most properties are built today with the intention of being sold on at a later date. As we can see from the sale analysis in the table on the following page, the market rate development will have a lower cap rate applied to it, and thus be more highly valued by the market, because it's not encumbered by restrictions on rent. Based on its cash flow and cap rate, it will be valued at $8 million ($403k NOI / 5% = $8.06 million). The Affordable development, conversely, might generously be valued around $2.65 million based on its cash flow. That's a $5.4-million variance for what is effectively the same building.

After the costs of selling the properties (6%) and the satisfaction of the outstanding mortgages are considered, we can calculate the returns for both projects. The market rate development returns $3.8 million in profits from an initial $2.5-million equity investment, for an annualized return of 13.5%. On a risk-adjusted basis, these returns are likely worse than if one were to hold all one's money in an S&P500 index fund, as one wouldn't have to deal with the many obstacles, illiquidity, and risk of a real estate development project. As such, it's unlikely that this project would get built. Ground-up development usually isn't greenlit unless annualized returns exceed 20%.

The Affordable development team would lose $3.2 million on their initial equity investment of $4.95 million. Each unit would generously cost nearly $620,000. A bargain in some markets, they would still be roughly 60% more expensive than our market rate units. Each apartment would require $14,500 in annual subsidies

Operating & Sale Analysis		
	Market Rate Development	Affordable Development
NOI	403,200	172,800
Cap Rate	5.00%	6.50%
Valuation	$8,064,000	$2,658,462
Cost of Sale	($483,840)	($159,508)
Debt Pay Off	($4,032,000)	($5,050,000)
Net Cash Flow (3 Years)	$241,920	($693,600)
Profits	$3,790,080	($3,244,646)
Multiple on Equity	1.67	(0.64)
IRR	13.50%	Does Not Compute

to cover basic operating costs, without factoring in the requisite additional administrative support, or unanticipated capital events like major rehabilitations after a severe weather event. The numbers simply don't work.

It's very difficult to justify deep subsidies in an expensive area where $3,000 apartments don't make financial sense, but if a public housing agency or nonprofit developer is committed to this path, these are the losses they must internalize, or find dollars somewhere to support the mission. To be clear, this requires a level of subsidy that doesn't exist. In 2023, HUD's entire budget was $72 billion, up more than 50% from $44.1 billion in 2019.[29] While this might seem like a lot of money, it's not for the scale of housing markets. If the entire budget of HUD was used to acquire homes with the goal of stabilizing them, it would only cover around 0.12% of the total supply.[30] Or 172,705 individual homes based on the Q4 2023 national median home value of $417,700.[31] However, most of these funds are dedicated to grant and rental assistance programs—demand-side protections that do little to add desperately needed housing. While vouchers and tenant protections are important, they're duct tape on the bottom of a periously leaking bucket.

That the agency tasked with overseeing national housing and urban development in a country 4 million homes short of demand doesn't create any new housing is a problem. The primary tool used by the federal government to encourage the development of more Affordable Housing, the Low Income Housing Tax Credit (LIHTC), only provided $10.9 billion in funding for 2022—the most it's ever received.[32] Since its inception, LIHTC has placed 3.44 million units into Affordable service, or roughly 100,000 a year. Credits cover around 22% of a project's cost.[33] Not all of these units are developed, however. Some are merely renovated, or acquired with the goal of sheltering them from the private market. In any given year, somewhere between 40,000 and 60,0000 units are newly built through Low Income Housing Tax Credits. Or, said another way, the number of homes built nationally through LIHTC falls somewhere between the amount that the metropolitan areas of Austin (42,000), and Houston (75,000) permitted in 2022 alone.[34]

Once again, though nearly $80 billion seems like a lot of money, it's not on the scale of housing. If we wanted to build our way out of our housing crisis by exclusively constructing Affordable Homes (as some advocate for), we would need quite a lot of money. At a fairly conservative estimated cost of $500,000 per unit, across an estimated shortage of 4 million homes, the federal government would need at least $2 trillion to solve the crisis, or more than 24 times the annual amount spent on LIHTC and HUD combined. All the funds would have to be used for new development. Presently, only $5 billion per year is allocated to new units, meaning federal spending would need to be ramped up 400 times higher than today's levels. This is simply not possible, no matter how well-intentioned the policy may be.

Let's say, however, that good-intentions win out—innumerate though they may be. If theory demands we move away from the private market, it strikes me as important to understand whether the public market can offer a better alternative. We can't simply trust that Affordable housing is superior because there's no profit incentive.

The New York City Housing Authority (NYCHA) manages 177,000 homes for 536,000 New Yorkers across 335 public housing developments. Most of these units are managed within their own properties, amounting to some 162,000 apartments across 277 NYCHA-built developments. Roughly 4% of New York's population, or 330,000 people, live in these buildings.[34] A significant operation, to be sure. And all the more distressing given how bad the conditions have gotten. According to NYCHA's former CEO Gregory Russ, the buildings they managed required $78.3 billion in repairs in 2023, or $442,000 per unit.[35] Considerably more than the cost of developing brand new apartments for every NYCHA tenant.[36] Bringing these buildings up to basic habitability would require the entirety of HUD and LIHTC funding for one year. Mind you, this is only for capital improvements. The problem is going to get worse. Only 20% of operating expenses in NYCHA buildings are covered by rent. Market rate buildings, by contrast, must necessarily cover operating expenses with revenue—often two times over—and still only yield 4–5% returns. Every year, NYCHA's funding pit will grow deeper. More and more subsidies will be required. Subsidies, as we've seen at the federal level, that do not exist. Such improvidence cannot be sustained.

$78 billion is a comically large number, so what does it mean on the ground? It means fixing dilapidated buildings where 83% of NYCHA apartments have at least one severe health hazard.[37] Where 75% of common areas (lobbies, elevators, hallways, and stairwells) have similar hazard levels.[38] It means fixing the more than 600,000 open work orders to deliver residents to the precipice of basic habitable conditions—not even desirable, but something approaching tolerable. It means prioritizing lead abatement in paint, walls, and water lines. Treating asbestos, mold, sewage leaks, exposed electrical hazards, and fixing long-broken elevators that leave residents trapped hundreds of feet in the air for extended periods of time. The disabled and elderly who cannot walk up and down many flights of stairs, and thus existentially rely on the proper functioning of mechanical systems, are effectively imprisoned when they break down.[39] Nearly one-quarter of NYCHA residents are older than 62. Another quarter are younger than 18. Depriving seniors of their autonomy, or poisoning children with lead, is unworthy of continued support.

This $78-billion repair bill wouldn't include making the apartments particularly desirable places to live. It wouldn't address the psychological or physiological ramifications of decades of mismanagement, or embodied environmental injustices. It can't change the fact that these areas were designed poorly from the beginning—as towers in the park that segregate, turn their backs on the city, trap residents, and limit opportunity—or the prejudiced ideologies that accompanied their creation in the first place. It's no wonder NYCHA was given the ignoble crown of worst landlord in the city four years in a row from 2018 to 2021.[40] Curiously, and one suspects after much shame and prodding to be removed from such lists, NYCHA didn't feature in the 2022 or 2023 rankings at all. The methodology for determining the worst landlord list is based on the average number of violations issued by the city's Housing and Preservation Department. In 2023, the worst landlord had nearly 3,300 open violations across 15 buildings and 306 units.[41] The top 100 worst landlords had 73,866 violations combined across 626 buildings and 13,451 units. NYCHA buildings aren't issued violations, so open work orders are used to determine a comparable number. By this metric, *NYCHA is 187 times worse than the top offender on the Worst Landlord Watchlist*, and more than 8 times worse than all of the worst landlords combined.[42] Beyond merely damning, these numbers should be a five-alarm fire necessitating a comprehensive overhaul of the authority. Too many lives are at stake for this incompetency to continue.

Proponents of public housing push back on these criticisms on two accounts. First, funding. If only NYCHA had enough money, they reason, these problems would be rectified. This is a claim worth interrogating, because if true, we're in luck that we can avail ourselves of such a simple solution. NYCHA's budget for the fiscal year 2023 was $4.41 billion. This works out to nearly $25,000 a year per unit in operating costs. According to "New York City's Rent Guidelines Board 2023 Income and Expense Study", the median operating and maintenance (O&M) cost per apartment in New York is $974 per month, or $11,688 annually.[43] O&M costs include eight major categories: taxes, labor, utilities, fuel (for heating), insurance, maintenance, administrative, and miscellaneous costs. It's not clear to me how NYCHA can be suffering from a lack of funding when it spends more than twice as much on expenses as the median market rate unit in the city, which, it must be noted, is managed to a much higher standard. Some may still push back, arguing that public housing expenses are not an apples-to-apples comparison to market rate ones. Though I would reject this premise, let's take the claim at face value and explore a closer analog. Rent-stabilized units—homes where rents are regulated by the city—are managed for a median of $1,091 per month, or $13,092 per year. This is still roughly half of what NYCHA units are operated for.

It seems that NYCHA has more than enough money on a comparative basis. The issue, more likely, is in allocation. Where does that excess money go? Some of it, doubtless, to fueling the sprawling bureaucratic apparatus that presides over the city's public housing. But dispiritingly, a lot of that money is lost. To put it rather charitably. Recently, 70 NYCHA employees were charged with bribery and extortion as part of a sweeping no-bid corruption scandal.[44] Borne of good intentions, no-bid contracts were implemented as a way to help the authority dig its way out of hundreds of thousands of open work orders without being slowed down by a competitive bidding process. People needed urgent help. On-site superintendents were thus empowered to quickly dispatch vendors for fixes under $5,000 (increased to $10,000 in 2019) without running it up the chain of command. This quickly devolved into a kick-back scheme where vendors would pay superintendents a portion of their bid (usually 10–20%) in order to secure a job. Contracts were kept under $5,000, and then $10,000, in order to escape suspicion. With little oversight, it was easy to do so. How much does it cost to replace a light bulb at NYCHA? At the Throggs Neck Houses in the Bronx, $708. At Brooklyn's Whitman Houses, 20 light bulbs were replaced at a cost of $4,851. Elsewhere in the city, a door was replaced for $4,985.[45] In total, the U.S. Attorney's Office for the Southern District of New York found NYCHA employees received $2 million in exchange for awarding $13 million worth of no-bid contracts. One suspects that if more rigorous probes were conducted, the unexplained variance in operating costs per unit between NYCHA apartments and all others would quickly be explained

Second, counter-criticisms might arise from the way public housing is operated in the U.S. more broadly. Proponents might point to the Faircloth Amendment, a 1998 provision of the *Quality Housing and Work Responsibility Act* that prohibited the net new creation of public housing units above the 1998 mark of ~1.28 million homes, as the reason for public housing's troubles.[46] But this doesn't quite pass muster, as public housing authorities cannot even manage the existing assets they have. If their current 1 million units were exemplars of management with excellent conditions, then this is an argument I could get behind. But they're not. For the nation's largest public housing authority, the amendment stands as protection against the expansion of deleterious conditions for those who can least sustain them.

And yet, many might still urge us to move forward, believing we can learn from our mistakes. Who am I to deny this bit of Optimism? Trudging forward, high per-unit costs of Affordable

The number of subsidized buildings in New York City (left) compared to the neighborhoods with the highest poverty rates (right) are very similar.

Housing remain. As such, Affordable Housing developers have to make tradeoffs in order to get projects built. They can try to build smaller units. They can try to cut corners in construction. Or, they can try to find land in cheaper areas, with more permissive zoning. Usually, they pull all three levers, as all tend to be necessary. This results in a heavy concentration of Affordable units in a few neighborhoods. These areas, overwhelmingly, are the most marginalized and economically disadvantaged of a given city. Or, said another way, *the development of purely Affordable Housing profoundly deepens racial and economic segregation.*

Back to New York. Despite being home to less than 10% of the city's population, the poorest 8 community districts in the city saw 41% of all new low-income housing built in the last decade.[47] These neighborhoods all had median incomes less than half that of the city ($72,150 in 2021), while the lowest income areas, Morrisania/Crotona and Belmont/East Tremont, had area median incomes (AMIs) one-third of the city's, with poverty rates above 40%.[48]

These community districts are disproportionately home to minority groups, meaning *the creation of new Affordable Housing is deepening racial segregation.* In New York, the median income of Hispanic ($49,554) and Black ($53,715) families is less than half the median income of White ($106,697) families. When maps of neighborhoods broken down by race are overlaid on maps of

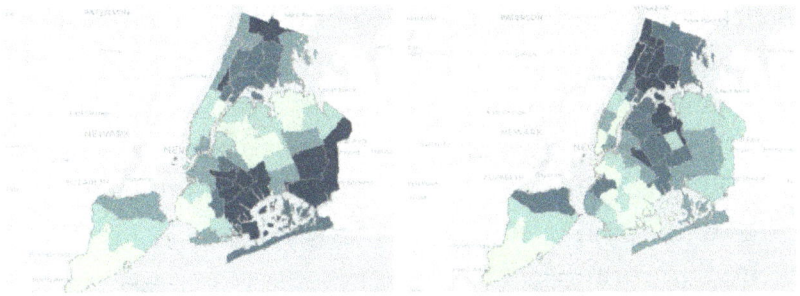

Areas in New York with larger Black populations (left) and areas with larger Hispanic populations (right) both eerily match Affordable developments.

new Affordable Housing development, they bear an eerie resemblance, heavily concentrated in East New York (Brooklyn) and the South Bronx.

The Furman Center, a highly respected urban policy research institution, has affirmed these troubling trends, stating: "New government subsidized units targeted to low-income households were built in areas with higher Black and Hispanic population shares, higher poverty rates, and lower prices and rents than those of new units overall. In addition, new units targeted to low income households that are suitable for families (with two or more bedrooms) were located in higher poverty census tracts than smaller units. These patterns raise concerns about whether the location of new income-restricted units is doing enough to counter patterns of economic segregation and to connect low-income children, in particular, to well-resourced neighborhoods."[49]

With findings like this, I worry we're failing to learn from the mistakes of the past. Indeed, there are deep parallels between the Affordable Housing units that are being delivered today, and those that rose in the mid-century period. The (significant) caveat being that today's aren't rising on the lots of newly demolished neighborhoods, as happened in urban renewal, but on the graves of failed policy from that generation. New Affordable Housing is unquestionably of better quality than the public housing of yesterday.

Both have delivered moments of progress, like much-needed housing and improved services that even market rate tenants would have found difficulty securing. Where elevators, gyms, and courtyards in new buildings are coveted in the free market today, central heat, running water, and playgrounds were the in-demand amenities of the past, in buildings likewise designed by prominent architecture firms.

But the generations have more troubling parallels, as well, including long wait lists and intense segregation. Where the first NYCHA projects received anywhere from 12 to 40 times the amount of applications as available units, today only one in every 592 applications is approved to live in an Affordable home, a system hardly better than the actual lottery.[50]

While racial integration is better than it was in the past (not by much, though), economic stratification is not. According to research from Pew, the share of lower-income and upper-income households living mainly among themselves increased markedly from 1980 to 2010.[51] In New York and Philadelphia—the cities with the worst economic segregation in the country—41% and 38% of low-income households resided in majority low-income neighborhoods in 2010. Segregation is expected to have only gotten worse in the last decade.

These are worrying numbers, not only for the danger they pose in creating an ever more polarized society, but also, and more importantly, because people's individual lives are at stake—potentially generations of families, as sociologist Patrick Sharkey has shown.[52] When marginalized groups are concentrated in neighborhoods—through force or by lack of choice—they get stuck, as it were, and are unable to mobilize themselves out of disadvantage. This is because, among many other factors, there are fewer resources invested in community upkeep, fewer jobs and economic opportunities, worse environmental/public health conditions, and increased violence—all of which further compound spatial inequality and marginalization.[53] The data is clear: when neighborhoods are segregated by class, those with concentrated disadvantage remain disadvantaged, and opportunity is severely inhibited.[54] There is nothing ideologically righteous about this. The furtherance of segregation is always a bad thing. So, why do we keep building like this?

Perhaps it's because new development and funding allocations are fabulously misunderstood, and funneling any sort of money into disadvantaged communities is seen as inherently good. I'm sympathetic to this notion, as disinvested neighborhoods getting money expressly dedicated to existing community members is a good thing. These places are, after all, where the justifiable fear of displacement is the strongest.

As millions of people have moved back into American cities over the last few decades, there have been tensions between accommodating that growth and protecting existing residents. When people who make more money than the average person of a given neighborhood move into that neighborhood (gentrification) and some long-time residents move out because rent has gotten more expensive, it makes sense to think the newcomers are to blame. Who else could have caused this? And so, not only has profit become pathologized, but so too have new residents and the newer buildings they tend to live in as well. This moves the burden away from the production of housing towards the preservation of existing housing for Affordable ends.

But this, empirically, is wrong. Though it might feel like that new glassy building that houses young, wealthy professionals is causing displacement, counterintuitively, it actually alleviates it. New construction has been found to reduce rents by 5–7% in a neighborhood, as more supply reduces competition for homes.[55] Austin, Texas has been the poster-child for this finding. From 2020 through 2023, Austin permitted the most homes per capita of any large metropolitan area in the country, and in the top 5 of metros of all sizes.⁵⁶ Rents subsequently declined 12.5% year on year from December 2022 to December 2023, among the highest in the nation.⁵⁷ Not only does building more housing result in cheaper prices, it also broadens housing choice as a higher share of older homes hit the rental market. For every 100 new market rate apartments built, 70 middle-income apartments open up elsewhere, as fewer wealthier people are forced downstream to find housing.⁵⁸ This effect is most pronounced in high cost areas, though it occurs across all neighborhoods. In a process economists call migration chains, each new unit of housing ripples outwards in a chain effect where the wealthiest people move into the newest, most expensive buildings. After moving into a new unit, the first person in the chain's former apartment becomes available, and a relatively less wealthy person can move into that home. When the second person moves, a third relatively less wealthy person takes their home, and so on, until everyone moves up to take the housing of the person who lived in the unit before them. Over many years, what was once new housing filters down to lower-income groups. If we want to accelerate this process (which we do), we need only build more housing.

Research shows that instead of low income families being displaced in this process, they actually move into (!) gentrifying neighborhoods, as new housing is created further in the chain.⁵⁹ To the extent that displacement does occur, it's only for the lowest income groups, and is only ~1% higher than one would expect in any given year, holding all else constant. If sufficient protection is given to the sliver of the most disadvantaged groups who are at risk of displacement, new development thus becomes a remarkable net benefit for neighborhoods.

Williamsburg, a metonym for hipsterfication and gentrification, and the neighboring Greenpoint, added more than 17,000 homes from 2007 to 2019 following a series of upzonings. A further 7,500 were under construction according to a November 2019

Department of City Planning Community Update.[60] Throughout this growth, the amount of people making less than $50,000—and even those earning less than $25,000—remained the same in the neighborhood, signifying that displacement, to the extent it occurred, was negligible. In study after study, and meta-analyses of studies, adding more homes moderates price increases, making housing more attainable to low- and moderate-income families.[61] This is how we build housing that is affordable: through outcome-based, empirical processes.

And yet, this common sense, data-backed solution faces perplexing opposition. It's become fashionable to ridicule any change in a neighborhood that doesn't comport with one's subjective experience as "gentrification". This is harmful for a few reasons. An aversion to any change harms those who are suffering in the status quo and actually need positive intervention. In a twisted bit of irony, those who purport to defend the marginalized through the lens of anti-gentrification are often their greatest oppressors. Their stubborn refusal to allow positive changes deteriorates the quality of life of a neighborhood and renders housing something that must be fought over, not enjoyed by a broader range of people. In areas that have been disinvested in, and are under-resourced, and in varying states of decay with poor-quality services, new investment is precisely what's needed! Constructing a grocery store in a food desert, putting up lights on dark and dangerous streets, or planning a new park on a vacant patch of land are all good things we should celebrate, not oppose.

Explicitly, this discourse opposes people who look or think differently than the extant community. That's bad. This leads to the aforementioned calls of unviable 100% Affordable Housing for local residents, which, when successful, deliver intense segregation and concentration of poverty. Very bad! More commonly, when these calls are unsuccessful, they lead to the displacement of those very same marginalized groups because wealthier people can simply outbid them without being accommodated with new market rate housing that they would otherwise move into. Rent control does little to help this, as it privileges a minority of those who already have housing and forces them to stay in place, while it deprives newcomers of opportunity as it discourages new development.

The solution to affordability isn't to preserve housing for the few who are fortunate enough to get it through lotteries or dumb luck. It's to build enough so that everyone is provided for. When we play zero-sum games in our built environment, everyone loses. For those who embrace diversity and immigration, housing policies that effectively make it impossible for refugees and immigrants to continue to come to the U.S. for a better life are not to be lauded. Immigrants built America, and they continue to do so today. Unless you're Native American (less than 1% of the population), we're all descendents of immigrants. There is no moral superiority in shutting the door on others who weren't fortunate enough to have been born here, at an earlier time, or with sufficient connections or resources to get in. Besides, this line of thinking is ahistorical. Neighborhoods are constantly changing. An archival search of articles on a given city block will tell vastly different stories about vastly different peoples depending on which decade one is reading about. More importantly, this opposition is self-defeating, as immigrants make our communities better. *People make our communities better!* The Malthusian notion that populations must be limited through cullings and controlled growth should trouble any person sympathetic to humanity.

The beauty of humanity includes people of all classes. Common sense holds that neighborhoods integrated along class and racial outcomes deliver better outcomes and reduce polarization. Common sense, amazingly, makes sense: when one interacts with people of different races, religions, beliefs, politics, and socio-economic backgrounds, one realizes we're not all so different. Othering is stamped out. No longer is someone different, or someone to be feared, but they may become a friend, a colleague, or a partner. This, of course, is a two-way street.

A lack of understanding of what goes into the costs of housing has pathologized any level of profit, and thus made it righteous to ideologically oppose. However, housing is not a game that keeps score based on ethical imperatives. What results from this way of thinking is a refusal to compromise within the nature that our built environment exists in, exacerbating our crises by raising emotion to the same level as empirical findings or operating realities, but with a moralization that unemotional data can't rival. Whether our political economic system should or should not rely on profit is a question this book doesn't seek to answer, and one this author is not qualified enough to opine on. All that can be proven, as I hope to have demonstrated here, are the current outcomes of theory's impact on municipal policy, and how it often leads to contradictions of desired goals.

The programs we use to realize new Affordable homes are antithetical to the stated mission of providing lovely high-quality housing for those groups who need protection the most. Instead of surface-level policy that does little more than ensure politicians will be re-elected, let's go beyond what people think works in theory, and focus on what works in practice. If the results don't align with our goals, it's time for a new system. We cannot accept failure, no matter how righteous the talking points, or shiny the social media campaign. Because the construction of Affordable Housing is so expensive, because the financing of Affordable Housing is so limited, and because construction of Affordable Housing takes so much longer than the creation of market rate housing, we know the solution to our housing crisis must in large part be based on the creation of more market rate housing.

So, while building 100% Affordable sounds like a great idea in theory, in practice, it's delivering poor outcomes. For the many hundreds of thousands who aren't able to find somewhere to live, well-intentioned policy makers and legislators must ask themselves, is it better to stick with an ideology that can only possibly help a small fraction of people, or compromise and embrace empirical findings to improve the livelihoods of people across the board? The answer should be obvious. Cities must unlock the development of naturally affordable housing that doesn't require significant (and often nonexistent) subsidy. They then must encourage it to be done in a fundamentally lovely way that imbues pride in residents, not feelings of anonymity, melancholy, and paralysis in the status quo.

Praxis in the Built Environment

If a city's goal is to truly become more sustainable, it must stop building for and around the car, and start building for people again. Instead of EVs, it needs EBs (e-bikes). Instead of new highways to new subdivisions, it needs wider sidewalks, narrower roads, and bike lanes that allow people to get to new infill sites within city limits, using pre-existing infrastructure.

Finding synthesis between goals and reality requires not just looking at the true, non-theoretical impact of policies as we explored in the realm of housing, but to do the math on those policies as well. For example, a new protected bike lane in a city costs around $100,000 per mile to construct. More expensive ones top out around $600,000. A new rural highway without any surrounding infrastructure, on the other hand, costs around $3,000,000 per mile. In the core of those cities who have sadly not learned from the failings of urban freeways, these costs can rise to $70 million per mile. It is that rare quadruple whammy for a city, with more expensive upfront costs, more expensive maintenance costs, reduced economic activity, and worse environmental outcomes. The roads don't tend to last for very long, either.

Across the board, we need to challenge the failing status quo with common sense. Instead of bike lanes being viewed as frivolities, and highways as sound and indispensable community investments, we need to analyze them for what they are, outside of the bounds of pre-established bias. Bike lanes are an eminently sustainable and critical piece of infrastructure. They generate meaningful economic development benefits at a human scale, confirmed in dozens of studies, peer reviews, and pilot programs. In contrast, in urban and suburban contexts, highways can act as an asphalt noose. This isn't to say all highways are bad, as many confer significant value in logistics, travel, and connectivity, but that doesn't mean they're always the right solution. Handmade pan pizza from Domino's is one of life's great joys, but eating it every day, and sometimes for breakfast (not speaking from experience, of course), would be very bad (again, not speaking from experience). Highways play an important role in connecting cities to one another, enabling rural areas to be integrated into the economy, and *can* make daily life more efficient. But orienting our communities around highways, or highway-like structures, is a very different thing.

Main Street, U.SA., is an ideal embedded in the consciousness of Americans. That lively, inherently local place where everyone knows each other's names, the diner is always open, and even the tax collector is welcomed as a friendly, familiar face. The buildings are charming, one can walk for many blocks continuously and carry out all their daily activities easily, and there is no shortage of interesting things to do. But the idea of Main Street, U.S.A., and the reality of it have been quite different for some time. Most Americans don't live on or near traditional main streets, but around anonymous commercial strips, characterized as much by their national chains and gas stations as their wide road widths. This is what orienting our built environment around highways looks like in practice.

These aren't highways in the traditional sense, but modifications. They're somewhere between the complex ecosystem of streets that community wealth is built around, which Main Street, U.S.A., embodies, and the roads designed for higher speeds that traditionally connected economically productive places. This marriage of street and road is called a stroad, a term coined by Chuck Marohn of Strong Towns. If you've ever driven somewhere above 40 miles an hour with (at least) three lanes, flanked by gas stations, fast-food chains, and strip malls, you were likely driving down a stroad.

Stroads are creatures of design in the same way hyper-rationally zoned residential communities are. Road widths are assigned by engineers working for state or local departments of transportation (DOTs), with the goal of accomplishing two things. Their first goal is to increase the flow of traffic. Anything that makes drivers slow down, or could potentially lead to more congestion and slower transit speeds, is reworked until the design of the roads allows for increased traffic flow.

One of the great detriments to traffic flow is when a driver has to think about driving. Traffic engineers do their best to take this burden away. If drivers have to worry about being too close to other cars, they will reflexively lower their speed. Wider lanes remove this worry, giving drivers more space to go fast. If one thinks there will be too much congestion, and is thus discouraged from making their morning commute at a given time, another lane can be added to rid the commuter of this concern. If a driver is worried about crashing into trees (or buildings) that tightly flank the road, vegetation can be cleared, and buildings can be set back. And if anything else should pop into a driver's mind (or phone screen), may as well make the roads a bit wider, add a few more lanes, and further clear the surrounding landscape. Just in case. Regular streets become more like highways, with commercial uses clinging onto the side of them.

These interventions are meant to improve driver safety, the second goal, at least according to traffic engineers. With fewer distractions, counterintuitively, drivers aren't actually any safer. When one doesn't have to think about driving, one is more likely to go fast and make reckless decisions. Accidents happen more frequently because there are no design elements to check impulses. If a street feels like a highway, someone will drive at speeds they would normally feel comfortable with on a highway, not a local street. Speed limit signs become less of a rule and more of a suggestion printed on laminated aluminum. But when drivers have to think about overhanging tree branches, the narrowness of right of ways, dining parklets, or pedestrians walking back and forth, they naturally go slower. That these "distractions" all happen to be elements of successful human-oriented streets is lost on engineers. If the town must be destroyed in order to facilitate more traffic, well, that's just the cost of doing business, they might say. But it doesn't have to be like this—and, for our sake, shouldn't be.

Neither of these goals is working that well. Congestion is high in core cities, and drivers still get into accidents with great frequency. Moreover, car-centric planning destroys the prosperity (and sometimes entire livelihood) of communities. The sort of businesses that rely on local foot traffic and community networks, the key components of Main Street, U.S.A., are unable to survive for long in these areas. The drive-throughs, national chains, and gas stations that populate stroads congeal in conformity, rendering them much like anywhere else in the country, and nowhere in particular. With dangerous wide roads, anonymous businesses, narrow (to non-existent) sidewalks, few cultural amenities, a seeming hostility to passersby, and bereft of trees, it makes sense that people don't want to spend time in these places, which further depresses economic development. For all of these negative consequences, it gets worse: stroads are fantastically expensive to construct and maintain.

Common sense would hold, then, that we need to preserve the core of our towns for streets and people, and build roads between communities that discourage the appendages of stroads. It means we should stop believing that speed limits or red light cameras can create safer places on their own, and redesign streets so that we move away from punitive policy with dangerous outcomes, to better outcomes at lower costs. And it means we should invest in strategies that are proven to deliver safety that generate more value for a city or town.

It's not easy to change the status quo, though. Many of these stroads are state roads, so localities have little power to change the harm inflicted on them. The obstinance of traffic engineers and byzantine nature that accompanies all state-level regulation makes change difficult. But not all of these wide roads are governed by state caprice. Some are written into the laws of localities, which has led to some perplexing results.

There is, perhaps, no weirder case of theory failing to meet reality on our streets than that of fire trucks. New streets for subdivisions or town expansions are subject to minimum widths just as they are for stroads. But instead of driver safety or increased traffic flow being the guiding imperatives, the logic for street widths is dictated by the fire department, where roads must be wide enough to allow a full-sized fire truck to make a turn on the street. This "turning radius" can be as narrow as 25 feet, but is often 30-, 40-, or even 50-feet wide. When combined with setback regulations that push homes 20 plus feet away from the street (so veering cars have a buffer before hitting them), residential areas begin to feel more like highways. This encourages speeding in what should be safe residential areas. It mandates that more asphalt be poured and maintained, which augments the heat island impact, worsens storm water runoff, and leads to more particulate matter finding its way into the atmosphere.

What's a more common sense solution? Reorienting our entire society around massive vehicles for fire safety, or ... building smaller fire trucks or retrofitting existing trucks with longer hoses and enhancing other fire safety protections? Billions of people around the world seem to make do in dense urban environments with narrower roads, and they haven't all burned down yet. While fires were a major concern for pre-industrial cities those cities were mostly built of wood; with the proliferation of brick, concrete, steel, and masonry buildings, as well as fire-treated wood structures in more recent decades, fires do not pose the threat to our urban cores that they once did. A brick building cannot easily burn down. Besides, when codes mandate robust fire-safety ratings and built-in fire breaks like setbacks that force buildings at least 10 feet apart from one another (as is the case in nearly all detached, single-family-zoned suburbia), are wide roads for further "safety" not excessive? It strikes me as not only redundant and destructive, but utterly senseless, as it leads to vapid environments that are no safer than narrower streets. In fact, it's likely easier to fight fires in dense cities because stations aren't so spread out. What good are wide roads for trucks to turn around in if it takes them far longer to get to the fires?

Common sense can only be avoided for so long, especially when the math is so strong. Some hold the belief that national chains along stroads are superior to Main Street, U.S.A., for the breadth of products they offer, lower prices they confer, and overall reliability. Their ubiquity is surely testament to their victory over mom-and-pops in the competition for commerce. For these people, advocating a return to Main Street, U.S.A., and walkable downtowns is grasping for an idealized past that doesn't match reality; we might not like it, but Walmarts and ExxonMobils are what the market demands. There's some truth to this, but far less than what's popularly believed.

It is true that many national chains are remarkably efficient, reliable, and cheap. But this comes at a cost. At a high level, we trade community for convenience. The spirit of Main Street is swapped for more utilitarian ends. If this weren't a big enough loss, it's

Aerial of a Walmart in rural Pauls Valley, Oklahoma

also a mathematically dubious proposition as well, for those less sentimental.

Big box stores pay a lot in taxes. To the casual financial analyst, this would be where the story ends. But when one compares the taxes that chains pay on a relative basis to those of smaller urban properties—for which "modest" would be a compliment to bestow upon them—some surprising data emerges. Based on surveys conducted by Urban 3, a data analytics firm that pioneered the use of value-per-acre analyses, while big box stores pay more in aggregate taxes, on a relative basis, they're valued far less than the types of buildings we might find on Main Street, and subsequently pay less in taxes. In Western North Carolina, the average Walmart—which might stretch across more than 40 acres—is worth $592,649 per acre.[62] A Dollar General is worth $603,647. In downtown Burnsville, a small community whose poverty rate is above 31%, the average value per acre is upwards of $3 million. In Sylva, North Carolina, an only marginally better off town, downtown buildings can be 10 to 30 times more valuable than the average Walmart on a per acre basis. For more sprawling Walmarts, it's not uncommon for values per acre to be less than $200,000. In more productive cities, small tax lots can be worth tens of millions of dollars in value.

What does this mean? It means that in addition to the other negative externalities that sprawling, car-dependent development patterns guarantee, they also ensure lower tax revenues and higher liabilities, as stroads and parking lots are far more expensive to maintain than sidewalks and bike racks. While a small salon on 1/20th of an acre might not look like much, it uses a fraction of the resources, utilities, and land that a big box on 20 acres does, while delivering far more value.

It's not enough that tax revenues are lower from big boxes—they're negative. According to a 2002 study analyzing commercial uses in Barnstable, Massachusetts: "Big box retail generates a net annual deficit of $468 per 1,000 square feet. Shopping centers likewise produce an annual drain of $314 per 1,000 square feet. By far the most costly are fast-food restaurants, which have a net annual cost of $5,168 per 1,000 square feet. In contrast, specialty retail, a category that includes small-scale Main Street businesses, has a positive impact on public revenue (i.e. it generates more tax revenue than it costs to service). Specialty retail produces a net annual return of $326 per 1,000 square feet."[63]

The myth that walkable communities and Main Street, U.S.A., are relics of the past is just that—a myth. We don't need to spend billions of dollars subsidizing uses that actively destroy our communities. Walmart received "$1.2 billion in property tax abatements, sales tax rebates, infrastructure and site improvements, and other economic development subsidies from state and local governments around the country" across two decades, according to a 2011 study.[64] That math doesn't work. These grim, soul-sucking, asphalt hellscapes bleed money from our communities from two directions. Supporting their proliferation in regions across the U.S. deprives untold trillions in value and billions in revenue, while increasing liabilities. This is a lose-lose situation.

A Common Cognitive Aesthetic

Throughout this book, I've referenced the need to build in a fundamentally lovely way. What exactly does that mean? It seems too subjective to even entertain. But a book is nothing if not entertainment, so why not try? Perhaps we could say that building something fundamentally lovely means building something beautiful. That's a start, but an uneasy one. Beauty has become something of a hot button issue in the built environment. While design professionals talk ad nauseum about sustainability, legibility, and dichotomies, strangely beauty is scarcely mentioned as an important virtue, despite it being a critical component of good citymaking. Heresy is the natural charge when one invokes it. Non-architects reading this section might think this sounds sort of crazy. *Of course beauty matters.* How else could one explain why 30 million people travel from around the world each year just to catch a fleeting glimpse of a place like Venice (a city near-universally believed to be profoundly beautiful), while only several hundred thousand go to Milton Keynes, somewhere that could charitably be described as a depressing geometry of concrete and bricks. The answer has little to do with the amount of people who are already there, and their subsequent gravitational pull. The two cities are of similar size (251,944 in Venice v. 287,000 in MK), but the population is significantly lower in the parts of Venice that most people travel to see, at around 50,000. A disproportionate amount of people go to Venice than its population would indicate, because it is enchanting, beautiful, and appeals to the highest ideals of the human spirit.

Many design professionals today seem not to appreciate this distinction. Trained in Modern and contemporary design, their personal aesthetic preferences skew towards Milton Keynes and places that look like it, scorning the use of older forms as anachronistic and regressive. Their designs invariably reflect what they like, which doesn't quite match up with the reality of what the general public tends to like. A "Design Disconnect" has materialized between those who design our built environment, and those who live in, work in, and experience it.[65] Psychologist David Halpern first observed this disconnect in a 1987 study where volunteers were asked to rate pictures of people and buildings in terms of attractiveness. Some of the volunteers were architecture students. Others were not. All participants agreed on which people were attractive, but curiously, "the architecture and non-architecture students had diametrically opposed views on what was or was not an attractive building". Consistently, the least popular of the 12 buildings shown to non-architecture students were the most popular among the architecture students. The longer architecture students had been studying, the worse this disconnect got.

These findings have been reproduced in a series of surveys conducted since, including a 2008 study in Chile, and a 2015 survey from British think tank Create Streets.[66] (Disclaimer, I'm a Create Streets fellow.) Create Streets found that 87% of respondents preferred a traditional block over a more contemporary one. Amazingly, of the 13% who said they preferred the newer, more innovative buildings, roughly half (46%) worked in planning, architecture, or the creative arts, despite only being 2.25% of the survey's respondents. This is worth restating. Nearly 90% of the general public prefers more traditional architecture forms, viewing them as beautiful, while eschewing novel forms. But of the 10% who prefer the more innovative architecture, half of the respondents are the ones who shape our built environment! In America, a 2020 Harris survey of more than 2,000 people found that more than 72% prefer traditional to Modern design.[67] This was true across racial, age, religious, class, and political divides. There's almost nothing that brings Americans together like this today. The only group who consistently preferred more Modern architecture? Architects. There's little mystery as to why so many people think new buildings aren't

164 BUILDING OPTIMISM

Results of preference surveys conducted on traditional versus Modern architecture.

very good—it's because architects overwhelmingly design places that the public consistently dislikes!

Why has design diverged so significantly from public sentiment? While there are a couple of ideas floating around, there's one I find most compelling. Before presenting it, I must preface some of these ideas. Architects are constrained by how much influence they can have, as building and land use codes shape design to a great extent. Moreover, as will be argued in Chapter 6, our perceptions of architecture are heavily influenced by factors it cannot control, like urban design, street composition, and neighboring structures. An unremarkable structure can become greatly admired if located on a charming narrow street with a lot of tree cover, while a very attractive building may become lost if it's located on the side of an 8-lane highway. With this qualifier considered, we turn to an explanation on the design disconnect.

Architects are taught a rigid theory of design during a time of formative brain development. By the time they enter the world to work on their own projects, the conditioning is complete. As humans, our brains aren't fully formed until we're around 25. Though the process of shaping what we know, and how we perceive the world, is most impactful in our younger years, there's still a lot of time between high school and our mid-twenties to round ourselves out. Architecture students typically enter A-school when they're 18 and spend four to five years (depending on the program) learning about theory, design, and the discipline generally, before entering a graduate program to study for another two to three years. In total, architecture students study for 6–8 years in a deeply impactful period of their neurological development. This is a particularly intense phase, as well, which strengthens the fibers of maturation, hardening ideology into a sort of orthodoxy. Long hours, little sleep, brutal criticism. If you've never been part of a design review or desk crit (a process where reviewers offer guidance, but more often criticism, of one's work in the middle of a project as a sort of check in) count yourself lucky. One can be yelled at for not adhering closely enough to a professor's subjective standards, shamed for going outside of the orthodoxy, and trained to appreciate environments that are provocative as renderings and social commentary, without much focus on real-world impact or viability.

What are young architects being taught to design? Precisely the kind of stuff that much of the public dislikes. Many architecture schools in America only teach derivations of Modernism buildings that take influence from our old friend Le Corbusier) or more contemporary design—a catchall for newer buildings that may not adhere to a certain school, but stand defiantly against traditional architecture. Though Modernism and its offshoots are just a few of the many hundreds of styles of architecture, oddly, they have been adjudged to be the end of architectural history by the academy. How have millennia of theory from influential thinkers like Vitruvius, Palladio, Confucius, Alberti, Filarete, Ruskin, and Alexander, and thousands of regional traditions from across the globe been reduced to just a few narrow styles?

From the time Modernism became the dominant style in America in the post-war period until about the '80s, there weren't really any universities in the U.S., and very few practitioners, that focused on traditional design. Practically all secondary education was centered around Modern and contemporary design. These same teachings were (and continue to be) reinforced in the professional realm, where the work environment is even harsher, and the stakes even higher. If one wanted a job in the industry, or to be respected by their peers (valuable currency in a profession as intertwined with the academy as it is), they had to adhere to the party line.

Step out of line, and risk being excommunicated from the industry entirely. Indeed, many prominent critics and practitioners view non-contemporary design with such revulsion that they label those who appreciate it—yes, including 90% of the general public—as either too uninformed to know what constitutes good design, or regressive for sticking to the past. This is, of course, lunacy, but difficult to fix. As we age, we become less capable of changing our views on things. Our brains are less accepting of new ideas. Neuroplasticity diminishes as we get older. Worryingly, this process is accelerated for young architects. Before they can even explore what styles they might like best, they're indoctrinated into studying a single design ideology.

This pedagogy and resulting orthodoxy explains how some contemporary architects can talk glowingly and at length about a building that to most other people might seem quite poor, or get downright uncomfortable when pressed about the notion of objective beauty in the built environment. Where non-architects intuitively know beauty when they see it, many contemporary architects don't, deflecting to their favored SAT words of choice to explain the complexities of what they're seeing, as their capacity to intuit has been modified. Years of groupthink internally validate their perspective as experts. They convince themselves that others just don't get it because they haven't put the work in. Moreover, a predisposition towards elitism (to be a world-shaper one has to have some level of ego) encourages closed-mindedness, as they're less willing to consider the perspectives of those who don't share their rarefied backgrounds. But one doesn't need to study for a decade to understand what beauty is. We intuitively grasp it.

Mercifully, if only gradually, this orthodoxy has been challenged, as the public has risen up to demand a better state of architecture. Public and private sponsors no longer implicitly defer to the supposed expertise of experts, worn down by a nearly century-long experiment that has delivered dreariness, gigantism, sterility, and anonymity. Architects, after all, are ultimately subservient to their clients' desires. Notre Dame implemented a curriculum based on classical architecture and traditional urbanism in 1989, one of the first schools in post-war America to do so.[68] It's been followed by others, like Catholic University, the University of Miami, Utah Valley University, and The American College of the Building Arts, to name a few. If the binary of traditional versus Modern has confused you (which is understandable, as it's a false dichotomy) it's worth noting that traditional architecture doesn't pertain to any one style. It simply means the vernacular of a region (local building style), which is itself a composition of many centuries of wisdom and styles built on top of one another.

There are thousands of regional vernaculars that get lumped into the traditional design bucket. Structures as varied as a Bhutanese temple in Thimphu and a Dutch gabled canal house in Utrecht might not seem like they have much in common, but under such a worldview, they are both labeled traditional.

Don't get me wrong, I love a great deal of contemporary design. Zaha Hadid, Bjarke Ingels, Annabelle Selldorf, and Kengo Kuma are among my favorite architects. I have great admiration for Thomas Heatherwick, Kazuyo Sejima and Ryue Nishizawa, and Jeanne Gang, among countless others. As a native New Yorker, I've looked up at the skyline in awe for my whole life. Where it all goes wrong, as far as I'm concerned, is when architecture forgets that it's architecture, and instead wishes to be an embodied commentary about our lives. It should not be, for instance, a dialogue between normative political economy and the effects of global capital, an explicit exercise in making passersby feel uncomfortable in order that they might internalize the many horrors of our modern world, or an expression of the "separation and fragility that man feels today in relationship to the technological scale of life, to machines, and the car-dominated environment" as voiced by Peter Eisenman in his famous 1982 debate with Christopher Alexander on the state of architecture.[69]

Architecture should principally be about three things. First, it should result in the creation of a building that performs the job asked of it. A school should not try to also be an office building, or vice versa. Second, those buildings should make us feel good and comfortable. Third, and only after the first two things have been accomplished, at its most elevated level architecture should strive to raise our spirits, not teach us a lesson. Architecture is the only art that one cannot opt out of. If you don't like a painting, you never have to step foot in a gallery. If you hate a song, you can turn it off, choose another, or in the public realm, put in earphones. No one will force you to go to a concert for an artist you can't stand.

If poetry makes you feel weird, you need never pick up a book of it. But architecture is unique. It impacts us all the time, whether we like it or not. If one lives across from a woefully austere structure that looks like it relishes in tormenting humanity (side note: it probably does), it's not so easy to avoid such a place. Similarly, if one is forced to work inside of a box that makes them feel sad, or vulnerable, or anxious, they cannot easily stop working there. And one can't very well pick it up and place it somewhere else. Well, not easily at least. Hope may come in the form of demolition, but there's little reason to tear down a perfectly functional building that just so happens to be ugly. And even then, it may well take several decades. As many have come to lament, salvation often does not come within our lifetime.

This isn't a simple matter of preferences, nor a frivolity of aesthetics. There are profound psychological implications to the way we design our world. Sarah Williams Goldhagen makes this point clear in her 2018 book, *Welcome To Your World*; when it comes to the human experience in a place, there are no neutral environments. Our surroundings are either nurturing or destructive. This doesn't mean we are fated to vacillate between extreme states of euphoria and malaise, but rather, as Goldhagen observes, "Our minds and bodies constantly, and at many levels engage in active and interactive, conscious and nonconscious processing of our internal and external environments."[70] The built environment directly impacts how we feel, and reciprocally, how we perceive it. We're attracted to places that make us feel good, and repelled by the ones that make us feel bad.

Imagine, if you can bear it, walking along the broad and blank wall of a concrete parking garage. You will feel more defensive and suspicious of passersby than if you were walking down a tree-lined street with cafes and people spilling from the sidewalks onto the street, even if you encountered the same pedestrians on both walks. You'd likely avoid walking by the parking garage if you had the choice. We spurn sharp and irregular forms, blank masses, and synthetic materials. They give us anxiety. Many social and cognitive deficiencies can arise from the condition of a space. If you spent all your time in and around hulking concrete structures without much greenery, devoid of compassionate, humane design, you might feel elevated levels of stress. Few would feel comfortable enough to have an impromptu conversation with a stranger under a highway overpass. Same as if you spent too much time in a room with low ceilings, hard surfaces, and a lack of light—who would willingly spend time in such a space if a viable alternative were available? And yet many of us are subjected to them. Buildings cannot be so utilitarian. They form the basis of our social connections and sense of belonging. How they are constructed can change the fortunes of our very lives.

As humans, we're attracted to natural, smooth, and warm surfaces like wood, brick, and stone. We are of nature and thus have an intrinsic connection to it (a concept known as biophilia). When exposed to synthetic mediums, we're unconsciously aware that something isn't quite right. This is why the subtle difference between two homes—one clad in wooden clapboard, the other in cheap vinyl—can feel so significant. Financially, vinyl is the cheaper solution, but it's also the cheaper solution neurologically. We know we're being deprived of the real thing, and feel a bit conned. Simulacra are improving, but as with most things, the real thing is always better.

When walking by unrelenting concrete or metal structures, one might find themselves feeling cold or even threatened. This is your brain at work once again. Thermoception deals with our discernment of temperature and subsequent response to it, whether imagined or real. As concrete and architectural metals reflect heat, and have the appearance of being colder (yellowish colors are typically associated with warmth and black/grays are cold), by extension, they make us warm-blooded beings feel colder, even if we're not actually experiencing temperature fluctuations. Furthermore, overly austere concrete, steel, and glass-clad structures can repel us by making us feel as though we're in danger. Evolutionarily, we've learned that sharp and imposing objects have threatened our survival. When you avert your eyes from an all-glass tower, in some sense you're experiencing a real-time application of Darwinian theory. Subliminally, your brain is telling you not to get too close.

Our brains crave visual stimulation as we move through space. We're intrigued by detail, and even if we're not consciously aware of it, are drawn to structures that are varied and intriguing. When we describe a place as feeling sterile or soul-sucking, our brain is giving us a cue that we're not being stimulated enough in that environment. These cues can morph into feelings of intense loneliness or distress. But these aren't just feelings; they have a measurable physiological impact.

Collin Ellard, a cognitive neuroscientist at the University of Waterloo, and Charles Montgomery, author of the terrific *Happy City*, conducted a series of studies in 2011 on how buildings affected the psychological state of pedestrians. Participants were given bracelets to measure their alertness and were asked to answer questions that assessed their emotional state as they walked along different areas.[71]

Across many locations, one dichotomy stood out. A group of participants was asked to walk by two different sites. One was a blank wall which belonged to a Whole Foods, while the other was a strip of vibrant restaurants and stores. The many doors and windows of the second site opened out onto the street and continuously activated it with many people. "When planted in front of Whole Foods," Ellard noted "my participants stood awkwardly, casting around for something of interest to latch on to and talk about." The biometric bracelets on the participants' arms showed that they were bored and unhappy. But just one block away in front of the lively, fine-grained row of buildings, pedestrians observed that they felt really good. Their bracelets confirmed this. "In front of the blank façade, people were quiet, stooped and passive. At the livelier site, they were animated and chatty, and we had some difficulty reining in their enthusiasm."

The team's findings were consistent over 39 tours of participants in three very different contexts: New York, Berlin, and Mumbai. When people are bored by something, they experience higher rates of sadness and stress, as measured by elevated levels of cortisol and heart rates, and lower skin conductance (arousal activated from internal or external stimuli).[72] Very little of our modern world is stimulating to look at. Everywhere we go, we're bored. We have limited exchanges with nature, which is a countervailing force to stress. We can't walk many places, and certainly not anywhere visually stimulating. Interactions with bad streetscapes are bad for our health, and yet bad urban design seems to be the norm in most of our cities. Fun, unique, colorful, and vibrant places aren't just vanities to seek out on vacation, but restorative elements of creation. Environmental psychologists have long been aware of the importance of they how spaces affect individuals, and we'd do well to heed their wisdom.

Ellard and Montgomery's surveys validate decades of study from the renowned Danish urbanist Jan Gehl, whose work centered on the observational study of how people actually respond to the built environment, not mere theoretical musings of what might do. Sorry to all the renderers of shiny renderings, but people rarely act as we hope they might. Gehl noticed that people walk more quickly in front of blank façades, hardly turning their heads as they unconsciously perceive there's nothing interesting to look at. Better to trudge forth and find somewhere more interesting. Contrast this with an open, active façade, and people suddenly open up in turn. Not only will pedestrians linger along these soft edges (even more so if they're given somewhere to sit), but they're more likely to talk with other people, shop in stores, and create

The Shady Hill School campus extension (Cambridge, Massachusetts) is a great example of a welcoming school environment. Designed by Machado Silvetti. Completed in 2009.

communal connections.[73] These are places where people are given space to live, not utilitarian realms that reduce human experience to menial tasks that require only the most basic of corridors to get from point A to point B.

Just as the design of stimulating and pretty streets positively impacts us, so too does the quality of building interiors. In a 2013 paper which studied the impact of built environment factors in British schools, higher quantities of natural light, better air quality, stronger connections to nature, bolder colors, greater choice and flexibility of space, and complexity of design (visual stimulation) were measured to positively impact student performance by up to 25%.[74] Students were found to attend class more regularly, have fewer behavioral problems, and even score better on exams when they were taught in more pleasant environments. Just consider: which classroom sounds more conducive to learning? An overcrowded one with stained and tired linoleum floors, bright white

LED lights overhead, CMU blocks on the walls, limited connection to the outdoors, and drab furniture that might give way any day, or a warm space flooded with natural light, constructed out of natural materials, filled with cushioned furniture and plush curtains, and with enough room for kids to have true ownership over their learning environment? The answer is obvious, and its impacts are profound. Barrett, Zhang, Moffat, and Kobbacy found that the difference between the best and worst classrooms can be up to a full year of academic progress. When variances in design compound year over year, educational—and life—outcomes can diverge rapidly. How much good might we accomplish if we simply designed better quality educational facilities?

Beauty may well be a tricky thing to define—eye of the beholder and all that— but we're neurologically hardwired to be attracted to certain things in the built environment. That's why, no matter where you're from or what you do (even if you're an architect!), we all generally find the same sorts of places attractive. There are (inasmuch as this is possible) universal aesthetic preferences.

This doesn't mean one architectural style reigns supreme. We can find places as different as Buenos Aires, Lijiang, or Bologna equally beautiful, and don't need to be trained to appreciate them. This is true within an individual city as well. Neighborhoods like SoHo, Forest Hills Gardens, and the Upper West Side in New York don't resemble each other very much, but are equally beloved. When we occupy these spaces, they fill us with an indescribable warmth. Butterflies swim in our stomachs. It is a wholly encompassing sensory experience.

While different places may look ... well, different, they're actually very similar compositionally. These neighborhoods are all mixed-use, so there's always something to look at, and always people moving about. Life follows life. The buildings of our favorite neighborhoods are also appropriately scaled to the streets, and subsequently to the people who walk along them. Passersby aren't made to feel too small, but rather there is a cozy intimacy, especially in older areas with narrower roads. Most of the materials used are natural, and buildings feature decorative elements meant to engage pedestrians. When visiting a place like Lijiang or Bologna, the words spoken may sound unfamiliar, the food might taste a little different, and the culture may well seem entirely at odds with one's own, but remarkably, the built environment has a strong comfort and resonance, as though one has been there before even when one has not.

People are fundamentally the same types of beings. Mostly, we're all predisposed to the same things, because we're all humans that have evolved in the same way. Whether one is from rural Nebraska or Kolkata, this holds true.

Perhaps we intuitively view traditional forms as beautiful because they have evolved alongside us, achieving the right balance between ease of understanding and complexity. Harmony, even among seeming chaos, exists in these places. Indeed, recent research into fractals from Brielmann, Buras, Salingaros, and Taylor has validated this.[75] A fractal is a series of patterns that repeat over and over again, at many different scales, such that any small part resembles the whole. The presence of multiple fractal patterns in traditional architecture has been observed to reduce stress and mental fatigue. The patterns we observe in traditional architecture are the same sorts of ones we see in nature. We are drawn to rolling hills, savannahs, and waterfronts without having to be told they're worthy of admiration. So when designs in traditional architecture mirror these patterns in nature, we subconsciously find them beautiful as well. The most widely disliked Modern and contemporary architecture, on the other hand, features low-fractal patterns. Such low-fractal architecture has been found through eye-tracking technology to catch so little perceptual attention that we barely register it. Our brains cannot adequately process what we're seeing, which leads us to reject it.

This isn't to say everything should look the same. Far from it. Even the most beautiful building in the world would get pretty boring if it were copied and pasted on every block. We need a bit of novelty, a bit of innovation, and a bit of disharmony. Contemporary interventions of older warehouses can be very compelling, where a glass and steel extension contrasts with the older brick in just the right ways. This injects some disunity, which keeps things interesting. A little bit of surprise is good. While walking along a row of 9 identical brick townhomes, we reasonably expect the 10th to be just the same ... when suddenly, hold on, corten steel shouldn't be here. That's interesting! (So long as it's not imposing ...) Regardless of how different natural environments and buildings might seem from each other, they can have the same effect on our brains so long as they feature multiple fractal patterns in harmonious, quasi-symmetrical structures. The best contemporary buildings embrace this. The worst ones—sharp, imposing, severe—spurn it.

As modern humans, we might think that we've mastered the world and become Gods of our own realm. It's difficult to argue with this. Not only have we have transcended many existential challenges that humanity faced for millennia with ease, we hardly think about this triumph at all. Driving to the grocery store to stock up on fresh food delivered from around the globe is as much of a birthright as taking a dose of medicine to eradicate a disease that in previous eras would have claimed the lives of millions. We have access to history's collective knowledge on a small device we keep in our pocket and take selfies with. We can travel across the world in less than a day and complain about how long it took, and when we're back home, have someone deliver us cuisine from anywhere that we might have traveled to, at the touch of a button, to our front door in about 30 minutes. If we teleported back in time even 100 years and told our ancestors how we live now, they would think we were hallucinating. If we brought with us the technology that fuels our modern lives (and were able to use it), they may well think we were indeed Gods. The further back in history we travel, the greater our deification would become.

But our brains haven't evolved as fast as our civilization has. We're still primitive up there, and no matter how smart we think we are, we're hardwired to be attracted to some things, and repelled by others. Someone from the year 800 might be able to go to the core of Amsterdam in the year 1600 and feel relatively at ease. Same for Paris in 1850 (sans electricity). The basic fabric would be intelligible to them, even if the scale and style of the buildings remained foreign.

Put that person in Brasilia, Dubai, or the plaza outside Boston's Brutalist City Hall, however, and their mind would melt. Our minds melt in these places today! They make us feel small, vulnerable, scared, bored. Our brains are telling us to get away from these places as fast as we can!

Though we have tools like biometric tracking, neurological studies, and brain-imaging techniques at our disposal, we don't really need them to understand what makes a good place good. We intuitively feel it. One doesn't need to use PhD language to express why walking down a certain street feels nice. We might not be able to describe it, but we just know it feels right. These good places are neurologically attractive. And because we feel attracted to them, we consider them beautiful. Taking such considerations seriously means elevating beauty to an inherent virtue of good placemaking, and setting it forth as a cultural value. Beauty cannot be exclusively reserved for the wealthy, nor can it be preserved as a relic of the distant past only to be worshiped behind glass cases. We suffer cognitively and physiologically when we do not live among beauty.

* * *

Though it may seem tedious to the reader, it's worth reiterating that how we shape our world has a profound impact on us. Our theories on housing, development patterns, and design have significant consequences on the affordability, sustainability, and desirability of our world. Optimism transcends theory to execute on noble ambitions in reality. Creating places that are not only financially viable, but fundamentally decent as well.

If an investment manager or financial analyst were to look at an Optimistic development pattern, they could find reason and common cause. Community activists would laud policies that deliver better outcomes for historically marginalized groups. Environmentalists—true environmentalists—would see reductions in particulate matter and pollution, and be able to enjoy far more green space and natural lands preserved outside the arms of nox-ious development. Fire marshals would have safer cities. Aesthetes would have more attractive places to admire. And everyday people would benefit from all of these disparate and salient disciplines.

At present, we adopt policies that make none of these groups happy beyond small coteries of vested interest. The goals of each one of these groups will never fully be met until we choose to priv-ilege reality over theory, and make common sense truly common. Our favorite neighborhoods are at once the most lovely, desir-able, and dynamic, while also being the most sustainable, safe, and economically productive. Common sense would hold, then, that we should maximize these places to such an extent that they can deliver on the major challenge they have consistently failed to address—affordability. When there are 500 places of the same quality as Beacon Hill as opposed to just one or two, demand can be more equally distributed, delivering the wonder of great com-munities to all who want to take part in them. So, why aren't there 500 Beacon Hills, or Lincoln Parks? Let's take a look in the next chapter, before we establish a series of foundations we can use to build a better world.

5.

Why Does Everywhere Look the Same?

If we're innately drawn to more beautiful, walkable, and human-scaled places, and they're the most quantitively common sense ones to build, why aren't we creating more of them? Why does our built environment look the way it does today—namely, bad?

You might be struggling to contain yourself, thinking that the obvious answer is zoning codes that have been copied and pasted from one town to the next. Don't worry, I understand the excitement, but you'd only be partially right. They're merely the foundation for why everywhere looks the same. Zoning codes ensure that places will compositionally be similar—residential subdivisions there, office parks over there, and commercial uses along stroads connecting the two—but they don't quite explain why buildings look the way they do.

For the structure that's made our places look the same, we must start with the laws that govern how buildings should be constructed: the building codes. Though building codes have existed in some form for centuries, the modern set of standards that informs most development in the U.S. today, The International Building Code (IBC), was created in 1997. In 2000, the International Residential Code (IRC) was created specifically to govern single family home construction. These sets were designed as model codes for jurisdictions around the U.S. to adopt, and that's exactly what they've become.

Smaller cities and towns don't write their own zoning codes from scratch due to the difficulty in creating them. Similarly, local building codes are heavily adapted—if not directly copied and pasted—from larger model codes that have already done all of the hard work. This makes sense, as towns, cities, and states don't have the capacity nor ability to create codes on their own, especially when they can run several thousand pages long and require frequent updates to ensure the latest safety standards are being met. If towns, cities, and states had to make their own codes from scratch, a meaningful gap in the quality of codes created for wealthier jurisdictions and under-resourced ones might arise, which is unacceptable.

When a change is made to the parent codes, it automatically applies to all the underlying sets in cities and towns across the country. Modifications can trigger significant changes to the way the construction industry works, almost overnight. This is precisely what happened in 2009 when a revision to the IBC allowed wood treated with fire retardant to be used in the construction of mid-rise apartment buildings.[1] Previously, the IBC had only allowed mid-rises to be constructed out of reinforced concrete, masonry, or steel. Building with these materials takes a lot of time and costs a lot of money, so not very many mid-rises were built. The numbers just don't pencil without significantly higher allowed density. But when the IBC allowed five-story buildings to be constructed out of wood frames over concrete podiums, suddenly, an entire new market opened up. A project with 100 apartments could now be built at 60–70% of what it cost before, which, overnight, made thousands of multifamily lots around the country viable for development.

These types of buildings have earned several names, some of which you may have heard of: Texas Doughnuts, Fast-Casual

Windsor by the Galleria in Dallas, Texas. Completed in 2015.

Architecture, McUrbanism, those big bad boxes that stretch across the block, Spongebuild Squareparts. But they're most commonly known as five-over-ones. Contrary to popular belief, they're not called this because there are five stories of apartments over one story of retail, but rather because of their construction method: type V (wood-framed) over type I (fire resistive, made of concrete and steel).

The changes to the IBC coincided perfectly with another major shift in multifamily development: the rise of institutional investors. As mentioned in Chapter 4, these are companies that invest on behalf of other very wealthy individuals or institutions. They're a kind of financial manager that oversees investments into a range of different asset classes for some of the largest investors on earth. Hedge funds that invest into the public markets, and private equity firms that invest into private companies, are good references to think of. They work on behalf of entities like pension funds, university endowments, and insurance companies, all of which sit on large amounts of cash that they've raised from retirement savings, donations, risk premiums, and funds from operations.

Institutions need to earn a yield on the money they hold, because their beneficiaries depend on it. Indeed, that's the promise. When a public sector employee agrees to set aside a piece of their paycheck to go towards their pension, they expect to have predictable streams of money when they retire that they can use to support themselves and their families. Without investing in productive assets, institutions can't hold up their end of the bargain, as the money will eventually run out. This spells catastrophe for hundreds of millions of people across the socio-economic spectrum, but most urgently for the working and middle classes, who have no other recourse. If you're a teacher in Iowa, a student who needs financial aid in Eugene, or someone who has broken your leg in New York, you rely on Iowa Public Employees' Retirement System (IPERS) for your retirement checks, the University of Oregon endowment for your education, or MetLife to cover your medical expenses, respectively.

The challenge for institutions is how they can deliver sufficient returns for those who depend on them without taking unnecessary risks that threaten those investments. One can't just YOLO this money into the speculative fad of the moment, after all. Institutions address this challenge in a few ways. First, they diversify risk into different asset classes. While investing in the S&P500 for an annualized return of around 10% would be a great outcome for most institutions, the stock market doesn't consistently go up 10% every year. A 40% gain one year ($100 → $140) and a ~13.5% drop the next ($140→121) results in the same amount of money after the second year as two years of 10% growth ($100→$110→$121). Psychologically, and actuarially, these two scenarios are very different. If all of one's eggs are in the stock market basket and subsequently they don't have enough reserves to pay out pensions or medical claims in a poorly performing year, many real and devastating consequences can ensue. So instead of investing all of their assets in the stock market, institutions spread that risk to safer investments, like bonds with lower rates of return, and alternative assets, like real estate, venture capital, private equity, and hedge funds with higher risk profiles that can deliver commensurately higher returns. When blending all of these investments together, their returns can approximate or exceed that of one asset class.

But institutions don't just need to diversify. They also need to work with an eminently credible firm with a long track record of managing large sums of capital. If you run a $30-billion pension fund, you can't just give your nephew who is, like, totally into day trading the keys to the retirement savings of hundreds of thousands, and potentially millions, of people.

That's all well and good, you might be thinking, but what does this have to do with apartment buildings? Well, before 1990, there was hardly any institutional capital in multifamily properties. They were thought of as kind of unwieldy and unsophisticated. And they were. People are complicated, and managing their homes is a messy business. Often literally. Where office buildings had long leases with quality tenants that led to some form of stability (historically), the risk of turnover, rent collection, and the unexpected in apartments was just too much for pensions or insurance companies to stomach, especially when there was little liquidity in secondary markets. All of this changed in 1990. The savings and loan crisis of the '80s saw federal regulators take over failed S&Ls in 1989, setting up the Resolution Trust Corporation (RTC). The RTC was tasked with disposing of the S&Ls assets, which included thousands of repossessed properties and delinquent mortgages.[2]

But the RTC wasn't properly equipped to manage real estate. The economic downturn of 1990 meant there was a need to quickly get assets off their books if they wanted to recoup any value. This is where Blackstone, then a relatively small firm who primarily worked in leveraged buyouts of assets like railroads and barges, entered the real estate game. Partnering with Goldman Sachs, they bought a package of recently constructed apartment buildings in the Sun Belt. Stephen Schwarzman, the co-founder of the firm, calculated that they could earn a 16% return without doing too much other than waiting for the market to turn around. With leverage layered on top, and the vacant apartments leased up, they did far better than 16%. Upon selling these buildings, Blackstone's first real estate investment delivered an annualized return of 62%, more than six times greater than the average annual S&P-500 return.

Around the same time that Schwarzman began buying garden apartment buildings in Arkansas and Texas, developers were finding great difficulty in raising funds for their projects due to a rising interest rate environment. Traditional real estate companies needed access to larger pools of capital, and seeing none in the private markets, they shifted their focus to the public markets, which were undergoing significant changes. Ambrose and Linneman (1998) explain: "Before 1993, "the 'five or fewer' rule limited the ownership position of large shareholders in order to promote REIT ownership among small investors, severely limiting the stock liquidity for institutional investors. The 1993 tax law modified this restriction, by creating a 'look-through' provision that allows institutional investor shareholdings to be allocated among their beneficiaries rather than being counted as a single shareholder."[3] This made it possible for institutional investors to take large positions in publicly traded real estate investment trusts (REITs) without violating tax law. With further changes like aligning fee structures to investment performance, as opposed to asset size (previously a manager could charge 2% and make $20 million on $1 billion of assets under management, even if the value of those assets dropped 20% year over year), the creation of UPREITs that allowed entities to contribute assets to REITs in exchange for shares without a capital gains hit, and greater transparency requirements for reporting in the public markets, the seeds that sprouted the forest of institutional investment in real estate were planted.

With access to robust returns proven by trusted allocators, and an ability to invest in an asset with growing liquidity and more stability than they once thought, institutions concluded that the risks of real estate investment were sufficiently mitigated for them to feel confident enough to join the fray. At year end 1992, there were only 89 equity REITs in operation with a total market capitalization of $5.6 billion. By year end 1997, the equity REIT market valuation topped $135 billion. This was only the beginning.

At the turn of the millennium, institutional investors allocated just 2–3% of their portfolios toward real estate.[4] Two decades later, target allocations have jumped north of 10%, a ~3–5 times increase.[5] This spike tracks eerily close to two salient markers. First, the increase in private construction spending since the mid-'90s, which grew from $400 billion in 1995 to $1.6 trillion in 2023.[6] And second, the balance of outstanding multifamily loans originated in the last 30 years, which have increased from $288 billion to nearly $1.4 trillion.[7] This trillion-plus number represents 40% of outstanding commercial mortgages, up from 22% in the mid-'90s.

In 2012, public pensions (retirement plans for teachers, policemen and policewomen, federal employees, etc.) allocated 6.3% of their total assets to real estate. By 2023, however, the average allocation for U.S. public pension funds had risen to 10.6%.[8] While a rise from 6% to 10% might not seem significant, a few hundred basis point move on tens of trillions of dollars is equal to tens of billions of dollars.

After a few decades of comfort, institutions have gone into overdrive in residential real estate investment. Cap rates have compressed as investors have viewed these assets as increasingly secure. For those uninterested in a deluge of numbers, you can skip this paragraph, and be assured that the quantity of this new investment is a very large number indeed. For those interested in quite how large, read on. Globally, institutions increased their allocation into real assets by more than $3 trillion from 2010, where total investment was $1.4 trillion, to $4.7 trillion in 2021.[9] It's tough to get an exact number because private asset managers (and private institutions) don't have to disclose their holdings to the public, but using some rough back-of-the-envelope math, with help from a few different surveys, there's likely anywhere between $1 trillion and $1.5 trillion in institutionally managed real estate in the United States.[10] The total market for professionally managed real estate now stands at $5.3 trillion in the U.S., which includes holdings from high net worth individuals and corporations that aren't overseen by institutional managers like Blackstone, Brookfield, or PGIM. The total commercial property market in the U.S. (which means any non-residential real estate, but includes multifamily buildings) is worth upwards of $20.7 trillion. That's a really big number. How does one even make sense of it? Is it the size of a city? No. All of the real estate in San Diego, the eighth-largest city in the country, was assessed at $335 billion for 2024.[11] Is it the size of a state? No. The assessed market value of all real property in Minnesota is $1.06 trillion.[12] Even the combined market value of all of the real estate on the West Coast (California, Oregon, and Washington) hovers around half the value of the total U.S. commercial property market, at $10.5 trillion.[13] There's a lot of money, and every day more is flowing into it.

Remember, though, the large capital allocators who are funding much of this investment are still risk-averse. They only want to give money to people who they trust will be able to return it, with extra yield on top. A big part of earning that trust is proving that you've successfully built, leased, and sold real estate development projects before. Not everyone can execute a real estate development project. It's risky, difficult, and requires a highly specialized skill set. Investors don't fully know who will be able to execute it at the onset of a project. The best they can do is to work with developers who have a long established track record. Even this is no guarantee of success. But it erects a fairly sizable barrier to entry

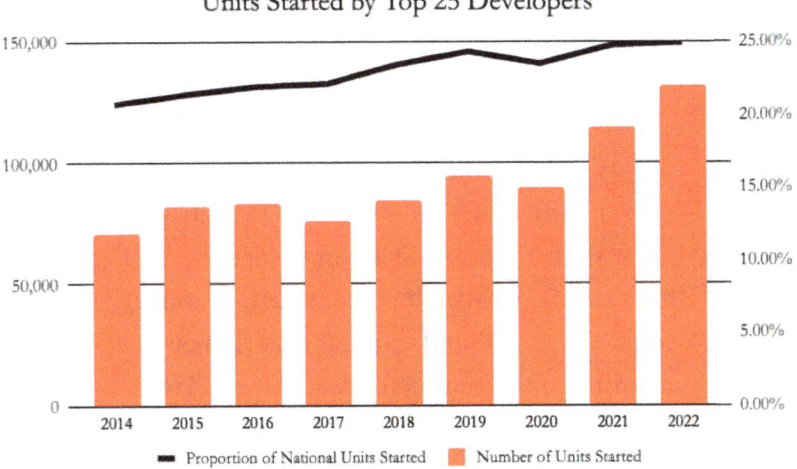

Proportion of multifamily units started by the 25 largest developers in the U.S.

for smaller, younger, or unproven outfits who don't have much of a track record to speak of, to say nothing of a proven one. With increased prices of land from artificial scarcity borne of restrictive zoning, and years-long permitting timelines that require long financial runways with many attorneys and consultants, small builders simply can't compete with their deep-pocketed counterparts. A catch-22 materializes.

How do small builders get into the game if they need a lot of money to start, but investors won't give them money until they've done several projects? Even worse, if they do manage to raise some money, banks are even more cautious of financing unproven developers than equity investors. Especially when they want to build something innovative or contrary to the status quo. If there were any federally backed programs guaranteeing mortgages for novel strategies, like missing middle housing, as the FHA does with single family homes, that would certainly help. But there really aren't, which leads to fewer comparable properties that could provide banks with comfort. If a small builder manages to get through all these hurdles, she would then likely be faced with onerous interest rates and highly risky personal guarantees where assets like her home are pledged as recourse at great personal liability.

The results of these imperatives have led to a meaningful concentration of a few firms building a disproportionate number of units. In 2022, nearly 25% of all multifamily units started in the country (more than 132,000) were commenced by just 25 developers.[14] That's a strikingly high percentage in a country of more than 60,000 developers.[15] Similar trends exist for new single family homes. According to the National Association of Home Builders, in 1989 the ten largest builders "captured 8.7% of closings. By the year 2000, the share was 18.7%; and by 2018, 31.5%, reaching above 30% for the first time." In 2022, that number reached 43.2%.[16]

It's very difficult to enter this loop without already being in it. It's sort of like how employers ask for a year of work experience for a job that's only courting recent graduates. How can one have a year of experience if no employer is willing to give out the year of experience required, because one doesn't have a year of experience in the first place? This forces out the types of small developers who created the built heritage and idiosyncrasies across America that we venerate. It deprives those who want to improve their community from being able to build wealth within it.

For those who do manage to break into this ecosystem, it's little surprise that they often choose to scale their businesses up to complete ever larger projects, raising ever more money, so as to not have to deal with the many difficulties smaller builders struggle through. Investors prefer this as well. It doesn't make sense to spread funds across dozens of small projects. Too much can go wrong. Investing $100 million in one project is 20 times less of a headache than investing it across 20 projects. *If you can make more money while doing the same amount of work, you'll choose to make more money.* Oftentimes, every effort is made to do the least amount of work possible to stretch dollars as far as they will go.

Institutional builders and investors have learned this lesson well. Back to zoning codes and land use regulations to explain how. Zoning mandates what can get built where, while a broader suite of land use regulations dictate the form buildings take. These regulations govern things like the mass, bulk, and setbacks of properties. When codes are written such to allow the full build-out of a site, the result is a rectangular box extruding up from the boundaries of its lot. This is called building out to a site's full envelope. It's done in order to create the most amount of units possible, and is often executed by stacking identical floor plates on top of one another, while eliminating any differences that may manifest as "headaches". This isn't without its efficiencies. Bathrooms, showers, and kitchens (wet walls) can all be located in the same place from floor to floor, reducing the cost of piping and making a building easier to manage. But it also removes any quirks that might give a building character, leading to more sterile feeling homes. It's a tactic that's been perfected in neighborhoods like DC's Navy Yard, San Francisco's Mission Bay, and Boston's Seaport, where buildings are constrained by how high they can rise, so they expand out as much as possible up until their height limit, identical floor after sterile identical floor.

After the maximum amount of units are penciled into their designated box, the next step for an institutional developer is value engineering. Value engineering is the process of reducing costs by stripping back the materials and design to the bare minimum needed to get a project built. This results in the cheap (and cheap-looking) housing that has come to represent today's epoch of development. Thin walls that make any private conversation a quasi-public one, paint that peels away when one scratches it, lights that flicker when someone jumps too hard upstairs. We've all been around these places, wishing desperately not to be there.

Once a single building is finished, replete with its boxy form, units jam-packed inside said box, and value engineered to the greatest extent possible, further economies of scale kick in. If an institution is happy with the returns generated by a given developer, and if that developer is happy with the architect, engineer, and leasing brokers on a project, why not bring the crew back for another job? Since they've already done it once, very little additional work needs to go into doing it again. Risk is mitigated that much more. A developer can simply copy and paste the program from one project to the next, regardless of the location. The work required to form new teams in each market is an intensive process of relationship and trust building, ingratiating oneself to that community. Out-of-town developers have little interest in doing such things, though, and their limited partners only care about yield. If you're investing from New York, Chicago, or San Francisco, you're not particularly bothered about the impact a building has on some random street in Columbus, Fort Worth, or Salt Lake City. It's not your neighborhood, and you have no true connection to it, so you can't be expected to care. This leads to a product with little personality—getting creative with design is a risk that might not pay off, after all. If you never pass the places you build, or aren't held accountable for what you create, there's little reason to care about the quality of a building beyond the bare minimum required to hit a certain return threshold unless you're inordinately driven to create something fantastic. In which case, you probably wouldn't have found yourself in the bullpen of a large institutional developer in the first place. While it's theoretically possible for these firms to deliver high-quality additions to the built environment, it's preciously rare, and painfully obvious in so much of what's built today.

Besides, many of these developers have backgrounds in finance or consulting, not architecture or planning. Certainly not the arts, sociology or psychology—disciplines that have much to teach about the world around us, and how it should be informed. Or not, according to some. The places we live in have become commoditized vehicles for securing institutional returns, devoid of identity or charm.

This is why a building delivered in Tampa can look the same as one completed in Fargo. Despite the opposite contexts, it's possible the same developer recycled the same design to create the same building with the same architects, engineers, and "designers" (who aren't truly designing much), leased to the same chain store retail tenants. These same people have proven they can create a project that has performed well before, and although the location may be different, the zoning and building codes are likely functionally the same, privileging a lowest common denominator design. Copying a proven success is the greatest risk mitigation strategy possible, so institutions double down on it. Sometimes, this even extends to the same vague and insufferable name like "The Point", which can be recycled for each new location. All one needs to do is replace the suffix. "The Point at Tampa" becomes "The Point at Fargo". *Et voilà.* Audaciously, institutional developers march forward, ignorant of what makes Portland, Maine, different from Portland, Oregon, or Philadelphia from Kansas City. Unique local traditions? Completely different climates? Hah! Joke's on us. A box fits just as well in any of these places. Any level of idiosyncrasy is just an opportunity for the market to withhold support, potentially reducing the prospects of cash flow. And we can't very well have that. Better to be cautious and deliver something that's overly austere that no one could possibly take offense to. Make no mistake. This is an entirely rational proposition, shepherded not by philistines and villains, but fiduciaries and regular people. And of course, that's the problem, because communities do not thrive on rationality, but quirks and idiosyncrasy whose value cannot be divined by a spreadsheet.

This overall effect is exaggerated when developers acquire entire city blocks, and made even worse when high parking minimums force parking decks within a structure's envelope that rival the size of the building itself. These banal and monotonous structures offer little relief or stimulation to passersby. Despite how soul-crushing they may be, the scale of institutional capital necessitates the assemblage and subsequent development of the largest site possible, built out to its full extent. It doesn't make sense for firms playing around with billions of dollars to spend time breaking up a site into several smaller, fine-grained buildings that might make for more interesting neighbors. A 25-, 30-, or 50-unit development is quite literally not worth their time. They're just too small.

As such, the biggest developers aren't building duplexes, quadplexes, or rows of townhomes. They're building projects that can absorb tens of millions of dollars—structures with hundreds of units. Five-over-ones. Texas Doughnuts. Spongebuild Squareparts. The uptick in new multifamily buildings with 50 units or more (the census doesn't track the size of larger complexes), has risen commensurately with the entrance, and increased allocation into real estate, of institutions. We've been on a 30-year up-trend, with one Great Recession sized dip.

With more big buildings, there are fewer small buildings. The sorts of places that people just starting out typically build. As everything becomes bigger, and anonymized, and value engineered, it's nearly impossible for smaller builders to compete with larger ones capitalized with billions of dollars. So most people don't, leading to an ever larger share of institutional development. This crystalizes the notion that all developers are nameless suits (or vests, to update the stereotype). As the data shows, this is increasingly true.

Indeed, as institutional capital allocations have flowed into real estate over the last decade, the share of apartment buildings with more than 50 units has grown exponentially. And it's not just that these are larger buildings, but that they are *all* the same buildings. Everywhere looks the same because everywhere *is* the same! We have copied and pasted ourselves into an identical world, and yet nothing brings the comfort of familiarity. Contrary to what some

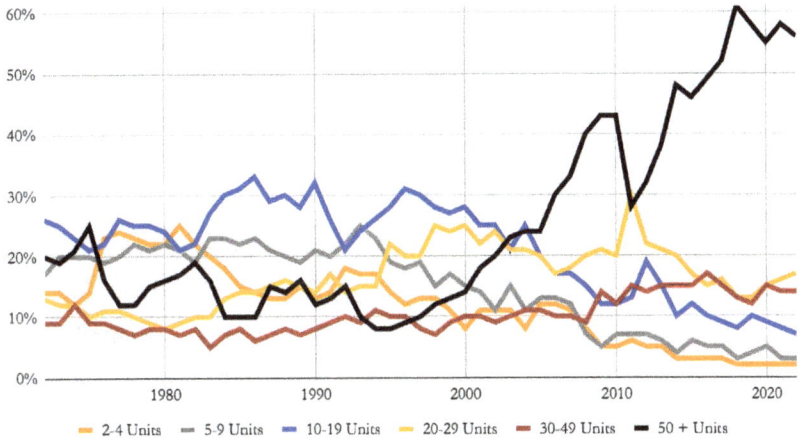

Proportion of multifamily buildings delivered by unit count.

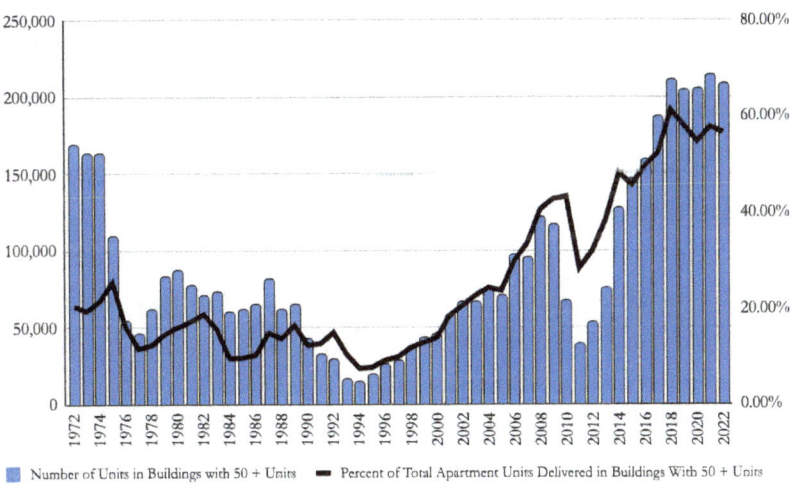

Number of new multifamily buildings with 50 or more units.

planning departments, boards of review, architects and developers might think, slapping several different materials and colors in various line styles across a facade doesn't, in fact, make a building look more compelling, but further disorients and confounds the passerby.

We need housing, though, right? Shouldn't we just be happy with what we get and be quiet? After years of battling, many of these new buildings have conceded to add mixed-use spaces, and have leveraged density to more positive community, economic, and sustainable outcomes. All the good buzzwords! But just having the right ingredients is not the same as cooking the recipe well. Trust me, and anyone I've cooked for, when I say I know how wrong this can go. These are deeply unsatisfying places. Our hearts yearn for more. It's little different than if we replaced all of our meals with a beige concoction of ingredients with essential nutrients. Are we getting all that we need to sustain ourselves? Sure, but nothing more. All of the enjoyment of food is stripped away. The sacred ceremony of gathering around a worn-in table for a home-cooked meal with loved ones, abandoned. We deserve more than the bare minimum, especially with the wealth, talent, and knowledge we possess—all the more so given the abundance of excellent recent examples that have been built at costs that are competitive with those of the vacuous status quo. One such example is Chevy Chase Lake, a 530-unit transit-oriented development in Chevy Chase, Maryland, a wealthy and historically anti-development DC suburb. There are shops, restaurants, a grocery store, and a central gathering lawn. It is likely the finest collection of mid-rise buildings that have been completed in North America in the last several decades, a testament to the power of deliberate, thoughtful design.

Most places are not Chevy Chase Lake. We've ground our spirits down to such an extent that we're happy with pretty much any improvement in where we live. But we shouldn't be afraid to demand better, as better work is being completed all the time. *A new apartment where I don't have to live miles outside of the city in a tract home? How exotic!* That it's located just off a highway with fumes to inhale and a constant soundtrack of rubber meeting asphalt is, of course, secondary. After decades of institutionalized

Chevy Chase Lake in Chevy Chase, Maryland. Developed by Chevy Chase Land Company and the Bozzuto Group. Designed by David M. Schwarz Architects and Martin Architectural Group. Construction began in 2018, buildings in the first phase completed in 2023.

single family home development following a nearly identical process, we have slowly begun to internalize the modern buzzwords of planning as saviors (density, mixed-use, walkability) but without the soft, qualitative aspects that give true power to these concepts. Density is oppressive if it isn't modulated with greenery and cognizant of human scale. We have much to improve on, but at least it seems we are moving in a better direction.

Housing is a relatively easy thing to examine because it's where we spend the majority of our time. Even when we don't want to think about how we live, we have no choice when our neighbor throws a one-person concert after midnight, there's no parking on the street, or our air conditioning stops working for the tenth time during the dog days of August. What's less explored, but has suffered a fate arguably worse than the places we live, are the places where we join together.

From Main Street to Chain Street

Walk down the Main Street of any reasonably prosperous city or town today and you might notice something off. It's not that the roads are too wide (though they are), or that the sidewalks are too narrow (though they are, too), or even that there's not much to walk towards (though this is usually true, as well). These are all known elements that North Americans have gotten used to over the last several decades. It's not even that what would be considered the Main Street for most communities isn't actually a Main Street at all, but rather a stroad amid sprawl, those highways masquerading as "commercial corridors". None of these things would strike the casual observer as deviations from the norm.

No. Look into the storefronts, or at their signs, and you'll notice something else. Something that contributes to the sense of sameness, dullness, and overall lack of character that seems to be a near-constant critique of contemporary places. They render our communities as spaces where we don't particularly want to spend much time, despite their being all that we have.

From neighborhood to neighborhood, city to city, Main Street to Main Stroad, these stores are all the same. The set of incentives that drives this sameness is prevalent in every community in the country. It's the story of how our basic needs have become corporatized through scale and credit, zoned to transactionalism, and rendered profoundly anti-human at the expense of the small businesses and idiosyncratic development patterns that lend spirit, intrigue, and meaning to our places.

Historically, the composition of a town's Main Street was fairly consistent; most communities generally had a grocery, a bank, a barber shop or salon, a few restaurants, and maybe a dry goods store or boutique. Nearly every one of these stores was locally owned, so even if two towns had the same type of stores on paper, the character, personality, history, and complex interpersonal dynamics imbued into those places would be so radically different that one could hardly say that either town was very much like the other at all.

This uniqueness was essential to the cultivation of the imagined spirit of Main Street. This, as the romanticization follows, is really only possible in the type of community that is deeply rooted, supporting its neighbors by default. Regardless of how true this notion was, it's easy to imagine it being so in a place where merchants have a vested interest in the success of a community they've known, and have been known in, for a long time.

Though these elements continue to exist in select small businesses and charming towns, they occupy a diluted and vastly diminished position in our society today. Same with our imagined spirits. No longer is our country one of small businesses and vibrant places. We are now a land of insipid chains and dreary power centers. Our psyche has transformed from one of strong, tight-knit communities (regardless of its historical veracity), to a series of individualized, transactional relationships within placeless places, devoid of any personality. Scenarios like the one illustrated below are commonplace:

After work, one may drive a car from an isolated office park 15 minutes to the hypermarket for some batteries, then another 10 minutes to a fast-food drive-through window, before finally ending the day fueling up at an international oil corporation's pumps that have been indiscriminately plopped down along a quasi-highway, only to do the same thing again the next day.

In all likelihood, in none of these stopovers would this person have had a meaningful interaction with another. There may not even be a proper place where they could spend time with their friends away from home, or a ripe setting to bump into someone else (more on that in a bit). They would've been wholly dependent upon a car, and their dollars would be sucked out of their community to some far, far away office tower, corporate campus, or McMansion. Indeed, when one shops at a national chain instead of a local business, less than 40% of those dollars stay in the communities where they were spent, roughly half of what would be the case if the business were locally owned.[17] Instead of the small business owner using profits to stimulate the local economy, those dollars are corporatized and sent out into the winds of global capital. A single town among 1,000 locations matters only in proportion to the amount that can be extracted from that place.

This isn't to say all chains are bad, or that they don't provide any value at all. Hardly. As mentioned, I love Domino's *and* my many local slice joints. But chains have so ubiquitously taken over the American landscape that there's no balance. We live in Chainland. How did we arrive at this pervasive pattern of development, prisoners to the dissatisfaction that has come with it?

Scale.

All things being equal, those with more resources have more power than those with fewer resources. This isn't revelatory. You already knew that. Most people also intuitively grasp how chain stores beat out local businesses: more selection, better prices, and brand loyalty that compounds each time one visits a new location. Not only does this fuel revenue for one specific chain, but it primes a consumer to look for, say, Subway when in want of a sandwich, rather than a local deli. This solidifies into a chain of demand from devotees new and old. Cynicism aside, there's much to be said for the psychology of reliability when one is on the road, or visiting somewhere they're not familiar with. To pass by McDonald's Golden Arches or Chick-fil-A's red script letters in an unknown land is to find comfort in a trusted friend. The importance of this shouldn't be understated. Demand-side growth can only go so far, though. At a certain point, if the only thing one is being served is a limited series of choices, true preferences cannot reasonably solidify. Preference only comes at the intersection of choice.

When a company like Walmart offers its price match guarantee, it doesn't do so out of benevolence or a sacred covenant with its customers, but rather for pure competition's sake. Chains leverage their economies of scale to drive down prices. Profits are earned on lower margins and higher volumes. Smaller businesses can't compete, because their relatively low volumes don't allow for lower margins. While many may love their local grocer or hardware store, if the prices are more expensive than a sufficient number of customers can justify, those stores will go out of business. We arrive at a situation where one community may have had a grocer, a hardware store, an electronics shop, and a bike repair center that all got subsumed into one big box, somewhere on the edge of town (or the middle of nowhere), mandating that one must drive to have access to those services they may have previously been able to walk to. The scale of chains doesn't fit easily into quaint and walkable Main Street, U.S.A., but instead offers anonymity and demands ample space for parking. This is anathema to proper community.

So, if Chainland's imperatives are crushing small businesses, how many are there left? Surprisingly, perhaps shockingly, more than 98% of all retail companies are small businesses (employing less than 50 people).[18] At first blush, this doesn't seem to make much sense. We see chains everywhere, how are they less than 2% of all businesses?

If we dig a bit deeper (using the best data available, which may have some holes in it), the picture becomes clearer. As of 2022, there were 1.06 million brick and mortar retail locations in the U.S.[19] Currently, more than 700,000 of these establishments are chains, with restaurants comprising the most of any category at more than 215,000 locations.[20] While less than 2% of unique businesses entities are chains, if the data is to be believed, 70% of physical retail locations are chains. This is a staggering number. All of our commercial streets look the same because 70% of our stores are chains!

The scale is almost difficult to comprehend. As of the end of 2022, Subway, the largest chain in the U.S., had 20,576 locations. Dollar General, Starbucks, and McDonald's had 19,146, 16,346, and 13,444 locations as of the end of 2022, respectively.[21]

To put these numbers into perspective, let's look to the past. In 1929, there were nearly 1.5 million retail stores in the country. 11% were chains. By 1948, brick and mortar locations grew to 1.77 million, with the proportion of chains shrinking to just below 6% of total stores.[22] How has this trajectory reversed so forcefully? The answer lies in development patterns that privilege economies of scale, accelerated by economic expansion.

In the latter half of the 19th century, a maturing economy enabled a burgeoning upper middle class of residents to move from crowded cities starved of open space out into the countryside. These proto-suburbs developed around regional rail and streetcar lines. Riverside, Illinois, was one of the first planned suburbs in the U.S. (1869), and among the most prominent. It had another claim to fame; Riverside was designed by Calvert Vaux and Frederick Law Olmsted, the duo who designed Central Park, among dozens of other venerated places. Suburbs allowed the erstwhile urban population to enjoy the privilege of open land. By 1910, rough estimates pointed to 7% of the country living in suburban areas.[23]

Economies developed around this new and growing class of commuters. Strips of shops, services, restaurants, and other essentials required to facilitate this new development pattern sprouted up. Romanticized tales of this era dwelt on the relationships new suburbanites could be expected to forge with their favorite vendors, getting to know the people behind the commerce in a way that wasn't easy to do in the hustle and bustle of the industrialized city. Even the most utilitarian of interactions became intimate as commuters and shop owners enjoyed a much closer mutual dependency than their counterparts in the city. Whether this spirit of Main Street was imagined or not, it was ephemeral.

By 1940, the share of the U.S. population living in suburban areas had ticked up to 15%, or 20 million people. During the postwar period, these numbers ballooned. The pace of growth was rapid. By 1970, more Americans lived in a suburb than any other kind of demographic area (37.6% of the country, or 76.5 million people). A majority of Americans, nearly 141 million people, were living in suburbs by the end of the century.

This population boom had a profound impact on the state of American retail and our built environment writ large. The 120 million who moved to the suburbs over just 60 years—and their cars—had to be accommodated somewhere. Downtowns were inhibited from supporting this growth with their newly adopted, highly restrictive zoning codes. Heavy subsidization of highways and subdivisions on cheap land meant that suburban areas were the natural settings to host the colossal migration flows. Gradually, and then with great haste in the last quarter of the century, retail was relegated to specific zones on newly cleared land in between communities, not within them. Merchants who were able to abandon downtowns to be closer to their customers did so. But this was not so easily done for modest local businesses. Not only would they have to build out new spaces at considerable expense (only partly subsidized by their new landlords), but they would have to create entirely new marketing, management, and organizational strategies too. While well-capitalized companies were able to thrive in an environment that privileged large scale, small-time shopkeepers who were better suited to the localized domain of people were ruined in the realm of the car.

Those businesses that clung to the old cores, either unable to afford a move, or unwilling to give up on their way of commerce, struggled mightily as their customers fled to new subdivisions out on the edge. Downtowns entered a vicious cycle. As many and more left the historic cores, shops closed. These closures led to fresh exoduses, which damaged the remaining shops further, leading to yet more closures, and so on and so on. Slimmer and slimmer were the reasons to go downtown, until eventually, emptiness was the only thing visited upon them.

In this vacuum our retail spaces transformed into highly controlled, segregated, and car-dependent realms—a far departure from the romanticized Main Street. All that mattered in this paradigm was getting what one needed and driving home. If your only way of getting around requires driving past an area at 50, 60, 80 miles an hour, you won't notice design flourishes, so a box will do nicely. Quite nicely. Gone was the tradition of imbuing one's storefront with the pride of one's business. Those finishes were antiquated, vestiges of pre-modern ideology. These things don't scale, and so in an era where expansion was king, they simply cost too much. Appearance was thus not valued particularly highly, so the design of malls (of mega and strip variety), pad sites of individual chains (think of a McDonald's in the middle of a Best Buy parking lot), power centers and more devolved considerably. Little wonder e-commerce was such a shock to this anonymous system. Why hold fidelity towards something that makes no attempt to earn one's affections?

The growth imperatives of publicly traded companies, which many chains were increasingly opting to become due to the public market's ability to offer deep pools of capital for expansion, kicked into hyperdrive. Remember, proven concepts are prized highly by institutional capital. Once one has achieved middling success, it's off to the races.

In 1948, profits from chain stores hovered around $310 million (adjusted for inflation), representing 23% of total retail sales. How high has this share grown in the last 70 years? Well, it's tough to get an exact number, as the data isn't fully available. Private sales data isn't available to the public, which necessitates doing some creative math and educated guesswork. But using some rough back-of-the-envelope calculations, we can get close to the share controlled by the largest chains. Total U.S. retail sales for 2022 were estimated to have been $8.123 trillion.[24] After factoring out car, car parts, and gasoline sales, this number drops to $5.856 trillion. Strip out 2022 e-commerce sales of $1.034 trillion so that we're only looking at bricks and mortar data, and we're left with $4.822 trillion in sales.[25] A qualifier: there's some overlap between some of these categories. Costco, for example, sells gas and car parts at the same stores as it sells double chocolate chunk cookies and Tommy Bahama beach chairs. But this estimate will have to do for our purposes.

Of this $4.822 trillion, $1.023 trillion comes from restaurants and drinking establishments, which includes caterers and food-service contractors, venues that provide entertainment (some comedy or jazz clubs may get roped into this category) and limited-service establishments, which aren't quite brick and mortar retail locations. Thankfully, we have data that's a bit more precise. According to a report from Technomic, a management consulting company, the top 500 chain restaurants accounted for 59% of total restaurant sales in 2022, or roughly $393 billion of the $662-billion industry.[26] The top 10 chains alone accounted for 25% of all restaurant sales in the country. One full quarter of all restaurant sales controlled by 10 chains! These chains were, in order of most sales to least, McDonald's, Starbucks, Chick-fil-A, Taco Bell, Wendy's, Dunkin', Burger King, Subway, Domino's, and Chipotle.

The remaining $3.799 trillion in retail sales covers pretty much all of the other sorts of stores: grocery stores, clothing stores, sporting goods stores, book stores, general merchandise stores, pharmacies, and home improvement stores. Similar to the restaurant industry, there's significant market share concentration among the top 100 chains in the general retail category. After excluding pure e-commerce retailers like Amazon or Wayfair, and backing out car parts stores and gas stations, the 93 largest brick-and-mortar retailers accounted for $2.538 trillion in revenue in 2022.[27] It's difficult to know how much of this number comes from in person versus online sales. Some businesses may do a higher share of their revenue online, while others will do a lower share. For our purposes, let's just assume that on average, the top chains sell the same amount of goods through e-commerce channels as the broader retail economy, at 15.4%. They don't, but let's imagine they do. At this proportion, the 93 largest retailers oversee $2.148 trillion in bricks-and-mortar revenue, or more than 56% of all general retail revenue. Less than a hundred chains dominate an industry with hundreds of thousands of discrete business entities. It is the precise opposite of whatever Main Street, U.S.A., was, or is meant to be.

This domination is reflected starkly in our built landscape, reinforced not just by zoning codes, car dependency, and development patterns, but a system of carefully constructed financial incentives and imperatives. A point that this book has stated, and will continue to state, is that a considerable amount of money is required to construct any building. As developers seldom raise the full amount of equity for any one project (mostly because using all of one's own equity dilutes returns when cheaper money in the form of debt can be borrowed), they go to banks to fill in financing gaps. Just as with five-over-ones, but even more acute with sites that have large retail components, lenders look to mitigate as much of their risk as they possibly can. The last thing a bank wants to do is take over a project midway if a developer can't follow through. They're not in the development business, they're in the risk management business. Collateral of a bad asset isn't worth very much. Sometimes even less than that. And half-finished buildings are pretty bad assets. Half-finished buildings with large unleased retail spaces that only a handful of tenants could possibly occupy are even worse.

The same catch-22 that exists for apartment developers applies for their retail counterparts. Well-capitalized developers, similar to large chains, leverage their economies of scale to compound their advantages, beating smaller parties into submission. Bigger buildings in sprawling landscapes are rubber stamped, while smaller ones in walkable fabrics can hardly even pass a preliminary review.

What's the best way to leverage economies of scale? You guessed it—copy and paste a design used from a previous project to prove to the bank that you can do it again, on the same terms. What better way to provide maximum comfort to your lender than building the same exact project as one that's already succeeded?

This process removes inefficiencies, reduces friction, and, most importantly, raises the bottom line without having to deal with the headaches brought on by smaller tenants. That it's devoid of local charm matters little, as Americans have become trained to expect nothing from the retail landscape. Whether a project is in New Brunswick or New Braunfels, San Jose or Saint Louis matters not at all. A lease-up strategy exclusively targeting national-chains can be successful anywhere because they have national relevance and loyalty. Mega-developers and mega-chains are two sides of the same coin, reaping and sowing the benefits of soullessness across the country.

These same dynamics come into play with existing properties, too. Just as lenders want security from those they're extending a loan to, they want security from those who will be occupying the building. This is reflected in a tenant's credit, a measure of trustworthiness that signals how likely they are to pay their rent on time and honor the terms of their lease. The higher the credit, the less risky a tenant appears on paper. The lower the credit, the higher the risk. If a property has many high credit tenants, it will be valued higher and receive more favorable financing terms because the cash flows are perceived to be more secure.

Chains are high credit tenants. They have well-known, trusted corporate structures that stand behind them, are generally very reliable payers of rent, and don't need to be babysat on simple management things like keeping the space in front of their stores clean, operating at normal hours, and not being a nuisance for their neighbors. Small businesses, conversely, are unknown commodities. Their owners cannot match the financial prowess of international chains, and worse yet, might not even have a tested business model. *Quelle horreur*! What security can a lender have from such a person? Despite the fact that community-based small businesses are the foundation of great, highly desirable neighborhoods, and often lend those areas their desirable characteristics, most landlords and lenders would rather take the sure bet of sterility than the uncertainty of dynamism.

Some might describe this as lazy, or an abdication of a landlord's responsibility as a steward of the neighborhoods they invest in. But the people who make such decisions aren't (often) intentionally commodifying their block. Sometimes they lament the changes that befell their street. But they cannot deny the uncaring truth of math. If you'll allow, a brief example:

Hallie owns a commercial building on Main Street in Middletown. When she was a kid, she admired the street's beautiful architecture, and loved the ice cream from the local parlor. The shop has long since closed down, but the buildings remain. She counts herself lucky that she now gets to own one of those very same structures. But Hallie has a problem. When she bought the one-story building at 112 Main, it was vacant. So with no income from a commercial tenant, there was no income at all.

Shortly after she bought the property, she was approached by a couple who wanted to open a coffee shop and gallery that supported local artists. They had big plans. Large comfy couches, cozy rugs covering salvaged hardwood floors, and coffee mugs the size of your face with $2 refills. Bless their hearts for not knowing the wear and tear on the couches and rugs would make them look shabby within months, and that they could charge much more for such large portions. Starbucks certainly knows these things, which is why they have polished concrete floors and durable chairs that don't easily wear the marks of humanity. Regardless, the presumptive cafe owners envisioned 112 Main to be a community hub, a place anyone could pop into for five minutes, or linger for five hours, without ever feeling any pressure to leave or buy something else. Acoustic guitar shows would be followed by late-night tattoo sessions for those whom the music sufficiently inspired into action.

As they were just starting out, the most the couple could have afforded to pay was $4,000 a month. After expenses, but before debt payments, the property would have generated $33,600 a year in net income. A leasing broker tells Hallie that with this tenant, the property would likely be valued at a 7% cap rate. What if the coffee was no good? What if the tattooist had dirty needles? What if an artist read subversive poetry out loud? Too much uncertainty. The idea sounded fantastic, and somewhere that Hallie would want to hang out at especially because there wasn't another coffee shop on Main Street, but she would lose money if she signed the lease. The property would only be valued at $480,000 ($33,600 / 7%), far lower than the $600,000 in debt she used to buy the property. So, she waited for another tenant.

Months go by. Years. Finally, a multinational bank agreed to sign a lease to open a branch in her storefront. Hallie was thrilled. While missing out on two years of rent hurt, the $67,000 she would have received from the coffee shop pales in comparison to the new valuation of the property. Though the bank only paid twice as much in rent as the coffee shop would have, the valuation of the property is more than 3 times as high at $1.6 million. This is because banks are among the highest credit tenants in the industry. Not only do they offer great terms—they usually pay far more in rent than almost any other prospective tenant—they offer great financial security, and are not very management-intensive at all. This results in lower operating expenses, compressed cap rates, and a higher valuation.

Building Valuation Variance Between High & Low Credit Tenants			
	High Credit Tenant (Multi-National Bank)	Low Credit Tenant (Small Coffee Shop)	Variance
Occupied Square Feet	2,000	2,000	0
Months Vacant	27	3	24
Gross Monthly Rent	$8,000	$4,000	$4,000
Annual Rent	$96,000	$48,000	$48,000
Rent PSF	$48	$24	$24
Expenses (%)	25%	30%	-5.00%
Expenses ($)	$24,000	$14,400	$9,600
NOI	$72,000	$33,600	$38,400
Cap Rate	4.50%	7.00%	(2.50%)
Valuation	$1,600,000	$480,000	$1,120,000
Loan Outstanding	$600,000	$600,000	$0
Profit after Loan Payoff	$1,000,000	($120,000)	$1,120,000

With these numbers, Hallie figured she could have waited more than a decade without renting the space and still come out ahead after factoring in the lost operating income and holding costs. She made the right choice. Don't blame Hallie, though. First, she isn't real. Second, hers is the story of commercial landlords nationwide, whose sensible financial decisions have helped to revive Main Streets across the country. Every vacant space is waiting for a white knight to save them and the valuation of their property. From a transactional perspective, long forgotten downtowns have benefited from the banks, fast casual chains, and deep-pocketed medical practices that have repopulated their storefronts, even if they don't offer much on the charm front. Financial incentives mandate America devolve into a sea of high credit, well-paying chains. That your Main Street has three banks, two dentists, and several popular lunchtime assembly-line cafes is just the market operating efficiently. How can we argue against math?

Math, as it's wont to do, has a funny way of changing. The last decade has marked a departure from more than a half-century of chain store dominance. In the wake of the Great Recession, many national chains have shuttered locations, formally ending a period of near-continuous expansion since 1950. While reporters have breathlessly remarked that this is a retail apocalypse brought about by e-commerce, that's not exactly true. In 2017, around the time when the notion of a retail apocalypse gained popular momentum, less than 9% of retail sales were coming from e-commerce.[28] Though this is a meaningful amount, it wasn't apocalyptic then, and it isn't now. While every closure of a Payless or a Sears was reported with near-religious zeal, more brick and mortar retail stores opened than were closed from 2017 to 2019.[29]

So, the story is about more than e-commerce. Legacy retailers have struggled to adapt to a changing world, doing little to update their antiquated businesses models and user experiences. To walk through a Kmart at any point in the last five years was to become intimately aware of how melancholy, insipid, and unsatisfactory the big box brick and mortar experience had become. And while it's true that the downfall of struggling retailers was hastened by other factors, like marauding private equity firms who levered them up only to strip them of their valuable parts and discard the rest, this is not exclusively, or even primarily, why those businesses failed. America was oversupplied with retail space. In 2018, the U.S. had more than 23 square feet of retail per capita, more than any other country on Earth.[30] An amount nearly 10 times greater than that of Germany, and five times the United Kingdom's. Closures of certain outmoded and overextended chains isn't an apocalypse, but a correction.

My intention is not to play down the real pain that many thousands felt in losing their jobs at these retailers, nor sneer at those who lost their beloved cultural touchstones. Sears, JCPenney, and Brooks Brothers, among others, were iconic brands, and the innovators of their day. Several generations grew up with malls as their central gathering space, finding their identities in food courts, enclosed promenades, and department store giants. However, the world has moved beyond requiring the services of many of these once revered institutions. Such is only the natural course of life. But this does not mean life ends for those who remain. We continue on. And so too has retail, refashioning itself to better suit the contours of our new age. Let's dispel the myth that retail is dying. It's not. Bad retail is dying after decades of woeful overbuilding. Even after the decade-long correction that's taken place, the vast majority of our commerce is still firmly rooted in the domain of Chainland.

There exists a window of opportunity to rectify our mistakes in Chainlaind, if only a sliver. Optimism lives! Despite all of the challenges, small businesses have proven resilient. The total number of retail stores has grown in the last few years, specifically small, specialty retail.[31]

According to The Center for American Progress, entrepreneurs filed 5.2 million business applications between January 2021 and December 2023, an increase of more than a third compared to 2017 through 2019.[32] Much of this entrepreneurial activity has been channeled at a grassroots level towards more local commerce. Consumers are prizing it more highly, and a greater share of landlords have proven a heartening willingness to partner with small tenants and help them grow. Returns may be somewhat diminished in the short term, but as stronger communities are cultivated, value in the long term (both financial and qualitative) will rise. We need more of this. These tenants may very well be the next great companies of tomorrow, or simply a beloved provincial shop, but they can't get there unless they have an opportunity. We must provide for that.

For those who want to cure themselves of the curse of homogenous and sprawling chains, to find identity and meaning through small businesses, there are a few steps towns and cities alike can take to get started.

First, we can't support our small businesses if the landscape is designed to favor big boxes. We must create conditions that are favorable to burgeoning entrepreneurs. This requires extensive zoning reform (more on that next chapter). But it also requires a rethinking of historical modes of American commercial development. We must progress beyond the romanticized linear Main Street of our collective imagination, so that retail becomes less like a parade one transacts along, and more like a comprehensive place one is integrated within. In other words, we should make downtown a place to be, not just pass through. Mid-block retail must be enabled (there are few things more charming than a cafe nestled unexpectedly in a residential row), and corner commercial spaces should be allowed as of right, without needing any special application or having to go through a years-long review process. These proposed changes extend beyond traditional retail to include other ground floor users like offices, civic spaces, and more novel tenants like ping pong bars and social clubs. Giving life room to live at all hours of the day, in all its varied manifestations, is the goal of a good commercial street.

Second, housing is essential. In order for commercial areas to be successful, they have to be of a mixed-use nature so that there is a built-in support network of neighbors to patronize shops and businesses. This absence is one of the critical flaws of Chainland, where every trip mandates the use of a car because no one lives there. Serendipity is foreign to this land of untethered consumption patterns. One can just as easily go to the shopping center three miles away in one direction, as three in the other, dispersing potential connections with neighbors and local characters to many small nodes as opposed to a singular large one. Location becomes depersonalized, and experiences commodified. Every place is somewhere to drive-through, not linger, compounding the challenges described in Chapter 2. When housing (and parks and civic spaces and etc.) is a part of a commercial development program, conversely, intimate walkable patterns form that can become a part of one's daily rituals, whereby the great challenges of our day are solved non-consciously by making the right thing to do and the easy thing to do the same thing.

Merchant's Square in Williamsburg, Virginia, an extraordinary recent commercial development. Designed by Quinlan Terry Architects, and developed by The Colonial Williamsburg Foundation. Completed in 2002.

It's not by chance that the places we love the most are those that have the most local businesses. Part of this is because in America, these areas have historically been older, located in more vernacular forms of architecture that we also love. These places get a lot of traditional urban form right, and are the last vestiges from a pre-Chainland society. But successful areas need not be old to be loved. We can create great places today, so long as we're thoughtful, and get the foundations right. When we treat our main streets and outlying retail districts as the only places where commercial value can pass through, they will necessarily be viewed as transactional domains. Owners will respond as such. But if we reimagine them as networks of interwoven, intimate streets that one goes to live in, rather than consume, a whole new world would open up.

In surrendering to Chainland, we've lost the gathering spaces that form the heart of community, those third places that are not home, neither the office nor school, and certainly not the drive-through, but where we come together to enjoy life and create our own memories. Perhaps the reason so many of our communities feel soulless is because we've eliminated the places where soul is created. With declines in church attendance, the loss of prominence of community organizations (like rotary and VFW clubs), and diminution of low-pressure, low-expense gathering places where people can simply spend time with friends and family, we're grasping at straws for opportunities to connect with one another. Many have sought out their own communities online, exchanging ideas and building relationships, but this is not entirely satisfying.

Moreover, self-selecting into narrow online groups shelters us from interacting with those who may look, or increasingly think, differently than us, driving polarization, and pathologizing those who don't align with our own predilections. Depriving us of a true diversity of experience and thought, a world of a million small tribes atrophies our critical thinking skills, capacity to initiate and maintain interpersonal relationships, and ability to respond to actions outside of the expected norms of our tribe. It's a simulacrum of what our bodies have evolved to crave, and indeed, need. Historically, gathering in groups protected individual members against their own shortcomings and vulnerabilities. Collectives who possessed diverse talents could lift one another up, where individual members who were weak in one area benefited from the support of others who were stronger in it, and vice versa. Without this support, vulnerability led to bad things. Things that haven't changed much in modern times. This phenomenon was masterfully detailed by Robert Putnam in his seminal *Bowling Alone*. With no places to gather, loneliness has risen, division has solidified, and many communities have died.

It's high time to rescue the narrative of commercial places away from the clutches of Chainland. We've sacrificed community, complex interpersonal relationships, our health, our environment, and the primacy of humanity itself all for a few dollars off of our fast-food receipts—savings which end up being offset by prices at the pump we're forced to use to fuel such daily tasks. This has been a penny wise, pound foolish bargain. A bargain that has deprived us of something more profound than any benefit Chainland can confer: the spirit of our places. A priceless treasure. Once it's gone, it's very difficult to bring back.

This is what we're up against. We must look the challenge firmly in the face in order to have any chance of defeating it. Shaking our fists at the sky powerlessly or shouting battle cries into the ether of social media, helplessly unaware of how we've arrived at the state we presently occupy, will do us precious little good. Such ignorance will only damn us to repeat the same mistakes over and over again. There is hope, though, as ever! And it doesn't take all that much. We must only adjust the series of decisions we make in our built environment. We must fix the guidelines we've written for ourselves. Though daunting, it is not an impossible task. Just as surely as we wrote ourselves into this situation, we can write ourselves out of it. Incrementally moving the zeitgeist of development, pulling the tides away from institutionality, and towards individualism. Moving from homogeneity to idiosyncratic wonder. It is my firm belief that we have the power to slay the worst manifestations of yesterday, through thoughtful policy written today, and implemented tomorrow. So, let's begin. Today.

6.

An Optimistic Foundation

Our world is shaped by a series of decisions. If we want a better world, we must start by making better decisions. It's really that simple. In theory, at least. As the baseball-player-and-aphorist Yogi Berra so astutely pointed out in his signature wit, however, and as we have already seen: "In theory there is no difference between theory and practice. In practice, there is."

While we must make new choices to alter our current trajectory, it's not as though we're operating from tabula rasa. We have to contend with decisions that have been made in the past and enshrined in code, which are very difficult to fight against. If a regulation has been on the books for 70 years and has had many overriding revisions visited upon it such that it resembles a palimpsest, it's not likely that it can be rolled back so easily. How can something be rectified if it's too difficult to make sense of what it even is? So sometimes, change doesn't come because it's too challenging to know where to even begin. But sometimes there are other reasons, like vested interests that uphold antiquated laws for the sake of personal gain. These agents remain in power for decades, often unopposed, because very few people have any level of interest in land use regulations. The structure of our world is thus left to the designs of a few opportunists, ignored by many, and subjected upon everyone. The burden falls most intensely on those who are least able to do anything about it. As opposed to being re-evaluated every few years to make sure they're still meeting the needs of the people, our land use regulations have become unresponsive and unassailable commandments: *Thou shall not build apartments. Thou shall not live within walking distance of a library. If Thou wants to bike, Thou shall feel the wrath of God when endeavoring to do so!*

This foundation is unstable. If we don't shore it up, it threatens to collapse. Not immediately, but as has been the case in cities like Detroit and San Bernardino, gradually, until the scale of the problems is too large to contend with. Thankfully, change is on the horizon after many years of tireless advocacy, failed interventions, and pleas for a more common sense regulatory environment have been ignored. In recent years, zoning has broken into the mainstream consciousness as an institution particularly worthy of modification, thanks to scholarship from figures like Richard Rothstein, Jenny Schuetz, Seymour I. Toll, Alain Bertaud, Sonia A. Hurt, and Edward Glaeser, among others. The many negative externalities exclusionary zoning has wrought, like segregation, environmental degradation, inequality, mental and physical health crises, and more, have been exposed to the general public. Some have even gone so far as to advocate for the elimination of zoning entirely, as M. Nolan Gray convincingly argued in *Arbitrary Lines*. While I wouldn't quite go so far as to call for the elimination of zoning codes, this position is closer to where we need to be than where we are today.

Advocacy has not stopped at zoning reform. The movement for improving our built environment has expanded to how we plan and build generally, which includes many non-obvious things like parking minimums and fire exits, that profoundly shape the way our world looks. Many have begun to question whether we can adequately regulate the countless known and unknown permutations of everyday life. It seems undesirable (and likely not possible) to anticipate and legislate for every subjective suboptimal case that sprouts up. Does it really make sense to require those who want to install a basketball hoop in their driveway to apply for a permit because one time a hoop fell down and hit a neighbor's car? Can we really know the exact amount of parking spaces a strip mall should have in order to meet peak capacity? What happens when a strip mall is 50% vacant, but the owner can't lease an empty storefront to a daycare because doing so would require more parking than the site can theoretically provide? Or if the local cookie store becomes a social media sensation overnight and suddenly the half-full strip mall now has a near-constant row of cars queuing up for two blocks? I can go further into the weeds, but you probably get the point, and almost certainly don't want to read it. Trust me, I wish I didn't have to learn these lessons the hard way.

How exactly to go about changing our current laws can get tricky, though. At some point, nearly all of the rules that govern our built environment had a sensible purpose, or still do in some narrow contexts. For example, it's a nice idea to have unit size minimums, so that people are not living in what are effectively closets. But when one law is layered on top of another without an understanding of how they might impact each other, they quickly devolve from pragmatic interventions to another bale of hay in a stack of chaos where the needle of common sense is slipping further and further from view. If a minimum dwelling unit size of 1,200 square feet is paired with a maximum lot area coverage of 40%, side and rear setbacks of 10 feet, and a minimum parking ratio of one car per bedroom, on a small enough lot, there may not be enough land left over to actually build anything. We have to analyze the causes and effects of these regulations in the context of our extant laws, uniting theory with reality. If the best of intentions can become grotesquely distorted through the complexity of our many laws, imagine what ill-intentioned laws can do?

In order to move forward in the pursuit of a better world, we must rethink the decisions that have delivered us to our present state. Only then can we ensure we will have the right foundations to start building the places of our dreams.

Rein in Superfluous Regulations

Here's where things get a bit difficult. How can we know which well-intentioned regulations are leading to negative outcomes, and which ones are having their desired impacts? It's hard to control for variables when there are so many regulations targeting so many different things. Is the minimum lot size to blame for why people are driving so much, because large lots push people further out? Or is it the parking minimums that mandate a parking lot at every property, discouraging other forms of travel? Or is it zoning, perhaps, which lowers the allowable density on each piece of land and inhibits people from living closer together? Or, some sociological factor we have no control over? If we tweak one of these variables there's no guarantee we'll get the results we want. Things only get harder when an attempt is made to address one of these regulations, only to realize its language is cross-referenced to a half-dozen other provisions strewn over thousands of pages, each of which may or may not have their own related external clauses and overlays. One finds rather quickly that everything is connected, and a single provision can't be modified without also changing many others. Our complex regulatory networks are near illegible. Land use policy in the U.S. is well and truly broken.

Rather than try to disaggregate and dissect individual pieces of code that may or may not be tangled among many dozens of other pieces of code, let's step back to ask ourselves what the purpose of regulations in the built environment are meant to be. Most of us can probably agree on what we want out of our towns and cities. We want them to be safe, have clean air and water, have solidly built housing that won't fall down on us in the middle of the night, good infrastructure, ample and quality education and employment prospects, fun things to do, and nothing that would actively sicken or imperil us. We want them to be beautiful. But these things look differently to different people. While one person might be grateful to send their kid to the public school within their district, another might not even consider sending their child to a private school that doesn't have a sufficiently high ranking.

There are core elements that we should regulate for, like making sure our buildings stand up straight, won't catch on fire, won't make us sick, and are accessible to peoples of all abilities. Far more nebulous, however, is whether a 300-square-foot apartment can accomplish these goals just as well as a 600-square-foot one. If someone wishes to live in a smaller apartment, whether because they want cheaper rent or because they just don't need very much space, we should let them do that. Arbitrary standards of what one person on a city council or community review board (who may never have even lived in an apartment before) believes constitutes a quality space may directly lead to worse conditions than what they were fearful of when commenting on a piece of legislation in the first place. Prohibitive costs may be imposed on the people for whom a specific piece of legislation was intended to help. As former principal urban planner at the World Bank, Alain Bertaud, has synthesized from his work around the globe in vastly different contexts, including New York, San Salvador, Bangkok, Sana'a, Chandigarh, Port au Prince, Tlemcen, and Paris: "when regulations do not allow the formal market to provide affordable housing, the informal market takes over".[1]

The informal market operates outside of government control. Whereas in the formal market developers and builders submit applications to a planning department for approval to build whatever structure they have in mind, there are no applications in the informal market. An informal builder in Jakarta, for example, might decide one day that they want to add a third floor to their home, and without permission, get to work right away. Usually this form of construction occurs in slums or neighborhoods where government oversight is lax (or nonexistent). Residents have to take matters into their own hands if they want to improve any aspect of their lives as public help is rarely available to them. Initiative, ingenuity, and resolve are all required in spades.

Ideally, the informal market could be supported with the help of basic foundations provided by a government like clean water, electricity, sanitation, and emergency services. People could then work their way towards higher standards of living over time, according to their means and initiative. Chilean architect Alejandro Aravena notably demonstrated this concept through his half built houses. The low-cost homes were only halfway completed when they were delivered to their eventual residents, and could be finished, remodeled, extended, or redeveloped whenever the residents had the funds or desire to do so. It's a highly creative solution that has resulted in many wonderful organic structures, each taking on the personality of their owners.

But when informal conditions are cracked down on and arbitrarily high standards are enforced, the vulnerable may be relegated into ever-worse conditions. Arguably the most prosperous city in the world, New York has anywhere between 300,000 and 500,000 people living in illegal basements across the city, deprived of light and air, overcrowded, and concealed from public view.[2] These conditions are bad. Very bad. Exposed electrical wiring, mold, rodent and pest infestations, and unsturdy wall constructions threaten many thousands. Many are located in flood zones, and become submerged in severe weather events.

These dwellings primarily house the workforce immigrant population that makes New York run—people who have risked everything to contribute to our society in pursuit of a better life. In turn, we have given our thanks by forcing them into dark warrens of danger, precarity, and neglect. Shame on us. I'm sure many of these essential figures would prefer a 200-square-foot private studio or SRO, if only developers were allowed to build them. Though small, these units wouldn't actively pose a threat to their lives. And there is much evidence that these studios are both a valued and essential form of housing.

Millions of people in the world's most prosperous cities live reasonably well in conditions that we have foolishly outlawed in the States. Paris' *Chambres de Bonne*—small former maid's quarters accessed via service stairs on the top floor of Haussmann apartment buildings—have long enabled students, the working class, and immigrants to trade space for proximity to jobs, amenities, and services. It's a trade many happily make, as a slightly bigger apartment an hour further away via transit may sever one's connection to the city. Besides, there's no guarantee that one will be able to find cheaper housing if they move further away, anyway, if those outlying municipalities have regulations that increase the cost of housing as well.

Lofted micro apartments in Tokyo, sometimes smaller than 100 square feet, can be rented for just a few hundred dollars a month in the city's most expensive, trendy, and centrally-located neighborhoods like Harajuku, Nakameguro, and Shibuya.[3] Contrast this with the difficulty many have in finding an apartment cheaper than $2,000 in the heart of a major global capital. In some cases, $2,000 is even a bargain. Despite their small size, it's easy to see why these unconventional residences are beloved by many. They allow people to pursue careers or passions that may not initially (or ever) be remunerative, but are deeply enriching to the soul. In other cases, they allow individuals to save considerably more money than they otherwise would be able to, boosting future quality of life prospects, especially given the close proximity to strong job centers. On the more prosaic end of the spectrum, modest affordable housing allows the essential cogs of a city's machinery to have a place as well. Sanitation workers, waiters, delivery cyclists, clerks, taxi drivers, pipefitters, warehousing staff, teachers and more can exist as equal citizens, as opposed to a secondary class that serves the whims of the more fortunate. Moreover, when a city has many things to see and do outside of one's home, some are fine with their apartment being no more than a humble place where they sleep.

In the U.S., we've deluded ourselves into thinking that an insular lifestyle is superior to a more sociable, communal one. Perhaps this belief is a coping mechanism to deal with the poor quality of much of our public realm. Were this mechanism true, however, it would only provide comfort to a subset of the populace. As we have explored, it's not as though we traded a universally ideal public realm for a universally ideal private realm, secured by sensible, measured regulations. We have sent out more than we've received, but still pay as though we all enjoy the highest quality habitations.

A recent analysis from the National Multifamily Housing Council found that 41% of all development costs are attributable to regulation.[4] Said another way, the average development costs 41% more than it otherwise would absent regulations. Additional studies have corroborated these findings, including a 2015 paper which explained "[t]he vast majority of studies have found that locations with more regulation have higher house prices and less construction".[5] With respect to rental apartments, the cost of these regulations are directly passed down to tenants. Applying our 41% number, $1,200 of a $3,000 per month apartment is attributable to legal standards. That's nearly $15,000 a year, an extraordinary amount of money to most people. The normative cost attributable to regulations isn't zero, of course, but it's definitely closer to the single digit percentages than half of a home's cost.

In a 2019 study in the *American Economic Journal*, Chang-Tai Hsieg and Enrico Moretti found that reducing (not eliminating) land-use restrictions in a few major cities would add 3.7% to the GDP of the United States.[6] That means we're losing somewhere in the magnitude of $900 billion a year due to artificial constraints. Not exactly nothing.

Some of these regulatory items might be obviously expensive, like parking minimums. A single parking space in a garage, below-grade lot, or multi-leveled structure can cost more than $50,000. For some of these regulations, there's no empirical reason why they exist as they do, despite their purported mathematical raison d'etre, other than the fact that the numbers sounded good enough when the regulations were initially crafted. And in some cases, there may be a thread one can follow that traces back to the origin of regulatory rationale, but once one gets to the end of the line, there's little there.

Take the parking requirements surrounding Black Friday. The phenomenon of retail stores dedicating the day after Thanksgiving to sell heavily discounted goods began in the 1950s, but it wasn't until the 1980s that the event rose to prominence and storefronts became overwhelmed by hordes of value-seeking holiday shoppers. In order to deal with this chaos, planning codes around the country were rewritten so that big box stores would be able to accommodate the high demand. No one would have to endure the misery of circling a parking lot and miss out on all the sales. Though Black Friday's peak demand is no more than a few hours in a calendar year consisting of 8,760, codes have forced excessively large parking lots for the .0007% of time that they *might* be fully occupied. In reality, they sit chronically vacant for the entirety of the year, wasting considerable space and resources. Imagine mandating that every home have eight parking spaces because on Thanksgiving several family and friends *might* come over. This is wholly ignorant of the fact that only some homes host Thanksgiving (non-hosters are leaving someplace empty, after all), and that not everyone drives. Some take buses, others hitch a ride with a relative, and still more make alternate plans altogether.

But of course, these situations aren't quite analogous because Black Friday's in-store importance has declined dramatically. The event is now spread over many days and a rising proportion of sales come from online, making the high requirements ever more nonsensical. In 2015, the last year I could find reliable data on brick and mortar sales for Black Friday, revenue was $10.4 billion, a $1 billion drop from the year prior, while e-commerce sales had risen 14%, to $2.74 billion.[7] Online shoppers spent $9.8 billion on Black Friday in 2023, with another $12.4 billion coming on Cyber Monday.[8] All told, $31.7 billion was spent online from Thanksgiving through Cyber Monday. These trends are only accelerating, while the need for parking is diminishing. Trading idle parking spaces for areas that could be used for nearly anything else, including untouched natural land, is very expensive. Beyond their direct price, parking minimums enshrine car dependency, and guarantee elevated levels of pollution, more dangerous streets, environmental degradation, and poor health.

As the case of Black Friday illustrates, it's not possible to anticipate every fluctuation of daily life through code. Where it's attempted, ephemeral events are given power to rule tyrannically over more permanent conditions. Some areas of town, and on select days of the week, may require more attention at certain times. Others may need less. If we can't reshape our world every day of the week to adjust for demand, why should our codes try to do the same?

Other, less expensive line items mandated by regulations, fly under scrutiny because they seem to have positive outcomes that more than make up for the costs they impose, or at worst are inconsequential to price. Of course new apartment buildings should pay fees to the local school district to support the kids who might live there. If there are a lot of birds dying because they're flying into transparent glass, mandating the installation of bird-safe windows is a benevolent intervention in order to protect local ecology. And if we want less stormwater runoff, requiring large developments to have bioswales and permeable pavement that can absorb water before it carries pollutants into crop lands, potable water sources, and diverse ecosystems is only common sense.

But dig just a little bit deeper, and the outcomes borne of these regulations aren't so rational nor inconsequential. Why do apartment buildings that only have small studios and one bedroom (where few kids are likely to live) have to pay school fees in order to receive their permits? If birds are constantly flying into transparent facades, the solution is to reduce glazing ratios with higher proportions of opaque products like wood, stucco, or brick, not opt for a more ornithologically sensitive glass. And while bioswales may indeed control runoff from an apartment building's parking lot, it's a drop in the bucket (or bioswale) compared to the runoff generated by a 60-foot-wide stroad mandated by the department of transportation, that doesn't have to abide by similar regulations.

Rarely are impartial cost-benefit analyses carried out on proposed regulations. What reports are commissioned often arrive at conclusions favored by their proponents' prejudices. So they remain with impunity. Politically, there's no appetite to strike plausibly good regulations. This makes sense. Why roll back policies that your constituents approve of, when getting such approval in the first place is no easy task? But it's absolutely imperative for our officials and planners to do the work of digging a little bit deeper than the surface level to see what the downstream consequences of their policies are. We must understand if our regulations are actually providing the benefits they're meant to. If they aren't clearly supporting the advancement of a desired outcome, they must be rescinded or reformed. This critique is not borne of some ideological doctrine of deregulation for the sake of deregulation, but the pursuit of employing common sense to make sure the outcomes we're getting are the ones we want.

The seemingly small changes required by inflexible regulations add up, along with a hundred other well-intentioned policies. In an industry where margins are already very tight, these extra costs, or months waiting in entitlement for permits, can mean the difference between a persistently vacant lot and 50 new homes. We must consider the implications of our policies and see if we're willing to bear the added costs of enacting them. There's only so many weights that a development can take on before it buckles under the pressure and meets its end in the ever-growing graveyard of places that could have been. This is what developers mean when they say a project "doesn't pencil". It either becomes too expensive to make an appropriate risk-adjusted rate of return (in the private market), or isn't able to secure the level of subsidy required (in the public market). Despite what many people think—and far too many city officials—a building has to make economic sense or else it won't be constructed.

For those who aren't compelled by the economic argument, perhaps another line of reasoning will do the trick. The neighborhoods that people love the most, and travel around the world to see, would be illegal to replicate today because of our regulatory environment. In Manhattan, 40% of the borough's buildings couldn't be erected today without violating at least one (and in many cases, a couple more) of the city's zoning, planning, or building codes.[9] Whether they are too tall, take up too much of the lot, mix too many uses in one structure, have too many apartments on a dwelling unit per acre basis, those apartments are too small, or any number of other reasons, these places couldn't be rebuilt today if they were torn down. These structures are the very same ones that are emblematic of the city itself. They comprise the places that people most closely associate with New York, and admire. Put simply, if the current regulations had their way, New York would no longer be New York, but an uninspired, banal, bulky, and institutional series of conforming cubes of varying sizes.

Across the country, the story is the same. If the most lovely structure in many small towns or cities were to be demolished, or existentially damaged in a major weather event, it likely couldn't legally be replaced, and the community would be mortally wounded. Whether it be a pre-war apartment building, a monumental bank, or a warehouse that has since been converted to any number of uses, these beloved structures would be illegal to build anew despite all of the utility they provide. That's patently absurd.

Distressingly, there appears to be some cognitive dissonance between the barriers erected by cities, and how they perceive themselves to be. If a city administration's alleged goal is to create more affordable housing, but its rules staunchly defend the sorts of things that make delivering such housing difficult, very little will get built. Intention is not enough to make these goals happen; policy must align with practice, and if policies are precluding progress, they must be redirected.

We cannot allow codes created a century ago—in vastly different contexts that had no way to anticipate the ways in which our world would change—to strangle us today.

Good Foundations

Few could object that much of what we're doing today is wrong, and that reform is in need. But opposition isn't enough to move us forward. It's essential to lay out an idea for what a better world looks like before we can go out and build it. After all, it's not possible to build anything without the right foundation. The foundation of an Optimistic philosophy starts not with buildings or theory, but urban design and planning. Despite what some might think, much of what makes a place attractive doesn't come from individual buildings, but from how the streets, parcels, and public spaces are laid out. Other elements like trees, streetlights, benches, art, and public facilities can further elevate a place. There needs to be some level of organization, though, or else chaos may overcome order.

The best organizing foundations don't stand in the way of much. They don't rigidly dictate how a place should be, instead, they allow it to grow into itself, however that may look. Making a left turn here, a right turn there, and a completely unexpected twist in a third place. There's an enchanting imperfection that can't be anticipated by strict planning, but somehow just makes sense. The streets are narrow, the buildings aren't set too far back from the property lines (if it all, as this discourages interactions and deadens space), building widths are not too wide (except for monumental structures), and heights aren't too tall. The scale is not just appropriate, but perfectly comfortable. If the streets wind a little, so much the better. Vistas can be terminated by monuments or everyday structures.

One of the most important foundations is the provision of a sense of enclosure. We prefer to interact with spaces that feel like outdoor rooms—four walls gently providing structure—which safeguard us from open spaces. A longing for protection is ingrained in us. Exposed to open areas, our ancestors ran the risk of being attacked by foes or predators, or getting caught in inclement weather. Millennia of intuition has solidified into a biological adaptation—thigmotaxis—a tendency to hug against edges. If your favorite seat in a restaurant is the booth in the corner where you can survey the room with your back against the wall, that's no mere matter of preference. It's a primal response. We like booths not only because they have plush seats, but also because our brains crave spaces where nothing can surprise us from behind. Should anything go wrong within our field of vision in front of us, we would have ample opportunity to respond.

This same principle applies to cozy public squares and narrow, meandering streets. Not so for expansive stretches of asphalt, orthogonally aligned on grids where the streets seem to extend forever. *Is that the curvature of the Earth on the other end of 6th Avenue?* How else are we meant to feel other than small and vulnerable? Neither of these things feels particularly good. Moderately narrow streets that wind gently through a series of tightly knit together buildings, on the other hand, make us feel like we're gently being hugged by the walls of the street, but in an intimate way, not a claustrophobic one.

Simply put, a good environment is one where the proportions of a space complement the dimensions of people. This is called a human-scaled environment. Human-scale relates to the height, width, and bulk of a place, but also the speed and the ease with which an average person can interact with a given feature of the built environment. Places dominated by cars rarely have much in the way of good human scale infrastructure. While a car moving at 60 miles per hour may feel right at home on a four lane highway, a person walking a few miles an hour on the buffering sidewalk might feel completely overwhelmed. For the most part, we should seek to build "Goldilocks" places, where we neither feel too big nor too small, but just right.

Traditionally, human-scaled buildings have risen five to six stories high, located on streets a few dozen feet wide, meaning the space in between buildings (known as the right of way) would be roughly half as wide as the buildings are tall. Move up the scale and ratios of 3:1 may seem a little snug, but a 60-foot-tall building on a 20-foot-wide street isn't fated to be imposing. The impact depends on how well the building is composed. This historical scale was partly limited by technology: without elevators or steel, we were limited in how tall we could build. Walking up and down 12 stories several times a day isn't exactly something most people want to do—if even they're able. Traditional urbanists also note that building any taller than six stories makes it difficult for residents of higher floors to interact with passersby on the street—important for maintaining a sense of neighborliness. Though there is some truth to this, it's still possible to build tall without sacrificing a human-scaled environment. Taller structures can be set back from the street so they don't loom over the people below. Wedding-cake towers, which set back in tiers as they rise, achieve this masterfully, gracefully soaring above the clouds without feeling too threatening. Twenty-story buildings can perfectly coexist with 50–75 foot tall neighbors, though of course several-hundred foot tall buildings can also function as monuments and focal points, scattered throughout an area as treasured jewels.

Regardless of style, getting the fabric right is what matters most. Streets, and the relationships buildings have to them, are more important than individual structures. Perceptions of space take care of most of our attraction to a street, which is why the massing of a building is so important. Five-over-ones, our friends from Chapter 5, wouldn't be so loathed if they didn't sprawl so much horizontally across entire blocks, and actively discourage streetlife. Though I believe a Victorian mansion block or Prague's Art Nouveau mid-rises are far superior to the architecture of five-over-ones, if the buildings of today's fashion were contained to 25 or 50 feet of street width, as opposed to several hundred, they might be much more welcomed.

Indeed, some of the most attractive cities don't have very many beautiful buildings at all. Individual structures can elevate a place from the very good to the sublime, but they're not a prerequisite. Over time, places can reinvest in themselves to get to this level, like Venice, or Buenos Aires, but they need not ever get there for them to be fundamentally good. Take Athens or Tokyo. These are terrific cities, but on the whole, they have pretty poor architecture. Athens' gray and dreary concrete apartment blocs known as *polikatoikias* won't grace the cover of retrospectives on good design, but when woven together, the fabric they enable through fine-grained density is as vibrant as one can find in all of Europe. Tokyo is almost unbelievably dynamic, but not chaotic. This is thanks to some level of mixed-uses being allowed by right in every neighborhood, even quiet residential ones. Though buzzing, core residential areas are seldom loud. Tokyo is composed of many superblocks, where large buildings line the periphery of neighborhoods along busy roads, leaving the interior a maze of ungridded narrow streets and low rise structures where walking and bicycling are the easiest ways to get around. Though cars are allowed within the superblocks, few have need for them. What cars enter the neighborhoods drive very slowly, cutting down on noise, and making the streets safer for pedestrians. Small lots, narrow streets, and mixed-uses mean there's always something new to see every few steps, which offers much stimulation and a sense of enclosure. Housing costs are some of the lowest in the world for any major city. One-bedrooms rent between $500 and $1,500 even in the core of the city, while two-bedrooms can cost less than $2,000 a month. As mentioned earlier in this chapter, this affordability grants much freedom, allowing people to pursue niche passions, and spend more time indulging in the city without stressing about how they're going to make rent.

How do we build these sorts of magical places? In order to promote better foundations shaped by many hands, ironically, we have to start from the top-down mandate of just a few, not the bottom-up of the many. As explored in Chapter 3, for much of the last century, we've been living in a bottom-up world where decisions have been democratized to the block and neighborhood level. While it might sound noble or desirable, this experiment hasn't quite worked. There are nearly 20,000 incorporated cities, towns, and villages in the U.S., each with its own sets of rules, laws, and norms. In fact, cities and towns incorporate precisely because it gives them more local control over things like police forces, trash collection, and of course zoning codes, as opposed to being subjected to the rules of a larger county or city. If a group doesn't like a city's rules, they can incorporate outside of its boundaries and make their own incorporated place It's surprisingly common, like in Los Angeles. Who doesn't love Santa Monica's pier, or Malibu's beaches? Beverly Hills is an iconic shopping destination renowned globally for its glitz and glamor. These places make L.A. what it is!

Except none of them are actually in Los Angeles. They are their own separately incorporated communities, catering to a certain kind of person, while conspicuously excluding others. You won't find much housing in Hidden Hills, or many strip malls in Beverly Hills, but drive towards central L.A., and you'll find most of what these places have excluded. Metro Atlanta has seen no fewer than a dozen new cities and towns incorporated in the last 20 years.[10]

These new rules don't lead to greater autonomy. They lead to more restrictions. It's not *really* about local control, but a different kind of box to be put into. Though Beverly Hills or Malibu may be unique in their cultural value, most incorporated communities in America generally look the same. It's a grand ruse. Residents feel like they have freedom because they're a part of an in-group which empowers them, but in reality they're more restricted than the places they came from. One often has more ability to do something interesting on their land in the cities of Atlanta or Los Angeles than in a newly incorporated municipality, where they might struggle to even paint their house depending on the homeowners association of the subdivision they're in.

This balkanized system of governance makes collaboration between neighboring areas really difficult, to say nothing of regional cooperation among dozens of communities. Why would two places work together when one of them explicitly seceded from the other because it didn't like how they were doing things? Scale this up to all of the municipalities that make up one metropolitan area, and it's easy to see how relying on each of them to incrementally adopt better zoning and building codes isn't likely to happen. Especially when few of these places have any planners at all. For those that do, they may not be capable of ushering in even marginal change. Should change eventually arrive, it may well take decades for its impacts to fully be made manifest.

As we look for an alternative to this factionalized system of control, we must be cautious of being overly top-down. We wouldn't want to repeat the mistakes of Moses, or implement the schemes of Le Corbusier at the expense of our urban cores. Instead of opt-out provisions where groups can secede from their larger city, we have to reset the default such that no one can shirk their responsibilities. Communities can then decide what makes the most sense for them—whether staying closer to the baseline or moving beyond it. The good news is we know that different models can work. Back to Japan.

Japanese zoning is set nationally, not locally, which takes away a lot of the perverse incentives, in-dealing, and general absurdities that arise when the connection between emotion and legislation is so close. It's a lot easier to implement policies that people might not initially like if one doesn't have to see them at the barber shop or cafe. Fear of a deli-run-in is no reason for not implementing better policies, however. Especially if that deli is within walking distance to a train station, but local regulations deny the land from being optimally used because a loud neighbor from down the block is worried about the shadow a few new floors may cast on their lawn on a late spring afternoon.

Japanese cities still maintain some level of local zoning control, but regulations are far more permissive than in the States, and they're very easy to understand. There are only 12 zones.[11] Unlike in the U.S., there aren't complicated overlays prescribing extra rules. Planners can thus more easily manage cities, and builders can more easily build in them, without needing the aid of specialized land use attorneys. Though there are restrictions on some uses, the biggest difference between Japanese zones is not the use, but the intensity allowed. Lots near train stations have higher FARs and lot size coverage ratios, allowing the higher demand to live close to transit to adequately be met, while more peripheral and rural neighborhoods have lesser densities.

In the most restrictive zone, developers can still build schools, temples, churches, clinics, and a slew of other small-scale uses, including modest offices, cafes, townhomes, and apartments in low-rise structures. This leads to far lower rates of segregation by class, because it's possible for someone who owns a townhome with their family to live next to an identical structure that's been carved out to house four apartments. As zones get progressively more permissive, all of the uses allowed in the lower zones are still allowed in more intense ones. Temples or small commercial offices don't ruffle very many feathers, so they're generally allowed everywhere. Cities are rendered mixed-use as a default in this paradigm, where there's always something interesting to see on a side street. Good foundations don't care what's within a given building, so long as it's not so disruptive. The only thing that could be described as exclusionary about Japanese zoning is that industrial zones home to heavy manufacturing are kept to themselves, which just makes sense.

Seattle, as a point of comparison, has 41 primary zones.[12] These range from Residential Small Lot (RSL) to Residential, Multifamily, Lowrise 1 (LR1) and Industrial Commercial (IC). Each of these zones has many different sublayers. In reviewing the city's municipal code and land use data, I found at least 286 (!) permutations of these zones—though I wouldn't be surprised if there were more.[13] Each is more complicated than the last. For example, in an LR1 zone, one can build an apartment building that has a maximum height of 30 feet tall, and is set back five feet from the street, so long as there isn't more than one home per 1,300 square feet of lot space. Whereas in an LR2 RC (M) district, one can provide some small commercial uses and build up to 40 feet tall, so long as—brace yourselves—the length of all portions of façades within 15 feet of a lot line don't comprise more than 65% of the length of that lot line. If a lot with the same zoning elsewhere in the city has an additional shoreline overlay because it's located next to the Puget Sound, the owner of that land may not be able to understand what exactly they could build, but they could be assured that there would be a few more letters and numbers on the back of the zoning designation. I can hardly write these examples without laughing, but also not without contempt and frustration. Such is the absurd micromanagement that American local zoning codes attempt to preside over. If these barely-decipherable codes delivered pleasant, desirable, walkable, and attractive communities, that'd be one thing. But they don't.

Up until very recently, more than 80% of the residential zoned area in Seattle was reserved for the same sort of low density, detached single family homes.[14] Despite the city's attempt to curate itself through complex code, most of the city looks the same. All that work for nothing. More than half of the land in one of the most prosperous urban areas in the world is effectively suburban. And homogeneously so. Seattle, sadly, is not alone in orienting its land use regulations this way. Much work is required to rectify the current state of affairs.

So, what's to be done? The solution isn't to apply Japanese zoning one-to-one to the U.S. Different cultural and governance norms make it unlikely to translate a national model of land use. But that doesn't mean states can't adopt better regulations from the top down. Unable to get around the collective action problem of needing many people to change their obdurate ways for the greater good, governments have begun moving towards preemption to supersede local regulations from the state level. If individual cities or towns aren't willing to do their fair share of housing, infrastructure and commercial accommodation, states can step in to override local zoning. Though this isn't the tabula rasa solution that some may call for—and state laws still have to be adopted, and then enforced, by uncooperative localities (no easy thing)—it moves us towards a more permissive building culture. Places like Oregon, California, and Maine have begun experimenting with preemption, passing laws that make it legal for people to build duplexes or ADUs anywhere in the state by right, without having to get special permission. This doesn't mean single family homes are illegal to build, but just that choices are elevated onto a level playing field. It should be just as easy for someone to build a three-unit walk-up with a coffee shop on the ground floor as it is to erect a McMansion with a three-car garage. People should have the ability to decide what they want to do with their land. That's freedom.

We can't rely on zoning codes to sweep the nation, town by town, as they once did. Things have become too ossified as inertia and acquiescence to the status quo have set in. State preemption represents a good opportunity to break that up. Similarly, we can't rely on individual towns to update their building codes to bring about more beautiful, common sense places, because these are even more complicated than zoning codes to modify. Luckily, just as changes to the International Building Code in 2009 filtered down to local levels and led to a massive expansion of five-over-ones, we can change the parent code again to allow for the types of buildings we love, but which are currently illegal. The same goes for revisions to the Manual of Uniform Traffic Control Devices, and standards administered by state-level departments of transportation which determine how wide streets can be, how fast cars can go, and where crosswalks and traffic signals can be placed. Making progress on any one of these fronts in a small, isolated part of one state can't have the wide impact we're so desperately in need of. But if changes are made at the highest level, the impact can be broad and give individual communities the agency to decide what's right for them.

To summarize, governments should lay out permissive foundations as an infrastructural layer, then let individuals fill in the gaps however they might see fit. This is autonomy with a set of bumpers. The bar for city building is set at a high base quality without being overbearing. It lets people generally do what they want (so long as it's safe), expressing themselves through local practices. Just as our current development patterns prescribe certain things and proscribe others, Optimistic foundations can do the same. Excise taxes can be used to disincentivize building things that make our cities worse (surface parking lots, wide/blocky buildings, congestion, etc.), and fund things we want more of.

Great Foundations in the Midst of Great Challenges: The Industrial City and Paris

Paris is perhaps the best example of sufficiently high-quality foundations being leveraged to create a wonderful city. While the Eiffel Tower, the Louvre, and Notre-Dame are extraordinary, what makes the city really special aren't its monuments, but the quality of its "average" blocks, which were created in response to a crisis as severe as any our modern world has known.

Mid-19th-century Paris was noxious and overcrowded. Philosopher Victor Considerant described the city in 1845 as "an immense workshop of putrefaction, where misery and sickness work in concert, where sunlight and air rarely penetrate. Paris is a terrible place where plants shrivel and perish, and where, of seven small infants, four die during the course of the year."[15] Something had to be done.

Emperor Napoleon III had some ideas. Louis Napoleon envisioned a grand renovation of the city. The first steps were taken in 1850 via a bold project to connect the Louvre to the Hôtel de Ville via an extension of the Rue de Rivoli. He expanded this vision in 1853, appointing a loyal civil servant named Georges-Eugène Haussmann as Prefect of the Seine. Haussmann, who asked for the title "Baron" in continuation of the honor bestowed upon his grandfather, was effectively given free reign to transform the city from a warren of dark, dirty, and dangerous passageways gripped by disease and crime into a modern capital.[16] He was instructed by Napoleon III to "*aérer, unifier, et embellir*" Paris; to give the city open space and fresh air, connect the disparate parts of the region into one complete whole, and make the resulting metropolis more beautiful.[17]

This mandate wasn't too dissimilar to the goals of the Social Reformers, who strove to improve the lives of the working classes in industrializing cities, but with one key distinction. Social Reformers operated at an incremental level, improving a tenement here, a block there, and, in aggregate, perhaps a whole neighborhood over a few decades. Haussmann's task was absolute: to transform the entirety of one of Europe's oldest and most important capitals.

He got right to work, cutting through neighborhoods to create a north–south. Haussmann connected areas that had effectively been inaccessible from one another before due to the difficulties of navigating paths whose obstructions were so plentiful they resembled the outdoor rooms of hoarders.

While the Empire had the power to initiate this project (and doubtless appreciated that Haussmann heeded counsel to make long and straight roads by which it was easier for the military to promenade along) its coffers weren't limitless. In exchange for financing the large-scale road building and infrastructure projects that provided light, air, sanitation, and connection, private investors were given development rights along these new boulevards to house the booming populace, and imbue the city with beauty. Regulations for this construction were strict and ruthlessly enforced. Sir Peter Hall explains in *Cities In Civilization* how Haussmann "retained building height at 17.54 meters [6 stories] as in 1784 building code. Streets under 8 meters wide, cornice height was set at 12 meters, a 1.15 ratio. same for buildings on streets of 10–14 meters wide. The largest boulevards were 18 meters wide. 5 floors and 2 balconies. Limestone could be cheaply transported from quarries into the city via rivers. French doors exactly 1.2 meters across."[18] Everything had to be exactly so. Deviation was not to be tolerated.

At first, this seems counterintuitive. How could this uniformity lead to much beauty? No matter how attractive something is, intense repetition dulls our brains and diminishes our perception of it. If one can mitigate that repetition with small details that make each edifice unique, however, monotony can be transformed from a tedious canvas into a masterpiece that highlights creativity. In Haussmann's Paris, so long as the aesthetic integrity of the street front was respected, and all of the regulations were met, freestyling and embellishment of ornamentation were permitted, if not outright encouraged. Working within these extremely tight constraints, and perhaps because of them, designers expressed their creativity in remarkable ways, producing, in Sir Peter Halls' words, "extraordinary diversity within uniformity".

When the backdrop is the same, our eyes pay closer attention to the finer details. This is true whether one is looking out at the ocean and sees an irregular wave on the horizon, or picking through a bag of M&Ms only to notice that one of the M's is misprinted. It's especially true in Paris. The baseline was built to such a high standard that it demands attention from passersby to appreciate all that it has to offer. Upon heeding these calls, a closer inspection of a given facade rewards the viewer. Here is where Paris truly shines, where the "average block" is not so much a place to live in, but a stage adorned, where passersby are but one in a revolving, infinite cast of characters. A door is a door until it's something else. It might seem normal at first blush, but look closer: these aren't normal doors. They're taller than your run-of-the-mill entryway. They're colorful. They're surrounded by precast ornaments that draw your eyes up, asking you to acknowledge their subtle grandeur. They might have circular inset windows, or geometric extrusions that offer depth and require deeper examination, if only for just an extra moment or two. Sometimes, if you're lucky, you can see one opening up, offering a glimpse of what's inside, but never fully revealing its secrets. The effect is compelling precisely because of the unknown, piquing our curiosity that has been engaged by the thoughtfulness put into the entryway, but never fully sating it. If the front door is this wonderful, what treasures are held inside?

Entryways in Paris. Pictures taken by the author.

And sometimes, a door isn't required at all. To stumble upon a covered passageway protected by caryatids is to be shepherded by guardians through a sacred portal to another realm, elevating what at first was nothing more than a span of stone or concrete into something magical. Divine. Such entrances are well and truly a celebration of transition, embodying the importance of distinguishing different spaces from one another. There is no flattening of meaning here, nor deprivation of identity. Paris' entrance ways are forceful expressions of value, virtue, and aspiration. They compel reflection, cultivate refinement, and celebrate the glories of the quotidian.

Or maybe columns are more your thing? When the constraints of structure are strong, but there are no regulations on adornment, opportunities arise to transform a simple pillar fortifying an entrance into a work of art itself, allowing what might be a utilitarian building element in less capable hands to be worshiped for its own splendor and artistry.

A covered entryway and shopfront in Paris. Pictures taken by the author.

These qualities extend to storefronts, which immeasurably improve the standard Parisian block. Many of the best stores are rather small, located in older buildings. As Jane Jacobs so astutely observed, older buildings have cheaper rent—even in wealthy neighborhoods. Small business owners can thus take risks on novel ideas, and not worry about higher overhead costs or programming merchandise across an area that may be beyond their means. Throw in a bulkhead, some robust mullions, a transom window or two, *et voilà*. An innate pride exists in these places that's rare in contemporary commerce, where supreme individual craftsmanship is united with the quirks of passionate merchants to realize wholly unique and fully compelling places. I think much of this beauty comes from contrast: colors are set against neutral tones. Wood or metal are juxtaposed with stone. Depth vies with verticality for attention. The storefronts themselves are almost more compelling than what's on offer inside, beckoning shoppers to come off the sidelines and pass into another world.

Yes, there are still chains in Paris, but because of the many small storefronts in older buildings and a remarkably high density of people, an extraordinary diversity of offerings, including the most niche ideas and specialty shops, can flourish. If the 11th arrondissement were its own city, it would be the second densest place on Earth, at just around 40,000 people per square kilometer. Nearly every other arrondissement would qualify as one of the 100 densest cities on Earth, with a majority of these earning spots in the top 50. This means there's always likely to be someone to try small batch perfume, bid on a collection of antique stamps, read avant-garde books, or explore a cabinet of curiosities.

Stores cannot specialize in these ways in lower-density areas because there aren't enough people who might enjoy a very unique thing. So they generalize, amalgamating all the goods one might conceivably want under one roof, sacrificing distinction and intimacy of experience. Newer, larger retail spaces privilege banks and large chains (as discussed in Chapter 5), which are all too common in contemporary developments and have precious little intrigue to them. Vapid glass panes that cover the entirety of storefronts allow would-be customers to see all without providing a sense of wonder. Do you need to venture into a store where you can already see its wares? Are you compelled to walk into a shop that hasn't put any effort into attracting you to come in, without even the faintest mystique to arouse curiosity? Likely not.

Ornamentation infiltrates every crevice it can in Haussmann's Paris, vying for the passersby's attention. A floral iron railing here, a gracefully arching corbel there. Pilasters with corinthian capitals layered on top. Street furniture does its best to transcend the confines of rigid practicality as well, as cast-iron lampposts draw one in like a moth to a flame, trees are manicured as finely as nails ready for their close up on the red carpet, and water fountains have more artistic integrity than much of what we'd consider "art" today.

In *The City as a Work of Art*, Donald Olsen notes of Paris that "No city anywhere has taken more seriously its duties to look and behave throughout as if the eyes of the world were on it and the honor of the nation at stake."[19] This is, gloriously, and incontrovertibly, true.

* * *

Necessity can give birth to tremendous places, but only when the solutions to our problems are humane, enlightened, and seek to raise the quality of life of the people who are meant to live in them. It's not enough just to build, as the Soviets or mid-century planners did. We have to build well. With attraction and concern for the human condition, cities can rise from the ashes of destitution to become greater than even their most ambitious benefactors imagined they could be.

Time and again, this lesson has been taught to us. Whether via the Social Reformers, Baron Haussmann, or Ildefons Cerda, the 19th-century Spanish engineer who designed Eixample, Barcelona's magnificent urban expansion. Cerda created the foundations for graceful expansion in a city which had previously very low prospects of hope; mortality rates were higher than anywhere in Europe. Life expectancy was just 23 years for the working classes. 36 for the wealthiest. Epidemics tore through a city twice the density of pre-Haussmann Paris to devastating effect.[20] All of this history is probably lost on the 20-year-old study-abroad student who loves the city for its mediterranean climate, walkable streets, and buzzy nightlife, but that's all right, and sort of the point. A city should evolve and transform, always seeking to be better than it was yesterday, and open for whoever takes the helm of it tomorrow. If we had allowed the challenges of poverty, disease, and destitution to overcome our metropolises, the world could hardly have progressed very far. In raising the standard for average quality to a level higher than we could have imagined in the face of our greatest difficulties, we raise the collective spirit of humanity as well.

We can bend the forces of stifling regulation and bureaucracy—the defining features of urban governance today—towards better ends, just as we have in the past, instead of succumbing to the inertia of vested interest that is failing so many of us today. These are far from utopian musings. We can work within the system we've been given, and agitate it towards the best possible outcomes. Our challenges are severe, but not nearly so grevious as 19th-century London, Paris, and Barcelona, or early-20th-century New York. We've created exceptionally good foundations in the States from scratch before, as in James Ogelthorpe's Savannah. It can be done again. We've produced an abundance of common housing within strict boundaries before, that are so beloved today that they've become some of the most expensive places in the country, like Brownstone Brooklyn, Trinity Philadelphia, or Victorian San Francisco. It can be done again.

We need a structural revolution in how and where we build. An Optimism that defaults to saying "yes" in the service of abundance, affordability, beauty, self-determination, and common sense. A structural reform that replaces documents thousands of pages long that are designed to stymie any level of change without a coterie of lawyers, with an easy-to-follow framework that brings artistry, eccentricity, and pride back to the built environment. A system whose barriers to entry are lowered to such an extent that non-technical, non-built environment professionals can take part in shaping the world around them, as opposed to only the most well resourced and connected who act upon it today.

I must reiterate this point: this is not inherently an aesthetic argument, as foundations care little for the design of the buildings that rise above them. San Miguel de Allende, Algiers, and Bangkok are all very different looking. Foundationally, though, they're actually quite similar. Narrow streets wind to places that reveal few of their secrets at first blush, but are so gravitationally compelling that they induce travelers to venture in and find out. Central squares all play host to civic events, grand celebrations, and markets. People who hold vastly different beliefs all attend gathering places where they commune in prayer with their neighbors, with whom they walk to eat food with afterwards in cafes serving varying cuisines, but cooked with similar ingredients. These cities might not look the same, but they are very similar. No single architectural school will ever reign supreme (nor should it), but with the right urban form, this matters little. We must allow people to go out and decide what is best for their own community, and run with it. I suspect we'll be amazed at what they'll do when they're allowed to do it, but shouldn't be surprised when the foundations bear strong resemblances.

Part Two
Optimism in Action

7.

How to Create Better Communities

With the right foundations in place, an eagerness to solve the problems of our day, and an interest in making the world just a little bit more lovely, anyone can leverage Optimism in their own backyards. You don't have to be the mastermind behind a mega development, have millions of dollars at your disposal, or be friends with the mayor to do something meaningful. The fight against the tides of placelessness, commoditization, and sterility can begin at quite a small scale. Plant a tree. Paint your door a playful color. Put some tiles on the facade of a building or along a walkway. These small interventions accumulate into something far bigger than themselves, and spur on ever more projects. You can put this book down now and make your neighborhood better almost immediately, at very little cost. I'd appreciate it if you kept reading on and did those things afterwards, though. It'll be worth it. Promise.

For those who want to improve their community by creating buildings, or are curious how one would even begin to go about this, don't worry, it's been done hundreds of millions of times before. Though it's quite a bit different than simply grabbing a can of paint, and even for modest buildings no small amount of money is required, the process is one that nearly anyone can take on, whether on their own, or among a group of friends and partners.

With the qualifier that for any project, a competent roster of tradespeople and consultants will need to be hired to carry out much of the work, where does one start? Presuming you have a plot of land you'd like to build on (this is the first step—if you don't have one, it's sort of an important piece of the puzzle), creating a good place begins with an idea. What type of structure would you like to create? A home? A candy shop? A data center? Perhaps a gallery with studios above for creatives to work out of? The structure will be driven by whatever predominant use is, so it's important to know what you'd like to build. All good buildings have a certain degree of adaptability, of course, but in order to create the most beautiful and functional space possible, a set idea is probably best.

To create the finest version of what you'd like to build, a great next step is to look at the world around you. Keen observation is the greatest skill any world shaper can have. To create the best places anew, we must study the best places of old, intimately and obsessively. Only through deep study can worthy projects be rendered easy to understand by those who haven't undergone rigorous analyses. Where do people like to hang out? Where do they stay away from? What sort of buildings do they like? Which ones do they hate? What materials are the popular buildings clad in? How far are their windows spaced out? Are there any crowning features on the tops of those structures? We must design how people actually live, and shape the world after them. We cannot be too proud to ask what the general populace likes or wants. We need to listen to people, not lecture them.

What does this tangibly look like? Finding that first bit of inspiration can be hard. There exists an almost infinite amount of design choices one can make, such that it can induce paralysis in coming to any decision. But take a step back. What do some of your favorite places look like? Are there elements you can incorporate from them into your own project? Could you copy it entirely? If you're having serious house envy from somewhere you saw online, why not take full inspiration from the design? After all, that's in keeping with the spirit of one of the most sacred laws of both art and city building: good artists copy, great artists steal.

Good Artists Copy, Great Artists Steal

Contrary to what some might think, copying (or taking generous inspiration from) isn't something to be looked down upon. It's sort of what we've always done. Before the advent of architectural publications, social media, and the ability to share designs from around the world in an instant, the only references most people had for other buildings were what their neighbors had built. So they did the same thing as them. Even for those who saw more of the world through trade or proselytization, their ability to bring back design inspiration from their travels was constrained by local materials and the technologies available to them. Limestone, ubiquitous in the Levant, couldn't easily be transported to northern Prussia, for example. Clay was more abundant there, and so brick structures were the default. Even if more exotic materials were employed, construction laborers would still be of a distinctly local nature who only knew how to build in accordance to a regional vernacular, making the buildings of an age look more or less the same.

Over thousands of years of accumulated knowledge, moreover, societies learned which building types worked best in which climates. Trades and craftspeople mastered particular ways of building based on their contexts. A mason in 1st century BC Rome developed a different set of skills than a mason in 17th century AD Beijing. In very hot, cloudless areas, builders learned that structures should be sited closer together to provide more shade. Structures shouldn't face southwards in such places, but rather should be sheltered away from the sun. Specific colors and materials worked better than others, like whitewashed lime plaster or light paint, to minimize solar absorption. Regions with a lot of snowfall or rainfall might have buildings with pitched roofs. Not to look pretty (though they often do), but so that water and snow could be more easily shed off of the structure, as opposed to pooling on a horizontal plane which might buckle under the weight. Grass on roofs in places like the Faroe Islands and Iceland provide natural insulation, keeping homes cooler in the summer and warmer in the winter. Copying wasn't a faux pas, in cases like this, but an imperative.

Over time, these lessons, ways of building, and local values come together to form a vernacular, the local language of a place. Importantly, a vernacular is not static, but evolves over time, making room for ideas that are good enough to weave themselves into the language and improve it. This is the basis for how we have historically designed and built things around the world.

Embracing regional vernaculars as building templates doesn't mean we shouldn't test out new ideas or try to do cool and interesting things. Many fantastic contemporary projects have been built, and more are being imagined every day. But if new ideas don't work, we shouldn't stubbornly stick with them hoping that one day they might. The Dutch architect Mieke Bosse has articulated this idea succinctly and beautifully: "Tradition is the sum of successful innovations."[1] When something is good, we add it to our canon of knowledge. I for one am glad that running water, air conditioning, and insulation are now broadly used, while asbestos, lead paint, and flammable materials have broadly been rejected. Similarly, buildings that don't respond to a local climate, or that make people feel uneasy or sad near them, should be rejected. Down with the Robarts Library at the University of Toronto, that wicked monolith! Encouragement to Craig Race and his quirky homes, strange and different, yet absolutely alluring.

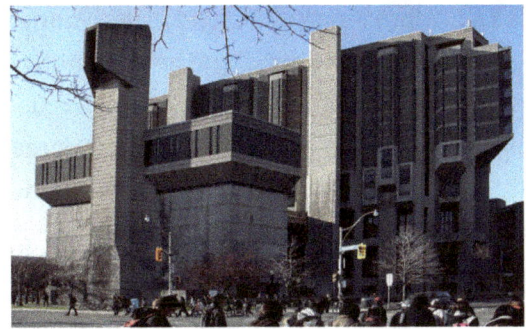

John P. Robarts Research Library (left). Completed in 1973. Race Residence II designed by Craig Race Architecture (right). Completed in 2017.

Traditional homes in select neighborhoods around the country have appreciated considerably in value in recent years. So much so that some have become convinced that these buildings are inherently more expensive than the McMansions and ranch-style homes that dominate modern subdivisions. Much of traditional architecture and urbanism, however, was relatively inexpensive to construct. What we perceive as expensive today historically comprised a meaningful amount of the middle and working class housing stock. The only reason some associate traditional neighborhoods as being unattainable is simply because they're in high demand, and short supply.

Take Brooklyn as an example. In 1840, 47,000 people lived in the borough. By 1900, this number had grown nearly 25 times, to 1.16 million.[2] By the outbreak of World War II, Brooklyn more than doubled its population again, to 2.7 million people. To accommodate all of this growth, the borough had to build a lot of housing, very quickly. The easiest way to do this was through rapid standardization, building as many homes as similarly as possible. Then as now, this allowed builders to leverage economies of scale to drive down pricing. It's like going to a Costco to buy croissants by the pound instead of *le petit boulangerie* down the block. When you buy in bulk, the relative cost per unit drops significantly.

William H. Reynolds knew this game well. Enterprising, young, and brash, Reynolds began his real estate development career buying land and building homes throughout Brooklyn in his late teens, growing to some prominence by his mid-twenties.[3] Acquiring large tracts and subdividing them into dozens, and ultimately hundreds of homes, he built quickly and cheaply, selling to the middle classes who were leaving Manhattan, or emigrating from overseas. Reynolds worked with respected architects of the day like Benjamin Driesler, Axel Hedman, and Magnus Dahlander to create a lookbook for his buildings with a set selection of design elements.[4] While few of the homes were identical, they broadly rhymed with one another because the list of decorative options only went so far. This strategy wasn't too dissimilar from what fast casual food chains do today, where there are many potential iterations of what your lunch can be from a set group of choices. You can get as creative as you want, but in the end, you'll still unmistakably be eating Chipotle. You might end up with a different bowl than the one your friend got, but there will be similarities enough if you both decide you'd like to have cheese and pico de gallo. Similarly, Reynold's buildings might have been Romanesque or Renaissance revival (the bowl, in this analogy), with a choice of roughly hewn stone, string courses, carved panels, reliefs, capitals and keystones, pilasters, round-arched windows, or cornices with dentils (the toppings). With a high-quality urban fabric and with fine-grained 25 by 100 foot lots tree-lined streets as the foundations, eminently handsome blocks could be built swiftly and at scale via bulk pricing discounts.

The process was no secret. Reynolds boasted publicly about it in newspapers, explaining how he could sell lovely houses for the equivalent of as little as $150,000 in 2023 dollars.[5] He purchased bricks by the million and kept a large labor force constantly busy, which allowed him to pay them a salary as opposed to the pricier option of contracting them out per each building. Reynolds bought land when it was low (as little as $5,000 in 2023 dollars a

HOW TO CREATE BETTER COMMUNITIES 255

An 1899 Brooklyn Daily Eagle ad for homes developed by William H. Reynolds in Borough Park, Brooklyn.

subdivided lot), built hundreds of homes at once, and paid cash for everything. *Everything.* Bluster aside, one can't say this wasn't a compelling pitch. And who could argue with the prices?

Though he rhetorically asked if anyone could compete with him, there were in fact dozens of similar builders throughout New York's boroughs who could. Eli Bishop, W.A.A. Brown, and Walter F. Clayton were only just a few. These small and medium-sized builders copied and pasted designs from one street to another, erecting nearly identical rows just a few blocks apart. Under this system of building, New York was able to absorb millions of people across many different housing typologies, from small townhomes to midrise apartment buildings. Ultimately, by the beginning of the 20th century, high rises serviced by elevators were being constructed with similar degrees of efficiency, if not quite so pervasively.

Grander single family homes of four, five and six bedrooms rented for the equivalent of $750 to $900 a month.[6] Even as late as 1941, stately triplexes were marketed for as little as $200,000 in today's dollars.[7] Land prices alone in the borough today can range from many hundreds of thousands to perhaps several million dollars for an individual lot.

Seeing the original prices for buildings that we now regard as lavish can be a bit disorienting. It doesn't need to be this way, however. When housing is viewed more as a product to be standardized and less like a scarce investment that needs its value to be maintained, prices will normalize. You may still be unconvinced. New York is New York and it's always been expensive. Surely building somewhere like New York is inherently pricier than some tract suburb today. Perhaps. But this theory wouldn't explain how the same patterns and modes of development were carried out in cities we don't think of as being particularly well off. Streets and neighborhoods in Baltimore, St. Louis, and Cincinnati are among the best North America has to offer. In some cases, far better than what one might find in the most prosperous coastal cities.

As it was in Brooklyn, so too in St. Louis. Cheap, mass-produced housing allowed the city to grow significantly, multiplying nearly 10 times between 1840 (16,500 people) and 1860 (160,800), peaking at 822,000 in the 1930 census. Though many of these homes were designed by architects, more weren't. Baltimore's terraces were most often built as speculative housing for immigrants, by those same communities, who had neither the connections nor the resources to hire the leading architects of the day. But they didn't need them. That's because they had pattern books, collections of architectural drawings of popular house designs (and their associated fixtures) with detailed instructions on how to build them. Plates and drawings in these books detailed the design of buildings, their dimensions, what materials were needed (and how much of them), how to stand the structure up, and how to garnish it with ornamentation afterwards.

Precise (sometimes exhaustively so) instructions allowed anyone to pick up a set of tools and get to work. Titles like Asher Benjamin's *The American Builder's Companion* (1806), Minard Lafever's

Rowhomes in St. Louis, built between 1860 and 1864 by the St. Louis Mutual House Building Company.

The Modern Builder's Guide (1841), and Alexander Jackson Davis and Andrew Jackson Downing's *Victorian Cottage Residences* (1842) were widely read among developers and builders alike, who copied and pasted designs, sometimes with exacting fidelity, other times merely as a foundation to jump off of.[8] These books were massively influential, sometimes giving rise and prominence to entirely new schools of design. Now inseparably associated with British vernacular, Georgian architecture relied heavily on the dissemination of pattern books, with thousands of publications sharing how best to construct the ideal home of the day.[9] Two of the world's most beautiful cities, Edinburgh and Bath, are quintessentially Georgian, with many of their most beloved neighborhoods taken directly out of the pages of pattern books. Though we marvel at James Craig's elegant plan for Edinurgh's New Town, and the magnificence of the now not-so-new neighborhood, we need not wonder how we might recreate a place so wonderful. We have the exact specifications to do so. Our favorite places weren't created by geniuses, but everyday people with strong discipline to stick to a set of instructions.

By the beginning of the 20th century, a middle-class professional could select their preferred plan from a catalog, have factory-cut materials delivered directly to their property, and be living in their new home 90 days later. These "kit houses" popularized iconic styles like Craftsmen and Cape Cod homes, though hundreds of manufacturers offered an equally high number of other styles that could be chosen from. 100,000 were built via catalog from 1908 to 1940, with prices for the plans and materials as low as $20,000 (2023 dollars), and sizes ranging from 750 square feet to a few thousand.[10] Many of these homes remain today. Built to a robust standard with charming design, they're arguably more desired now than when they were first produced.

But builders weren't limited to simple cottages and townhomes. Pattern books included plans for grand country estates and prominent cultural sites like churches and city halls. This was no modern innovation. Vitruvius set forth this precedent in *Ten Books on Architecture* (1st Century BC), standardizing the planning and construction of military camps and towns throughout the Roman Empire. Relying on the Classical orders, he delineated just how columns, entrance ways, and even siege machines should best be designed so as to lend strength, utility, and beauty.[11]

Andrea Palladio's *Four Books of Architecture* (1570) were critical in defining American architecture, and, by extension, the idea of America itself. Thomas Jefferson was profoundly influenced by the Italian master, referring to Paladdio's work as his "architectural bible".[12] He believed classical architecture could be used to legitimize the idea of the American Republic as a direct descendent and successor of the Roman Republic. Jefferson's personal designs, most notably his residence at Monticello and The University of Virginia, borrowed heavily from Palladian concepts. And in James Gibbs' *A Book of Architecture* (1728), templates were provided for aristocratic estates, prominent homes, and civic buildings across the Anglosphere.[13]

Where costs have risen to several million dollars today in some cities for pattern book homes, in St. Louis, row homes can still be bought for less than $100,000. Even large homes in sought-after neighborhoods rarely surpass $500,000 in value, while veritable palaces can be bought for around $2 million.[14]

Were St. Louis' streets to be transplanted completely into Boston or New York, the price for homes would surely be worth ten times that much or more. In Philly or Richmond, these properties might be worth three to five times as much. That's because what makes these properties expensive is not the building itself, but the land value, which is far higher in larger, more prosperous cities.

San Francisco is an excellent case study of much of what has been discussed so far. Individual examples of its vernacular of mass-produced housing—the Victorian—now regularly sell in the millions of dollars due to high land costs. The decorated elements we now appreciate in Victorians are veneers, cheap ornaments slapped on facades to lend the illusion of extravagance, catering to middle class tastes. Professor Richard Walker of Berkeley explains: "Victorian architecture was not one style, but a hodgepodge of historic references to Gothic, Italian, Dutch, Egyptian and Arab pasts, which home-buyers dipped into as suited their taste. Houses of that time are nothing if not a playful pastiche of decorative bric-a-brac. Streetfront variation came from personalized facades, oddities of lot sizes, and the small scale of building; a vigorous degree of freedom was possible within an otherwise rigid system of building. Victorian houses are all surface, however: the house is a simple upright box onto which are pasted all the gewgaws the buyer wished. These were thoroughly modern, mass-production houses, built with standard floor plans, industrially cut wood, standard balloon-frames, pattern-book blueprints, and machine-turned pieces selected from catalogues."[15]

Even when taking the increased wages of labor into consideration, the cost of housing is primarily downstream of land prices. Few of the structures profiled in this section were very expensive to build. An observation which I hope will harden into a lesson: building better structures isn't principally about construction cost—though it's important—but rather mitigating land prices. To understand why, let's take a deeper dive into a few case studies.

Creating Better Places Isn't About Cost

Graceful wood sided homes adjoin one another wearing all colors of the visible light spectrum proudly. With modest sconces, trim around the windows, and a surprising-but-not-unwelcome inclusion of brackets, they stand together as a quaint representation of the best of American city-building. Built for less than $200,000 in 2023 dollars, their inexpensive construction cost has not cheapened their integrity in the years since their completion. Are these another series of 19th-century row homes in Baltimore? Or perhaps a set of kit homes from 1916 huddled together in a leafy neighborhood of Seattle? Not quite. They're a part of a (relatively) newly completed neighborhood in a deindustrialized part of West Virginia.

Historic North Wheeling and Wheeling Heights in the city of Wheeling share 150 homes between them, funded by a HUD Hope VI grant in 1999.[16] Designed by Urban Design Associates of Pittsburgh, the developments were completed in 2002 and 2004 for around $17 million.[17] A mix of public, Affordable, and market rate housing, they rose on the sites of the Lincoln Homes and Grandview Manor, housing complexes in various stages of disrepair after years of mismanagement. In this forgotten pocket of the world, a fundamentally good place was created. More than a good

HOW TO CREATE BETTER COMMUNITIES 261

Historic North Wheeling Affordable Housing in Wheeling, WV. Designed by UDA. Completed in 2002.

place—one of the more lovely housing projects that has been built in the 21st century. Painfully simple, but resting on good foundations. Who could have imagined something like this would be possible in Wheeling, West Virginia, of all places?

Well, it is West Virginia, that's why the costs were so cheap, the skeptical reader might be tempted to think. Though this isn't the case, other references are merited to bolster the argument. So to the expensive coasts we go to explore two projects: one utterly simple—a great piece of urban fabric that provides for essential community needs—the other, pure luxury that proves craftsmanship is not inherently pricey.

Kevin Cavenaugh is not your typical real estate developer. After graduating from architecture school at Berkeley, he spent time in the Peace Corps in Gabon before returning to the U.S. (with a Gabonese dog) for a new adventure.[18] First acquiring a modest house in Northeast Portland for $16,000 in the early '90s, Cavenaugh has made a name for himself and his company (Guerrilla Development) in the Rose City by creating successively more whimsical and inventive projects. Names match the eccentricity of the designs. There's "Dr Jim's Still Really Nice", an early-1900s vintage Standard Dairy building that was redeveloped to house four apartments inside the unassuming structure by cutting a courtyard into the middle of it, and hanging swings on the exposed wooden trusses. "The Fair-Haired Dumbbell" is a 56,000 square foot speculative office building consisting of two canted six-story towers connected in the middle by a sky bridge. Vibrant and abstract original artwork adorns a facade that wouldn't be out of place in the notebook of an imaginative tenth grader's least favorite, and most boring, class.

"Jolene's First Cousin", as you might by now expect, is not a person, but rather a mixed-use apartment building in the city's Creston-Kenilworth neighborhood. Designed by Brett Schultz, the project features 13 apartments and three retail units. It was completed in 2020. 11 of the apartments are designated as Single-Room Occupancies (SROs) for formerly homeless individuals. This is real estate with a profound social impact and tangible community benefit. While it could hardly be mistaken for a palace, it's a beguiling little project. Situated on a corner lot, the colorful siding (made of

HOW TO CREATE BETTER COMMUNITIES   263

Jolene's First Cousin in Portland, OR. Designed by Brett Schulz, developed by Guerrilla Development. Completed in 2020.

fiber cement panels) is punctuated by large glass openings trimmed in wood, presided over by local merchants.

The total bill for the project was $2.2 million. Excluding land, it cost $1.62 million.[19] On a per square foot (psf) basis, this is a very reasonable $334, of which just $246 psf were attributable to construction costs. To put these numbers into perspective, all in, each unit cost just $137,500. Low construction prices have supported Cavenaugh's social mission—units rents for just $425 each.

Make no mistake, this project required great discipline and effort to deliver the results that it did. Cavenaugh had to get creative with how he financed the project, planned it, and found partners to occupy it, "soliciting online investments of as little as $3,000 ... 'to allow a librarian or a mechanic to invest in my buildings with me, not just a high-net-worth individual.'" An impressive degree of resolve was required—resolve that left a lot of money on the table. It would have been far easier to ignore the social needs of the community, deliver an uninspired box, and raise money from traditional limited partners who would have required above market returns, and likely taken much of the spirit out of the building. Instead, Cavenaugh bucked the status quo, gracing the neighborhood with charming buildings that meaningfully support those in need. Soul is abundant despite the project's simplicity. We can be optimistic that good things are indeed possible where vision and determination are enabled by land use regulations, if not outright supported.

On the other end of the spectrum of inexpensive housing costs, and on the other coast, we have $4-million luxury townhomes in New York.[20] Before you get your pitchforks out, allow me to explain! Fairfax & Sammons designed this infill row of eight townhomes on State Street in Downtown Brooklyn. They were developed by Strategic Development and Construction Corp. A quote from Richard Sammons (the eponymous Sammons of Fairfax & Sammons) proves insightful: "Unbelievably, this project was done for under $300 per square foot ... It proves that good design can be done on a low budget; the only cost is brain power."[21]

The sub-$300 psf Sammons refers to are the development costs, which aren't considerably higher than the $246 psf in construction

Newly built townhomes on State Street in Downtown Brooklyn. Designed by Fairfax & Sammons. Completed in 2013.

costs at Jolene's First Cousin. And this is despite the many superfluous regulations in New York which drive up prices. At first blush, this is a bit shocking. What explains the difference between a $425 rental and a $4-million townhome if the costs per square foot aren't too far apart? Part of the reason is the return threshold. Cavenaugh's investors only received 5% returns in Portland, not unlike Alfred Tredway White's philanthropy and 5% model that was explored in Chapter 1. As the data is private, it's difficult to know what the returns were on State Street for the sponsors of Fairfax & Sammons' townhomes, but it was likely a few multiples of this. Lower return thresholds allow for more flexibility in pricing as there's a lower bar to clear for returning capital to investors, but a rare sort of investor who will willingly accept lower returns is required.

Another reason for the variance in costs is the size of the Brooklyn homes. They're big, ranging from 3,400 to 3,800 square feet. On the larger end, this means that the development costs were just over $1.1 million per home—no small sum. This is lavish by any standard, but especially when compared to early American tract townhome developments, like Philadelphia's modest townhomes that seldom reached 1,500 square feet at the larger end.

Land is the largest determinant here, however. As there were several transactions between related parties in the years leading up to development, it's a little tricky to get a definitive answer on acquisition cost, so we must tread carefully. We do know, however, that the mortgage for the land on State Street was $8.45 million.[22] At ~9,500 square feet, or less than a quarter of an acre, the land cost nearly $900 per square foot. That's an extraordinary amount for eight homes. An amount that doesn't even factor in the interest payments owed on the loan. For perspective, Cavenaugh paid just $523,000 for his land, or $105 psf, 1/9th of the cost of the Brooklyn townhomes.

At 17,913 built square feet, the total development cost was ~$5.3 million. With the mortgaged land and holding fees considered, this project likely cost somewhere in the $14 million range. Spread across eight homes, this averages out to $1.75 million per unit—not exactly cheap. If we were to strip out the land cost for a second, the units would only cost ~$660,000 per door—much more reasonable, but still pricey. Let's go a layer deeper.

If this row were built exactly the same but inwardly were broken up to allow for several smaller, discrete units on each floor of equal unit mix and access to light, 20 condos could easily be accommodated at the following breakdown: 750 square feet for a one-bedroom and perhaps 1,000 sf for a two-bedroom. At 20 homes, the total costs of construction would drop to ~$265,000 per unit. Of course, we can't strip away land cost, which can only be modulated by allowing more density, but this example is illustrative in proving that exceptional quality of design isn't the driving force in price. If we can bend the conditions of programs designed by world renowned firms towards affordable ends, it cannot be argued that design is incompatible with accessibility.

It must be reiterated that these projects, along with nearly every real estate development project, are bound to the constraints of targeted returns required from limited partners. Not all developments can be as noble or as uniquely financed as Jolene's First Cousin. Guerrilla had to filter its way through an ocean's worth of interest in order to distill a capital stack that supported their vision. But there were a sufficient number of investors willing to support the novelty of Cavenaugh and Schultz's vision to get the project built. Now that it is a proven success, future capital raises for similar schemes should prove much easier.

Good design, whether simple or elaborate, is not the reason why our places have gotten more expensive. In fact, much of what fundamentally appeals to us doesn't cost all that much. There seems to be a national confusion that misattributes what is good for what is expensive—a market signal for taste. Nothing could be further from the truth. A slice of pizza can be delicious whether or not it's topped with $2,000 worth of gold leaf and caviar. In many cases, such superfluousness detracts from the foundational perfection that is baked bread, sauce, and cheese. As with pizza, so with buildings. Marble columns, soaring windows, and stone gargoyles may improve a building, but if the underlying structure is no good, these elements are worse than lipstick on a pig. At least a pig wearing lipstick is cute, and thus confers some utility in our enjoyment at seeing it. Not so with gaudy ornamentation. And yet this belief in expense-as-inherently-good persists in ignorance and defiance of good reason. Some of the best places consist of almost offensively simple structures, like Florence, where stucco rectangular boxes line narrow and well-enclosed streets. Hardly any ornamentation adorns their facades beyond a few shutters around the windows and tiled eaves crowning the box. Some Florentine structures, over time, may have gained rusticated bases and bas-relief, but these were built after solid foundations had already been established. Besides, many sumptuous finishes are not as luxurious as they might seem. August-looking building elements often deceive us into believing they're stone when in reality they're scored stucco.

The key determinant to nearly any home's cost in an expensive city is the land, not the building itself. Go look at the assessments for homes in wealthy communities or unaffordable cities. The land is often worth more than the improvements, and significantly so. High land costs are a function of high demand that's not properly addressed. Often the value is artificially inflated through a suppression of zoning (like a limited edition art print). While the price of land wouldn't become cheaper if one were able to add more units to a lot—in fact, it would increase—the relative cost of the homes on top of it would. If only one home were allowed on a $10,000,000 lot, for example, the relative land basis per unit would be $10,000,000. Very pricey. But if 200 homes were allowed on that lot, the relative land basis would be $50,000 per unit. Not so bad! This math matters.

When enough density is allowed throughout an entire city, prices will stabilize. This requires a reshaping of how North American cities might look. Instead of towers packed with as many homes as possible in a concentrated core to offset high land costs brought about by a restriction of building elsewhere, a gentle density can permeate neighborhoods extending well beyond downtown, where apartment buildings need only rise three to seven stories. Far shorter than skyscrapers, but importantly, more dense than prevailing development patterns of single family homes on large lots. Manhattan or Hong Kong these neighborhoods would not become, no matter how forcefully fear mongering opponents might try to argue. Mostly, these neighborhoods will become home to more townhomes and walk-up apartments, with some apartment buildings taller than seven stories sprinkled in, but only in the most expensive or transit accessible areas. Public officials have a responsibility to respond to the intensity demanded by a given market, not preserve the home values for a subset of the population.

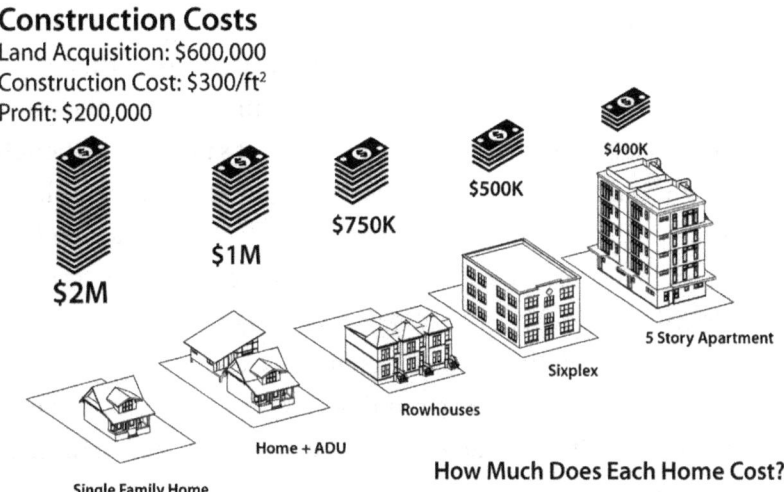

Construction Costs
Land Acquisition: $600,000
Construction Cost: $300/ft²
Profit: $200,000

Diagram illustrating how building more homes on a lot reduces a unit's relative land cost. Courtesy of Ryan DiRaimo.

Creating good and affordable places requires the cooperation of planners and developers. Planners must lay out the right foundation for communities, and be willing to be responsive to the demands of a market. Developers, for their part, must give a damn about the communities they're building! This, admittedly, is tough to legislate, but we need not be so prescriptive. In city after city, and neighborhood after neighborhood, the most expensive places are those with the best design. If we simply allow for more neighborhoods like those we venerate, the price of good design would drop because it wouldn't be so scarce, allowing more people to experience it.

Under this new foundational paradigm, there's no excuse for developers who build subdivisions on cheap land to not deliver attractive projects. The most expensive part of the project is effectively mitigated. If a development is still a homogenous morass of sprawling lots, wide roads, and poor design, it cannot be dismissed as one's "preference", but rather a laziness subjected upon those who are looking for reasonably priced housing and space enough for them and their families.

There exists, I believe, another reason beyond costs or codes why our places are less beautiful than they used to be. Unsatisfying, and perhaps a bit dispiriting, it is the underlying ethos that courses through modern building practices. It's not greed. Though this might play a part in our scarcity of good places, I think it's marginal. Value engineering, the process of cutting back embellishments in a construction project to the bare minimum, is often blamed for the banality of contemporary design. But it occurs later in the development process, after plans have already been submitted. Value engineering takes plans that were already bad and makes them worse, but it's not the reason those plans were bad in the first place. Besides, there's a pretty direct correlation between the quality/beauty of a place and the returns it yields. If developers were so greedy, they'd be building the most audacious places in search of the highest yield. Instead, they opt for a lesser route.

No, it's not necessarily greed that compromises our building culture, but systemic laziness. It is a lack of thoughtfulness, and perhaps no small degree of fatalism, that has led us to our diminished state. Combatting this isn't a matter of spending more money, but rethinking (and thinking generally, a paradigm shift in its own right) about how our places should be shaped.

Perhaps the most important driver of this disease of thoughtlessness is who's building our places today. While in the past our communities were shepherded by craftsmen, artists, designers, proud community members, and developer entrepreneurs who valued the creation of proud structures in their own backyards (and had the freedom to do so), that's not the case today. As explored in Chapter 5, most new development is carried out by institutionally backed firms who care little about the street-level impact their projects have. These firms tend to be out-of-towners who have little stake or vested interest in the neighborhoods they build in beyond their stabilization cycle. So long as the economics work and the units are occupied, the project is deemed successful. Any qualitative impact it may potentially have is deemed superfluous, or not considered at all. Or worse, and unfortunately more and more common, the language of good design is laundered in an attempt to pull the wool over the general public's eyes, where a generic building is given fawning treatment; *Experience the paragon of design on Broadway,* marketing strains to seduce us. Cheap advertising can only go so far, however. Passersby can see that whatever box has risen on Broadway is very much not the paragon of anything, least of which design.

I don't say this in jest or animosity. But the honest truth is that these aren't the best place makers we have. Combine this with the fact that those overseeing development in the public realm are hamstrung by decades of codified rigidity and it's little wonder our world looks the way it does.

While economies of scale are partly to blame for yielding the uninspired structures that dot our landscape, mass produced housing can still be of exceptional design quality as we saw in the last section. The bulk of the issue comes from those who direct the design, and the limitations imposed on them. While architects may refine and execute a given project, developers drive the process, setting forth the vision of what a building should be, based on the ground rules of zoning and land use regulations. Architects, as they'll be loath to tell you, are contractors subject to their client's desires. If a developer doesn't agitate for better design or, more often, explicitly expresses a need for efficiency without embellishment, the lowest common denominator reigns supreme. This has become the default. Being 10% more thoughtful on design, to pick an arbitrary number, doesn't cost any more money, maybe just an extra meeting or two with an architect or consultant. But to do that, one must be interested in design in the first place. That's not happening.

This is because the kind of people who are interested in creating thoughtful, attractive projects don't typically find themselves in the rooms where the vast majority of our places are created. These folks don't operate in many-screened open-floor-plan bullpens wearing formal workwear (or increasingly ever-so-generously allowed by these institutions, business casual), guiding institutionally scaled development. That tends to be the purview of number-crunching efficiency hawks, who don't think much of the qualitative aspects of real estate development beyond whether a building should have a gym, rooftop deck, or "game room", whatever that means. Very little consideration is given to how buildings meet the street and interact with their neighborhoods.

The *shrugging of shoulders, temporarily raising palms upwards, pursing lips downward, and errant escape of "eh" from one's vocal cords* that accompanies design decisions at institutional firms doesn't leave much room for thoughtfulness. If one one's keyboard strokes might have on Nashville or Boise is both unknown and uncared for. In short, the people driving much of American development are indifferent to the impact their projects have on communities.

Let's say, though, that through a stroke of remarkable luck or administrative oversight, a smaller developer who cares deeply about the quality of the built environment has secured land, sailed through entitlements, and is gearing up for construction. What then? Presumably, they should be able to move forward quite easily? Unfortunately, no.

Typically, around 60–70% of the funding for the construction portion of a market-rate development project is financed by banks. They're notoriously difficult to work with. Motivated by a series of imperatives not dissimilar to those of institutional equity explored in Chapter 5, banks also must hold some blame for the quality of our built environment. When one entity controls such a high proportion of the capital stack, it holds a lot of influence over what ultimately gets built. Not only do the developers who propose a project have to be thoughtful, but so too do their financiers. Lenders are risk-averse, de rigeur. If they think a project is too bold to be accepted, or deviates too materially from the status quo, a loan proposal could be shot down, preventing the project from moving forward. Same goes for the quality of the developer herself: if she doesn't have the right track record, or doesn't have enough capital to backstop the loan (with dreaded personal guarantees), she will be summarily dismissed. How is a small developer ever expected to get started with these hurdles?

None of these lending protocols are necessarily about costs at the outset. But they soon factor in. Every provision a bank requires adds expense to a project. Provisions that may not be required by a locality, but which loan committees mandate in order to take certain risks off the table. In a remarkable display of self-defeat, idiosyncrasies are waived away as unnecessary risks instead of being recognized as the most salient aspects of a project. The craft of building is ground down into a risk-averse assembly line, inhibiting intervention from artful, non-industrialized contributors. It is an eminently rational process that's been taken to its most logical extremes.

Even Le Corbusier, the 20th century's great hyper-rationalist, rejected the idea that costs or technology had anything to do with not being able to build well in the modern era; "Do we not possess the means? Louis XIV made do with picks and shovels ... Haussmann's equipment was also meagre; the shovel, the pick, the wagon, the trowel, the wheelbarrow, the simple tools of every race before the mechanical age."[23] If Paris could be built so excellently via simple means, all the technology we possess today should be able to deliver us places of at least comparable wonder, if not greater. If only we set our minds to it. Haussmann set his mind quite succinctly, and the fruits of his motivations are readily available for all to feast upon: "I venerate the Beautiful, the Good, and all things great; Beautiful nature, on which great art rests—How it enchants the ear and charms the eye!"[24]

Building better doesn't cost more money. It merely requires stakeholders to think critically about what they're building. This may require tactically spending dollars in some places (glazed, higher-quality bricks with terracotta ornamentation on the front of a structure, and cheaper bricks or vinyl without detailing on the sides and back, as one example), or making the overall design simpler, yet still elegant. It will require spending a little more time, and a little more brain power, but this mental exertion and inter-party cooperation is worth more than its weight in gold.

Through embracing an Optimistic philosophy, developers would be motivated out of their laziness for two reasons: principally (one hopes), their pride would impel them to create something that they can find satisfaction in, and which their end users can have affection for. Second (and more likely to be the driving force in the U.S.), other developers who embrace Optimism will sell their homes, and lease their apartments, offices, storefronts, and warehouses for more money than the status quoists. Competition to create the best-quality structures should be encouraged, and is conspicuously missing from contemporary city-building practices.

8.

What Better Communities Look Like (and What They Do Not Look Like)

If creating better places isn't about cost, but standardizing development on top of high-quality foundations to unlock creativity, what other elements should be layered on top of those footings? And how should they be composed? After all, a city is more than just its housing, which has consumed most of the pages pace of the book thus far.

If there's nothing for someone to do, or nowhere for them to work in an area, why would they live there? Especially at a time when technology has liberated us from spending the duration of our lives where we were born. If one doesn't like where they live, and is in a position to do something about it, they can simply drive, train, boat, or fly to a place that's more appealing to them. Communities who have suffered from brain drain (where talented residents move away to seek opportunities elsewhere) and deindustrialization (where a lack of jobs forces people to move away even if they might not have otherwise) have unfortunately known this painful truth for some time.

What do successful places do to garner our affections? A little bit of everything, so that there's something for everyone. The best ones have institutions that ensure a steady supply of new life and ideas. They are magnets that attract and retain. Students matriculate into universities every year. Museums host rotating exhibits that compel with new perspectives, and safeguard cherished treasures. Cultural organizations and philanthropies nurture, and sustain, the soft tissue of community. Institutions are often expressly committed to a city in a way that employers and transients are not, and perhaps cannot be. Patrons with emotional attachments to a city—whether because it was the place of their birth or adolescence, where they went to college, where they fell in love, or where they became acquainted with rapture on some other terms—are an institution unto themselves. They endow fruits of the sweetest variety. Whether they come from little or great means, their contributions are definitionally of the community, and thus carry wisdom that outside actors cannot bestow, so manifest which has special local resonance that all can enjoy. One doesn't need to be from Florence to appreciate the works of Da Vinci, Michelangelo, Brunelleschi, or Botticelli, but it's unlikely that such brilliance would have been without the nurturing support of the Medici.

Places that are deficient of these sorts of things and patrons are not doomed to failure. However, a lack of them does make things harder. A young designer from Paris, France, can more readily imagine themselves creating the next great work of couture, being enmeshed in the capital of fashion as they are, than a similar aspirant from Paris, Idaho. Without institutional support or natural advantage—a magnet in its own right, as people will always seek to live among, or in close proximity, to natural beauty—it's even more imperative for cities to focus on getting every other aspect of city building right. And if these efforts are well-directed, they will compound into forms of unknowable wonder, capable of spawning institutions in their own right.

The best way to start this process is by bringing all productive uses close to one another. If a city's businesses, amenities, and best attributes are far apart, their impacts get diluted by distance. If the shortest path between good things is a mile by car, it's quite hard to use these elements as foundational pieces to build off of. When mixed uses are concentrated next to one another, even with limited resources, a virtuous cycle can begin. If enough people go downtown to get their nails done, perhaps another enterprising resident will open a bakery to serve the post-nail crowd.

If that bakery becomes an attorney's favorite place to take meetings, perhaps she'll lease office space down the block, bringing half a dozen employees with her. Imagine what might happen next? An accountant who works closely with the attorney doesn't like having to shlep back and forth to meetings, so he might decide to lease office space in the same building as her. Our accountant prefers to eat at the Thai restaurant on the other end of the street, though. Seeing that more people are downtown, a developer plans to build a small apartment building for those who'd like to be closer to the action and shorten their commutes. This could serve as a signal for another restaurant to open up, as there are now more people downtown, and securing a coveted table to eat pad see ew at lunch has become near impossible.

The city, long hesitant of investing resources downtown because no one used to go there, might decide to clean up a vacant plot of land. Neighbors could be welcomed to plant flowers and trees in this new park. A local artist might donate a sculpture. The owner of the hardware store might then hang string lights so people can hang out after dark. Moms would doubtless watch their kids run around on the lush lawn in equal parts amazement and horror, as they're still not tired after practicing for two hours at the dance studio down the block. All of this activity would beget more activity, at a higher density than would be possible if all of these things were in different places.

These events don't happen as easily as I've described, of course, but the way this cycle works really isn't too far off. When a community is freed to leverage its positive assets (every community has at least a few), those assets compound. Quality of the assets matters, however. A place with mixed use isn't automatically good. A few apartments over a lawnmower testing center probably doesn't make for the best place to live. Too noisy. Same with a row of gas stations lining a wide avenue with austere office blocks behind them. Too soul-crushing

On the topic of offices, their future will likely look similar to what retail experienced in the 2010s—the best assets will thrive, while the bottom 20-30% will gradually, and unspectacularly, wither to redundancy. This could spell trouble for the health of our cities at large. In December 2023, the U.S. office vacancy rate hit 13.6%, the highest ever recorded—and this number doesn't include "shadow" vacant space that's being paid for but not being used.[1] Low commercial occupancy rates can create a negative domino effect, or doom loop, because of how dearly some municipalities rely on commercial tax dollars to fund their services. 36% of Boston's general revenues come from taxes on commercial properties.[2] If those buildings remain vacant for a long time, their assessed value will drop, and so too will the taxes their owners have to pay. Boston may need to cut certain programs like after school activities, pensions for public employees, and parks maintenance, in order to balance its budget. Soon, in some cities, empty office buildings, not poison, might be why middle school Romeos and Juliets can't share the stage together. For the first time in modern history, office parks in the suburbs, which have historically been less desirable, have seen their vacancy rate equal that of buildings in central business districts (CBDs).[3]

There are two issues at play here. First, convenience. The rise in remote work is one of the most significant transformations in the way we've orientated our societies since at least the Industrial Revolution. Though I'm sure most of you reading this will be tired of hearing about the impact remote work has had or will have, it's worth reiterating. A broad class of workers are untethered from where they work for the first time in human history. Never before can so many people derive their livelihoods in a place separate from the one they spend most of their time in, and certainly not so efficiently. It's true that there's always been remote work of some sort for creatives who were unaccountable to bosses, or a privileged few who had the ability to delegate their tasks to others. The leisurely aristocrat earning an income off of his lands comes to mind. But it was rather demographically limited. Not anymore. This will have immense, though untold, consequences on the composition of our societies. For anyone who has endured a multi-hour daily commute in and out of a stressful city center, a five-minute drive to the drab office park might not seem so bad. Even better if the location of remoteness is a trendy cafe or beachside locale. Driving next to bleary-eyed people in traffic or sitting alongside them on trains and buses in the morning, many of whom are dreading going to work themselves and wear it on their faces, doesn't exactly make one want to go to the sorts of places they're headed. Better to opt out, if possible, and only go to the main office when absolutely necessary.

The second issue is optionality. If someone is able to work from anywhere, they gain advantages as a consumer who can decide where they want to work, as opposed to an employee resigned to whatever bloc their company has chosen for them. This is bad news for CBDs that don't offer a compelling user experience. With imposing and anonymous structures rising out of the ground vertiginously, large blank walls that meet the ground floor with seeming disgust and turn their back on the public rights of way, windswept plazas, oppressive parking structures, and sad fast casual chains that reduce meals to a transactional, commodified experience wrapped in sterile corporate branding, CBDs zap the livelihood out of their guests. Workflows in these areas resemble modern assembly lines that reduce one's experience to that of a cog in a machine, depriving humanity and soul. You could be anywhere at all, but nowhere you'd particularly want to be.

Contrast the bleak downtowns of Hartford or Dallas with compelling neighborhood-scale offerings, like Portland's Albina Yard (2016) designed by Lever Architecture in 2016, or Sam Day's Live/Work units in Oklahoma City's Wheeler District (2020). Where large office buildings cloister themselves away from a city, erecting invisible moats that warn passersby of their presumptive passage through inhospitable realms, neighborhood-scale office buildings enmesh themselves in the fabric of a community, considerate of their impact on the street, and complement their neighbors, instead of dominating them. Small office buildings find success through their fine-grained nature—they're rather narrow, so one doesn't have to walk very long to get past a given building. As mentioned in Chapter 4, this provides stimulation for our brains, and an opportunity to quickly move past a facade we don't find particularly engaging. And because they're rarely owned by institutional investors, their owners can take more risks with tenants that provide far more intrigue than, say, a generic salad chain can. Their rents tend to be cheaper, as it's less expensive to construct a three-story walk-up than a 50-story skyscraper, the tax bills are lower, and it's far easier for a tenant to manage 2,000 or 10,000 square feet than many hundreds of thousands. These spaces have proven themselves to be remarkably resilient, not to mention eminently attractive.

The lesson here, then, may perhaps seems counterintuitive, with how poorly offices have been performing: build more of them. But not as we used to. Make them better neighbors, with complimentary amenities and mixed uses, fine-grained, and closer to where people live. And by closer, I mean next door. Or downstairs. There's no logical reason why an office building can't happily exist next to an apartment building, both with shops or cafes on the ground floor. Offices can also fare quite well when they're located on the ground floor, directly engaging with the street. In this way, new

The lovely infill office building Albina Yard in Portland designed by Lever Architecture (left). Completed in 2016. Spoke Street Townhomes, a mixed-use project in Wheeler District, Oklahoma City, designed and developed by Sam Day of Dryline Architecture (right). Completed in 2020.

commercial space will be both convenient and attractive, providing a viable alternative to the drab office parks that are close by and the larger mixed-use (but not totally desirable) CBDs that are further away. In this way, offices can return to being an integral part of a community, and not some sterile, segregated place.

On their own, offices and apartments don't add up to from a proper community. There must be third places where one can spend time when they're not at work or at home. This can be as simple as a McDonald's, a pub, a movie theater, or a gaming cafe, but ideally, one shouldn't have to pay to access public life. Having to spend $7 at a Starbucks just to meet with a friend or be around other people strikes me as dystopian.

Community centers and libraries are two of the best types of third places any city can build, because they're purely public amenities. Anyone can use them and feel as though they're a part of something, which is a core psychological imperative that has gone missing in recent years. This is especially true the more attractive these places is, as it instills a certain pride in all who pass through its threshold. No matter what else might be going on in our lives, for a brief moment, we can feel as though we're a part of something that matters—without needing to pay to feel as though we're worth something. Shabby, austere, and unloved structures confer little of this dignity. The benefits continue. Free public Wi-Fi can allow those who don't have it at home to become full participants in our modern society. Getting a laptop and connecting to Wi-Fi can be a fairly expensive endeavor, but not doing so may preclude someone from pursuing job opportunities, talking with their family, or simply doing the things online that they enjoy, like watching their favorite shows, reading articles, or being a part of an online community that gives them an additional sense of belonging.

As we age, the role of these places becomes even more important. When our abilities diminish, we may no longer be able to drive or make trips to see the people that we'd like to. Instead of being damned to isolation, a good community center or library within walking distance can be a haven for those who suffer from loneliness at an older age—a deadly condition.[4]

With library systems routinely facing budget cuts, threats of closure, and neglect, it can be easy to forget how important these spaces are. We'd be wrong to deprive ourselves of the "palaces for the people", as coined by Andrew Carnegie, who funded more than 2,500 libraries around the world, including 1,700 in the United States.[5] This abundance granted even the smallest of communities, like Loup City, Nebraska (population 1,045 as of 2021) to take advantage of the benefits of third places. A similar program today would be a potent national economic development and mental health initiative.

Of course, people don't only want to spend their time inside. Parks, trails, and gardens are equally important as community assets. By locating them next to public buildings, there's potential

Loup City Township Carnegie Library, Loup City, Nebraska

for an indoor/outdoor interplay where one public asset can augment the other. Every public place should do three things. First, provide clean, safe space. Second, allow for people to come together, whether in large groups, couples, or anywhere in between. There should be ample opportunity for people to choose what they'd like to do—and when they don't want to do anything at all. This extends to individuals who use public realms as settings of repose, reflection, relaxation, and somewhere to get work done. The third goal, often forgotten but absolutely essential, is to raise the spirits of all who pass through. Public spaces should always assume elevated importance, as they are the distillation of an entire people in a single place. If the collective best foot isn't put forward, a message is sent that the community as a whole isn't valued, or doesn't value itself. Only when public spaces are well-maintained, furnished with high-quality urban furniture, and offer spaces for both activity and quiet solace (so that two people in very different moods can enjoy the same space), do they truly live up to their name.

Located in the heart of Northampton, a small college town in western Massachusetts, Pulaski Park is one such asset. As the only

Pulaski Park in Northampton, Massachusetts, designed by Stimson Studio. Completed in 2016.

significant green space in the city, it was important for the design team overseeing the project, Stimson Studio, to deliver a place that could offer a little bit of something for everyone. There are lawns for sunbathers to take in the rays on warm days. Tables and chairs allow people to take their lunch away from the office. String lights illuminate the night so that residents can enjoy a few extra hours outside of the house when it gets darker. Benches are tucked away from the busier parts of the park—perfect for cuddling up with a good book. Smoothly paved paths and ramps offer accessibility to those who might find getting around difficult in other parks. And for those with more energy, boulders, logs, and water features for climbing on and splashing around in are abundant. Importantly, all of these design elements are crisp and nice-looking. This is no trivial thing. Not only do people have room to come together, but the space is somewhere that they'd *want* to come together. Few are in a hurry to leave Pulaski Park.

Contrast this with so many other parks that depress our landscape. Barren. Unloved. Weeds overgrown, grass browned by too much sunlight and not enough water. If benches do exist, they're of the moments-away-from-collapsing-under-the-weight-of-an-average-person-sitting-on-them, chipped-wood variety. These aren't welcoming areas. That's why they're almost always empty! Even if people wanted to spend time there, how could they? There isn't much to do. An open field that only someone equipped with a powerful imagination could make use of is not the right model for producing good public space. Oftentimes, there are scarcely any trees in many of these parks, which is senseless, as planting trees is one of the most cost effective, least time-consuming, and most agreeable things any town or city can do to improve itself.

The benefits include improved air quality, as trees absorb pollutants like carbon dioxide and filter particulate matter. Temperatures are reduced via the shade trees provide over heavily-paved areas, reducing the amount of heat that gets absorbed. Stormwater run-off is mitigated, as is noise pollution. High-frequency sounds are absorbed and blocked by thickets of branches and leaves. We gravitate towards trees; impelled by the pull of biophilia. When we're deprived of greenery, our ailments get augmented. So powerful are their calming and restorative effects that just a few minutes surrounded by trees is enough to bring down elevated blood pressure. In one study of patients recovering from surgery, those who were placed in rooms with views of trees were released from the hospital a full day earlier than those who looked out on brick walls.[6] They also noted they felt less pain as measured by how frequently

Before and after view of a road diet with many new trees planted on Lancaster Boulevard in Lancaster, California.

they asked for pain medication. With findings like this, it's not an overstatement to say that trees are critical infrastructure for mental and physical health. For just a few hundred dollars in upfront costs, and limited supervision thereafter, any place can improve with a couple of saplings. Even the most banal.

Lessons from trees hold true for cities writ large; focus on getting the little things right. Just as humans have a Maslowian order of needs, communities too have their own hierarchies. At the base level, is a city clean, safe, and green? Does it have grocery stores and healthy food options? Reliable public transportation, good educational infrastructure, and strong economic prospects? Is it easy and pleasurable to walk around? Moving up the hierarchy, is it capable of arousing affection? Is it attractive? And finally, at the top of the hierarchy—rarely met in our mortal world—does it inspire a higher form of humanity in its residents and guests? Does its mere existence make us better for having lived and visited there? No city can achieve this feat without an uncompromising and determined pursuit. Even that is often not enough. Gulf metropolises, though shimmering reflections of modernity from afar, irk many upon closer inspection. This is likely because they have sought to begin at the top of the hierarchy, neglecting the foundation which must necessarily support the pinnacle. It is only over time, after doing a lot of small things right, that these little actions can compound and form the base for bigger things. After having been naturally arrived at, they are worthy of our admiration, and capable of captivating our souls. This is Optimism in full force.

But if a city doesn't get its core foundations right, there's little chance, that further efforts will be meaningful or endure, it no matter how hard its stakeholders try, as there's nothing stable to grow out from. What good is an arts district, a luxury casino, or a shiny new convention center if no one wants to visit? Curiously, some places have worked hard to find this answer out for themselves.

No Silver Bullets: The Wrong Way to Build a City

Off exit 38 on the Garden State Parkway, there exists a locale that used to be one of the premier vacation destinations in North America. It had everything: beautiful beaches, luxurious resorts, world-class dining, celebrities, and star-studded shows nearly every night of the week. In the 1930s, more than 16 million people visited a year.[7] Synonymous with boardwalks, gangsters, glamor, and Monopoly, yes, Atlantic City was *the* place everyone wanted to be. Until it wasn't.

After World War II, travel patterns changed. The trains that once shuttled beachgoers from Philadelphia and New York were falling out of fashion. Post-war vacationers opted to drive their new cars to other beaches on Long Island, the Jersey Shore, Cape Cod, or anywhere else they wanted to go that had previously been inaccessible to them via public transportation. At the same time, the parlors of vice that had once made Atlantic City so alluring to those who sought relief through the various illicit pleasures offered were cracked down on. City officials who allowed such debauchery to prevail found themselves a bit too close to the sun. Their convictions in corruption scandals became routine. Police openly conspired with criminals and mobsters. Rock bottom must've looked pretty high up from the depths Atlantic City fell to. It had entered a doom loop, a vicious cycle where the loss of jobs, people, and economic vitality gave way to poverty, crime, and blight, which drove more jobs and people out of the city, leading to more destitution, and so on and so forth.

Looking for a silver bullet to restore it to the golden days, the city turned hard towards legalized gambling. After several tries, a referendum on the cause was ultimately victorious in 1976. And it worked. Sort of. The city's property tax revenues increased from $21 million before the passage of legalized gambling, to $69 million just a few years later in 1981. Spending on schools rose commensurately. 40 years on, Atlantic City spends $41,000 per student per year in its public school system. Triple times the national average, and about double the state average.[8] Funding, it must be mentioned, does not always correlate with success—a lesson for the city writ large. The performance of Atlantic City's schools is still among New Jersey's worst.

The city's public functionaries have also earned failing grades in their stewardship over the windfall. In that worst sort of recurring pattern, Atlantic City's officials couldn't steel themselves against the temptation of redirecting public funds into their private reserves. The first mayor post-legalization was indicted by federal agents for bribery and extortion in connection with the mob. His successor was arrested just a couple of years later, with similar charges (sans mob). But this time, the mayor brought friends. More than a dozen other city officials were indicted in this second sting. In the years since, mayors and public officials have routinely been shamed and brought to justice by both the law and the court of public opinion. Aides have been paid hundreds of thousands of dollars a year for seemingly nothing other than being close with those in power. Kickbacks, tax fraud, bribes for city contracts, and generally unsavory behavior were, and continue to be, table stakes. While the people may have left Atlantic City, corruption and vice have remained as permanent residents.

It should come as no surprise, then, that these sorts of officials didn't exactly have the best interests of the city in mind while governing. Instead of reinvesting casino tax revenues back into the city to improve quality of life, those funds were diverted into personal coffers and handed out to friends and associates in patronage schemes, all while crime worsened, vacant lots became more numerous than grocery stores, and the city's deprivations worsened. In desperation, more silver bullets were turned to.

Instead of fixing boarded-up homes where people might be able to live, raise a family, and contribute back to the community, a convention center was built for $268 million in 1997 ($507 million in 2023 money). It's chronically underused. In 2014, just 380,000 people visited, for an occupancy rate of 28% of the annual capacity. This number grew to 500,000 in 2022, for a still paltry 37% rate. Atlantic City is the place where street life goes to die. Who wants to be anywhere near a quarter mile of loading bays, blank facades, and horizontal monotony? Totally dispiriting. Even worse, the siting of the center kills any access to what might otherwise have been a transformative bayfront development.

Rather than focusing on a base Maslowian need of making the streets safer (Atlantic City's homicide and violent crime rates are among the highest in the country), a minor league baseball stadium was built. Just a few years after completion, its team folded, and the stadium fell into disrepair. Even after being "revived" it enjoys only sporadic use a few days a year, playing host to one-off concerts and community college baseball games with near nonexistent attendance.

And instead of investing in small business owners, a 1.3 million square foot outlet mall was built in the heart of the city. Tanger

Outlets (formerly known as The Walk), would be more at home on the side of an exurban highway than the core of a once-prosperous city. Grasping at straws, seeing little success elsewhere, Atlantic City has tripled down on casinos. This hasn't gone so well, either. The city's latest great hope, the $2.4-billion Revel hotel, shuttered its doors two years after opening in 2012, filing for bankruptcy.[9] Twice. More recently, the city courted a $100-million indoor water park. Opening up on the boardwalk, the consortium behind it seemingly forgot that they're located only a few steps away from the beach.[10]

Time and again, Atlantic City shoots silver bullets that hit nothing as much as its own feet, paralyzing it from moving forward, and punishing the city in a doom loop where bad dollars are thrown after bad. While external forces have played their part in Atlantic City's downfall, in my estimation the city's responses to these exogenous events have inflicted just as much damage, if not more. Trying to recover lost glory is a recipe destined to go foul when other places, notably Las Vegas, can play the casino, nightlife, and entertainment game so much better. There can only be a few winners of this competition in our globalized, inter-connected world. Unfortunately for A.C., this is not a contest that cares for old sympathies, but a savage zero-sum battle that demands extraordinary resources. And even this is no guarantee of success. If one city builds a billion-dollar stadium today, some other city can build a nicer one five years from now. Bigger, too.

Smaller regional casinos in the northeast, to say nothing of the more than 2,000 others spread throughout the country, have proven that doubling down on casino-oriented development is a game that often ends in futility for the cities that host them. Why drive, fly, or take a train to Atlantic City when you can go to one closer to home? All the better that you don't have to walk by boarded-up stores, open and rampant crime, vacant lots, and destitution on one of your few days off from work. I've taken the bus down to Atlantic City many times to see family in South Jersey, and the Orient Express it was not. No word describes it as simply nor as well as "sad". No amount of silver bullets will give cause for redefinition if the city continues to be perceived as dismal and unsafe. Rightfully so.

Instead of trying to attract people from outside of town, and neglecting those inside, Atlantic City must reverse the script and focus on making the city a good place to live first and foremost. The rest will follow. No locality should try to do everything at once, or become a must-see destination overnight. They almost certainly won't be. Besides, Atlantic City has tried this and failed for a half century. But by slowly building up its foundations—repairing boarded-up homes here, investing in park cleanups there, offering incentives for small businesses and partnering with non-extractive institutions to put roots into the city—it might gradually become a place people will want to spend time in, not one they'd rather avoid.

If a city is populated by students, nurses, accountants, clerks, construction workers, families, artists, scientists, and hard-working professionals, rather than those whose chips have dwindled down, others will gravitate to spend time there, too. This characterization may sound harsh, but it doesn't make it any less true. Like attracts like. Every city must decide what it wants to be like, and who it wants to attract. It is a continuous and constant process that, when ignored, delivers banality at best, and destitution at worst.

Sick of its peril, Atlantic City has begun to chart a more hopeful future. With support from the city, Stockton University opened a new campus in 2018, which features an academic building and a 543-bed dorm. In 2023, 416 more beds were added in a new 135,000 square foot complex, along with another 56,000 square foot academic center.[11] Tens of millions of dollars have been invested, replacing vacant lots near the beach with life. This initiative has catalyzed growth. Students, more than 1,500 of them now, have been connected with the largest employers in the city through various partnerships, with the goal of keeping talent in town.

Immigration, that long-successful antidote to faltering communities, has been helping to cure Atlantic City, too. Bengali script can now be read on many storefronts and converted mosques. Mexican and Central American immigrants are leaving their positive marks on the city, as well. As any visitor can see, though, there's still more work to be done. One hopes the city has learned its lessons from the past, and can continue its upward ascent, building off of recent victories and prudently mapping out a course for yet more.

The best communities are an amalgamation of many good places strung next to one another. Not world-defining bits of starchitecture or mega-developments, but good, solid projects. We can feel their energy. There are promenades to walk along, many different stores and restaurants to pop into, and unique buildings all in relatively quick succession. The closer doors are to one another, the better. 20 or 25 feet is usually a pretty good benchmark to shoot for. If one building or store doesn't appeal to us, we can quickly move past it. When buildings are really wide, or developed by the same firm, we can't escape them. They deaden their surroundings. There's no shortage of these sorts of boring and lifeless streets, or mega-development projects that may have the veneer of action, but in reality are uncanny, insipid monoliths populated by anonymous national chains. So called "town centers"—those loathsome open-air assemblages of corporate sterility which exist as simulacra of traditional downtowns and whose central arteries could never hope to hold as many people as the ambitions of their parking lots would have one believe—are little better than the gratuitously ordained "office parks". Both are public relations contrivances of urbanism that leave many disquieted. After visiting, one has an inescapable feeling that they have been, in some essential ways, duped.

Town centers are as useful in creating community as a chicken pot pie is in the drafting of a national constitution. Though there may be some conceivable reasons for their presence, it isn't clear

WHAT BETTER COMMUNITIES LOOK LIKE   293

The Cotton District in Starkville, Mississippi, is the anti-town center. Realized through the driving, but not exclusive, force of Dan Camp over 50 years (beginning in 1969), the Cotton District has incrementally developed into the heart of an entire community. Home to many small businesses and off-campus housing accommodations, and playing host to events most weeks, it is a true community center.

how they're particularly useful in furthering the stated goal. Yes, a town center might have a promenade that one can walk along, but it is still fundamentally a piece of car-dependent infrastructure, inseparable from anti-social behavior. They exist as a sort of oxymoronic "drive-in urbanism" that's self-defeating. They are dead malls of a different name. I expect their demise will come shortly. Town centers can not, and will never, create proper communities. The reason is in the formulation. Neo-dead-malls are almost exclusively the product of a vision from a single institutional firm, tenanted by large national chains, and built to a finished state such that any change, even when necessary, is very difficult to carry out. They are thus inhibited from doing what buildings and neighborhoods must do in order to survive: breathe, evolve, and change to suit the needs of the people who live there.

Even if one believes oneself to be the most enlightened thinker on the built environment since Da Vinci, no place worth spending time in can ever be created via the vision of just one person. It must be conceived and shaped by many hands, over much time. Embodied wisdom results from the crowds duking it out in the marketplace of ideas. When one entity controls all of the buildings, this process is arrested, as all thoughts must be subsumed by a single vision. Worse still, fresh ideas and new committed stakeholders are prevented from being introduced into the fray.

When hotels, apartment buildings, and office spaces are added to these places, they're a further corruption of mixed-use development, applying the concept in name but hardly in practice. While a hotel within 500 feet of a restaurant is technically mixed-use, if that hotel is a Holiday Inn, and that restaurant is a Chili's, and there are a hundred parking spaces shared between them, it's not quite what most placemakers have in mind when they campaign for a blend of different uses. Proper mixed-use neighborhoods are efficient, vibrant, and offer much choice—a far departure from the grim and limiting vapidity of town-centers.

There is an unfortunate shortage of places that get this mix right. The few that do exist, following the foundations of good development, are quickly usurped, as they're identified by chains and larger investors as good investments. Upon successful infiltration, once desirable neighborhoods ironically lose much of what made them successful initially. Places like quirky restaurants that couldn't exist in high-rent neighborhoods due to their novel appeal, comic stores that care more about whether their heroes are being misrepresented in the latest Hollywood blockbuster than turning a meaningful profit, and thrift shops that exist to offer affordable clothing for those in need, not a wardrobe-in-waiting for influencers, all make way for higher credit, sanitized alternatives. These lovable pockets exist in a sort of Goldilocks zone, short-lived and magical for the time that they're around, but ultimately (inevitably?) succumbing to their own success. Better than what they were in the past, but more compelling than the future that's in store. Abbot Kinney (Los Angeles), Bedford Avenue (Brooklyn), 14th and H Streets (D.C.), Frankford Avenue (Philadelphia), Milwaukee Avenue (Chicago), Ballard Avenue (Seattle), and many more than my heart is able to dwell on have gone through this insipid transformation.

Though we may feel a reflexive disdain for this state of affairs, a moment of pause for analysis is required. Such qualitative changes must be measured against the benefit of more homes, grocery stores, and new local businesses that have managed to survive or prosper. Increased tax revenues are inarguably better than vacant lots and storefronts. But residential displacement where erstwhile residents do not get to participate in the upside of their own neighborhoods (the more commonly recognized effects of gentrification) is a much different story.

Direct involvement is a potential cure to this, where public-private partnerships are leveraged to ensure better local outcomes. Not building is not a choice in our current housing crisis, as this will only lead to displacement or, in the cases where certain policies like rent control are adopted without strong carve outs for new supply, disinvestment as developers and landlords fear losing money. But if the members of a rapidly changing community are made to feel like they're part of that change, moving in a more positive, inclusive direction, great things can happen. The wrong way to do this is through community review, where the only real power residents wield is the veto. There's one thing to say yes to, and a thousand to say no. Objections are the natural result, especially when planning hearings become an "us versus them" affair. Let's get rid of this dynamic. On publicly owned lots, cities should openly court private developers and bring residents into the discussion so the process can be demystified, with all costs, schedules, and challenges openly shared. Designs can be crafted alongside architects and voted on by residents, leading to immediate pride in their creation, which will increase the probability of enduring support. What stands a greater chance of success—a banal box proposed by an anonymous non-resident, or a bold display of local identity created in part by the community? The answer is obvious.

Beyond partnerships, a city might be able to sell municipal lots at market rate, and include the people of a neighborhood in the economic upside of that sale by making them a party to the agreement. Perhaps they could be given limited partner rights, receiving dividends from any rents and capital events (refinancings, sales) from the future property, where funds are paid out directly to participating local households. For those who might want longer-term stability, a community investment entity with a simple mandate to manage low-cost index funds—potentially ones that deliver some dividends—could be set up for the benefit of local residents and paid out in quarterly distributions.

And if a neighborhood wanted to get really ambitious, agreements between their city and developers could be structured as ground leases, where timelines are not in the order of a few years, but a century. This would demand that a community think long and hard about what type of places they'd want to create. As the land increases in value, adjustments to the underlying lease every five years or so could be made to bring payments up to market value. This strikes me as a much more favorable solution than getting a meager supply of new "Affordable" housing, whose benefits rarely flow completely through to an impacted community. Incentives would thus be changed from vetoing new development (and exacerbating existing challenges), to embracing it. In this way, a city would be shaped by many hands, not just the transactional grasp of an institutional few.

*   *   *

These ideas on how to create better buildings and communities might sound great in theory, but is it happening in the real world? Are there places embracing new development? With practitioners executing projects in fundamentally lovely, novel ways that are bucking the status quo, forcing us to rethink what's possible? Well, I think you can guess the answer to that. You might be surprised to learn about the extent of it, though. In the next chapter, we'll explore a few cities, where many great new places have been built by scratch which have had profound impacts. The flywheel of Optimism is mighty. Once it gets going, it's remarkable to see all that it can create.

9.

Why Are Some Places More Optimistic Than Others?

Despite all of the challenges inherent in building beautiful, people-oriented places, it's being done all around North America. Regrettably, it is not pervasive. Not yet at least. There are oases of exceptional new development in deserts of bad status quo. Sprawling status quo deserts are no reason for us to abandon our mission, though. On the contrary, it should be a celebration of sorts, if only a small one. Hardly two decades ago there wasn't much worth celebrating outside of a few case studies and flights of fancy from eccentrics with money to spend. Now, triumphs can be found in every corner of the country.

Concentrated pockets do pose a difficult question for us, however. Why are some places more likely to have high-quality development than others? In this chapter, I've chosen three cities to profile that each explain part of the story. In some cases, there's a strong historic fabric that serves as direct inspiration for contemporary developers. This is the story of Charleston, where many traditionally inspired projects have popped up because there's an easy and accessible template for local builders to reference. In others, like Santa Barbara, a strict design code and uncompromising aesthetic vision has raised the bar on the quality of new development. And finally there are some places, like Portland, that have proven that outstanding projects can be supported by iteratively tweaking land use regulations that enable designers to dream up new and compelling visions of the future.

Importantly, all of those laboring to do great work in these cities share a relentless zeal to create attractive places. It might sound simple, but disregarding this truth would be foolish. Intention is the fuel that drives any initiative. If one doesn't start from a base of trying to achieve something lovely, it's nearly certain one won't end up there by chance. To build with spirit is as important a goal as achieving a certain price per square foot. Indeed, it is a virtue which exists on a plane higher than mere commerce can achieve. Transactional developers who build placeless places in placeless places would do well to internalize this.

Some of the routes these cities have chosen to take may feel a bit more prescriptive than we might wish them to be, but it's hard to argue with the results. Over time, I hope the pathways forged by these cities function like training wheels that can help others get on the right path, only to be quickly taken off to allow for more freedom in the future once they've got their bearings straight.

The projects profiled in this chapter may represent a small portion of what's being built today, but they are a rapidly growing piece of the total pie. Developments like Catfiddle Street in Charleston, or El Andaluz in Santa Barbara are no longer one-off curiosities, but the mold from which other projects are being cast. Imagine how many incredible places will be built once the barriers to creating them are removed, and the lessons from this generation of work are learned? As you'll see in the pages that follow, there is already so much to be excited about. Let's dive in.

Charleston

Charleston may have the highest quantity of excellent new developments per capita of any city in North America, so it's a natural place to start our survey of regions where a lot of good is being done. Charleston is old. 100 years older than the United States, old. Perhaps counterintuitively, it's because of its age that the caliber of its new work is so high. Here's why. When cities around the country were tearing themselves apart in the 20th century with highways and housing projects, Charleston was working hard to keep itself patched together. Susan Pringle Frost—an activist and early suffragette—laid the foundations for this work. She began by buying historic homes in her native Charleston in order to save them. First renovating, and then selling them on to others, creating a living tradition of historic architecture. But she couldn't renovate every building, nor protect each one from demolition. And so in 1920, Frost and a group of kindred spirits came together under the banner of the Society for the Preservation of Old Dwellings (now known as the Preservation Society of Charleston) to protect as much of the city's built heritage as they could.[1] Their first major effort was to preserve the Joseph Manigault House. A stately 1803 brick mansion designed by Gabriel Manigault (Joseph's brother), it adhered to classical principles of order and form promoted by Robert Adam, the architect of masterpieces like the Old College at The University of Edinburgh, and Pulteney Bridge in Bath. Despite challenges along the way, the preservationists won.

This victory led to another, and another, until ultimately a historic district was formed in 1931 protecting much of Charleston's downtown Peninsula.[2] Frost's accomplishment was well before its time, predating the federal designation of the National Register of Historic Places via the *Historic Preservation Act* by more than 30 years. To this day it remains one of the country's largest historic

42 South Street, a Carolopolis winner from the 68th annual Awards in 2022.

districts, at more than 500 acres. Compared to other American cities, the core of Charleston is remarkably well preserved.

Since 1953, the Preservation Society has awarded the Carolopolis Awards for "significant undertakings in historic preservation, rehabilitation, restoration, or new construction" which go beyond routine maintenance to promote excellence in the built environment.[3] Far from a vanity contest, the Carolopolis Awards encourage practitioners to do good work. This isn't trivial. When people are praised for the work they do, they want to do more of it. Research confirms the importance of adulation. From the classroom to the conference room, people are more productive when they feel valued.[4] With this reward comes pride, which propels the pursuit of ever better work with each successive attempt as one tries to augment (or at the very least maintain) the good standing they've earned. Jealousy is also a powerful motivator. Seeing others rewarded for work which you might reasonably believe to be of lesser quality than your own can fuel you to go that much further in your own efforts.

This motivation is especially powerful for new developments, as rewards signal what type of work the city values writ large, which can be remunerative for honorees in the form of future opportunities and higher sale/rent prices. Sometimes, as in the case of San Diego's Orchids & Onions Awards, emulations of projects that are broadly disliked are disincentivized. Bad projects are awarded Onions—sorry onion lovers!

Without centuries of heritage to reference, contemporary builders in Charleston would have little to go off of. They might have even arrived, via circular reasoning, at the false notion that any structure from the past that was demolished deserved to be knocked down simply because it did not survive to the present day, and therefore wouldn't be worth taking inspiration from. But because Charleston didn't tear itself apart, and because the community values high-quality places, a signal has been sent to developers that they should aspire to build the same sorts of places that have always been successful (both qualitatively and financially) in the city.

This signal wasn't always transmitted clearly though. Charleston had fallen on hard times by the 1980s. Waves of post-war progress that washed over other parts of the country in the preceding three decades had mostly passed the sleepy southern city by. Its population was less in 1980 than it had been in 1950. Downtown could be a dangerous—and in certain areas, dilapidated—collection of buildings. There wasn't much going on. Some people liked the quiet. Others were determined to chart a new path.

As told in Witold Rybczynski's fabulous *Charleston Fancy* (a book all would-be city builders should read), Charleston's renaissance began in 1985.[5] After some years leaning into the bohemian lifestyle that the city enabled, George Holt teamed up with his wife Cheryl and an air force captain named Jerry Moran (whom George met in a bar and bonded with over their shared love of buildings) to buy one of those run down homes and renovate it. They paid $37,000 (just over $100,000 today) and set out to restore it to its former glory. When they finished the project, they were pretty happy with how it went. So they decided to renovate another, and then another, not unlike Susan Pringle Frost. George and the team accumulated experience, learning more about construction and architecture with each new job they took on. They learned what people seemed to like in a home, and what they didn't. Eventually, they scaled up their practice to include ground up projects which rose on empty plots of land.

One of these early projects, Tully Alley and Charles Street, has laid the foundation for Charleston's Optimistic development over the last three decades. In 1991, George, Cheryl, and Jerry bought a lot with four vacant homes on it for $175,000 (2023 dollars). Almost immediately after closing, one of the homes collapsed. Bad foundations—how apt. But this presented an opportunity. George designed a duplex for the now-vacant patch, their first ground-up project, and set about renovating several of the dilapidated structures on the lot. This was a wise decision as these buildings had been, until very recently, drug dens filled with the sorts of things most people don't particularly want to live near or be around.

After completing this work, the back half of the lot was still vacant. Eager to live in their own spaces after sharing a smaller house they rented downtown, George, Cheryl, and Jerry set about building their own homes. Jerry's design was more conventional. George and Cheryl, however, dreamed of something not exactly common to Charleston. While the outside looked normal enough by the standards of the day (it was simple and elegant, and only had a few quirks that would cause a mostly-conscious observer to turn their head), the inside was Byzantine, with stone floors, soaring vaulted ceilings, and a covered pool. It was here that George flexed his burgeoning skill and uncompromising design vision, opting for masonry construction instead of cheaper wood, and polished green columns with ornate capitals resting on top of them as opposed to more standard load-bearing walls. The Byzantine House might be viewed as anachronistic. Not because it has no

The Byzantine House, built in 1996 by George Holt.

place in our time, but rather because it exudes a character, ambition, and execution that one would be hard-pressed to find in even the most luxurious newly constructed homes today. Instead of spending dollars on incrementally "nicer" marble countertops or appliances, money was spent on transcending the basic idea of what a single family home could be. For these reasons, the Byzantine House may well be one of the most important structures completed in the last half century. Certainly in the region, but I'd argue beyond it as well. It proved definitively that not only can we build exceptional places, but that we can do so where people least expect it. The neighborhood, Elliotborough, was not a very nice or safe place at the time. Crime was rampant, drive-bys were frequent, and many homes were boarded up or vacant. Slowly, however, with each successive development, life was breathed anew into an asphyxiated neighborhood.

When the property next door went on the market for the handsome sum of twice what the trio paid for the original lot (which came with the added bonus of an illegal bar whose pugilistic patrons occasionally shot at each other), George brought in his brother Bob for some needed capital to acquire it. Between 1996 and 1997, four homes were built and designed by local architect Randolph Martz, who also happened to be George's landlord when he was in college. Bob lived in one, Jerry's sister Mary lived in another, a friend of George's bought the third, and a fourth was sold on the market a few years later. Mary selected the name for this burgeoning community, Tully Alley, as an homage to her Irish heritage. As lots adjoining Tully Alley became available, the group bought them, either renovating the homes that were on them or building anew according to what was needed.

Two of the most striking new constructions were the Moorish House and Roman Villa. With pointed arches, stepped gables, and unmissable orange-painted stucco, the Moorish House (2001) would seem Disneyish if not for the sturdiness of its construction, and the reverence it holds for its immediate context, fitting in perfectly despite all reasonable expectations that it might stand out were it executed by a less careful hand. The Roman Villa (2002), not to be outdone, likewise features a stepped gable and is finished in a bright color. Yellow in this case. It's a courtyard house, but not in the way we might normally think of one. Rather than being located on the ground level, the courtyard is raised above the first floor, serving as an external passageway between two sections of the house. Perhaps most beguiling to contemporary observers (but hopefully perfectly normal to future readers), the Roman Villa features three apartments on the ground floor. It is perhaps the most unique quadplex in North America, enchantingly weaving in modest apartments that don't sacrifice the grand nature of the primary residence.

Something remarkable was happening. Completely organically, George, Cheryl, and Jerry had built their own community. These were people designing intuitively in compassionate ways that reflected their care for one another, and their community. Love, pride, and sturdiness are manifestly legible on their buildings, materializing in intriguing ways. Homes jutted out into the lanes here and there, but that was okay. Each slight meander gave a new perspective to view the pocket community from, and opportunities to do interesting things. Here, a small garden. There, an extra dwelling where it might not normally be allowed, charmingly adorned with tile and artwork. It was, and remains, a truly organic habitat molded around the needs of its residents, not shoehorning them into nondescript boxes. Having spent some time in the homes of Tully and Charles, and walking around the community, I can confirm that they render a miraculous sense of serenity. The extent of the contrast between what one feels moving through these spaces and the generic sprawl, parking lots, and sad squats that dominate much of our built environment cannot adequately be described. One can easily imagine how divergent the

psychological and physiological outcomes between those who are fortunate enough to live in these sorts of communities, and those unable to access them, might be.

When these homes were first built, they sold for as little as $80,000 ($180,000 in 2023 dollars). Architectural marvels like the Moorish House sold for $595,000 (~$1 million in 2023). Rents for smaller apartments hovered around $1,000 a month, and were sometimes far less. The different home types and sizes create a varied aesthetic that fostered a diverse and mixed-income community without much coercion. Students or minimum wage service workers could afford to live next to enterprising businesspeople, and importantly, benefit from the sorts of connections that might otherwise be unattainable had they lived somewhere else. There is richness to life on Tully and Charles, much of which comes from its intimate scale. 17 homes now exist on just under an acre of land, though it's not claustrophobic or overcrowded. A marked contrast to tract developments where homes are often allocated between 1/4 of an acre to a full one, whose residents somehow still feel their neighbors closing in on them, and thus rarely spend time outside. Everyone seems to get along well. Surprising some critics, the world hasn't buckled under the weight of this density. On the contrary, it is an innately comfortable place because it mirrors how cities have evolved for millenia, pleasing our primal brains. Prices bear this out. Homes on Tully and Charles have gotten so expensive that they're now out of reach of what most people could afford. But they were built not for the rich. They were mostly affordable when they were first completed. Prices follow quality. George, Cheryl, and Jerry added extraordinary and enduring value through an unexpected, charming, irregular, imperfect, idiosyncratic, but ultimately

Moorish House (top left), and the Roman Villa (top right) built by George Holt. Completed in 2001 and 2002 respectively. View from the Roman Villa's terrace onto Charles Street, including Jerry's first home which was built in the late '90s (bottom).

Homes along St. Philip Street, built in the late '90s to early 2000s, with entrances to Tully Alley (left), and Charles Alley (right).

humane development grounded in the scale and context of Charleston. The market has rewarded them.

For those who might be sympathetic to the idea of gentrification as purely a malicious force, Rybczynski disabuses us of those predispositions: "When George, Cheryl, and Jerry rebuilt their small portion of Saint Philip Street, they displaced the owners of an illegal bar and a single tenant—who left voluntarily. On the other hand, they added a dozen new homes to the city's housing stock, repaired four vacant houses, and put several new rental apartments on the market." Beyond its direct impact, the incalculable effect of greatly increased neighborhood safety and charm must also be considered, as well as the many indirect events that resulted from this benefaction.

To this cast of influential characters, we must now add two more. One, I'm lucky enough to call a friend, the developer Vince

Graham. The other, I deeply admire and believe to be one of the best practicing architects in the country today, Andrew Gould. Vince and Andrew's contributions have built off of the foundations that George, Cheryl, and Jerry laid out, extending them further, and pushing the region to what it has become today—the epicenter of great new development on the continent.

Andrew was brought to the Charleston scene by Witold, the eminent architectural critic and professor, in one of those remarkable intercessions of fate. Witold taught Andrew in a graduate class on architectural criticism at UPenn. When the time came for Andrew to graduate, he had been planning on moving back to his hometown of Brookline, a streetcar suburb that borders Boston to the west. Around the same time, George was in need of some help on his latest project. It was to be an Eastern Orthodox church that would serve as a critical civic and community space at I'On, an ambitious community that Vince was developing in Mount Pleasant, just a few minutes away from the heart of Charleston over the Ravenel Bridge.

Witold, who was introduced to Charleston initially by Vince, recommended that Andrew and George talk. After a few phone calls, a bit of prodding (Andrew had never been south of Philadelphia and Andrew's decision to convert with his then fiancée (now wife) to Orthodoxy, the project moved forward. Naturally not without many hurdles and deviations from the initial plan. That's par for the course in design and construction. Time forgets these challenges, but remembers the quality of the product. Holy Ascension Orthodox Church is worthy of such remembrance. Magnificent in execution, the 2008 structure would not be out of place in a 19th-century Russian village, albeit with some Lowcountry complements. Just as George, and his protege Andrew, would have wanted.

Holy Ascension is nestled in a residential area in I'On. Unlike other newly conceived town centers or tract developments, this civic structure is integrated into the community, not a pad site on its periphery. The church's placement is just one of the many lessons Vince Graham learned from his decades of experience in real estate. After developing a few projects elsewhere in South Carolina, most notably in Beaufort at Newpoint (commenced in 1991), where the much loved homes and streets were copied from the historic core of the city, Vince was looking to do something on a larger scale.

Serendipitously, the land for what would become I'On became available not long after the first homes at Newpoint were delivered. At nearly 250 acres, a planner was needed to map out what the large-scale development would look like. Though there are some purists who might have liked to see something like this constructed ad hoc over time without planning up front, 1) that would never pass zoning or planning due to its unwieldiness, 2) it would be difficult to get financing for an incrementally phased project so large, and 3) economies of scale privilege doing all work at once, so horizontal development costs (land grading, lot subdivision, road creation, utility line installation) and any vertical expenses taken on by the master developer can enjoy reduced bulk pricing.

Graham requested bids from two of the most prominent planning firms in the country, DPZ and Dover, Kohl & Partners, for the project. The lead partners Andres Duany and Elizabeth Plater Zyberk at DPZ, and Victor Dover and Joe Kohl at Dover Kohl, decided a joint bid would make for a better project, and so combined their efforts into one superstar team. After a few years of planning and permits, I'On received approval in March of 1997.

Approval didn't come without some work, however, and unfortunately, many compromises. Though Mt. Pleasant unanimously adopted a master plan which incorporated Traditional Neighborhood Design (TND) principles in 1992, and a strategic plan in 1994 which encouraged development to take the form of local precedent like Mt. Pleasant's Old Village, the town hadn't updated its zoning code. The strategic plan was thus completely toothless. Any changes to the city's zoning code would require approval from the town council. No easy feat. The I'On team originally planned for 800 single-family lots, 440 multifamily units, 90,000 square feet of commercial space, and several civic sites like houses of worship and community gathering spaces to tie the plan together. This would not be legal under Mt. Pleasant's R1 zoning, with its 10,000 square foot minimum lot sizes, large setbacks, parking minimums, and low lot size coverage ratios. While the planning commission nearly unanimously recommended rezoning to the town council, there was no shortage of local opposition, which threatened the project's viability. And so, the team was forced to go back to the drawing board to pacify the opponents. The number of proposed single family homes dropped to 730 in the second iteration, while multifamily units fell to 120. This still wasn't good enough. Mt. Pleasant's town council rejected the application in 1995, narrowly, by a 5–4 vote. In the design that was ultimately approved, all multifamily homes were stripped out. Despite its grand ambitions, the neighborhood effectively became an 800-home single family community—albeit a lovely one—save for a small area of commercial uses spread across 30,000 square feet.

Reflecting on the project, Vince has written that "The Founders had deep regrets about making these compromises as they felt the neighborhood would be less diverse and less affordable, thus reducing the overall quality of I'On. However, political circumstances made these compromises necessary to get anything approved."[6] Elaborating with great clarity and eloquence, "Prior to World War II people were excited about growth. Their expectations were that what was built would be beautiful and contribute to their quality of life. However, the overall quality of the built environment of the last 50 years has been poor. This makes people distrustful of anything new, and gives rise to a legitimate belief that anything new will, by association with most of what has been built over the last 50 years,

Homes overlooking East Lake (left) and a canal at I'On (right). Construction began in 1997, with homes delivering throughout the early 2000s.

necessarily be bad; The private/exclusive mindset embodied in the suburban mentality (which has spread to many urban areas) leads people to believe that any more development will degrade their privacy and exclusivity; and it is in the best short-term economic interests of existing property owners because limiting supply of new homes, puts upward pressure on existing home prices." But ultimately, he felt that I'On "demonstrates that it is still possible to build in a beautiful manner". Despite its quality, I'On presents a cautionary tale, which may dampen some of our hopefulness. Even when town officials explicitly plan for an enlightened mode of development, certain motivated actors within a community can exert disproportionate veto power to quash, or materially alter, that vision. Those who might be in favor of a project rarely mobilize themselves as forcefully as those who strongly oppose it. Hate (or motivated vested interest) is a more powerful force than passive support. Until the pendulum of development wrests some control back from individuals, these challenges will remain.

And yet, I'On has become one of the most successful masterplanned communities in the country in both financial terms, as measured by sale values, and qualitative terms, due to its impact on the real estate industry, in spite of the compromises it had to make. Vince and the Founders (including Geoff, Vince's brother, who I'm glad to also call a friend, and Tom, their dad) wanted to replicate a pocket of Charleston. While I'On is unfortunately not that, the result is eminently lovely. Walking around, it feels like a Lowcountry single family streetcar suburb. It's decidedly not the heart of the city, or even necessarily urban, but walkable, more dense than comparable suburban developments, and fundamentally beautiful. There are smaller lots (some 1/20th of an acre, 5 times smaller than what prior zoning allowed for), streets are narrower than one would expect, and the architecture is very good, thanks in part to a strict code reviewed by a local architectural historian, and rigorous standards guiding new construction.

The Founders interviewed more than 100 builders, and whittled this list down to just 10 who would be responsible for building all of the homes. Equal parts discerning and flexible, this process allowed I'On to maintain high standards while still allowing for a diversity of styles. Witold Rybczynski, in describing Vince's work at I'On, noted that in order "To develop what he called 'a culture of the right way to do things,' he organized dinners, ran workshops, and held an annual ceremony with awards in categories such as Best Carpentry and Best Masonry." This culture is palpable when one walks through the development. A celebration of quality is embodied.

When sales were first launched in the late '90s, homes ranged from $160,000 to the high six figures, with building lots starting at $30,000. That homes now regularly sell for more than $3 million, with several valued at more than $4 million, is again not an indictment of the developers, but a sign of demand for high-quality communities.[7] If there are fingers to be pointed for the current lack of affordability, the town council and local oppositionists have earned a few in their direction for reducing the amount of homes that could have been built, and subsequently the number of people who might have enjoyed the excellence of I'On.

Back on the Peninsula, George, Cheryl, and Jerry were dreaming up a new project. In 2005, George's brother Bob offered to buy the first house the trio developed at Tully Alley. Jerry owned it at that point and was using it as a rental, but agreed to sell it to Bob. In order to defer taxes from the profits of the sale, Jerry initiated a process known as a 1031 exchange. Exchange buyers often reinvest proceeds from the sale of a riskier asset into a more secure one, say, a single-user retail building with a long term, triple net lease where the tenant pays for all of the expenses. As we explored in Chapter 5, the higher credit the tenant has, the better. More often than not, exchange buyers will acquire a building leased out entirely to a Starbucks, McDonald's, Meineke Car Care, or another tenant of this sort. Triple net deals are pretty simple. Tenants agree to

Homes on a tree-lined street in I'On.

pay the owner a fixed amount of rent, but unlike traditional lease agreements, they also cover all of the other expenses at a property, like taxes, insurance, utilities, and any capital improvements. This gives a tenant more autonomy, and the landowner fewer headaches. A win-win. They're a particularly attractive investment because owners don't need to do much management, as everything is the tenant's responsibility. Year after year owners can sit back and collect 4%, 5%, 6% or more on their initial investment, with the potential upside of appreciation.

As one large landlord in Brooklyn told me of his triple net tenants, in a beautiful exhibition of New York character, "They can

"The Blue House" at 23 Catfiddle Street, designed and built by Andrew Gould and George Holt. Completed in 2008.

do whatever the hell they want with the property, even knock it down for all I care so long as they pay their rent. But by the end of the lease, the building better be in the same condition I leased it out to them in." That covers it pretty succinctly. The downside risk is that if the tenant leaves, all of one's cash flow is gone until another one is found.

But Jerry wasn't like most real estate investors. He 1031'ed into an asset with more risk than his stabilized rental—a rotting, modest cottage on Ashley Avenue in much need of some love. Jerry brought in George and Andrew to help restore the home, and they did just that, completing it in 2008 with their characteristic style and idiosyncrasies. But the work wasn't done there. Just as Jerry wasn't like most real estate investors, this wasn't like most lots. At 180 feet deep, there was potential to add several more homes to the property. Similar to what was done at Tully Alley and Charles Street, but this time, bigger and better.

On less than 300 square feet of land, the first house of what would become Catfiddle Street was constructed. A simple 13.5 foot by 21 foot home with three one-room floors stacked on top of each other was erected. Smaller homes confer affordability by default, as they're often simply designed and, owing to their limited footprint, relatively cheap to construct. It's the same logic behind Alfred Tredway White's cottages in Brooklyn, and Philadelphia's Trinity homes. Great beauty can often be found in modesty, reflecting a philosophy Andrew espoused: "We like to build things the way they used to be—solid, purposeful, and understated."

Incrementally, structures began to fill out the irregularly shaped lot. Andrew designed his own home in 2009, a masonry Anglo-Dutch colonial fortified by rebar (for hurricane protection), with heavy shutters, double-glazed windows, and an interior paneled in tongue-and-groove wood. A geothermal heat pump provided heating and cooling. He built all of the millwork himself. An extension, which can be seen in the corresponding images on the following page, was added in 2018.

As homes were completed, contiguous lots became available. Jerry bought the back half of his neighbor to the north's lot, and acquired a house next to the original cottage on Ashley. This nearly doubled the footprint of the original lot. Consistent with the tight-knit, familial community (often literally) that sprouted on Tully and Charles, Andrew's parents approached Jerry about buying a portion of the lot to build a retirement home. Andrew and George designed a house for them, as well as three others elsewhere on Catfiddle to present for approval to the Board of Architectural Review (BAR). The tall, Charlestonian style buildings passed, but there was a bit of a negotiation over the shorter, squat house that Andrew had designed for his parents. A tedious reminder that working with design boards often requires a lot of back and forth. Ultimately, it was approved. But not without compromise. Instead of a second home on the lot as originally planned, Andrew's family opted to build a modest mixed-use office structure. Well, more of a cottage with a small home office on the top floor and a guest room on the

Andrew's house at 21 Catfiddle Street (left), completed in 2009, with a 2018 addition. 25 Catfiddle (right), the small mixed-use office building Andrew designed next to his parent's home. Completed in 2013.

bottom floor. This allowed it to pass zoning as it was viewed as an extension of the main house, and not a discrete dwelling.

The neighborhood was starting to take shape. While there were a few architectural marvels (some might say curiosities) like a Palladian villa (24 Catfiddle, 2011) and a yellow Elizabethan home with dutch gables that cantilevered over a few parking spaces (26 Catfiddle, 2012, designed for Jerry's sister Mary of Tully Alley naming fame), most of the homes were rather simple. Their success comes predominantly in how they interact with one another, their relationship to sightlines, and how they front the lanes. This was, as much as is possible today, an ad hoc plan. Homes were built as needed, and according to principles of traditional urbanism. If one jutted out into the common walkway a few feet, or if a mature tree forced another to be pushed back, constraining cars to park wherever they could fit in, that was okay. Better, even. Intimacy via imperfection was created, an effect unknown in all but the oldest of North American streets, like the lanes of Vieux-Québec or Boston's

North End. This impact was augmented by a generous canopy of trees. Speckled light filters through sublimely in the little pockets created by amorphously placed homes.

This, however, is only the first half of Catfiddle's story. The second would come with the deeper involvement of Reid Burgess, a blues musician turned developer of the Palladian Villa. Reid was introduced into the fray via George, whom he befriended over email in 2009. Their friendship grew digitally until Reid moved down to Charleston, where he began doing work with George on a few projects, primarily at Catfiddle.

Getting a taste for design and development, Reid was eager to dive in deeper. That opportunity would come in the form of an irregular L-shaped lot, wrapping behind the original homes on Ashley with a small frontage on Bogard Street. The price tag was $540,000. How times had changed from years before when lots double the size would go for half the price. Reid didn't have the money, but desperately wanted to create a fantastical cluster of buildings. Luckily, his longtime friend David Coles had just come into some money. David joined Reid and his partner Sally to buy the land, forming the development company Reverse Sprawl. They closed on the Bogard site in December 2013, and quickly got to work. Design

Villa Witold, designed by George Holt, Andrew Gould, and owner Reid Burgess at 24 Catfiddle (left). Completed 2011. 26 Catfiddle (right), designed by George Holt and Andrew Gould. Completed in 2012.

would come from Andrew, along with George and Reid, who partnered up to launch the design-build firm Urban Ergonomics.

This confluence of actors was sort of like Jerry, George, and Cheryl 2.0, except George now had decades of experience and a much broader base of personal projects and international precedents to go off of. Reid supplied the eccentricity, verve, and passion. The comparison is apt for another reason. As Jerry had to take a step back from the day-to-day of development to take care of family, Reid stepped in to bridge the legacy of the original Ashley section of Catfiddle, connecting the two lots into one cohesive whole. There were to be 10 new homes, including one for Reid and Sally, who planned on moving out of their then-residence at Villa Witold in a manner very similar to what Jerry had done at Charles Street. Sally formally named the new community Catfiddle.

In addition to combining the lots that George and Andrew had built on, Reid was able to convince a few other neighbors to join a Planned Unit Development (PUD). This would allow them to create a special zoning district that would enable more creativity in developing the site, without having to receive a variance from the city for an unauthorized use (arduous) or rezone the neighborhood (good luck). In a PUD, individual lots are still owned by their respective owners, but the common space is common, so all owners benefit from flexible parking programs, pedestrianized lanes with shared access, and gardens. No individual owner has any individual claims beyond the home that they own. In total, Reid was able to combine 24 lots into one PUD. Some had existing homes on them, and others were newly created lots that were either acquired from, or contributed by, neighbors.

Reid and George note, in describing their goals for Catfiddle, that "Buildings and cities last a long time, so it's worth taking trouble when we build them. With this in mind Catfiddle Street is intended as a haven for buildings that inspire longevity, caretakership, social interaction and good physical as well as psychological

Reid Burgess and Sally Eisenberg's courtyard house, Highcourt. Completed in 2017.

health."[18] These goals have been realized. Standing in the courtyard of Reid and Sally's home, Highcourt, one is overcome by serenity and grace. It's a Russian nesting doll of sorts; Highcourt is a secret oasis hidden from the already tucked away Catfiddle Street through a series of exterior stairwells and covered passageways, a paragon of inner-block urbanism. Upon discovering the court, it's as though you've stumbled upon a hidden world, not meant for mere mortals. Walking through their home, the quality of craftsmanship and personality imbued into it is ineffable. With handmade built-ins, salvaged doors, artifacts from around the world, cozy nooks, high ceilings, and the fruits of artisanal care hammered into every square foot, it feels as though it shouldn't in our cheap commodified world. Certainly not in the U.S. But it does exist. Despite how unexpected Reid and Sally's home is, it works fabulously well, leaving the visitor with a sense of profound awe, and not a little bit of melancholy that for all the money in the world, few people can buy taste as good as this. Taste whose expenditures, it must be noted, amounted to dramatically less than what some insipid scion, inheritee, or mogul might pay for a contemporary hillside manse. Highcourt cost around $1 million in combined hard and soft costs. Not cheap, but not exorbitant for the quality of the product delivered. The style is tricky to pin down. A bit of Roman influence here, Spanish Colonial there, dashed with smatterings of New Orleans, Renaissance, and even industrial warehouses if you look hard enough. In this curious mélange, the building is difficult to define, but easy to appreciate.

Since 2005, the consolidated neighborhood of Catfiddle has been rounded into form. Vince has since developed a lot there, as well. Work continues as of writing this in 2024. At 26 units per acre, Catfiddle is remarkably dense. To give a sense of how many people this fits, after accounting for 25% of the land area being dedicated to public right of ways, Catfiddle has a comparable density to Newark, New Jersey, at around 12,500 people per square mile. For all its density, it is utterly tranquil. As this chapter has shown, density in the abstract does not seem to be a problem.

Urban Ergonomics was not alone in designing homes for the second phase—if it can be called that—of Catfiddle. Kenny Craft of Craft Design Studio and Julie O'Connor of American Vernacular contributed a few excellent schemes. So too did Jenny Bevan and Christopher Liberatos, who run the architecture firm Liberatos Architects. They are fierce defenders of classical and traditional

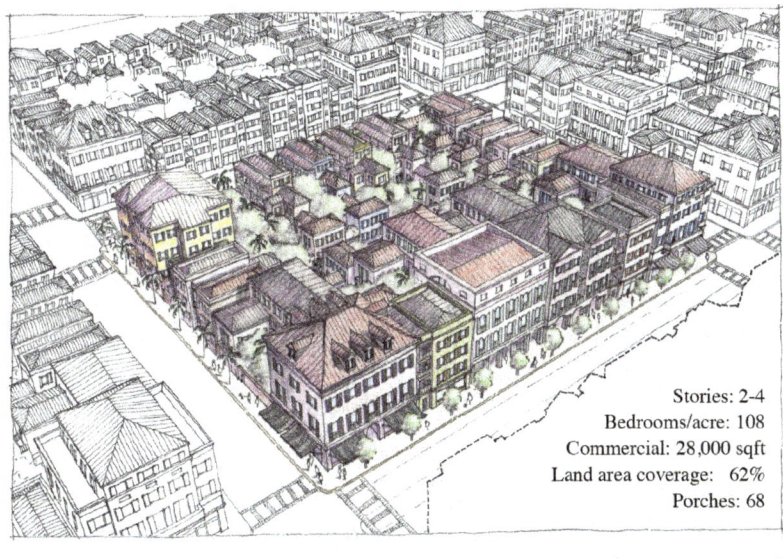

Stories: 2-4
Bedrooms/acre: 108
Commercial: 28,000 sqft
Land area coverage: 62%
Porches: 68

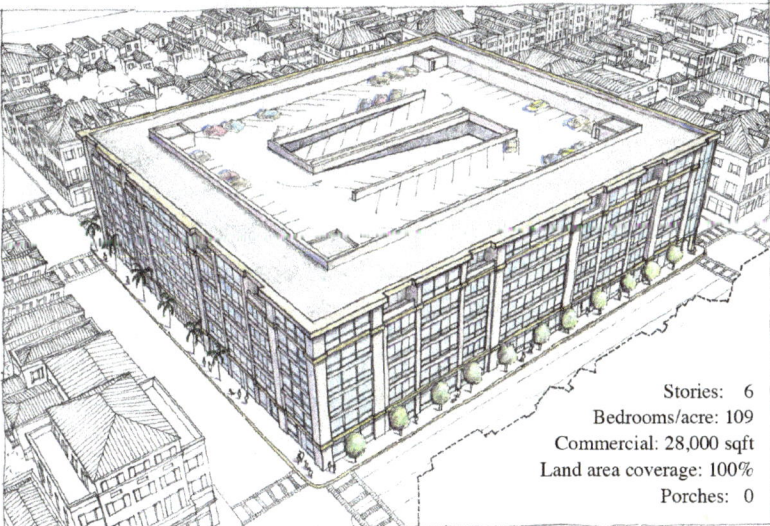

Stories: 6
Bedrooms/acre: 109
Commercial: 28,000 sqft
Land area coverage: 100%
Porches: 0

Liberatos Architects counterproposal to the WestEdge apartment complex in Charleston. Isometric view.

architecture. No one can mistake what they stand for, and what they stand against. There is perhaps no better illustration of this than a pair of drawings the duo created, which contrast prevailing multifamily development patterns with their preferred traditional vernacular. In response to a particularly bad example of a Texas Doughnut, Bevan & Liberatos proposed what an alternative in the Charlestonian vernacular could look like.[8] The counterproposal still meets all of the core elements the developers required, but is inarguably qualitatively superior. It was an inherently Optimistic vision, leaning heavily on local precedent to explore how Charleston could become even better through large-scale new development, not submissively accepting institutionality foisted upon them as in so many other cities.

Rising six stories, the Texas Doughnut covers nearly 100% of the lot, yields 28,000 square feet of commercial space, and has 109 bedrooms per acre. Bevan & Liberatos' design has roughly the same amount of units and commercial space, but because of its arrangement in the traditional Charleston manner, 38% of the lot is reserved for open space, creating a far more permeable, neighborly, lovely, and green development than the anonymous pastry. While the counterproposal might require more money to be spent on design and construction owing to the refinement of the scheme, its lack of elevators, large parking structure, and complex building systems would likely offset the difference between the costs of a five-over-one, if not make it even cheaper to build dependent on a number of togglable choices like materials, finishes, and paved surface area. The Charleston vernacular would allow more individual owners to have a vested interest in the community—a community based on inclusive walkability as opposed to the status quo—leading to improved civic and economic outcomes. This is the sort of Optimistic common sense that's difficult to ignore. We can have our cake and eat it too if we're intentional with how we build, and can often do more than we might expect.

As Charleston has gained in popularity thanks to its famous hospitality (Southern), suitability for bachelor(ette) parties, and enviable weather for much of the year, it has grown in population and become more prosperous. This prosperity has attracted larger,

The northeast corner of Columbus and Meeting in Charleston's East Side, before (2015) and after (2019) redevelopment.

national architecture and development firms eager to contribute to its built fabric. Charleston is not unique in having good weather, delicious food, and welcoming people. But its spirit of building is nearly peerless, which is seductive to the most talented practitioners in the built environment.

As it turns out, this spirit is scalable. Tremendous large-scale projects have been executed in recent years. Greystar, one of the biggest apartment managers in the world (800,000 units and counting), completed development of Courier Square and The Guild in 2019. Designed by the prolific Robert A. M. Stern Architects (RAMSA), Courier Square is Greystar's new Greek Revival influenced global headquarters. The Guild, for its part, is an eight-story loft-style brick apartment building.[9] With 220 apartments, it's a big building, but not without some elegance. A clock tower rests on its main elevation, dignifying what could have been a cumbersome, bulky building had a lesser firm designed it. Over the course of my research for this book, I took a few trips to Charleston. Walking by this part of town, I didn't even consider that this building could be new, and thus worthy of inclusion in my survey, such was its fidelity

The Guild, designed by RAMSA, developed by Greystar. Completed in 2019.

to traditional design. But as I later learned, and as striking before and after pictures confirm, this is very much a new project. Where surplus materials and construction equipment made their home on a vacant lot not ten years ago, now stand two excellent buildings, dramatically improving the corner of Columbus and Meeting.

A bit further down the peninsula, Fairfax & Sammons (who designed Brooklyn's State Street townhomes) and developer Bennett Hospitality collaborated on the Hotel Bennett, which opened its doors in 2019. The 179-key hotel is prominently located on one of the most important nodes in the entire city, the northwest corner of Marion Square along King Street. In another case of an underutilized site being improved through large scale intervention, the corner was previously home to a tired, dreary, and, given the location, offensively average structure. Important sites deserve important buildings. Hotel Bennett is precisely that. Though not everyone will be able to stay there (as of editing this section in September 2024, the average rooms were going for more than $600 a night), everyone who passes by will be able to appreciate its beauty.[10] One's spirit is raised by merely being close to it—no trivial thing.

For those who are frustrated by the price of the rooms, I understand, but land prices for prominent sites demand a certain yield. While a less graceful architecture might have been employed, I have my doubts as to whether the costs would be more reasonable if some lesser structure were erected. In this hypothetical scenario, the apartments or hotel rooms that would've risen in place of Hotel Bennett would still be objectionably expensive to some subset of the population because of the high prices demanded by the location. But in this counterfactual, that same subset would not have the opportunity to be soothed by a powerful aesthetic marker and monument to beauty. Charleston is better for Hotel Bennett's existence. Passersby who don't stay in the hotel arguably get the better side of the deal—we get to look at the building, while those inside can only look out from it.

Beyond private actors, public officials and municipal departments have played a critical role in Charleston's renaissance. One of the more consequential, for better or worse, has been the city's Board of Architectural Review. The BAR is tasked with reviewing

The northwest corner of Marion Square along King street before (above) and after (below) Hotel Bennett was built. Designed by Fairfax & Sammons, developed by Bennett Hospitality. Completed in 2019.

all new construction, alterations and renovations in Charleston's historic districts, which cover most of the downtown peninsula. On the one hand, strict architectural standards have set a pretty high bar for the quality of new development, which has largely been met. On the other hand, they can add considerable cost (mainly through added time), complication, and arbitrary considerations. When George, Cheryl, and Jerry first began building, the BAR was more lax due to the part of town they were in, and the lower stakes of development at the time. As the city has evolved, these dynamics have reversed, limiting the type of developer who can navigate the system, privileging larger institutional firms.

Though successful in some respects, stewardship cannot exclusively rely on code. Strong municipal leaders who see themselves as champions of progressing the discipline forward are essential. Leaders who see their job principally as setting forth a vision and executing on it—not finding excuses to obfuscate.

Vince Graham points to former mayor Joseph P. Riley as one of the most important catalysts for the success of Charleston today. Elected 10 terms in a row, Riley led the city from 1975 through 2015, a period which coincided with significant growth locally and elevated prominence nationally. Serving uninterrupted for 40 years brings a consistency that's rare in politics today. This stability does a few things. First, it gains back the time that's lost between administrations, and avoids the distraction of continuous campaigning at the expense of leading. Distractions that can waste several months, if not more, in a term of only four years. Second, consistency of leadership also removes the pressure for new administrations to take disproportionate risks in order to make their name and establish their legitimacy. Many of Atlantic City's silver bullets were shot by wide-eyed newcomers. Rarely do you see stable governments approving casinos or outlet malls in the heart of town. Cities are thus inured from short-termism motivated by winning the next election, and the outlandish things mayors might do to secure votes. They can instead work on enacting policy that takes a holistic and long-term approach. When one plans for a city across decades or centuries, as opposed to months and years, the quality of that city will inevitably rise. Perhaps this is easier said for a place like Charleston whose people can see first hand that good things don't come overnight, but only with the passage of time. Regardless, the lesson stands.

Third, consistency provides public officials cover to do what they feel is in the best interest of their constituents, even if it's not immediately popular, as they have built up enough goodwill and credibility to be trusted with doing the right thing. This might take the form of allowing for more housing in areas that have historically opposed it, rejecting a highway expansion that would make it easier for suburban residents to get into town more quickly at the expense of those downtown, or promising programs that are of dubious value but sound theoretically compelling.

Riley epitomized the benefits of mayoral consistency. Of consequence to the built environment, he was a devout and vocal champion of high-quality design. He often publicly expressed his wishes for excellence in architecture and construction materials, and encouraged a certain caliber of development to be built. How many other mayors in the country have said similar things, much less had a tangible vision for what they wanted the future of their city to look like? Troublingly few. Riley's uniqueness shows in the results he delivered. In his nearly half-century of leadership, Mayor Riley restored many of Charleston's most prominent civic buildings, revived the city's famed King Street, created outstanding new public parks, and oversaw Charleston's boom into both a tourist mecca and a permanent destination for people from around the continent to move to.

"Many have joked that Riley is a frustrated architect, and his interest in city building details ranging from paint colors to signage to lighting is well known. He often has talked about the influence a mayor can have on the design of his or her city ... 'as mayors, the decisions we make about the design and development of our city will be with our city 25, 50 or 100 years from now. [...] It is our opportunity and responsibility to make sure those decisions achieve excellence'" noted a 2015 article in the city's *Post and Courier*, which highlighted the many honors Riley received over the years for his efforts.[11]

Good leadership extends to city staffers who feel empowered to create a better city, not throw up barriers to thwart change. George Holt, reflecting on his career observed: "I don't think we would have been allowed such architectural exuberance without the support and encouragement of the city architect, Charles Chase."[12] This was not empty praise; George honored Chase by naming Charles Street after him. Unelected champions within the staff of a city are desperately needed in the pursuit of building better places, and deserve to be celebrated for the important, but often unheralded work they do. Without them, a new paradigm of development would not be possible.

The ideals shared among the municipal officials of Charleston have set a high standard for the city. Reflecting on how Charleston has arrived here, Vince shared with me, in his poetic way, that "An alphabet with rules and grammar doesn't spontaneously result in *War and Peace*." It's all well and good for a city to know the language of good urbanism and design, but if it doesn't know how to string that language together, there's little chance anything valuable will be created.

Beyond municipal leadership and the vision of a few developers and architects, a city must have a competent roster of subcontractors, which can be in short supply. Vince assured me that the right people are out there, even if they're not currently working in the construction trades. Maybe they're driving an Uber instead of woodworking, but there are countless people who would be capable of doing a good job if only they had the opportunity and the

Gaillard Center, a 2,700-seat auditorium and office building designed by David M. Schwarz Architects. Completed in 2015.

training. Wouldn't some people prefer to work with their hands if the chance presented itself, rather than sitting behind the wheel of a car eight hours a day? Especially if, as is the case, these craftsmen can earn upwards of six figures a year?

Charleston's secret advantage isn't necessarily that there are more people in the city predisposed to these sorts of professions than anywhere else, but that it has patrons who value the work, and importantly, an institution that provides the training. American College of the Building Arts (ACBA) is the only institution in the United States that teaches traditional building arts. Professional training is integrated alongside a more standard college curriculum. Part liberal arts, part trade school, matriculating students can choose from one of six craft specializations to study, including timber framing, architectural carpentry, plasterwork, classical architecture, blacksmithing, and stone carving. The model of education is based on France's Compagnons du Devoir, where students travel throughout the country completing apprenticeships with master artisans over the course of a ten-year academic program. Mastery is hard earned. Founded in 2004 in the aftermath of powerful coastal hurricanes which damaged (and in some cases destroyed) many historic buildings, ACBA condensed the ideas behind Les Compagnons into a four-year curriculum "where educational methods are rooted in the medieval guild system, training craftspeople to master a trade and teach it too".[13] The first degrees were conferred in 2009 to seven graduates. Now, the school enrolls more than 100 students annually, with plans to double this count over the next few years. Professors and graduates have worked on projects throughout the city, including I'On.

This pedagogy creates a virtuous cycle of its own. Students, who often do externships locally, know they can get consistent work that will be broadly appreciated if they stay in Charleston after graduation. So they do. One graduate, Guyton Ash, founded Artis Construction, a general contracting firm that specializes in historic preservation. Recently, Artis has begun doing ground-up projects. Ash has hired many ACBA graduates, allowing the company to offer services in masonry, timber framing, millwork, furniture design, and more. When employees inevitably move on to another firm, or set out on their own, their skills are shared across a larger population. This proximity raises the quality of the average building as others copy what seems to be in demand, creating a market across varying levels of cost and execution.

All who have been profiled in this section, and those who have not been as intimately studied but whose work attests to the same conclusion, revere beauty and pride, regarding them as virtues worth pursuing. Something that can't be said for many other contemporary builders. Lamenting the state of the current orienting principles of the world, and by extension how they've filtered down to architecture, Andrew Gould put it succinctly: "Nowadays we don't live in a beautiful culture."[14] Dreariness sucks the very life out of us. But as the stories of Andrew, Vince, George, Cheryl, Jerry, Reid, Sally, Jenny, Christopher, Kenny, Julie, Randolph, and many others have demonstrated, we can reinvigorate the world around us, shaping its compositions towards magnificence and grace. From just a few seeds, a forest of great new buildings has grown in the Lowcountry.

Though I admire each of these figures for their contributions to the built environment, none were prodigies. That's good news for us, because it means what they have accomplished is replicable. Most of what they learned came through experience on the job, or observations in the real world, driven by an ambition to build what others scarcely thought worthy of conceiving. Charleston's enviable historic fabric, walkability, culture of preservation, and respect for high-quality architecture certainly has given it an advantage, but there's no reason why other groups can't effectuate meaningful change wherever it is they might live. The result may not be Charleston, but that's a good thing. Every city should forge its own path, seeking to maximize what it does well through the power of self-determination. Those that have most fully embraced this spirit have presided over extraordinary outcomes.

Santa Barbara

At the same time Charleston was preserving its past, another city on the other side of the country was creating a springboard for its future. It similarly benefited from a few pioneers who were able to bring together many different types of people under the banner of a single coalition to push the city forward. That city, as the subheading denotes, was Santa Barbara. And those people were Bernard Hoffman, known in some circles as the father of Santa Barbara architecture, and Pearl Chase, a leader in the city's preservation movement. Both were integral forces in establishing the city's now-ubiquitous Spanish Colonial identity.[1]

Hoffman arrived in Santa Barbara in 1919 seeking treatment for his daughter's diabetes. She was ultimately well cared for by Dr. W. D. Sansum, one of the developers of insulin, and the first physician in the U.S. to administer the drug to successfully treat a diabetic patient. Grateful for the life-saving care, Bernard was eager to give back to the place that had given his family so much. He was well equipped for the task. Hoffman had a background in community building, with roots in the Village Improvement Societies, a civic phenomenon that began in the antebellum period in his hometown of Stockbridge, Massachusetts. Its core tenets emphasized basic sanitation, a strong division of land uses, the erection of monuments, and the cultivation of greenery and plant life, all in the service of civic beautification.[2] If some of this sounds familiar, that's because Village Improvement evolved into the more widely known City Beautiful Movement. At their heart, Village Improvement Societies were aspirational, yet practical. A romantic pragmatism for a young America, they aimed to lift people up in ways that could be readily achieved through the efforts of enterprising volunteers.

Pearl Chase was also a Massachusetts transplant, hailing from Boston. She moved to Santa Barbara as a girl with her family, where her father became a real estate investor of some prominence. Chase studied history at Berkeley, which inspired her love of preservation and lent her a critical eye.[3] Reflecting on her career later in life, she noted that upon returning home from a break at school she "was ashamed of the dirt and dust and ugly buildings and resolved then and there to devote my life to making Santa Barbara beautiful".[4]

Hoffman was a founder of Santa Barbara's Community Arts Association (CAA), which had the dual goals of beautification and progress. Chase was his key partner, serving as the CAA's secretary and chair of its Plans and Plantings branch, one of five committees dedicated to the betterment of the city. This gave her de facto status as Santa Barbara's urban planner before the position formally existed, as the committee was the primary vehicle for the improvement of the built environment. She used this platform to spearhead competitions and invite architects of national prominence to lend their talents to Santa Barbara. Chase registered the Plans and Plantings branch with Better Homes in America, a post-World War I organization which promoted home ownership, maintenance, and improvement as the critical levers for motivating a better class of citizenry. Goals that were similar to those of the 19th-century Social Reformers of London, Chicago, and Philadelphia, with equal levels of paternalism. James Ford, Executive Director of Better Homes in America, proclaimed in the 1931 introduction to the *Better Homes Manual* that "The improvement of homes is a primary means to the development of individual character…because through the conscious selection of environing factors in homes which are the chief environment of children it becomes possible in the long run to redirect the trends of civilization".[5] Better Homes Weeks celebrated the sort of homes and gardens that could orient civilization in the right direction. At its peak, more than 6,000 cities and towns took part in the annual campaign. The CAA hosted Better Homes Weeks for a decade, erecting demonstration projects and encouraging the community to appreciate the natural wonders they were surrounded by on the California Coast. Through enumerating and verbalizing their gratitude, Chase believed, Santa Barbarans would cultivate a spirit of emotional stewardship that would lead to the preservation, and improvement, of all they were blessed to have.

Neither Hoffman nor Chase lacked the capacity for such reflection, nor were they incapable of uniting that reflection with action. The robust organizational fortitude of CAA, along with other civic groups, was leveraged to execute carefully conceived long-ranging plans. Plans that made Santa Barbara into the city it is today. Contrary to what some might think, the city didn't always enjoy its particular hue of Spanish Colonial vernacular. Without the intent of its leading civic patrons, and a peculiar stroke of fate, Santa Barbara may have withered into obscurity like so many other towns that have either been forgotten, or were never known by the caprice of public affection.

The story of this Spanish Californian city is a hopeful one, because it proves that any place can make something great of itself, fueled by little more than ambition, pride, love, and a clear idea of how to move forward. Ambition, pride, and love came from its patrons. The idea of Santa Barbara came broadly from two unlikely wells of inspiration—a World's fair, and a World War.

In 1911, Bertram Goodhue was selected by the Panama–California Exposition Company as Consulting and Advisory Architect for their planned World's fair. Based in what is now San Diego's Balboa Park, the fair was intended to be a celebration of the soon-to-be complete Panama Canal, which promised much prosperity to the American city that was closest to the transformative project. D. C. Collier, a prominent real estate developer, served as president of the exposition during its earliest phases. Bold in scope, Collier hoped the fair would, "illustrate the progress and possibility of the human race, not for the exposition only, but for a permanent contribution to the world's progress".[6]

Goodhue was tasked with making this dream come to life by creating the general plan of the fair, and overseeing the design of all of its buildings and infrastructure. Early in the design process, several architects in his office, notably Carleton Winslow, recommended that the exposition's sponsors consider a Spanish colonial style as the unifying design language, with its pristine white stucco, red tiled roofs, wooden beams, and thick insulating walls.[7] Already known in the region, the style was well suited to the climate. Of salience to Goodhue and Winslow, Mexican Colonial architecture was Baroque-influenced, featuring concentrated elaborate sculptures and moldings which contrasted pleasingly with the bare stucco walls, grand curving lines, and bright colors. Known as Churrigueresque, this school was referenced to deliver awe and joy to fairgoers.[8]

Collier, Goodhue, Winslow and the fair's other stewards succeeded in their goals. More than two million visited Balboa Park in 1915. A profit was even turned, despite the fair's extravagance where little expense was spared. Impressively, a half-dozen buildings that lined the original axis of the fair (El Prado) still remain today. A handful of others were reconstructed to a more permanent status in the 1970s and '80s owing to the continued central role the Prado played in San Diego civic life in the decades after the exposition.

Fairs are definitionally ephemeral, lasting a predetermined amount of time. Their impact rarely lives much longer than their existence. Not so for the Panama–California Exposition, and its magnificent Cabrillo Bridge and California Quadrangle buildings, which remain among California's most visited tourist destinations more than a century after they were first completed. However, the exposition's most enduring legacy, I would argue, was its legitimization of Spanish Colonial Revival as an architectural form that could capture the hearts of Southern Californians, and reliably be employed as a vernacular elsewhere in the region.

For all its success, the exposition alone could not provide an idea of what Santa Barbara might one day become, 200 miles north. It was one thing to prove that a given school of design could be used within a temporary and uniquely aspirational context, but quite another to assume that it could easily be mapped onto the fabric of everyday life. A deeper analysis would be required, one situated in communities that had successfully lived among the style.

Since the 16th century, it has been common for the sons (and eventually daughters) of nobility to embark on the Grand Tour of Europe upon coming of age. Venturing to Paris, Vienna, Berlin, Florence, Rome, Venice, and usually completing their southward trip in Naples, though sometimes continuing to Athens, young travelers gained exposure to classical antiquity and the Renaissance, and were tutored in the lessons of the Enlightenment. Though there were guidebooks that helped usher tourists along, there was no set itinerary. Travelers might choose to stay in some places longer than others (sometimes for years), or venture off the beaten path to see family or sites that were particularly intriguing to them. For young architects, much time was spent sketching prominent buildings, measuring proportions, talking with craftspeople and engineers, and studying intensely how the best cities functioned. Naturally, immersion might often involve discovering, and indulging in, one's vices after hours. What better way to learn about a culture, after all, than when it lets its guard down? Students today might know a thing or two about this from their Study Abroad programs.

Aristocratic revelry and self-discovery were mostly put on hold at the outbreak of World War I, preventing access to much of the traditional Grand Tour. One of the few places travelers could go to study was Spain. Particularly for young architects. Andalusia was the most visited region, owing to the classical purity of its architecture, warm climate, and beautiful natural landscapes. Seasoned practitioners visited as well, notably Austin Whittlesey, who spent months exploring, cataloging, drawing, and writing about the buildings he came across. Whittlesey's influential account of his experiences, *The Minor Ecclesiastical, Domestic, and Garden*

Architecture of Southern Spain, resonated with architects back home who saw strong parallels between the region and their native Southern California.⁹

Inspired by their travels and readings, and encouraged by the success of the 1915 exposition, architects like George Washington Smith, James Osborne Craig, and Carleton Winslow established the roots of the Spanish Colonial school in Santa Barbara in the 1910s. Bernard Hoffman and Pearl Chase watered the seeds of this movement, promoting the style and hiring its devotees for select projects. Had it not been for war, Spanish Colonial architecture might not have been introduced to the city. And had it not been for natural disaster, it might not have lasted.

Just as momentum was growing to adopt the Andalusian style as a new domestic style attractive in June of 1925, a 6.5 magnitude earthquake destroyed much of downtown Santa Barbara. Of the few structures that managed to survive, the recently built Spanish Revival buildings stood most prominently. Civic boosters jumped into action, extolling the resilient (and virtues of these buildings. It was the convincing the city needed. At the behest of Pearl Chase, Santa Barbara established the first Architectural Board of Review in the country, to be helmed by Bernard Hoffman. It reviewed more than 2,000 plans for buildings in the first year after the earthquake alone. Hoffman even developed several projects in the style himself, including the beloved El Paseo commercial complex and the Lobero Theatre.

A community drafting room was established before the earthquake with the mandate of giving "the right" design assistance to property owners. It provided more than a thousand free plans that ultimately went before the Spanish Colonial-sympathetic Board, ranging from gas stations and factories, to shops and homes. Optimism was high. A newspaper article published shortly after the Civic Arts Association formally put their support behind the Spanish Colonial style reported "The chair of the committee believes this image will be worth millions of dollars to the city in the future. 'We're not going to attract major industry or business. Our image is our fortune.'"[10]

Given the paucity of strong aesthetic direction in most 21st-century communities, it's difficult to imagine such a claim being made today. If a presumptive mayor ran a campaign based on improving the quality of life of a city's residents primarily through the lens of beauty and experience, she might be accused of gross vanity and neglect of the common good. *Only a naive idealist could focus on beauty when potholes need to be paved, and trash needs to be picked up*, the cynic might observe. Eschewing cynics, while still provisioning municipal services, Santa Barbara's discretion would prove as prescient as it was bold. The CAA's plan worked. A mass adoption of wonderful buildings via pre-approved plans turned Santa Barbara Andalusian within a few years. The city, near universally admired for its beauty, did not become so spontaneously. It took a lot of work, and a great deal of intentional civic improvement. There's much that municipal governments and private patrons of the present can draw from this history. Today's housing crisis offers a similar opportunity to reshape our communities in rapid, lovely, and necessary ways. One hopes it can be done without the prodding of a World War or natural disaster. Though a World's Fair might be fun.

Building off of the legacy of Pearl Chase, Bernard Hoffman, and the Grand Tourists, the current generation of Santa Barbara architects and builders are reimagining what the city's heritage can look like for the future. Though this vision still rests on a foundation set by the Architectural Board of Review, it hasn't been static. There's been much ingenuity and iteration from the base. Importantly, the new stewards of Santa Barbara carry the torch of deep civic commitment, and a passion for realizing excellence. A thread that has existed more or less continuously for more than a century. As with G.K. Chesterton's famous aphorism, "Men did not love Rome

Ablitt Tower, a single family home designed by Jeff Shelton in downtown Santa Barbara. Completed 2006.

because she was great. She was great because they had loved her", so too with Santa Barbara.[11]

There's no better representation of Santa Barbara's contextual evolution than the city's master architect, Jeff Shelton. Shelton, a native Santa Barbaran, grew up admiring the vernacular of the region, marveling at the imaginative derivations of the Andalusian style which manifested in an "architectural creativity" of human-scaled design. It inspired him on a visceral level. "I soaked them into my bones," Shelton has said of these artists.[12] The reverence is clear in his work: unmistakably Californian, drawing from its Mediterranean base, but jumping off of it in wholly novel and exhilarating ways.

One of Shelton's most whimsical projects is Ablitt Tower, a single family home completed in 2006. Commissioned by a private client with deep roots in the city (multi-generational dry cleaning business), the home was an investment back into a city they had long loved. Far from monumental in scale, it is nevertheless a monument: organic, bumpy, hand-crafted, colorful, perfectly imperfect, idiosyncratic. Enchanting. Rising 53 feet up from a twenty by twenty foot lot (the area of about two parking spaces), this Dr.-Seuss-meets-Santa-Barbara structure defies all normal conventions of what a custom home should be. Where's the large backyard? The several car garage? The twee shutters? Ablitt Tower rejects all of this. It demands to be acknowledged, but not in the ostentatious, narcissistic sort of way so many contemporary projects do, ignoring (or shunning) their surroundings. By embracing his context and riffing on it, Shelton is like a great saxophonist whose classical training shines through in an original composition of new age jazz.

As fantastical as Ablitt Tower is, daring single family home schemes are not altogether unique as a typology. Many thousands of case study homes have departed from normal practice in order to make a statement, or attempt to change the way people live, like

El Andaluz, designed by Jeff Shelton Architects. Completed in 2009.

Villa Savoye, Fallingwater, The Glass House, and Farnsworth House. Famously, 36 case study homes designed by figures like Charles and Ray Eames and Richard Neutra rose in Los Angeles in the postwar period thanks to the sponsorship of *Arts & Architecture* magazine. For many centuries, patrons have indulged daring designers, offering up the places where they live as canvases for the artists to work. Leon Battista Alberti established many of the principles for what would become Renaissance architecture through the sponsorship of the merchant Giovanni di Paolo Rucellai, who commissioned Alberti to design his family's private residence (Palazzo Rucellai, 1446–1451).

But what about apartment buildings, or mixed-use structures? Might I introduce you to El Andaluz? With seven condos and two retail units, it's not exactly the sort of project one would typically expect to chart a bold new course of design. Too small to leverage the economies of scale that larger buildings enjoy (whose creativity, dispiritingly, usually amounts to a rooftop pool or alien architectural fins slapped onto facades in an attempt to ... well I'm not

The interior court of El Andaluz.

really sure what they're attempting to do), but too large to be a case study that is either enabled by, or takes advantage of, the tastes of an eccentric client. Often, projects like this can end up in an architectural no man's land. There are enough costs that a mistake can be devastating, but not enough upside that the result is life-changing. And so, sub-10 unit projects tend to be fairly pro-forma structures, even when they contain expensive homes.

But not El Andaluz. Where lesser firms would have pushed the rentable or sellable area to the greatest extent possible, the centerpiece of this condo development is a vast courtyard that even Moorish caliphs would feel comfortable in (though they might be a little thrown off, momentarily, by the colors). Indeed, the name is a Hispanicization of al-Andalus, the Muslim-controlled area of the Iberian Peninsula between the 8th and 15th centuries. Decorative tiles adorn every walkable square foot. They creep up on fountains, planters, and even elevations of the facade. El Andaluz is entirely original in its composition, yet the core of the project still retains trademark Spanish-colonial elements—white stucco walls and red roof tiles, de rigeur. If there's been a better condo building completed in the last 15 years on the West Coast, I don't know about it. For the enterprising reader, this isn't just idle praise. It's an invitation to challenge the claim.

Barry Berkus, a fellow Santa Barbara architect, has said of Shelton that he "has brought a whimsy, an appreciation for art and designs that relate to people. What Jeff has done in Santa Barbara is to enlighten it with a sense of freedom, shifting the dialogue while staying within the vernacular, much like Gaudi did in Barcelona".[13] The comparison is apt. Leaning on local precedent, Gaudi redefined Catalan architecture in the 19th and early 20th centuries in his wholly unique way, *sui generis*. There is an organic, playful nature to his work. In contrast to other early Modernists, there are precious few clean or straight lines. His designs elegantly curve, embrace unevenness, and bring together varying colors, textures, materials, and themes in unexpectedly harmonious ways. Whimsy delivers wonder. Gaudi's La Sagrada Familia is rightfully entitled a masterpiece, and among the world's finest structures, precisely because it defies convention so forcefully. La Sagrada's mastery

El Jardin, designed by Jeff Shelton. Completed 2014.

comes in its ability to still be comprehensible, and appealing, despite its distinctiveness. In a similar vein, Shelton's projects are most easily understood as heirs of two other exalted Gaudi works, Casa Batlló and Casa Milà, where private residences exist more as artistic expressions than four walls and a roof bounding family life.

The parallels continue as the Catalan proves an unmistakable inspiration for the more minute aspects of Shelton's work. Interiors and courts are neither forlorn nor neglected as they are in so many other developments, but often become the focal points themselves. This is somewhere that doesn't take itself so seriously, and perhaps that's the key to its success? Inspiration of joy is its guiding design principle. To make us stop for a second (or several) and appreciate it. The structure is not meant to embody the latest esoteric philosophical movement for normative orientation, but rather simple (though not simplistic) appeals to those things we're most naturally drawn towards.

Magnificence of this order wouldn't be achievable without a skilled team, as Shelton is quick to point out. His brother David is an ironworker who produces many of the marvelous railings, sculptures, doors, lanterns, and other pieces of metalwork that embellish the projects. In an interview with the *Santa Barbara Independent*, Shelton characteristically praises the local artisans and builders he works with; the trust he has in their relationship is evident. "'The talented tiler Juan Rios and his crew 'are always saving my ass.' And Upton, his longtime contractor, never 'squelches ideas out of the box and makes it all happen.'"[14] Key collaborators have their names enshrined on tiles in all of Shelton's projects, a celebration of their craftsmanship and an acknowledgment of the impossibility of creating these sorts of places without their collective efforts. The genius of a building is not due to the vision of one talented architect or developer, but through the totality of those whose labors brought it to life. Shelton's dreams would remain just dreams if no contractor built them, developer sponsored them, or tiler adorned them. "We strive to build it the way it ends up on paper, and it's built by hand— it's not a catalog building," Shelton told *PRINT Magazine* in 2022.[15] "People put their heart and soul into it, just as I do into the drawings and ideas." This spirit brings a tangible warmth and humanity into Shelton's buildingsThere are very few, if any, other buildings in America that are so earnest, endearing, or enchanting.

Oak Tree House, designed by Jeff Shelton.

When his career is over, I believe Shelton's work will be among the finest completed of any American architect in the last century. Whether he's rightfully acknowledged for this honor is another matter. That he is a master has doubtless benefited Santa Barbara in many ways, but mastery is not necessary for others to impact the built environment in similarly profound fashions. Jeff himself is the first to admit this, observing how the villages of Southern Spain that provided the inspiration for Chase and Hoffman were "mainly built by non-architects; just by people putting up these villages. You can see everybody's handiwork in every one of those buildings, and there's tile and ironwork".[16]

A city doesn't need to have a once-in-a-century figure like Shelton to create high-quality places. Though of course it's wonderful to have someone concentrating their genius in one place at a time we're fortunate enough to be able to track the progress as it happens, eagerly awaiting what might come next. I digress. It's possible to find talented architects wherever one might live, or at least import talent enough to get the virtuous cycle started. This is more true in regions like Santa Barbara that have a long legacy of championing high-quality design. Similar to Charleston's Carolopolis awards, Santa Barbara has its own set of prizes, Santa Barbara Beautiful, that have been honoring high-quality new developments since 1965. This is nearly 60 years of indicating to builders and designers alike what the public values. Awards serve as a valuable feedback mechanism for what successful projects look like, and how they operate.

The Santa Barbara Beautiful Awards are fabulously simple: they identify and reward beautiful places. Habitual winners, like Cearnal Collective, unsurprisingly design very attractive structures. The most prominent of their projects, the Santa Barbara Public Market and adjoining Alma Del Pueblo apartment complex (developed by Victoria Street Partners and completed in 2014), replaced an old grocery store and large surface parking lot in the heart of town with

The Santa Barbara Public Market, designed by The Cearnal Collective, and developed by Victoria Street Partners. Completed in 2014.

12 small businesses and 37 homes. From the perspective of someone who wants core downtown space to be activated rather than fallow, 37 homes is a marked improvement over several dozen parking spaces in the heart of a bustling city. Though less than a decade old,

Alma Del Pueblo apartment complex, designed by The Cearnal Collective, developed by Victoria Street Partners. Completed 2014.

Cearnal's creations feel as though they could have been standing for more than a century, seamlessly blending into their local context, without feeling pastiche, owing to the crispness of their execution.

Beyond a shared architectural heritage, Santa Barbara's new projects are also all built at a human scale: not imposing, not too tall, nor too wide without relief. They feel eminently approachable, and comfortable. Courtyards—the most sociable element of residential housing—help this feeling greatly. Paseo Bonito (6 units located in townhomes designed by Cearnal and completed in 2007), Arlington Village (31 apartments designed by Cearnal and RRM, and developed by Bruce Corwin & Urban Developments in 2018),

Paseo Bonito (top), designed by Cearnal Collective. Completed in 2007. Arlington Village (middle left), designed by Cearnal and RRM, developed by Bruce Corwin and Urban Developments. Completed in 2018. Chapala One, (middle right) designed by designARC, developed by Don Hughes. Completed in 2008. Mayee Plaza, (bottom), designed by Cearnal, developed by Kibo Group, completed in 2021.

Chapala One (46 apartments designed by designARC, and developed by Don Hughes in 2008), and Mayee Plaza (26 units designed by Cearnal and developed by Kibo Group in 2021) all leverage human scale, courtyards, greenery, and ornamental detailing to tremendous effect.

Artisan Court (top) designed by Christine Pierron for HACSB. Completed in 2011. Casa De Las Fuentes (bottom) designed by RRM for HACSB. Completed in 2002.

Despite Santa Barbara's well-earned reputation for its luxurious housing stock (as of December 2023, the average single family home would have cost you $1,970,000, according to a Zillow Market Overview), many of the best new projects have either been developed by the Housing Authority of Santa Barbara, or other affordable housing developers.[17] They stand toe-to-toe with their market-rate counterparts, proving affordable housing doesn't have to be grim, austere, and discourteous as it is much elsewhere in North America.

Casa de Las Fuentes (42 apartments designed by Peikert + RRM Design Group, completed in 2002 with rents between $811 and $1,351 per month), Artisan Court (five units designed by Christine Pierron, completed in 2011, where rents range from $777 to $1,295 per month), and El Carillo (61 SROs with supportive services for formerly homeless individuals designed by Cearnal, completed in 2006, where rents range from $733 to $978 per month) are all wonderful projects in the middle of town with deeply affordable rent.[18] Jacaranda Court, a proposed 63 unit development that will rise on top of a city-owned parking lot, promises to continue this positive momentum. In total, the Housing Authority manages nearly 1,500 units, and facilitates vouchers for another 3,000 in its system (with less control over design or quality).[19] In a city where the median one-bedroom rental was asking $2,950 as of December 2023, and the average two-bedroom $4,500, this is noble work.[20] Converting vacant land and parking lots into housing for the working class and formerly homeless has proven not only to be a viable strategy, but a lovely one as well, providing dignity and decency in those for whom it has too long been deprived. But for the more than 5,000 households on waiting lists for Affordable Housing in a city with 36,932 total households, they would doubtless benefit if zoning codes were loosened up to allow for more housing in highly restrictive zones, rather than waiting to get to the bottom of a very large funnel.[21] Restrictive zoning codes put an undue (and unnecessary) burden on a Housing Authority already doing so much.

Santa Barbara isn't just building great housing. Office buildings, an asset class much in need of new life to be breathed into them these days, have been completed to an extraordinary level of quality. New structures often rely heavily on the Spanish Revival vernacular, but because of their scale, they have more shared DNA with some of the city's new housing developments than their more traditional office brothers and sisters. A simple bank (The Santa Barbara Bank & Trust, designed by Cearnal Collective, completed in 2001) is more reminiscent of a stately villa; a district attorney's office—usually one of the more dreary typologies in a city—rises on top of a former surface parking lot in an elegance rarely matched by even the most determined builders (The Cearnal Collective, District Attorney's office). Parking garages are even given the

The Santa Barbara Bank & Trust (top) designed by Cearnal. Completed in 2001. Santa Barbara County District Attorney's Office (bottom left), designed by Cearnal. Granada Garage & Office Building (bottom right) designed by Watry Design and Henry Lenny Design. Completed in 2006.

Santa Barbara treatment, as exemplified by the Granada Garage & Office Building (designed by Watry Design, and completed in 2006). Rather than rising as an oppressive concrete superstructure, this 572-space project (which might otherwise be a suitable target of derision) embraces the street, leans into the adopted vernacular, and includes 10,000 square feet of commercial space.

Perhaps the most impressive of this impressive young generation of buildings is located just a few steps from the beach. In what has become a most welcome trend, Entrada de Santa Barbara transformed several surface parking lots into a new public plaza for the city, 123 hotel rooms, and 22,000 square feet of commercial space. Entrada connected the long divided Wharf and Lower State neighborhoods through some of the highest quality new architecture leaders on the continent. Once barren realms to be avoided wherever possible, these streets are now welcoming, comfortable, vibrant, and attractive.

The original Hotel Californian was constructed in 1925 immediately after the earthquake that infamously rocked the city that year. It was one of the first buildings to be completed in the Spanish Revival style. Due to years of neglect and decay (it closed in 2001) much of the building wasn't salvageable, and had to be torn down. The eastern facade, fronting State street, was able to be saved, however, serving as a tangible link between the Santa Barbara of Chase and Hoffman to this new era of enlightened civic leaders, architects, and developers.[22] In incorporating this historical detail into what was effectively a brand new building, the Hotel Californian rose again, a phoenix delivered from the ashes of its past. Developer Michael Rosenfeld of Next Century Associates oversaw the construction of the three new structures that were designed by DesignArc, and completed in 2017. During meetings with the community, Rosenfeld emphasized the importance of craftsmanship, thoughtfulness, and building in enduring ways, something that has evidently been achieved, thanks in part to the diligence of MATT Construction, the firm hired to carry out the redevelopment.

That many of the best new projects in Santa Barbara have been completed by only a handful of firms is unsurprising. Developers want to work with established and known commodities. The reader will notice that a lot of the projects I've featured have come from Cearnal Collective, helmed by Brian Cearnal. Cearnal is an important architect-as-civic-leader, helping to shape the future path of the city. In addition to his day-to-day work, he has served

Entrada de Santa Barbara, including Hotel Californian. Designed by designARC, developed by Next Century Associates. Completed in 2017.

as Chairman of the Board of Directors of the Santa Barbara Region Chamber of Commerce, President of the American Institute of Architects Santa Barbara chapter, and was a former Chairperson of the Architectural Board of Review. As in Charleston, it's imperative for a city to have as to who not only work in the community (and thus have a vested interest in making the city as good as it can be), but who can effectuate change in it.

Reflecting on the lessons from Santa Barbara, it seems that the restrictions that require new structures to be designed in the Spanish Colonial style has been a key determinant why so many lovely buildings have been completed in the recent past. The entirety of the city's aesthetic character is deliberate, after all. Far from scorning the practice, the local design community seems to greatly appreciate it. Santa Barbara architect Henry Lenny has observed that "Creativity without constraints is easy; it takes a higher level of creativity to design within the lines".[23] Shelton has voiced a similar opinion, "A lot of architects complain about the Spanish Revival criteria. They complain it stifles creativity ... I think the rules make it easier. They force you to be creative. They make you get to the point faster." It's difficult to argue with his results. Philip Suding, who chairs Santa Barbara's Historic Landmarks Commission, agrees: "Shelton has succeeded because he has paid homage to Mediterranean architecture while executing his own distinctive vision."[24]

This is the key that many communities miss. It doesn't matter what style(s) a city chooses to embrace, but rather how forcefully they march towards that vision. All chisels hammering with the same intention will lead to a better overall effect. If the vernacular is easy enough to replicate with sufficiently high-quality and relatively inexpensive materials, it can be readily adopted. This need not be a permanent condition. If a city is so inclined, styles can be varied every 20 or 30 years, such that history can be read in the built fabric. *From 2030 to 2060, ours was an Art Deco City. From 2100 to 2160, Neo-Gothic.* And so on, and so on. Only the best examples of each style will last. Clarity and efficiency of leadership can increase the probability that what is built is built well enough to have a chance to survive.

Others are not convinced. Some commentators on architectural affairs deem review boards as unnecessary obstacles along the path to better cities. The level of prescription they impose can be too exacting, they reason, leading to paralysis. Perfect becomes the enemy of the merely great, where too much control leads to stasis—that favored mode of death for many communities around the country. I'm sympathetic to the idea that the pendulum of control needs to swing a little further away from these entities, but the real challenge arises when design boards operate in cities without a strong heritage to review against, or when bureaucracy grinds the process of building to a halt. Or both.

To emphasize how well Santa Barbara's system works, it's useful to look at another city that has failed to do the same: Seattle—a municipality that seems determined to provide us indelible lessons on what not to do. Seattle and Santa Barbara are similar in that they are both set among some of the most glorious natural scenery our continent has to offer. Meaningful divergence, however, has come about in what each of these cities has chosen to do with their edenic gifts.

Where Santa Barbara's built environment magnificently compliments its natural analog, it's not clear that Seattle has any sort of idea about what relationship it would like to forge between these worlds, to say nothing of what course it would like to chart for its future. It's true that Seattle has a design review process. There are eight boards which review and approve the appearance, siting, massing, and street orientation of nearly all multifamily, mixed-use, and commercial projects proposed throughout the city. Boards are volunteer-run, consisting of one design professional, two community members, one developer, and one business or landscape design professional. The idea behind this system was that direct civic commentary would improve the quality of new construction. But as the aesthetic preferences of the volunteers are disparate, and the city hasn't bothered to lay out any vision of what it would like to look like, the process has led to some disastrous results.

In a city starved of housing, the average project took more than two years (805 days) to be reviewed as of the most recent survey.[25] "Streamlined" projects for townhomes and smaller apartment buildings have fared only marginally better, taking an average of nearly 500 days to be approved. Critiques lobbed by volunteers range from the colors of the facade to childcare centers occupying ground floors of mixed-use buildings. In one infamous case, a 324-unit apartment building anchored by a Safeway grocery store (the holy grail of large infill development for urbanists) took seven years to work its way through the process. Several architects and developers cycled through the project over this time, all subjected to the same inanity. Brian Runberg, one of the architects in charge of the design, worked with his team to prepare dozens of studies of brick colors, patterns, and articulations for the facade, none of which meaningfully changed what the building looked like, nor how it was composed. Reviewers squabbled over red storefronts that could perhaps look a bit more burgundy rather than auburn, fought for years over what style of brick was most appropriate, and how tall the roof's parapet wall should be.[26] Suggestions as futile as trying to explain the concept of Norway to a dog. Idle comments, these are not, costing hundreds of thousands of dollars in billable hours for the architects and attorneys on the development team, and potentially millions in holding costs of taxes, insurance premiums, and debt service payments due to meaningful delays over inconsequential puttering. Volunteers are regular people—officious though they may be—who have little accountability to the consequences their trivialities deliver. Seattle has given Monday morning quarterbacks the starting job. Is it any wonder they've fumbled around so much?

The Urbana Apartments in Seattle's Ballard Neighborhood, a project deemed worthy enough to have successfully made its way through the city's Byzantine Design Review Process.

If the buildings produced from this process were very beautiful, that might at least soften the blow. However, this is a counterfactual, as most of the buildings that pass through Design Review are very bad. Instead of a north that star guides reviewers, or an existing precedent they can reference, Seattle's process is completely arbitrary, and inconsistently applied from one plot to the next. It grinds down the quality of a building to each individual component, missing the forest for the trees.

Buildings become mashups of many architectural ideas, rendered absolutely incoherent and cheap-looking, as each individual volunteer must have their unique desires satiated before giving the all-clear. As many of the structures proposed are quite large, facades are called on to be "broken up", to make it seem like the buildings are neither as wide nor as tall as they really are. Architects are told to "articulate" their facades, or add design elements that provide visual interest. While this *can* introduce intrigue, so far that has proven elusive. Articulation tends to be an aluminum line running up the side of a building, painted yellow for verve, or some strange undulations that might seem interesting to the orthodoxy's well-trained eye, but induce nausea to almost everyone else.

Where Charleston has its rich Lowcountry vernacular, and Santa Barbara its Spanish Colonial, Seattle doesn't quite have a local style to call its own. As Tokyo, Athens, and the beginnings of Santa Barbara's story have taught us, that would be alright so long as Seattle's patrons decided on a set vision from either an urbanistic or architectural perspective, adopting a comfortable coherence in some fashion. However, no choice has been made, so design review exercises reduce Seattle to little more than an amalgam of things that feel right to one person, but in totality amount to grotesque masses of stick and synthetic stucco that only fleetingly resemble what we might call an apartment building if we squint our eyes close enough together. Someone can enjoy the wildly different art of Rembrandt, Caillebotte, and Koons, but just because different inspirations are good on their own (in the above example, two) doesn't necessarily mean they'll be good together. Even worse is when they're misunderstood and misapplied. Design review in this case is fueled by empty directives moving incoherently in all directions. A proud, and unknowing embodiment of absurdity.

The lesson here is not that design reviews shouldn't exist, but that they must be wielded towards a definitive end, as Hoffman and Chase sought to do. And they must do so in the spirit of proactively improving a community, not defending it from imagined terrors.

We can hardly say that Santa Barbara's Architectural Board of Review hasn't had its successes. Santa Barbara is one of the continent's most beautiful and expensive cities, a result not only of its majestic location on the California coast, but also of its deliberate adoption and superb execution of a given style. How else could someone explain why Santa Barbara is far more expensive than Ventura or Oxnard, cities closer to Los Angeles that also have world-class beaches but little architectural charm? Or, if one doesn't hold proximity to L.A. as a favorable amenity, why is Santa Barbara so much more expensive than more isolated communities, like Pismo Beach or Morro Bay?

Design review need not be an exhaustive process. So long as some core objective parameters are met, such as buildings not being more than a certain number of feet wide, limited front setbacks, a regulation on the amount of primary facade materials, etc., subjective qualitative interpretations can flourish. One can be purposeful in trying to create a new tradition in a given style (or mix of styles), but the exact school itself doesn't matter. Santa Barbara's civic and architectural community chose a mélange of Andalusian and Mission Revival, but yours may well choose Tudor, Neoclassical, or Neo-Andean—it doesn't matter. What matters is coalescing around an idea, valuing the end product, and iterating on it in the pursuit of becoming ever better with each successive attempt.

In Santa Barbara, a robust professional community was cultivated precisely in this way, where each booster, architect, builder, and gardener raised their skill by learning from others in the service of marching towards a singular vision, not selfishly executing their own dreams of petty fiefdoms supported by unwitting clients. For a more Optimistic community, a city must have a definite vision it wants to move towards, or else it will devolve into chaos and placelessness.

Portland

Charleston and Santa Barbara have enjoyed so many advantages, for such a long time, that a reasonable observer would be justified in thinking they might not be the most realistic models for other cities to base their futures around. Fair enough. Though I would caution against this being the sole takeaway from this chapter thus far, there's definitely some truth to it. The good news is that there exists another city which has made remarkable progress in positively improving its built environment over the last few decades, without the legacies of civic boosterism or a particularly noteworthy design tradition. That place is Portland, Oregon.

Portland has long been admired in planning circles as a pioneer of innovative land use. Biking is embraced, charming mixed-use corridors are abundant, and the region has enacted policies in the last half-century that have boldly diverged from prevailing national development patterns. Following the passage of Senate Bill 100 in 1973, Oregon became the first to implement statewide land use planning via the Oregon *Land Conservation and Development Act* (LCDA).[1] LCDA was predominantly focused on preserving the region's majestic natural beauty. This law required cities to establish urban growth boundaries (UGB), encourage smarter use of land within their borders, and protect the natural resources and farmlands outside of them. Portland was one of the first cities to adopt an urban growth boundary via its regional government, Metro, which was created in 1979. To this day, Metro remains the only directly elected regional government and metropolitan planning organization in the U.S.

There are a couple of interesting things going on here. First, urban growth boundaries are very rare in the States. One feels the remarkable impact of this while driving through the interior of Oregon. One moment you're in stunning, verdant, well-watered lands, and a few miles later you're in a city. This isn't to say there aren't any low-rise car-dependent communities, but just that there is a discrete delineation between town and country, instead of an ooze that trickles outward as far as it feels like. It's noticeable when compared to the rest of the country, and as far as I'm concerned, is good. More open land in proximity to urban areas is a win-win for all involved.

Metro has mitigated one of the more intractable issues other regions have to deal with, namely, wealthier suburban communities opting out of participating in regional housing production. Through collective governance, accountable collaboration exists between municipalities, as opposed to individual mayors or town managers warring with one another, who view their boundaries as medieval keeps to be defended at all costs. Regional light rail (MAX, run by TriMet) connects these communities, strengthening bonds. The system, however, is not necessarily robust. There are only five lines that service 94 stations, carrying an average of 67,000 people per weekday—a number much diminished in the aftereffects of COVID-19 and the city's struggles with maintaining basic standards of quality of life. MAX has not lived up to what it was dreamed to be, but its foundations still offer hope of future investments in connectivity.[2]

Portland's urban growth boundary is not without its critics. Separated by the Columbia River, the city is bordered by Washington State to the north. Development patterns outlawed by Oregon simply leapfrog to Washington, which doesn't enjoy as firm protection. A lot of rural land in Washington (with natural beauty identical to that being preserved in Oregon) is thus cleared in favor of exurban development. Out of the more than 3,000 square miles that make up Multnomah, Clackamas, and Washington Counties, only 245,000 acres (~380 square miles) are restricted under the growth boundary.[3] 295,000 acres are reserved for future UGB expansions, or a little more than 460 square miles. All told, around 1.82 million people live on 2,160 square miles within Portland's urban growth area. This works out to a population density of 843 people per square mile, comparable to Tampa, a place not exactly known for being particularly dense. Should the UGB receive praise for delivering results similar to one of the least sustainable metros in the country? Especially when it can simply be expanded when politics renders doing so expedient? I'm not so sure. Moreover, opponents are quick to point out that artificially restricting the amount of developable land within a growth boundary can lead to higher housing costs as plots become more scarce.

The Brookings Institution, however, found these fears to be misplaced. Housing costs haven't risen any higher in Portland due to the UGB when compared to other cities without growth boundaries.[4] The price to income ratio of Portland, which is measured as how many years of median income it would take to acquire the median home based on recent sales data, is 6.[5] The U.S. average is 5.25. Seattle and Miami are 7.5 and 8.1, respectively.[6] San Francisco's is nearly 10.

The real issue, it would seem, isn't the existence of the growth boundary, but rather a lack of complementary bills that allow for more supply within it. Recognizing this, the region has worked to allow more housing within the UGB. In 1981, Portland became one of the first cities nationally to allow for Accessory Dwelling Units (ADUs) in residential areas. The law was fairly restrictive, as only homes older than five years old (ostensibly to discourage more intense infill development) were allowed to convert existing interior space to another unit of housing. Not many homes were built, but it was a stake in the ground for more to come. A set of further reforms came in 1998, where owner-occupancy restrictions for the development of ADUs were lifted. As were minimum requirements for parking spaces, important in a city whose small lots can't often fit an extra space. ADUs were allowed to be built as of right without special approval nearly everywhere in the city. Permit applications trickled in, averaging around 27 per year, before the next series of

Retirement home ADU for homeowner's parents, designed by Webster Wilson Architect. Completed in 2018.

changes in 2010 removed development fees for homeowners who wanted to build an additional unit.[7] The maximum allowable size of an ADU under the 2010 reforms was increased to 75% of the square footage of the main house, with a cap of 800 square feet.[8] By the end of the 2010s, more than 500 units were being permitted a year, representing nearly 4% of all units approved in the metropolitan area.[9] That's not nothing!

Of course, it's also not everything. ADUs were just a starting point for the city. A valuable one, but a starting point nonetheless. Because ADUs are small and tucked away, they're far more palatable to communities who might otherwise be resistant to more visible change. As the vast majority of ADUs are developed by local builders and residents who live in the area, and not large anonymous corporations, they're also more likely to be accepted as organic iterations. This isn't to say they've been cheered in the streets. They haven't. No one cheers new development in the public realm, much to my chagrin. Should positive thoughts of new buildings manifest in the hearts of neighbors, they're secured in the innermost chambers, lest they be outed as sympathetic to the work of developers—verboten in this age where such support is akin to championing an authoritarian of yore. But Portland's ADUs have earned the most praise that any form of new development can hope for in today's climate; passive acceptance of their existence. One hopes this current generation of projects (and this book) will give permission for passive acceptance to graduate into more passionate support, especially because preliminary initiatives haven't proven as cataclysmic as opponents feared. They have even, dare I say, garnered some intrigue. We shouldn't dismiss this tacit approval in our chronically distracted age.

Portland's ADU laws have also provided a platform for smaller and burgeoning firms to prove themselves. At less than 800 square feet, and only a couple hundred thousand dollars in total costs, the creation of an ADU is, in relative building terms, not that risky or expensive. This means clients can take a chance on a less proven architect and get the benefits of someone who won't be as expensive as a more established entity. Presumably, smaller firms will more diligently oversee their projects, as there aren't as many jobs competing for their attention. Though small in scope, they represent a big opportunity. In some cases, a firm's only opportunity. Less established outfits are hungry to show what they can do. This seems to be a fruitful relationship, which has yielded lovely results.

As noted, however, ADUs are small, and on their own cannot be relied on as a panacea for a city's housing needs. Local officials, policy researchers, and developers in the aughts and early 2010s pressed hard for more intense zoning reform to help alleviate the pressures wrought by a population boom. Portland grew from 437,000 people in 1990 to 583,000 by 2010. The city grew by a further 70,000 people by 2020. Housing production couldn't keep up with this significant rise in demand, mainly because it wasn't allowed to. At the time, more than 70% of the land in the city was exclusively reserved for

Greenwood Avenue Cottages, an early example of the new generation of cottage courts. Designed by Ross Chapin in Shoreline, WA. Completed in 2001.

single family homes.[10] Prices were rising. Fast. One local developer had a novel idea that he thought might solve the challenge well.

In early 2014, Eli Spevak wrote a letter to Portland's then director of planning, Susan Anderson. With a subject line reading "Code Updates to Meet Portland's Future Housing Needs", Spevak, along with more than 40 local building and design professionals, requested that the city consider changing its codes to allow for a diversity of housing types in the service of creating more affordable, right-sized, environmentally-friendly, and community grounded places.[11] The letter called for a series of concrete policy changes, like allowing for more experimentation of low cost housing typologies and micro kitchens (that still adhered to basic life-safety standards), the elimination of discriminatory definitions that prohibited non-nuclear families from living with one another in a single residence, and the legalization of cottage courts.

Spevak was the perfect spokesperson for these changes. As a developer, he had enough financial and technical knowledge to intimately understand the challenges in actually getting housing built. But he was no vessel of avarice. Spevak made a name for himself as a compassionate community builder who looked out for those who weren't being provided for in market rate housing. He began his career as a volunteer construction supervisor for the Portland chapter of Habitat for Humanity in 1994, and over the next decade developed more than 250 units of affordable housing for non-profit organizations.[12]

Spevak ultimately founded his own development firm in the mid-2000s. At the outset, Orange Splot provided general contracting, consulting, and research/policy services, with a stated mission "to pioneer new models of community-oriented, affordable, green housing in Portland." One of these models was the cottage cluster.

A cottage cluster (synonymous with cottage court) is a form of sociable multifamily housing comprising, you guessed it, clusters of small one- and two-story homes oriented around a common landscaped courtyard. Rarely are there private backyards or cordoned-off spaces, as the courtyard is meant to serve as a collective outdoor gathering area. Though it's tough to pin down the genesis of the cottage court in North America, some of its earliest manifestations were the bungalow courts of Pasadena, California. St. Francis Court, the city's first, was designed by Sylvanus Marston in 1909.[13] Over the next 30 years, many hundreds were built around the city, of which around 100 still exist today. They took the region by storm, stretching the entire length of America's west coast from San Diego up through the Pacific Northwest. Their prominence among builders would not last, however. Viewed by post-war zoning codes as an invasive species that needed to be sterilized, bungalow and cottage courts were effectively outlawed by the adoption of land use regulations that made their creation impossible. The quaint, humble homes were presumed to be out of step with modern sensibilities of spreading out over as much interior living space as possible. Mixing single family homes with apartments was, of course, impermissible. And forget about the lack of parking! And so, for many decades, there was practically no construction of cottage courts.

It wasn't until the mid-'90s that they were revived, and in the unlikeliest of places. Jack Lynch was the planner of the tiny town of Langley, Washington. An hour-plus ferry ride away from Seattle on Whidbey Island, less than 1,000 people lived there. Attempting to counter the consumptive development patterns that were claiming more and more land on the picturesque Whidbey Lynch sought to enable more efficient and affordable housing forms in existing communities. And so, he crafted the Cottage Housing Development (CHD) Code, the first ordinance in the country to explicitly allow (and encourage) cottage courts in more than half a century.[14] Applying a novel incentive, developers would be allowed to build twice the level of density of regular residential zones (5,000 total square feet of buildable area became 10,000), so long as each cottage was small (less than 1,000 square feet), and oriented around a shared common court. Parking would have to be shielded from the commons in a lot sequestered to one part of the site.

Ross Chapin, Jim Soules, and Linda Pruitt were the first to make use of this code, teaming up to form The Cottage Company. Their first project was an eight-unit court on Third Street fittingly named Third Street Cottages. Completed in 1998, it was a resounding success. The homes were quickly sold under a condominium model, which allowed for the use of, and responsibility over, common spaces to be distributed more easily. Observers from around the Pacific Northwest looked on with envy at the prospect of living in such a genial, charming, and attractive form of habitation. Designed by Chapin, the cottages weren't overly complex structures. Small in footprint, clad in vinyl siding and topped by asphalt roof shingles, each home had a small porch that opened onto the commons, creating an intimate sense of neighborliness. "Beyond their appearance," Chapin has written of the project, "it became

Third Street Cottages, the pioneering cottage court in Langley, WA, which started a cozy, communal revolution. Designed and developed by The Cottage Company. Completed in 1998.

immediately clear that they tapped a deep, unmet longing for community. Soon after their completion, word got out about them, and the response from across the country was electric—from single women to young families, empty-nester couples, and children with elderly parents, calls and letters came in yearning for more 'real' communities like this".[15]

Meeting market demand, The Cottage Company and Chapin expanded throughout Washington state, completing pioneering projects like Greenwood Avenue in Shoreline (2001), Danielson Grove in Kirkland (2005), and Conover Commons in Redmond (2004 and 2008). With their intimate scale and forceful rejection of insular tract subdivisions, one would be forgiven for assuming these were prototype communities for some clandestine social experiment, never meant for public dwelling. Surreptitious, these communities were not. They were simply nice places to live, attracting curiosity only because they had been illegal to build for so long that much of the region (and by extension, the country) didn't know it was possible to create something like them.

Back in Portland, Orange Splot teamed up with architecture firm Communitecture in 2008 to build a couple of garden cottages in the back of a 50 by 100 foot lot. Technically ADUs, the cottages were just 170 square feet, with dimensions of 12 by 14 feet. Each had

Homes at Cully Grove. Designed by Communitecture, developed by Orange Splot. Completed in 2013.

a commensurately small front porch as well.[16] Two of these tiny homes flanked a comparatively larger main house, measuring 526 square feet. The entire front half of the lot was preserved bucolically for a garden and collection of fruit trees.

Elsewhere in the city, Spevak and Communitecture had just finished Sabin Green, a co-housing project consisting of four buildings oriented around a central lawn with ribbons of gardens running throughout the site. Of these four buildings, one was a new home, and one was a new detached ADU. Sabin Green has a special sort of coziness because the lot isn't very large (75 by 100 feet), and the buildings aren't aligned in an orderly row. This creates little moments of refuge within a more permeable site, allowing residents to convene or find privacy according to what one is in the mood for.

While not cottage courts per se, these two projects made use of nascent regulations (ADUs, infill development) that incrementally moved the needle to allow for more ambitious projects. Projects like Cully Grove, a 16-unit cottage cluster completed in 2013, whose design was overseen by Green Gables and Communitecture. Building Cully Grove not only gave Spevak credibility to advocate for creating similar sorts of projects, but it was executed to such a high-quality that it set the standard for this reborn typology. When Spevak wrote his 2014 letter to the city imploring them to update their codes, he did so having recently delivered one of the region's most successful projects. Who better to inform the creation of future places?

Set on two acres in Northeast Portland, not too far from the tiny garden ADUs, all of the homes at Cully Grove are characteristically sited around a shared garden. Each has access to a Common House, where residents can cook meals, play music, host movie nights, or just talk with one another outside of their own homes. It's a simple, but powerfully executed concept. Not quite a third place, as it's an extension of the residents' homes, reminiscent of areas in dorms where people are encouraged to make the space their own. It's this level of comfort that creates a genial atmosphere, where one can lower their guard and truly have a home space away from home.

Cully Grove was approved as a Planned Unit Development (PUD), giving Orange Splot more flexibility in how they could lay it out than if they had opted to follow the default land use regulations, which would have resulted in subdividing the site into individual lots adhering to a generic rectilinear platting model. Receiving PUD approval may have been the most critical factor in Cully Grove's ultimate success. As parking can be manipulated in any number of ways in a PUD, Spevak relegated it to the periphery of the lot, freeing up much space that would have otherwise been used for the marginal convenience of residents driving directly to their front or back door. This meant more green space and less paved surface area—environmental and communal wins. By clustering parking, Spevak was able to preserve the extant mature trees, plant a new 4,400-square foot garden, and lace winding pathways throughout the site, instilling a sense that one was living in a new Eden. Residents could walk outside of their front doors and naturally come into contact with one another, as opposed to processionally exiting via cars in their garages, breeding anxiety over interactions, and subsequently anti-socialness. Walking a few extra steps to a cloistered parking area seems a small concession for unlocking a whole new world of warm and frequent bump-ins with neighbors. "This is an example of infill density that looks good and feels good to live in," Spevak has said.[17] He's quite right.

Though it might not look like it due to their quaint, and even twee appearances, Chapin and Spevak's cottage courts are stealth initiatives to deliver more housing in communities that might be fearful of increased "density" and its supposed ills. At eight units an acre, Cully Grove is far from the height of urbanity, but it's twice as dense as a typical ¼-acre lot subdivision, leading to more affordability without sacrificing the form's idyllic nature, which is so often assumed to be a necessary tradeoff. While inside, one would be excused for forgetting they're within a major coastal city.

Portland's planners and local officials took notice of the success of these burgeoning experimental models, and worked to legitimize them in order so that they might be expanded. In 2016, the city council unanimously agreed to legalize duplexes and triplexes on corner lots.[18] Reversing the 1924 and 1959 bans on these two basic forms of housing that had been applied across a majority of the city's land was a sea change. Three years later at the state level, the legislature passed a bill that permitted the expansion of triplexes, quadplexes, attached townhomes, and cottage clusters in cities of more than 25,000 people within Metro, effectively ending exclusionary single family zoning in the region.[19] The city of Portland took this one step further in 2020 with the passage of its Residential Infill Project.[20] This allowed for quadplexes to be built on almost any lot in the city, removed all parking requirements from 75% of its residential land, and allowed for six-unit structures to be built anywhere if at least half of the homes were made available to low-income residents at affordably designated prices. How

Portland's Residential Infill Project
Re-legalizing "middle housing" citywide

A sketch created by Alfred Twu depicting the housing options legalized by Portland's Residential Infill Project.

fast times had changed, when only a decade prior three-quarters of the city's residential land was exclusively reserved for single family homes.

Okay, this all sounds well and good, but what have been the tangible impacts of these policy reforms? Over the last 20 years, total building permits have remained remarkably stable, save for a Great Recession sized dip from 2008 to 2012. So have the policies failed? Not quite. Though there hasn't been a housing boom, interestingly the proportions of unit types permitted has changed meaningfully.[21] In 2000, more than 75% of all housing permits issued in the Portland metropolitan area were for single family

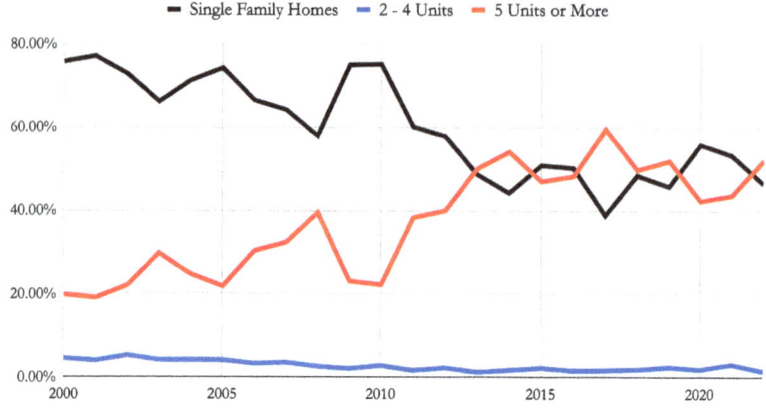

Permits Issued by Building Size in Portland 2000–2022
(Proportion of Total Permits)

homes. By 2022, that number fell to 46%. Surprisingly, perhaps even disheartingly, two- to four-unit properties didn't make up this ground as one would expect, given reforms at the more incremental end of the spectrum. This is likely because more changes are necessary to fully realize the development potential of smaller lots, like allowing for more square feet to be built per plot. Buildings of five units or more took the lion's share of the gains, rising from 19% of units permitted in the early 2000s to more than 50% today. This can partly be explained by the rise of institutional development and its imperatives that we discussed in Chapter 5, and it is partly due to a surge in demand from younger people priced out of a predominantly low-rise city that didn't have a large enough supply of apartments, and needed to build them. It's a reversion to a sort of normalcy. The average size of buildings comprising five units or more has more than doubled to 33 units in 2022 from 13 in 2001.

In 2000, the median value for a home in Portland was $154,700.[22] Rent was $633. As of the latest American Community survey conducted by the Census (2018–2022), median home prices have more than tripled to $523,100, while median gross rent more than doubled to $1,530 a month.[23] Though this might seem like a crisis in pricing, it's not. On an inflation adjusted basis, $633 in 2000 was worth $1,076 in 2022. So, median rent only grew by around $450 in real terms over 22 years, which isn't all that significant. Especially not for a major city. And set against comparable cities, it's doing quite well. According to Zumper, Portland ranks as the 41st most expensive among the country's largest 100 cities.[24] Impressive, considering it's the 28th largest city and 20th largest metropolitan area overall, meaning it is disproportionately affordable. Combine its size with its highly desirable location, and one would expect costs to be far higher than what they are.

Portland's affordability has been aided by the creation of relatively more housing units as compared to its peer set. As of 2022, it's metropolitan area permitted 5.21 units per capita, considerably more than Boston (2.98), New York (2.98) and San Francisco (2.39), which is in part why rent has grown more slowly.[25] Beyond keeping rent growth in check, the production of new housing in Portland has provided more opportunity for designers to scale up their careers and experiment on a broader array of typologies. One illustrative trajectory is that of Polyphon Architecture. Founded in 2013 by Ryan Austin and Schuyler Smith, the duo had worked with one another at Vallaster Corl Architects before setting out on their own. The first few projects they took on were rather modest—some small ADUs, renovation work (including an Airstream trailer), a studio, and even a treehouse (this is Portland, after all). But in time, they've risen to become a consequential firm.

From their first ADUs, Polyphon grew with the maturing infill regulations that were passed in the city. One of their more inventive projects is The Village, a co-living community in the city's Boise neighborhood, just off of the dynamic Mississippi Avenue. Working with local developer and contractor Owen Gabbert, three new contemporary, yet familiar, pitched roof buildings were constructed around an existing Craftsman home from 1890. A courtyard carves

The Village Co-housing, designed by Polyphon, and developed by Owen Gabbert. Completed in 2019.

its way through the middle of these four buildings, festooned with string lights. According to the project's description, "A primary goal in the development process of this co-living community was the creation of communal spaces and sharing resources to lower the per-unit cost of construction—less private space, but more space overall."[26] This has allowed OpenDoor, the operator of the co-living units, to provide below market rents while offering a more inclusive and welcoming living experience than what one might get in a traditional apartment building. When the property was initially leased up, the 26 bedrooms rented for between $850 and $1,150 (with an extra $100 a month for utilities). Four kitchens and 24 bathrooms were split between them.[27] Couples were and are allowed, but each has to pay an extra $100 a month. Love, it seems, does have a price. Perhaps not so expensive as one might think, though: the notion of potentially spending as little as $525 a month (($850 + $200) / 2) to live in a new development would be unthinkable in most other major cities, a delusion of the sort that only a naive emigre from some provincial town could harbor before realizing life in the big city is expensive.

Such is the power of properly written legislation that enables creative architects, developers, and operators to provide great spaces at reasonable costs. When we prevent this from happening by applying overly strict codes, utilitarian transactionalism of the sort that saps our spirits predominates.

Despite the rise in buildings larger than five units, Portland remains a single family home city at heart. As such, many people still want to live in a neighborhood where the buildings look and feel like single family homes from the street, even if they are not. One of my favorite projects I've come across in this several-year survey of the contemporary development landscape in North America has been Polyphon's Berkeley 6. Scaled to feel like a single-family home, as the suffix suggests it's actually a six-plex. Built on a small lot in a quiet area, when looking at it straight on from Berkeley Avenue, it really does like like a single house (despite the two gabled elevations). Harmonious in scale, there's only one front door visible from the street. Don't let the mailbox with 6 different addresses ruin the picture.

Walk to the south side of the site, and a different story materializes (a story that explains the mailboxes). Five additional townhomes unveil themselves to the viewer, with a pathway leading to the entrances of identical two-story units comprising two bedrooms, two bathrooms, and a private outdoor area. In total, each residence is just under 900 square feet. Built by Ethan Beck Homes, they were originally all listed for $389,000 before the business strategy changed and they were leased out as rentals.[28] The finishes are thoroughly modern, the spaces are bright and airy,

Berkeley 6, a six-plex built by Ethan Beck Homes, and designed by Polyphon. Completed in 2019.

and yet there's a character that's often not found in newer homes. The units ultimately rented for just under $2,000 a month. To give a comparison, glorified closets not dissimilar to the one I'm writing this paragraph out of in New York City that are less than 500 square feet, have no outdoor space, no air conditioning in the summer (builds character), and where one must walk up several flights of stairs (good exercise), can easily cost 2–3 times as much. For an adequately comparable unit, 4–5 times as much, if not more.

But, as New York rents have no relevance to Portland's, and I merely wanted to express this as a form of grievance because living in such a place for such a price is an impossibility here, a more applicable perspective is in order. Polyphon's townhomes would meet HUD's affordability threshold for a family of two earning less than 90% of the area's median income ($79,920) without any form of subsidy.[29] A dual-income household would only need to make around $40,000 each in order to afford one of these homes without spending more than 30% of their gross income on housing. If that couple had two kids, this would be affordable at 70% of the AMI for a household four. This is extraordinary—a triumph to be celebrated. Cities around the country will routinely spend millions of dollars in rental assistance to provide housing at or above these rates.

A key reason why the price of these newly developed homes is so low is because the cost of land, one of the biggest expenses in any development project, is spread across six units as opposed to just one. If more developers built gentle density such as this, the relative cost of land could be diminished even further. There are 156,068 single-family homes in Portland.[30] If just 5% of these owners (7,803) developed their land similarly to Berkeley 6, nearly 40,000 new homes could be created without really changing the scale of the city. Even for people who might prefer lower density in their neighborhoods, clusters of three to four homes oriented around courtyards similar to Spevak's projects would still yield nearly 20,000 new homes if an equal number of three- and four-unit clusters were built.

But as we've already seen with Portland (and Charleston as well), inner block urbanism can deliver far more homes than three or four on a lot while still remaining utterly charming. If Portland took all of the reins away from cottage court development such that they became a favored typology, and sprinkled in some fine-grained infill apartment buildings, the region's estimated shortage of 60,000 homes would be swiftly dealt with.[31] There would doubtless also be more than enough housing to go around to accommodate the more than 5,000 people who were homeless on any given night in the city in 2022. Whether this strategy could be capably carried out is another story. Portland is that rare city with higher vacancy rates and relatively low rents, yet high rates of homelessness. This is likely due to municipal incompetence and poor administration. Strong leadership, as ever, is needed.

Compared to the Charleston and Santa Barbara case studies, Portland is more legislatively oriented, unlocking their zoning code to allow people to construct new buildings in whatever style they want, so long as they're furthering sustainable practices through infill development. That's not to say, however, that there aren't a few prevailing styles. One of the most commonly observed is sleek and sophisticated, but grounded in familiar forms, like that old house on the block that's been painted all black but has a yellow door and gives out full-size candy bars for Halloween. Small-scale "Contemporary Traditionalism" might be one way to describe it. These buildings often have traditional elements like pitched roofs, porches, use natural materials (or those that mimic natural materials), and are well-proportioned to people. They're very often, though not always, black or white. Elsewhere in the country, particularly the South, this spirit has been captured in the "Modern Farmhouse" style. Contemporary Traditionalism is differentiated from the Modern Farmhouse aesthetic in that it employs slight irregularities that toy with what one would expect a traditional home to look like, providing enough intrigue to be interesting, but not so much so as to overwhelm. We're preconditioned to look for a symmetrical window layout, or to believe that facades should not be interrupted by outward projections. A solitary oversized window might not be common in historic buildings (for both technological and practical reasons), but its presence in a new one might bathe a room in light to grand effect.

These sorts of projects aren't afraid to try new things out. Drawing on Mieke Bosse's aphorism of tradition as the sum of successful innovation, embracing this architectural school means adopting what works from creative experiments, and rejecting what doesn't. Contemporary Traditionalism is perhaps the best example of this process in action.

Notable examples include Polyphon's Berkeley 6 and The Village, and Webster Wilson's ADU featured at the beginning of this chapter. Another excellent precedent comes from PARCEL, a fully integrated design and development firm. They embody the spirit of Optimism, noting on their website that "We build in the same communities we live in and we take pride in sticking around and managing the projects we build instead of packing up for the next best thing. We have a love for equitable, ecological in-fill housing and mixed-use projects that are woven into the neighborhood".[32] This pride is palpable in their Kite Lofts project. Tucked away between a rail line and the end of a cul-de-sac on what appears to be a forgotten patch of land in Northeast Portland, PARCEL completed three stark townhomes. The contractor was Ethan Beck, the builder of Berkeley 6. Land for this development was very cheap at $165,000, or just $55,000 per door.[33]

A low land cost allowed PARCEL to create generously sized and graceful homes without skimping on construction quality. Each townhome is 1,300 square feet, with three beds, two baths, dedicated parking spaces, and a private outdoor area. Family sized in an era where most who seek more space are forced to the suburban or exurban periphery. The third floors are all pitched with modified roof lines.[35] Asymmetrical windows and stark black and white cladding complete the aesthetic. Though the lot is amorphous and small, it has a common yard. Maybe not quite a cottage court per se, but close. When the homes were completed at the end of 2019 and began leasing up in 2020, the asking rent was just $2,475, or $825 per bedroom. Perhaps best of all, even though this

Kite Lofts, a three-unit infill development in Northeast Portland designed and developed by PARCEL. Completed in 2020.

project is in a somewhat suburban location, it's only a few blocks away from a light rail stop at Northeast 82nd Avenue, making this a transit-oriented infill cottage cluster (ish) development. If that's not a bingo-winning buzzword project, I don't know what is!

One of the more prominent practitioners of Contemporary Traditionalism is Ben Waechter of Waechter Architecture. Founded in 2008, Waechter is a highly acclaimed firm, winning many awards at both the regional and national levels. And for good reason; the firm has designed some exceptional buildings. A few standouts are worth taking note of.

Origami is a striking 12-unit townhome project that takes up a full block in Northeast Portland, and yet it's not imposing as many other full-block projects have proven to be. As the name of the building makes allusion to, its design was carefully considered. "Looking to avoid a strategy of either fragmented individual buildings or a monolithic block," the project description on Waechter's website reads, "our solution took inspiration from the process of origami, in which a sheet of paper can be manipulated

Origami, a 12-unit townhome development designed by Waechter Architecture and developed by Project^. Completed in 2019.

through folding to produce complex figures in its form and play of light and shadows. Adopting the fold as the formal driver of the project, the overall mass of the development was broken down, providing an individual articulation of each unit while maintaining the sculptural impact of the whole".[34] This is not an easy thing to execute on.

So often, block-wide buildings are dreadfully monotonous. Or, in an attempt to introduce variety to break up the massing, they become confused. Not origami. Jagged peaks fold in and out elegantly, and provide articulation without disarray Though taller than their neighbors, they're still single family homes, ranging from 1,000 to 2,000 square feet, with garages to boot. One hopes the success of this project can open the door for similarly-scaled buildings with apartments, as well, to broaden housing optionality.

Waechter has done some excellent work with more conventional building envelopes as well. Claybourne Commons is a 20-home project located in a sleepier part of Southeast Portland. Developed by Anlon Construction in 2017, a parking lot and two

Claybourne Commons, a 20-unit townhouse development designed by Waechter Architecture and developed by Anlon Construction. Completed in 2017.

home lots were transformed into four rows of attached townhomes. Claybourne has many of the hallmarks of Contemporary Traditionalism—it's built at human scale, has a stark black and white color scheme, pitched roofs (with standing seam for a little flare), and sleek finishes that make the whole place feel refreshing. Reminiscent of 19th- and 20th-century row home developments, each home is serviced by an alley with a first-floor garage and dedicated areas for trash collection. As with Ross Chapin and Eli Spevak's cottage courts, provision is still made for those who need off-street parking in a more car-dependent neighborhood, but Claybourne doesn't cede a large amount of land to cars nor compromise on the integrity of the urban design. In the middle row of the development, there's even a common courtyard.

Not only did Claybourne Commons deliver a net gain of 18 homes (which each sold in the low $400,000s, or less than $300 a foot, cheaper than the hard costs alone for many projects in more expensive metros), but it's also a part of a successful neighboring

Milwaukie Way with Claybourne Commons in the background, designed by Waechter Architecture and developed by Jim Morton & Drew Prell. Completed in 2016.

mixed-use project. Collaborating with local developers Jim Morton and Drew Prell, Waechter designed two new commercial buildings to wrap around a historic 1929 Spanish Colonial structure, acting more as background pieces to highlight the main star. Separating the new and the old is a paseo of sorts, where ground floor businesses set out chairs and tables for patrons to hang out, and sandwich boards that beckon them to come in. Milwaukie Way, as this portion of the project is known, is clad in vertically ribbed black metal, and spreads out across more than 7,000 square feet of retail and commercial space. There is an intimacy to the alleyway because of the tightly enclosed spaces. The juxtaposition between the old and the new, and the light and the dark, creates an intriguing interplay where passersby can't help but be drawn in. Oversized windows augment this effect. Though the new buildings aren't very large, their important role in defining the space makes it seem as though they have a much larger footprint than they do without feeling imposing. As the reader can see from the pictures, Over the course of just a few years, a place to be ignored was transformed into a one that is sought out. Waechter's work in Southeast Portland proves that it doesn't matter if one builds in the heart of a bustling downtown core or a quieter enclave: if one builds well, the people will come.

If we break Contemporary Traditionalism into its two component parts, contemporary and traditional, Portland's designers and developers are doing great work at both ends of this spectrum as well. The city's new cottage courts are unmistakably traditionally inspired, evoking the spirit of the charming historic bungalows and kit homes that populate Portland. The built heritage of the region extends beyond that, though. Some buildings don't have a distinct style they can be identified with, they're simply vernacular structures. One can't easily say *look at those pointed arches, it must be Gothic*, as there are no arches to be seen, nor gargoyles protecting entryways. An unnamed vernacular may one day assume a formal title like "Colonial" (which originated in New England), and bloom into a formal school of architecture that's applied well beyond its home turf. More often than not, however, most vernacular buildings progress through life unnoticed due to their humdrum nature. This simplicity of form can be wonderful, as the structure fades into the background and frames life around it, as opposed to being in the center of the picture itself. Just as frames can be gilded or highly polished, however, vernacular buildings can be elevated to augment the setting of a particular location.

Kevin Cavenaugh, the Portland developer we first encountered in Chapter 7, employed this tactic on Jolene's First Cousin, riffing on the Pacific Northwest vernacular. He used a very similar design language on "The 2/3rds Project", which was also designed by Brett Schulz. Colorful plank siding is accented by natural wood window frames and doors. The building is little more than a box; a box with human-scaled proportions and warmth that makes for a reassuring neighbor, but a box nonetheless. Architects and developers

The 2/3rds Project, designed by Brett Schulz Architect and developed by Guerrilla Development. Completed in 2015.

1930 Alberta, a 33-unit mixed-use building designed in an Art Deco inspired style by Emerick Architects. Completed in 2018.

would do well to internalize the simplicity of a design like this, and embrace its proud modesty in the service of building more affordable and robust cities.

Other neo-traditional buildings take more direct inspiration from historic schools of architecture, like Sera's charming Victorian NW Portland Hostel or Emerick Architects' Art Deco gem at 1930 NE Alberta. Remember, we can create great places by simply copying what we admire from the past. If it worked before and people still seem to like those structures, why not do it again? It's not so complicated. That's not to say we can't put new spins on old ideas, but the foundation doesn't require wholesale reimagination.

Where wholesale reimagination is desired, Portland answer the call capably. The city doesn't stake its identity to one particular school of design in the way that Charleston or Santa Barbara do. The rise of mass timber as a construction material and aesthetic finish is a great example of this. In 2016, Lever Architecture completed the first building in the U.S. created from domestic cross-laminated timber, Albina Yards, the excellent infill office project that was profiled in Chapter 7. "The project's primary goal was to utilize domestic CLT in a market-rate office building that would pave the way for broader market adoption of renewable mass timber construction technologies in Portland and the US," a description on Lever's website reads.[35] They did just this.

Waechter also took up the mantle of commercial timber construction, completing the Mississippi Building in 2022. It became the first commercial project in Oregon to use timber construction for all of the components of the building's structure (most commercial buildings are constructed via steel-frame and concrete, smaller ones use flimsier two-by-four stick frames). The exterior is clad in a weathering steel, which offers a nice contrast to the warm woods inside. A courtyard was carved out in the middle of the building, increasing the amount of light that could be brought into the structure and commensurately increasing the property's leasable area. The benefits of courtyard typologies have been known for millennia, but it's good to see a departure from the core and shell style office buildings of the mid-century period, where expansive floor plates offer the privilege of natural light only to those closest to the windows, while those nearer to the core must strain under a sky of artificial LEDs.

The Mississippi Building, a mass timber mixed-use office building designed and developed by Waechter Architecture. Completed in 2022.

The PAE Living Building, a mass timber mixed-use office building designed by ZGF Architects, and developed by a consortium of Downtown Development Group, Edlen & Co, Walsh Construction Co, Apex Real Estate Partners, PAE, and ZGF. Completed in 2022.

Pushing the envelope even further, ZGF Architects designed (and partly developed) the PAE Living building in the Old Town Historic District. Built on the site of a former parking lot, the PAE Living Building is a mass timber structure that was the first in the city, and one of the first in the country, to receive full Living Building certification, which is defined as any structure that produces more energy than it needs (carbon negative), processes its own water (in this case an in-house treatment center with a 71,000-gallon cistern), and uses sustainable building materials (like cross-laminated timber).

The design and development team's aim was to show that mass timber could be used to reduce the carbon footprint of commercial buildings at a large scale while still being profitable. This is not some throwaway goal. Commercial structures cost millions of dollars. It's not possible to build them with a speculative, wide-eyed experimentalism. They must work, or else their sponsors will lose their money and no more buildings like them will be built for some time. Having to revert to steel, concrete and rebar, and wood-framed buildings as opposed to the far more resilient mass timber would be a significant setback in our fight to create a more resilient future. PAE has proven that we can chart a new course ahead, one that's sustainable, lovely, and viable.

For cities that want to be more Optimistic, Portland offers a compelling path forward. While there is no singular design vision that propels new development like in Santa Barbara or Charleston, the city has established excellent foundations that have allowed a mélange of styles to come together to create someplace wholly unique and intriguing. The lesson from Portland is that if a city takes proper care of its legislation, arduous and prolonged though the process may be, it can become fresh, exciting, affordable, and allow people the freedom to pursue whatever idiosyncratic, abnormal, or ambitious thing they might want to do. Though Portland learned the hard way over decades of research and experimentation, other cities need not go through all the prolonged trial and error. Remember, good artists copy. Great ones steal. The same is true for cities. There will always be some level of trial and error, of course, and stopping and starting, and political bargaining, and forming towards local conditions. It's not possible to anticipate and legislate the perfect city from scratch. As I've argued, we shouldn't try.

Despite all its progress, there is still much more work to be done. Anyone familiar with Portland is well aware of its challenges with municipal governance, homelessness, public waste, and safety.

But with its strong foundations in place, relative affordability, and embrace of the wonderfully strange, I'm more hopeful of its ability to solve its challenges than others might be.

10.

The Optimism of Universities

Rising costs of tuition, overly competitive admissions, and resort-esque amenities are among the common, and justified, gripes of colleges today. Less considered, however, are the spaces and the buildings themselves. Historically, universities have been settings of great aspiration. By design. When on campus, the world is at one's fingertips. One is more likely to feel this, and act on one's passions, when one is in a place that makes one feel as though anything is possible. As such, there is a deliberate effort to be attractive. Would you rather study in a concrete bunker with eight-foot ceilings and white LED lights shining above while your feet rest on a stained carpet, or under the dome of the Low Memorial Library at Columbia University?

There's a reason people come from around the world to tour, and attend, the University of Virginia or Oxford University, but few have ever heard of SUNY Fredonia. Beauty and awe matter. This is a lesson many elite schools have learned. Great architecture is not only an inspirational force for those studying within it, it's also a marketing tool. If one wants to attract the best, they must be the most attractive. When prospective students visit a campus, they'll imagine how they might live there one day. It's far easier to do this in a place where they'd not only want to be, but cannot believe they have the privilege of living in.

While having a campus designed by a president or with nearly a millennium of history helps in this attraction (yes, talking to you again, UVA and Oxford), for schools that aren't as lucky to have, these legacies they can take solace in knowing that we can build structures that rival the best of yesterday. Three schools stand out in the success of their efforts in the past decade or so. Non-coincidentally, these are also some of the best schools in America: Yale, Vanderbilt, and Notre Dame.

At Yale, Robert A. M. Stern Architects have done much work renovating and expanding old structures, while also delivering new icons. In 2009, RAMSA completed the Greenberg Conference Center, its first project in New Haven. Attention is drawn to "the wood-paneled walls and arcuated wood ceiling ribs and beamwork of the dining room", which "evoke the dining halls of James Gamble Rogers's Yale residential colleges".[1] Rogers, a graduate of the university, is a seminal figure in New Haven, and an important link tying the Yale of the past to the Yale of the present (and future).

In 1917, James Gamble Rogers was commissioned to design the University's first residential quadrangle, entitled Memorial. Hamstrung by delays due to the U.S.' entrance into World War I, it opened in 1921. The impact it made was significant, as noted in a glowing review in the October 1921 edition of *Architecture: The Professional Architectural Monthly*: "The students ... are unanimous in their approval. But it is particularly gratifying to observe how strongly the Quadrangle appeals to the general public, who visit it in daily increasing numbers from all parts of this country and from foreign lands. Those who heard the tremendous applause which greeted the architect at the Yale Commencement last June could not but be thrilled by this spontaneous and enthusiastic public tribute to architectural achievement."[2]

Branford College, originally a part of Memorial Quadrangle. Designed by James Gamble Rogers in 1921, expanded in 1933.

"The Quadrangle has quickly taken its place in the affections of New Haven's people. It is already a cherished feature in the city's life. 'The buildings stand, in the midst of traffic, a monument to the life of beauty, to the life of the spirit,' writes Professor William Lyon Phelps, who gracefully expresses the common tribute of admiration when he says: 'For my part, the Memorial Quadrangle gives me actual happiness every day of my life; for a thousand years to come it will educate, inspire, and civilize those who live within its enclosure, and those who come to see it; century after century people will come from all over America to gaze at its mysterious and inspiring towers and walls, and no intelligent European will return from an American sojourn without having visited Yale.'"

Though this praise might strike us as hyperbolic today, it's a testament to the power architecture can hold over people when it's executed well. With such passionate reception, Rogers was the natural selection when it came time to design an expanded campus. Enrollment had roared in the 1920s, nearly doubling from 1920 to 1930.[3] Overcrowding was common. The lack of facilities to accommodate this growth led to social alienation and diminished undergraduate cohesion. Societies and student groups who were able to get off-campus accommodation did so. Those who weren't members of these groups were simply left behind.

Looking to rectify these challenges, a "Quadrangle Plan" was proposed by the university's President, James Rowland Angell. Modeled after Oxford and Cambridge, the plan required a significant endowment to be undertaken. Edward Harkness, an alumnus who was also fortunately a large shareholder of Standard Oil, was turned to as the primary benefactor. Harkness' $15.7 million donation in 1930 ($288.6M in 2023 dollars) was contingent on Rogers designing the eight planned residential colleges.[4] This was not only a gesture of friendship between the two men, but reflected Harkness' admiration for Rogers' work, which had grown to include Yale's Sterling Memorial and Law Libraries (which were both wrapping up construction in 1930) along with a few frater-nity houses (Beta Theta Pi, Psi Upsilon, Delta Kappa Epsilon, and Alpha Delta Phi).

Central campus required significant reconstruction in order for the plan to be executed. Several buildings in the core were demol-ished, making way for what was hoped to be a vast improvement on what came before, both in utility and in beauty. It didn't disappoint. Rogers' efforts culminated in what is widely acknowledged to be one of the most beautiful campuses in the country. 8 of the 10 pre-war colleges were constructed according to his vision (with Sillman and Calhoun—now Grace Hopper—the exclusions). Memorial was reconfigured and broken into Saybrook and Branford Colleges. Other prominent structures followed, like the Hall of Graduate Studies. Nearly all of these were built in what is now recognized as the campus' trademark style, Collegiate Gothic. And similarly to Santa Barbara, it was totally contrived. A century later, few care

Harkness Tower, designed by James Gamble Rogers. Completed in 1921.

that this style was adopted according to the aesthetic preferences of a few people, or that it was a marked departure from the Colonial roots of the city. Quality, however it looks, will always win the day.

By 2008, it was time to expand the university again. Robert Stern, of the eponymous Robert A. M. Stern Architects, was the dean of Yale's School of Architecture at the time, and was selected to create the new structures. Helmed by lead partner Melissa DelVecchio and a project team of Jennifer L. Stone, Graham S. Wyatt, and Stern, RAMSA opted to follow Rogers' vision with a neo-Gothic design. Unlike the warm granite and sandstone favored by Rogers, however, the new residential colleges were clad primarily in brick and trimmed in stone, a reference to four of Yale's original residential colleges which are red-brick Georgian. Though they have a different hue, the new Benjamin Franklin and Pauli Murray

Exterior and interior photographs of Pauli Murray College and Benjamin Franklin College at Yale University. Completed in 2017.

Colleges, completed in 2017, are a fitting homage to the original quadrangles. Drawing deep inspiration from the old campus, their detailing is exquisite. An extensive program of carved stone, totaling some 400 pieces, adorns the structures, including a sculptural depiction of Robert A.M. Stern.

With highly ornamented buttresses, archways, windows, finials, and extravagantly furnished interiors, the new colleges were not cheap. Housing 904 students across 532,000 square feet encompassing dining halls, lounges, study rooms, classrooms, and multi-purpose space, the project is estimated to have cost between

$500 million to $600 million in 2013 dollars.[5] More than double what Rogers' original colleges cost when adjusting for inflation (due primarily to material inflation and increased labor costs) while only housing around 1/4th of the students. It's tempting to think this was little more than an imprudent venture in vanity, squandering funds that could have been otherwise used for scholarships. Especially when public universities—in California of all places—can build dorms on the lower end of the price range between $200,000–$300,000 per bed (albeit at spartan accommodation) compared to the $550,000-$650,000 Yale built theirs at.[6]

Spartan Californian dorms and New Haven's residential colleges aren't quite an apples-to-apples comparison, though, as Yale's new facilities are a unique model that goes beyond simple lodgings: they're part academic space, part residential space, and part leisure space. In order to get a better understanding of their relative cost, it's useful to assess the expense of the other typologies in the region that are wrapped into the residential colleges. The cost of new academic buildings in Boston and New York (New Haven is firmly located between the two) range from $500–$675 per square foot.[7] Still lower than the ~$1,000 per square foot Benjamin Franklin and Pauli Muray were built for. Attempts were made to keep costs from rising further with the use of cast stone (which James Gamble Rogers had also used), to produce "more repetitive elements, like the student room window surrounds" according to DelVecchio.[8] But there is a limit to how much money can be saved through building 1.5 miles of richly detailed facade, landscaped gardens, and a soaring monument (the 192-foot Bass Tower) that would give skylines around the world envy. Yes, Yale's new residential colleges are expensive. They are also a triumph, executed to a caliber unparalleled nearly anywhere else in the U.S. in the last several decades. There is a cost to the highest quality of architecture, to be sure, but it's not 3, 5, or 10 times more expensive than the standard typology. It may well be 1.5 to 2 times, with efficiencies in construction technology promising to reduce this number further still. And remember: Cost is a concern to which posterity is ignorant. I suspect Yale Students and New Haven residents will be blissfully ignorant for generations to come.

Much like how RAMSA's ubiquitous touch shepherded a new chapter in Yale's campus history, in Nashville, David M. Schwarz Architects (DMSAS) have transformed Vanderbilt University. Work began in 2003 with a master plan for the accommodation of 5,200 students across 330 acres in a residential college model. Likewise drawing on James Gamble Rogers' original vision, the goal of DMSAS's plan was to bring students of varying backgrounds together in places they could share as one, with the added benefit of close proximity to faculty members who, through their leadership, could guide discussion and discovery outside the classroom.[9] Through breaking up the traditional monolithic accommodations of dorms and housing students in smaller groups, the designers hoped to reduce the anonymity and intimidation that can accompany large-scale housing.

The first set of buildings were completed in 2008. Known as The Martha Rivers Ingram Commons and designed by Orcutt Winslow, 10 residential colleges were completed across 300,000 square feet of space.[10] Facilities include dining halls, campus utility infrastructure (like electric, telecommunications, and water lines), and a 24/7 commons building (designed in part with Simmons Studio) with room for studying, breakout space, and round-the-clock food options. While not extraordinary architecturally—decent enough, though—they proved the viability, and desirability, of the residential college model.

Two more followed in 2014, Warren and Moore, which house 670 students between them and feature lounges, study spaces, and communal kitchens.[11] Designed by Goody Clancy and EOA Architects, these structures were a bit more ambitious than the first set of residential colleges. Detailing is finer and of better execution.

More consideration is given to the programming of the landscape architecture, and there's proper enclosure of spaces, providing a fully immersive community.

These would all prove to be stakes in the ground for a more remarkable intervention, though. Replacing the Vanderbilt and Barnard 1950's vintage residence halls, and their 240 beds, DMSAS designed the 350-bed, 205,000 square foot E. Bronson Ingram College. Students moved in for the fall semester of 2018. Without exaggeration, and in this author's humble opinion, it is one of the most magnificent new buildings in America. Working in collaboration with Hastings Architecture Associates, a firm local to Nashville, the project is estimated to have cost around $115.5 million. For perspective, this works out to $340,000 per bed, and $560 per square foot—around half of what Yale delivered its new residential colleges for. Some of this cost variance is likely due to the lower wages and streamlined construction processes in the South, as the end result is in no way diminished in its quality, though perhaps slightly in its scope. By design, it is almost indistinguishable from a building that might have been constructed a century ago. Many elements harken back to a lost era of proud craftsmanship, like steel windows, as opposed to vinyl, so they don't feel as cheap.

Ingram College's windows recall a rule from Christopher Alexander's seminal text, *A Pattern Language*, on small panes: the smaller the panes of a window are (or the more a window is broken up into smaller component pieces), Alexander explains, the better we connect with the world on the other side of the glass, as more perspectives are framed than the one offered by large plate glass.[12] Molded bricks were favored instead of extruded ones, which make the surfaces look a bit irregular, solving the problems of uncanniness and perceived inauthenticity many new buildings clad in brick seem to inspire in observers.[13] Masonry used on newer structures tend to look a little too perfect—the mortar lines between rows are

E. Bronson Ingram Residential College at Vanderbilt, a 350-bed, 205,000 square foot community designed by DMSAS. Completed in 2018.

too straight, and the bricks themselves are little too smooth, seeming somehow fake when compared to the rough nature of bricks on older buildings. Not so at Ingram. Three different stones were used for accenting the brick work, arcades, stringcourses, archways, quoins, and other parts of the facade. Modern components like mechanical, electrical, and plumbing systems are hidden by chimneys, downspouts, and other architectural concealments.

With great deftness, the massing of the building is broken down into smaller elements that make it feel less imposing than a 200,000 square foot structure might otherwise be. Projections from the facade offer the equivalent of Collegiate Gothic bay windows. Dormers carry symmetry through sloping portions of the roof, in line with peaked gable elevations. Articulation has been executed with coherence in mind, not as an afterthought mandated by codes. A tower punctuates the sky, lending identity as a fitting focal point for the campus.

Along the University's northwestern border, on West End Avenue, DMSAS recently finished an even more meaningful intervention. As part of a $600-million project, three new residential colleges rose on the former site of several parking lots and a collection of brick monoliths set atop tall, blank concrete walls set back from the street. These structures, known before their demolition as Carmichael Towers, represented the worst of mid-century architecture: anonymizing, spartan, and dreary boxes that stored beds for 1,200 students, offering nothing stimulating to the skyline while actively spurning the street. Their implosion was celebrated with mugs, T-shirts, and buttons.[14] There was little lament for the loss of the "cinderblock jail", according to one former resident who commented on the demolition on a Reddit thread—an unimpeachable barometer of public sentiment, to be sure.[15] Nicholas S. Zeppos, the Chancellor of Vanderbilt who has overseen the building spree on campus, celebrated the new plan, lauding, "With timeless architecture that will last for generations, communal dining and creative spaces, every detail is designed to build a lasting community grounded in civility, respect and friendship."[16] Throughout every phase of the university's transformation, officials have been quick to mention their deliberate attempts to create beautiful buildings that students and faculty would feel more comfortable in. Shockingly to some (but not others with a bit of common sense) this seems to have worked quite well.

Nicholas S. Zeppos College, designed by DMSAS. Completed in 2020.

These buildings have character, and soul too. They all happen to be in a traditional style. That's not to suggest contemporary buildings can't have these qualities—many do. The issue, it seems, is a contingent of high-profile practitioners who are content with substituting anything comforting or attractive in favor of something that feels novel or inventive, uncaring about its impact on the people who are meant to live with it. These practitioners also have yet to learn—or care about—the fact that materials borne

Rothschild College, designed by DMSAS. Completed in 2022.

of industrial modernity are not a shortcut to high-quality. Glass, on its own, does not mean sleek. Articulation, without expressive detail, does not confer soul. Sharp, amorphous shapes are not inventive when they are incoherent. Moving away from the concrete blocs of the midcentury means little if one is not moving in the right direction.

In 2020, Nicholas S. Zeppos College was completed, comprising 335 beds across 260,000 square feet. 2022 brought Rothschild College and another 330 beds across 205,000 square feet. Oliver C. Carmichael College—the new Carmichael—just completed in June 2024, made room for 305 students in its 160,000 square feet. If we were to look at the cost broken down by square foot of residential college space ($960) and price per bed (~$600,000), again, they seem quite high.[17] But again we must remember, these numbers include grand academic, dining, and lounge space, and the extensive demolition required to dispatch the old eyesores. Five dated fraternity homes were likewise taken down (sorry, brothers), with six new homes taking their place. The $600-million project included the construction of a 20-story tower rising 310 feet tall, with 22 residences for visiting scholars and an executive boardroom. It's an icon in every sense of the word, a tower that wouldn't be out of place in the collections of the finest skylines in the world. So, what I'm trying to say is that the price paid was a steal! Okay... maybe not quite. But in less than two decades, for a bit more than a billion dollars (no small sum, but not an unthinkably large one, either), Vanderbilt has been able to overhaul itself. If you're the sort of person who cares about college rankings, the school has risen the charts of the most prestigious and desirable institutions. Without question, architecture has played a meaningful role in this ascent. If you're the sort of person who could care less, the buildings are handsome and they'll no doubt inspire the creation of places that likewise house those who find revulsion in annual listmaking.

We'll wrap up this section by taking a brief look at the University of Notre Dame, the vanguard of (and one of the few schools that teaches) traditional architecture and urbanism in the States. It's where many of the associates who were a part of the design teams of the buildings profiled in this section went to school. Classical and traditional architecture was revived at Notre Dame, and subsequently America, in 1989 by Thomas Gordon Smith, the chair of the School of Architecture at the time.[18] He did this by first restructuring the School of Architecture to become independent from the College of Engineering, with which it had previously been connected. This freed it from the more practical sentiments, shall we say, of prior faculty members and curricula. The School's website reads, "The program's pedagogy is based on the assumption that in the design of cities and towns, neighborhoods, homes, offices, and parks, architecture should reflect our highest aspirations... The School of Architecture emphasizes the timely and timeless principles that encourage beauty, community, and sustainability."[19]

Without Smith, it's unlikely that there would be much of a sustained, broad revival of traditional architecture in America.

Dunne and Flaherty Halls, designed by Goody Clancy. Completed in 2016.

Doubtless, there would have been renegades who rebelled against the status quo (as the New Urbanists have), but without Smith providing a formalized structure of training to young architects, it's difficult to say whether the learning of traditional and classical design would have been sought out by more than a small group of eccentrics. Smith's legacy was secured by the appointments of Deans Michael Lykoudis (2004–2020) and Stefanos Polyzoides (2020–present), highly respected practitioners. In the more than 30 years since this revival began, several thousand architects have matriculated from the undergraduate and graduate programs to beautify the world. South Bend, where the university is located, has not been left out.

Expansion of the campus in the 21st century began with Duncan (2008) and Ryan (2009) Halls, both designed by Mackey Mitchell Architects. Duncan, a men's dorm, was built at a cost of $17,000,000. With 232 beds across 68,500 square feet, it was built for just $73,000 a bed, and $248 per square foot.[20] The chapel inside may well be testament to the fact that achieving costs so low required divine intervention. Ryan Hall, a women's dorm, is a bit bigger, at 248 beds and 74,000 square feet. Costs are assumed to have been similar, though I wasn't able to find reputable numbers. 2016 brought the completion of Dunne and Flaherty Halls, designed by Goody Clancy, (the same firm who designed Vanderbilt's Warren and Moore residential colleges). Dunne and Flaherty were each funded by $20 million gifts, measure 71,000 square feet, and feature exercise rooms, study and social spaces, laundry facilities, hall kitchens, and chapels large enough to fit most residents in the halls, de rigeur.[21] With 450 rooms split between them, they're comparable to the cost of Duncan and Ryan Halls, when inflation is considered.

The template of constructing one new men's dorm and one new women's dorm with each gift was used again with the completion of Baumer and Johnson Family Halls (2019 and 2020). Both Goody Clancy (Baumer) and Mackey Mitchell (Dunne) returned for design, with each hall housing 251 and 230 students respectively. A similar program was used for all of the new dorms, which is likely why costs have been able to be controlled. If it's built right the first time, at affordable costs, why deviate from the established system? The new Collegiate Gothic buildings feature golden bricks, which have become the university's distinct calling card. Limestone is used for exterior trim and detailing, while slate protects the structures on the roofs. Though attractive, these buildings are far more restrained than their analogs in New Haven and Nashville, especially their interiors. Intrigue exists in some key areas, but for the most part, they are relatively simple and focus more on massing and relationships to space, proving that quality does not have to be excessive.

There have, of course, been structures more richly executed at Notre Dame, notably HBRA's Jenkins, Nanovic, and McKenna Halls. Though new, McKenna Hall shares a name with the building

Old McKenna Hall (top) and the new McKenna Hall (bottom) designed by HBRA. Completed in 2021.

it replaced. A place that, upon reflection, doesn't look like it would've been much fun to spend a great deal of time in. The new McKenna Hall was built at a cost of $37.5 million.[22] It is a gorgeous 87,000 square foot Collegiate Gothic structure, whose many symmetrical small-paned windows demand to be observed from within, and admired from without. It is the type of building that might not be considered iconic itself, but is so visually intriguing and versatile that its presence elevates the campus around it.

For an academic building at an elite institution to be completed for $430 a foot is impressive, but for it to be done at this level of quality is truly commendable. Even cities that don't have college campuses can take inspiration from these efforts. Strip away the bells—though perhaps leave some of the whistles—carve out a courtyard, and make a simple residential or commercial building instead of a residential college, and the costs should come down meaningfully enough to use this as a viable template for development off-campus. Prices no doubt influenced by lower labor costs in Indiana, but as we've seen, even in more expensive markets, the costs of construction are not as high as we might expect them to be.

11.

Moving Beyond Utilitarianism: In Defense of Beautiful, Aspirational Places

To stand under the dome of St. Peter's Basilica or the Pantheon, or to view the Taj Mahal from a hundred meters away, is to have a transcendental experience that has little to do with the religiosity imbued in these buildings. Louis Kahn, the famous 20th-century American architect aptly remarked, "There's something about a 150-foot ceiling that makes a man a different kind of man."[1] Architecture, at its best, has the ability to move us on a spiritual level. Humbling, powerful, and profound.

Architecture, at its worst, can crush us. It can be dispiriting, draining, and depressing, whether we're consciously aware of it or not. I won't burden the reader by showing any examples here, as I don't think anyone would be particularly interested in seeing them, and we're already subjected to far too much dreariness in our everyday lives. Even the middle ground leaves much to be desired. Our contemporary built environment suffers from being overly utilitarian. As has been explored, but is worth reiterating, in most communities, we have a box that we sleep in, a box we drive to the office or school in, and then, once we're there, a box to work or study in. At lunch, we often go to a generic box that can be found in one of several dozen cities, and repeat the same thing every day. Occasionally, but less and less frequently, there may be some other box that we go to the movies in, see a show in, or go out to eat in. These places are often devoid of any ornamentation, special details, or contextual elements that would ground them in a specific community. Structures of cheap materials are hastily thrown up, only sometimes detailed (with similarly cheap finishes), resulting in a harsh and bare exterior experience, concentrating efforts on insular spaces (if they even do that). These places do not elevate our collective experience. Just the opposite. They threaten our psychological well-being and grind down our humanity in their mundanity.

Instead of reinvesting into our cities and towns, we've value engineered them down to the lowest possible, extent thinking that design itself is superfluous. *Who cares about higher quality materials, considered massing, good urban fabric, or ornamentation?* the average participant in the built environment might ask, continuing, *Life seems to be working perfectly fine now without all of that. We don't do that here, and based on my subjective quality of life, we get it right.* Yet, as has been discussed at length in this book thus far, people travel around the world to merely exist in the presence of remarkable structures that have the power to stir emotion. Domains of spirit, personality, grandeur, and excitement, so places missing these qualities can't be getting it all *that* right.

As I will continue to reference, much of what makes a city good is attributable to its underlying foundations of urban design, the relationship between streets and buildings, a mixing of uses, and a generous allocation of enclosed or programmed green space and trees. This much we've explored. Magnificent cities, however, rise beyond these core basics. They're filled with extraordinary structures, monuments to society (both literally and figuratively), that are grandiose dreams embodied in stone, wood, concrete, and brick.

Too many monuments, however, makes a crowd. If every structure tries to stick its neck above the others, our cityscapes will become egotistical and disoriented. No building can ignore or opt out of its location. Any attempts to do so will certainly worsen the surrounding area. We can protect against the fear that simpleness will prevail by elaborating on select monuments so that only a few buildings jump out at us among a series of background buildings. When they do, we can more fully admire them. Paris and Florence are exemplars here, as is so often the case. Their core fabric is certainly very good. But what makes these cities great are the monuments that punctuate the skyline. One can read the story of Paris' ambitions by looking up; Notre Dame, Sacré Cœur, the Louvre, the Eiffel Tower, and several dozen more serve as guideposts of history and pride among the sea of Haussmann's uniform apartment buildings. Florence's Duomo, on the other hand, is the single defining feature of the city. It commands attention. Any visitor is immediately compelled to walk towards it, as if in a trance, to take in the wonder of Brunelleschi's dome from up close. The only other competitor on the skyline is the Palazzo Vecchio—an extraordinary building in its own right, but one that stands shorter in deference.

Contrast this with the effect of standing outside of St. Paul's in the city of London, or St. Patrick's in Midtown Manhattan. Inarguably, these are among humanity's great achievements embodied in stone, but they're swallowed whole by their surroundings. In Midtown, one can pass a structure that would be the crowning jewel of nearly any other city, without so much as registering its existence beyond being a large peripheral mass. How many people could even recall what Harde & Short's masterful Alwyn Court looks like? Or John Cross' General Electric Building?

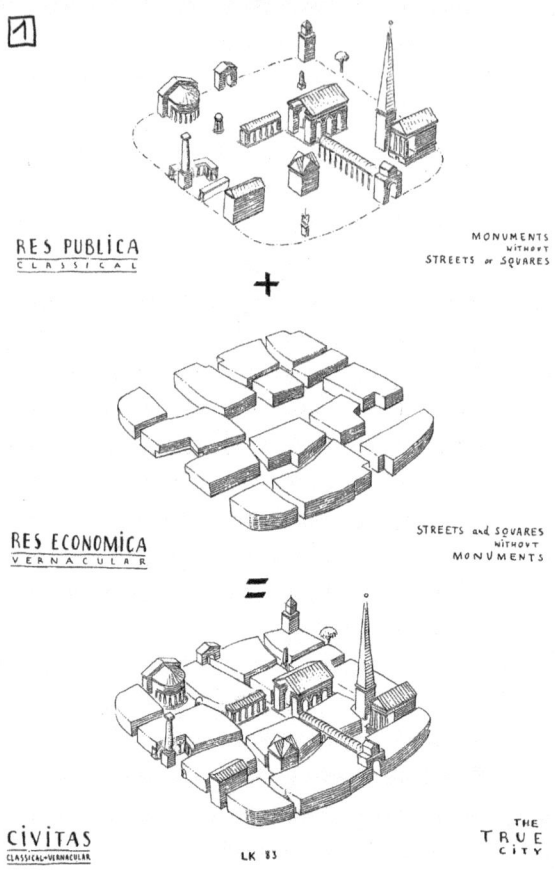

Leon Krier's Res Publica Res Economica Civitas diagram.

Architect, planner, and theorist Leon Krier has described the special power monuments have as effectively as I've come across. In his famous *Res Publica Res Economica Civitas* diagram, Krier postulates that proper towns and cities are made up of two realms—public and private. Res publica is made up of civic and community structures, monuments and monumental buildings. Res economica is the fabric of a place, the streets and the background buildings which are necessarily simpler. If a city only has monuments, it will devolve into an overwhelming and incoherent tourist trap. If it's purely economical, with unactivated streets and the barest of buildings, it's drearily utilitarian. But take some of both, sprinkling monuments, squares, and civic buildings around a city, not just in one area, and you've got the best of all worlds.

Structures that tell a meaningful story of the people or institutions of a place should be larger, and more richly adorned, so their importance can be sufficiently acknowledged. This orients us. The best cities have a rich fabric of human-scaled buildings interspersed between grandiose monuments, never yielding primacy to cars or large built statements devoid of connection to people on the ground. Implicit in their success is that they're conducive to life. If res publica doesn't make sufficient room for res economica, as in the master planned cities of Canberra, Astana, or, at the most extreme, Naypyidaw, an eerie emptiness washes over the landscape and renders civic structures oxymoronic—palaces meant to be awed by the public, with few people in sight. If a city has no life, it cannot truly be a city. It's more of an open-air museum: lovely to look at but with very little practical appeal. Greatness does not occur spontaneously, it is the careful cultivation of aspiration. Under this perspective, little of what we've built in the last several decades would classify as great.

It didn't always used to be this way. Historically, leaders, families, and institutions used architecture, and specifically the ornamentation of architecture, to legitimize their wealth, power and longevity. At great expense, and sometimes at their own expense, they invested their wealth back into the built environment. Sometimes these projects embraced the public realm, as with Florence's Loggia dei Lanzi. Other times, as in Versailles, opulence was reserved for the most privileged eyes, only to be opened up to the public in later centuries. The pride exhibited by these sponsors and artisans is difficult to ignore. In schools of design as varied as Art Nouveau, Baroque, and Gothic, craftspeople rarely missed an opportunity to adorn a facade in service of the goal of bringing more wonder to the passerby, more glory to God, and more prestige to themselves, with the smallest niches and alcoves treated as seriously as focal points. One can spend hours mesmerized by all of the intricacies of the Hagia Sophia or La Sagrada Familia, in awe of the labors that led to their creations. As excellently synthesized by philosopher Alain de Botton in *The Architecture of Happiness,* "Belief in the significance of architecture is premised on the notion that we are, for better or for worse, different people in different places—and on the conviction that it is architecture's task to render vivid to us who we might ideally be."[2]

Modernism, as has been detailed in this book, eschewed ornamentation as needlessly excessive. Two reasonable people can argue in good faith about the subjective attraction of Modernist structures, but there is no escaping their austere nature. While some can be superbly elegant, most are simply too banal in their execution. Thomas Heatherwick in a 2022 TED Talk suggested the reason we spurn the prevailing functionalism of the world is that it leaves something very important absent—emotion.[3] Even the smallest and least heralded buildings should be imbued with some emotion that rises beyond utilitarianism, because every single structure affects us. It should come as little surprise, then, that when most of what we build is characterless and boring, without personality, texture, or imperfections, our world feels unwelcoming to us. It has become inhumane.

Don't mistake this for a naive historic romanticism that imagines everything in the past was better than it is today. It wasn't. There exists a survivorship bias where only the best from the past has remained. We don't still live in the shanties and huts that preceded the buildings we now revere. Our world is a far superior place to live in today than it ever was in the past, and boring but functional places have conferred a fundamentally decent quality of life for billions of people. This is far more desirable than extravagance for the few and poverty for many. My argument, however, is that we don't need to settle for the utilitarianism that has brought us to where we are today. While it has improved the outcomes for many, why have we decided to stop here, freezing the world as it currently exists? We should not be satisfied with our status quo, deeply flawed as it is, deciding that we've reached a finished state. That would be ahistorical, and against our nature.

In the past, the construction of a simple building was not a promise that it would last forever, but the seed of a burgeoning garden that could be nurtured and improved commensurate with the means of its steward. Over the course of a lifetime, a modest wood building might be replaced by one of stone, have an addition built on top of the first floor, or be reimagined altogether in the belief of creating something better. Hope was inherent to this pursuit. Demolishing a building out of dissatisfaction was okay because something better was sure to replace it.

This is consistent with evolutionary psychology. Our brains have a negativity bias, an evolution our ancestors developed as worrying about what might harm them was far more valuable than focusing on what was pleasant.[4] Studies of brain activity, notably Reisch, Wegrzyn, Woermann, Bien and Kissler's 2020 paper in the journal *Human Brain Mapping*, confirm this; our brains respond more actively to negative images than positive or neutral ones.[5] If we were always content, we wouldn't have any motivation to seek food in response to hunger, shelter in response to harsh elements, and protection in response to danger. In preserving our world in amber through the morass of bureaucracy, zoning codes, and endless regulations, we have inhibited a primal response to improve our condition of life.

This preservation has metastasized and hardened into a prevailing cynicism, but not without an underlying sense that something isn't quite right. This is partly why we feel such dread moving through monotonous rows of homogenous tract homes, strip malls, or office parks. Surely this can't be it, right? What stories do our prevailing development patterns tell about us? That we worship cars? That our communities can easily be replicated with identical placeless structures? That we're cheap? That we value corporations over the idiosyncrasies of local businesses within a unique neighborhood fabric? Few people would say these things about their own communities, as they appreciate them for the rich networks of social relationships and intimate connections they provide. But that's precisely the story their built environment is telling. We no longer imbue our intangible ambitions, successes, and stories into our cities and towns. We have severed the very soul of our communities.

It's true that we don't technically need anything more substantial than a simple box to live in. Everything that doesn't directly contribute to survival is, strictly speaking, superfluous. But what kind of life is one that accepts the bare minimum? Certainly not one that has any relation to the long march of prosperity humanity has made over millennia. With this march, we've mobilized out of brutish subsistence and demanded more of our world. Even the most ascetic worship at the feet of grand monuments. From the Great Pyramids of Giza to the Ziggurats of Ur, and through sky-scraping medieval churches, humanity has always sought to reach higher, express ourselves more completely, and give to posterity collectively that which may be limited in our own day. These buildings and places come to define us for generations, and represent a power greater than us as individuals.

Would our lives not be improved if we had more of this sort of enchantment? Is life not more fun when what's around the next corner is not only unexpected, but full of wonder? Whether a fleeting moment that gives us a temporary reprieve from our day, or an immersive experience that transforms our perception, our built environment powerfully influences how we perceive the world.

While changing the status quo isn't an overnight process, it's something we can kick-start today, even at the smallest scales, just as those who came before us did. It doesn't take much. Indeed, this is how many of our most magical places evolved. They weren't built to a finished state on day one. The patina of age has worked its way to confer a romantic charm on these places, that's only earned on the other end of an arduous passage of time. We revere the stories that are carried in their bricks and glass. We strive to learn their mysteries. Inevitably failing, but still we are compelled to push forward. There's a thread that ties us to this past and continues into the future, a linkage of humanity that's forged in a common bond. And if we're lucky enough, we may be able to add some small piece to this great tapestry, to pull fantasy ever closer to reality. This can't be said of the mundane.

Thankfully, as ever, there are reasons for hope. Contemporary architects have begun to relearn the lessons of old. Audaciously, relentlessly, weaving with magic strings. Though some critics may initially wave their work off as vanity projects, and attack them as idealists (or enablers for whoever they may be working for, if said critic, in their estimable self-estimation, deems that person unworthy), they can often become massively popular among the general public, and eventually work their way into the hearts of even the most cynical nonbeliever over time. This has manifested in a few different ways, from starchitects carrying out fantasies dreamed up by the super rich, super powerful, or both, to historically marginalized communities charting their own path in humbler but no less enchanting ways.

Starchitecture, as the practice of hiring celebrity architects has come to be known, has taken the world by storm in recent decades. Though the practice of hiring world-famous designers to create iconic buildings isn't new (think Michelangelo, Bernini, and Bramante's contributions to St. Peter's), it's taken on an elevated form in this era of globalization. Operating within a globally interconnected culture and economy, it's never been easier for the wealthiest patrons to issue proposals to the world's elite firms. It matters little

Frank Gehry's iconic Guggenheim Bilbao. Completed in 1997.

if a site is in Abu Dhabi or Singapore; the best architects from Chicago, Amsterdam, Hong Kong, or London can be flown in and let their imaginations run wild. Indeed, that's encouraged. Through the power of social media, the jealousy of various developers can be leveraged towards creating ever bolder and more imaginative structures, and broadcast out to the world. Not every project with such lofty aims is special, or even good, of course. Most may not be. But that hardly matters to some sponsors who lust after glory. Architects have assumed a near deified role in this paradigm, thanks to their ability to anoint any place as globally relevant with the magic touch of their brand.

Take Bilbao, Spain, as an example. It saw significant growth in the first half of the 20th century, more than quadrupling its population. The latter half was not so kind. Bilbao struggled in the throes of deindustrialization, mid-century urban renewal projects which decimated swathes of the city, as did sectarian terrorism. Basque's capital was in need of rejuvenation. To achieve this, a competition courting starchitects from around the world was launched with varied goals, ranging from tangible metrics like improved economic development and tourism, to more ineffable pursuits of instilling dignity in Bilbotar and forming a favorable civic brand. Frank Gehry, the Canadian-American whose most notable projects at the time were the Weisman Museum of Art at the University of Minnesota, and Prague's Dancing House, was ultimately selected.

Building off of forms first introduced at the Weisman Museum, the Guggenheim Bilbao represented an epochal shift in the history of architecture. Wildly creative, and more like an abstract piece of art than a museum thanks to the use of computer-generated models that enabled a previously impossible curving form, Gehry's shimmering titanium centerpiece delivered all that was asked of it and more. So transformative was his intervention that it even has a name, christened the "Bilbao Effect", whereby daring architecture serves as a key driver of tourism, economic development, and civic pride generally. The impact has been more than simple rejuvenation, though. Bilbao has become an international destination.

Not every project needs to be sponsored by a multi-billion-dollar institution or multi-hundred-billion-dollar sovereign to be successful. They don't need to be wholly inventive masterpieces, either. Where the demands of basic survival have largely been satisfied in the secular West, our societal values have shifted to privilege individual quality of life and personal experience as the peaks of self-actualization as opposed to previous era's esteem of religion and royalty. Under this value set, parks serve particularly well as cultural attractors because there's no special test, entry fee, belief, or pre-requisite understanding needed to move about the space. Anyone can enjoy a good park.

And what about a great park? In 1999, Joshua David and Robert Hammond founded an advocacy group for the preservation and adaptive reuse of New York's old West Side Elevated Rail Line, a viaduct that was abandoned in 1980. Through a design competition not unlike Bilbao's, 720 proposals were submitted for ideas on how to reimagine the disused infrastructure. The potential to add a signature building block to the fabric of one of the world's great cities was too compelling of a siren's song not to heed.

Friends of the High Line, as the organization was called, had very modest beginnings. The prominence of the site and the novelty of converting erstwhile rail tracks, however, led to a groundswell of support, and backing from the highest levels of the city. After hundreds of applications were sorted through (including a proposal to build a mile and a half elevated lap pool), James Corner Field Operations, Diller Scofidio + Renfro, and Piet Oudolf were selected to collaborate on the first phase of the grand transformation.

Since opening its first section in 2009 (4 additional phases have opened as of the time of writing), the High Line has been a success of almost unimaginable proportions. In less than a decade, the West Chelsea neighborhood that surrounded the High Line evolved from a seedy row of auto body shops, gas stations, vacant lots, and light industrial buildings and warehouses, to one of the most expensive areas in the country, home to arguably the greatest architectural parade of neighboring structures in the world. Just 15 years ago, the notion that this area would regularly see multi-million-dollar condos would have been laughable, to say nothing of multi-billion-dollar buildings. While updated figures are not readily available on every desired metric, each year the High Line welcomes more than 8 million people to its elevated surface, who are important contributors to the tens of billions of dollars in

The High Line, with Zaha Hadid's 520 W 28th Street (completed in 2017) in the background.

economic activity and billions of dollars in taxes that the park has generated since opening.[6]

Many of the buildings that rose alongside the High Line did so on former parking lots, and those abandoned or underutilized structures mentioned in the last paragraph. Freeing up space for people in cities at the expense of cars is an unqualified good. The area has also become much safer thanks to more activity on the street, and fewer dark corners where crime can proliferate. Despite the neighborhood failing to provide an adequate amount of affordable housing or stability for long-term residents, that's no fault of the park, but rather the city and the planning department. They can be somewhat excused, though not completely, as few could have fully anticipated the park's success. Qualifiers included, in many ways the High Line is one of the great achievements in modern economic development history.

There's no practical reason for the High Line to exist as a park. Much less for it to be as excellently designed and diligently cared for as it is. And yet, it is now one of the most delightful and beloved places in all of the world. It features some of this century's finest examples of urban design and landscape architecture, and has served as a catalyst for placemaking around the world. There's no doubt New York is better for it.

As cities take note of the success of others, they naturally want their own Guggenheim or High Line, or at least the positive effects that places like these generate. Projects with aspirations of greatness have been announced around the world at a rapid pace in the last decade. The problem many of these initiatives face, however, is that they lose sight of the values that underpin the creation of popular projects. They don't truly understand why they've been built in the first place, nor who they've been built for. They don't internalize the contexts that made other projects successful, and ignore the needs of their own surroundings. While a museum or a leisure park might not seem to have the same practical value as a church, temple, or public housing complex, both the Guggenheim Bilbao and the High Line were built with specific missions of regeneration in mind.

This much can't be said for London's recent Marble Arch Mound. The Arc de Triomphe, it was not. Designed by Dutch starchitecture firm MVRDV, the Mound debuted to a chorus of critiques, and quickly closed after just six months of existence. Though its stated goals of supporting businesses and adding greenery to offset the impacts of climate change were well-intentioned, they weren't apparent in this project. The Mound was oafish, looking

One of London's latest vanity projects, Marble Arch Mount has failed because its existence adds neither beauty nor utility to its surroundings.

as though it was thrown up haphazardly without much thought given to it. It was an embarrassment to its neighbor, John Nash's graceful Marble Arch (from which the mound took its name, but did no justice). While the Westminster City Council claimed the failure was due to the structure opening before it was meant to, launching a few months later wouldn't have made a difference for this ill-conceived plan.

There's no discernible reason why the Mound should have existed in that place at that time. It was a glorified flight of stairs without much beauty, didn't provide anywhere to sit, and didn't serve any community needs. An ignoble cash grab for transient tourists' dollars is all that it can honestly be chalked up as, though tourists likely wouldn't have even used it for the aforementioned reasons. It wasn't even a true green space, but an abstraction of it. Manicured grass, which comprises most of the green space on the Mound, does little to offset the impact of carbon emissions. Indeed, building and maintaining the Mound was likely more destructive than beneficial, owing to the use of pesticides, diesel-powered leaf blowers, and its short lived, wasteful life. A white elephant of a tourism initiative, it was so brazenly lost in its search for desired self-importance that it repelled many people from wanting to spend time on it or near it. That it cost $6 to effectively walk up a set of stairs didn't help its case, either. It was vanity for vanity's sake without even providing something nice to look at.

Projects can also fail because of the assumption that what worked in one place will automatically work in another. At the most extreme level, this might look like a replication of the Eiffel Tower in China. Hangzhou is not so felicitous as the 7th arrondissement, in this case. Unlike fabric buildings, duplitecture (copying and pasting icons) is guaranteed to feel like a pastiche, inauthentic and kind of pathetic.[8] We cannot divorce meaning from its context. Once this bond is broken, authenticity is impossible to achieve. We prize originality and value the unique contributions that distinct historic events and cultural touchstones around the world have given us. These contextual episodes cannot, definitionally, be divorced from place. For a place to be great, it must rely on, or forge, its own history.

Rowan Moore, the architecture critic of *The Guardian*, has argued that public- and private-led regeneration through attempted iconic design is: "the use of spectacle to distract attention. Public authorities might not want you to notice that their regeneration plans are flimsy. Developers typically use eye-catching design to justify their stretching of planning restrictions, or to obscure the fundamental sameness and ordinariness of their products, or to sell buildings before they are realised—in some cases too to deodorise the dirty money that pays for the projects."[8]

This feels apt for both the Mound and the copied-and-pasted Eiffel Tower, but a bit too cynical for all projects of this type, which are rarely so vacuous. Some projects are easy to ridicule when they're obvious failures of superfluous design. Not every vanity project will be good, even those with considered and noble aims. But this doesn't mean we should stop the pursuit of building more exciting and inspiring places. It means we must try harder. The good places will last. Those that aren't beloved or valued will fade away if there's no desire to maintain them, leaving room for better projects to take their place.

New York's Little Island recently opened its gates as the most prominent vanity project of the early 2020s. Settled atop 132 concrete tulips in the Hudson River, the 2.4-acre park features 350 species of flowers, trees, and shrubs, as well as a nearly 700-seat amphitheater. Meticulously cared for pathways carve elegant slopes through the air. It is my belief that this is an excellent place that is both beautiful and a worthy addition to the already superb series of public spaces that line Manhattan's West Side.

The park was made possible through a $260-million gift from the billionaire couple Barry Diller and Diane von Furstenberg (this amount does not include a further $120 million pledged for future maintenance in the coming decades). Disapproval from the media has been strong, though it should be noted that the public seems to have broadly and excitedly embraced the island Critiques have stemmed from three main sources: private actors shaping public spaces, the location of the project, and the usage of the funds donated by Diller. While these critiques all have some merit, on the whole I think they're misguided.

Private actors have been shaping cities for all of civilized history. Recently, this has become more true in the U.S. as the public sector has receded from building initiatives, leading to higher proportional shares of construction from the private sector. Even some places that are most associated with the public realm aren't truly "public" spaces in that they aren't actually publicly operated. As *Slate* columnist Henry Grabar notes, "Central Park, Bryant Park, and Union Square, are run not by the city parks department but by local groups funded by property owners and civic grandees".[9] There are, moreover, many fantastic privately-owned spaces that are accessible to the public, like Rockefeller Center, Santa Monica Pier, and Pike's Place Market, to name just a few. A moral purity test that believes public spaces cannot be owned by private individuals, such as has been advanced by the many critics of projects like Little Island, is the wrong metric to gauge whether someone can enjoy a space or not. What matters is not who built it, but how it performs.

This doesn't mean there aren't negative impacts, Grabar continues: "The corrosive long-term consequence is that private money flows in ever-larger amounts to flagship parks while support for taxes ebbs, inequalities grow between public spaces in rich and poor neighborhoods, and government is made the caretaker of last resort. At those parks dependent on philanthropy, meanwhile, donors dictate the path of new investment." Privately funded spaces can be exclusive, denying access to those of lesser means or even whose appearances are deemed unworthy. We must create spaces where all members of society can congregate and enjoy. But that doesn't mean we should limit the creation of privately funded spaces because they *might* exclude, when we have a shortage of quality places from the public sector and an almost limitless desire for quality third places in our cities and towns.

The critique I'm most sympathetic to is that of the location of the project. The West Side of Manhattan surrounding Little Island (consisting of Chelsea, the Meatpacking District, the West Village, and Tribeca) is one of the wealthiest pockets in the world. It's within a stone's throw of the Whitney Museum, Chelsea Market, 8-figure townhouses, and five-star hotels. The High Line runs in parallel two blocks away for nearly 2 miles . If ever there was an embarrassment of riches in the urban environment, this would be the place.

Frankly, Hudson River Park (the 4-mile stretch Little Island is situated along), is one of the last places that needs a project like this. Before Little Island came along, it was already the standard bearer for waterfront parks globally, attracting 17 million visitors a year and receiving billions of dollars in cumulative investment.[10] Adding Little Island to HRP is like adding gold leaf to a Maraschino cherry-topped ice cream sundae made of the most delicate cow's milk that has been painstakingly overseen by a team of round-the-clock dedicated professionals. But that's the benefit of compounding: the rich get richer. Doubtless, other places in New York would have also benefited from what is assured to be a future landmark of the city. Ultimately, however, the location was up to the discretion of the sponsors of the project, who just so happen to live and work within close walking distance of the site.

The loudest source of criticism surrounding Diller and Von Furstenberg's Island has been the way it was financed from the outset. Many detractors have prescribed just where Diller's nearly $400-million gift *should* have gone, as well as the city and state's $21 million (though they've not taken into account that much of the public funding will be recouped through events and concessions revenue). Would that money be well spent on affordable housing? Yes. Food kitchens? Absolutely. Improvements to public transportation? Of course. Education in marginalized communities? Unquestionably.

But these critiques and suggestions ignore something fundamental: Little Island's funding is of a private nature that has only been made available to the public for the specific use of this project. If the money wasn't used for this park, it would have just stayed in its owner's pockets. These funds were not a discretionary item that the public could have voted on. It's a gift that we can enjoy. Many have. Further, it's not as though Diller and Von Furstenberg would have spent the money on any of the critics' charities or causes of choice. In a grossly simplified way that opens itself up for misinterpretation, it's like telling someone the money they budgeted for a weekend kayaking should be spent on organic groceries.

Kayak money was never going to be spent on groceries, organic or otherwise.

Moreover, Diller and von Furstenberg have already given generously to education, health services, and community development groups, among other sectors. They've pledged to give more than half of their $5 billion fortune away to charity by the end of their lives.[11] We should celebrate investments back into the built environment, and encourage more people to make them. Instead of spending their money on a super-yacht docked in some exotic enclave, or a Rothko sheltered in a free port that will never see the light of day, Diller and Von Furstenberg have chosen to spend it in a way that allows millions of people to enjoy an iconic park. One that is sure to inspire future iterations in New York and beyond.

Thomas Heatherwick, who designed Little Island, remarked in an interview with Fred Mills of *The B1M*, "This isn't a substitute for a project in The Bronx, or Harlem." He continued, "Projects should be happening of this level of ambition in every borough and in every part of all types of cities."[12] He's absolutely right! Of course not every neighborhood has the ability to support a project of this nature, but they should seek to create their own commensurate representations. We must focus on making our places better and more enjoyable for all, not succumb to the vapidity of utility that dulls our senses and strips excitement out of where we live.

Architecture critic Paul Goldberger distilled Heatherwick's role as the frontman of this era of vanity building well: "In general, Heatherwick ... does not design the kind of conventional projects that mayors and city councils, strapped by tight municipal budgets, would be inclined to commission on their own; his unusual and ambitious work generally requires both more vision and a larger pocketbook, which is why he has become the embodiment of a new type of privately sponsored public place, underwritten by billionaire benefactors, such as Barry Diller and Stephen Ross, who would like to be remembered as patrons of a new kind of urban planning."

MOVING BEYOND UTILITARIANISM   437

Aerial of Little Island overlooking Chelsea and Midtown Manhattan. Completed in 2021.

Goldberger continues, "He is also convinced that his projects will benefit their cities, and that he has the opportunity to take advantage of an unusual moment in history, when the owners of private wealth ... are showing interest in the public realm."[13]

Much as it may be looked down upon by elite sentiments, there's a reason why millions of families travel to Disney theme parks every year: we revel in the ability to simply have a good time. We'd do well to transpose some of Disney's placemaking into our everyday lives. If our goal is to create places people will enjoy, we could do worse than taking a few lessons from Theme Park Urbanism, which is expressly designed to cultivate joy.

Perhaps the issue many are grappling with when confronted with this age of vanity projects is what our new societal values are—not the built environment's reflection of them. The monuments we build today aren't to Gods, the church, the state, science, industry, or corporations (mostly), but to places that are built for enjoyment's sake, which can sometimes manifest in graceless and indelicate ways. Murals are more likely to be designed for pouty-mouth selfies to be taken in front of rather than deep contemplation. It makes some deeply uncomfortable that our values privilege this vanity—which is understandable; I've often been frustrated by this as well. But it's also a signal of what people broadly want. In economics terms, this is the market speaking pretty clearly to us. Who are we to turn our noses up at it? Rather than sneer, we should seek to present these new values in the best light possible.

The disconnect between what our societies ought to build and what the masses value is no modern phenomena. Edwin Heathcote of *Financial Times* elaborates, "Architects are loath to talk about fashion but starchitecture is exactly that, a fashion. The history of architecture has been one of styles—Gothic, Neoclassical, Art Nouveau and Art Deco. Modernism came with ideology, with theory and then the 'isms'—from Constructivism to deconstructionism, late modernism to Postmodernism. Now fashion itself has replaced ideology, the form is the content, the medium the message."[14]

Heathcote, in defense of vanity, writes, "At least with a starchitect system there is a chance of getting something good." This is an important point. At a basic level, people just want nice things in their neighborhoods. In a time where value-engineering and spreadsheet architecture have become so soul-crushing that dreadful monotony reigns, people are desperate for anything they can cling to in order to shape their identity.

For everyday buildings and streets, the desire of embodied expression has trumped utilitarianism. Living in boxes of artificial materials that facilitate nothing more than our base needs is a recipe for dissatisfaction. We aren't utilitarian beings any more than the limitations of our resources constrain us to be.

Yes, we have pressing housing and homeless crises to solve. Yes, climate change threatens to alter or destroy the livelihoods of hundreds of millions globally. Yes, many are impoverished. Yes, there are wars. And yes, there are hundreds of other issues I won't be able to mention here that likewise merit attention. But building vanity projects and solving these challenges aren't mutually exclusive. What happens when we (hopefully) address these crises? What would the world look like if we focused solely on satisfying utilitarian demands without giving any consideration to our spiritual and emotional needs? Not one that's worth wasting keystrokes and ink dwelling about. A world that prioritizes only the most basic needs for survival would still be chillingly bleak if it didn't include provision for beauty or joy. Vanity projects, then, serve a critical psychological purpose. One that cannot be denigrated. There will always be new challenges to face. The goal posts will always move. We can't wait until we've solved every issue to begin building a better world, because that will never happen.

A difficult reality to face is that we possess the ability to solve a great deal our most pressing challenges at current funding levels, but our society has been plagued by misallocations of resources and crises in inefficiency. Administrative bloat, corruption, special interests, and pet-priorities see dedicated funds misdirected and squandered. The solution, for many of these challenges, does not reside in the avarice for ever more funding, but rather a prudent and accountable management of the money that has already been allocated for them.

Should political winds necessitate it, perhaps additional proceeds for a given challenge, where needed, could be raised through special fees levied on the profits derived from certain vanity projects. But killing them is senseless. In that case, the public loses twice over, as we're prevented from having a place we might have used and loved, and we don't see potential tax dollars and economic development. Should we sacrifice quality because of the ineptitude of those whose demands we continue to fuel? No.

As people, we have a tendency to view what exists today as always having been there. It's difficult to conceive of a world without an Eiffel Tower or the Statue of Liberty, even though they're brand new on the timescale of civilization. We're not bothered by the hundreds upon thousands of failed cultural attractions that preceded one single Eiffel Tower, because we don't think about their existence. We value the monuments of today, but rarely question how they came to be, for better or worse.

Our most beloved places are the result of long consideration, years of tireless work, an ambition to deliver some bit of extraordinariness, and the winds of fate carrying them to the present day. They didn't just spontaneously come into being. Identity creation in the city-building discipline is a dynamic process. If cities knew what would succeed, they'd simply do it. But they don't, so they must try, try, and try again. As well they should.

This requires much investment: of time, financial resources, and physical space. As previously noted throughout the book, this process can start with pop-ups or bits of tactical urbanism to test what people gravitate towards. After careful observance, builders can double-down on what works, and set aside what doesn't. Feedback loops are important.

For larger projects, cost overruns and lavish budgets are easy subjects to pin blame on. But to a certain extent ... does it matter? Neither the Duomo, the Pantheon, nor Grand Central Terminal adhered to a strict budget that required value engineering. The resulting places are phenomenally enriching pieces of functional art that are among humanity's greatest creations. Cost is a concern to which posterity is ignorant. While this isn't a justification for cities or benefactors to be profligate, there are circumstances for which the value of a given thing is far greater than whatever the dollar amount it took to create it. No price tag exists for such treasures. For projects of deep spiritual, cultural, and societal importance, we must play the long game, not just the next election cycle.

Make no mistake—monuments cannot rise without solid background buildings to support them. And none of these structures matter much if municipal services aren't properly administered. But these are basic Maslowian needs. We aspire to higher stations. Refusing the potential to improve the quality of a people's life for the sake of parsimony mistakes sympathy for the beleaguered with kinship for their poverty. The marginalized do not live in shortage because that is their will, but this false belief deprives them of amenities they would readily enjoy. A family living in poverty has no less desire than a wealthy one to go to a well-tended park, or admire a work of public art. They simply don't have access to them. What cruelty would lead one to believe this? To view marginalized communities as requiring nothing more than the bare necessities is to deprive them of higher-level humanity. Not merely patronizing, it is villainy.

We shouldn't bemoan the effects of compounding from vanity projects, nor ignore their existence. We should lean into their ability to improve the quality of life of all people, and take steps to fuel economic growth in the most marginalized places that have historically not had access to them. We can't ignore our neighbors. Projects like the Bronx's Concrete Plant Park along the Bronx River represent small interventions that can play a meaningful part in turning around the fortunes of a neighborhood.

Should we continue to build aspirational places, of sometimes dubious utility and excess ornamentation? Yes. Absolutely. We should seek to make them as exceptional as possible. They make our lives more exciting. Give our hearts a little heart jump. Imbue this world that's so quick to shut down joy with a little bit of it. We encourage the creation of more green spaces, imaginative third places, and thought-provoking installations in the public realm that bring together those of all colors, classes, and creeds to rub shoulders with one another and deliver on the limitless potential that is the project of the city. We must work towards adding more great places, in all places, for all.

Just as it's important to celebrate special days, and, arguably more importantly, to celebrate nothing in particular at all, we must herald the superfluous and the ordinary in our built environment. Life is meaningful to the extent we give meaning to it. If one reverts to nihilism in the belief that nothing matters, nothing will matter. In my opinion, that life is quite sad. But, if we find joy in the little things, and come up with fantastical reasons to celebrate (whether it's "a 100th anniversary of an important event in my culture", "I won my swim meet today", or "I simply felt like indulging myself") and carve those commemorations into the built environment, the world will be a better place.

12.

On Stewardship

An Optimistic philosophy is predicated on the belief that we should create wonderful places in accordance with human needs, organically evolving in a resilient mode such that we can maximize our quality of life today without it coming at the expense of the world around us, or our successors' futures. In this way, it's similar to Danish architect Bjarke Ingels' idea of "hedonistic sustainability". By making sustainable architecture more exciting than the severe and forbidding design that informed by, among other beliefs, Mies van der Rohe's utterance of "Less is more" (the phrase originally comes from Mies' boss and teacher, Peter Behrens), more people will become interested in creating a greener, cleaner future. We can do this, he believes, without having to reduce consumption or lead ascetic lifestyles. If improving the planet isn't sufficiently compelling to people, after all, they won't want to do it. Hedonism is an important motivator. Drawing on Robert Venturi's "Less is a bore" maxim, Ingles' twist of "Yes is more" taps into a key insight.

The most sustainable places are the ones that will be cared for over many generations. All things equal, people would much rather preserve an attractive, enchanting place than a boring and sad one. The consequences of this extend far beyond aesthetics. Of all sources of global emissions, construction is the third largest polluter.[1] Tearing down structures only to build them anew every generation or two guarantees carbon emissions will remain high. Unfortunately, that's exactly what we do. According to an EPA survey from the late '90s, the U.S. demolishes nearly 1 billion square feet of residential and commercial space per year, amounting to some 65 million tons of waste.[2] These are really high numbers to wrap one's head around.[2] To give some perspective, a study from Brookings found that based on the 2004 trajectory of development patterns, over a period of 25 years, the U.S. would have demolished and rebuilt one third of its entire building stock, for a total of 82 billion square feet.[3] California's power needs could be supplied for a decade based on the energy this process would consume. Our pace of demolition and construction has only accelerated in the 20 years since this report was released. Every year, 1–2% of a growing national supply of housing is torn down and rebuilt.

Transportation is the second largest source of emissions. This is also bad news for our single-generation building practices. In our globalized world, it's possible (and likely) for a condo tower built in Miami to be made of steel from China, furnished with marble from Italy, wood from British Columbia, copper from Chile, and furniture from Denmark, with hundreds of other materials and component parts making the trip to South Florida from around the world. Simply shipping the materials to the site is a massively carbon-intensive exercise. Now multiply that over many millions of buildings.

This illustrates a key flaw in the prevailing discussion and regulation of "green" building in North America. One can build to a Passivhaus standard (airtight, highly energy and thermally efficient structures), or other more arbitrary point-based sustainability systems, but if those structures are not built to last more than 50 or 100 years, gains from efficient energy usage during the life of a given building will be wiped out by the need to construct another. A report by the Preservation Green Lab at the National Trust for Historic Preservation confirms this, finding it could take up to

Love Lane Mews, a 38-unit condominium property realized through the conversion of five prewar parking garages in Brooklyn Heights. Designed by SBJGroup, developed by Donald Zucker Real Estate Company. Completed in 2013.

"80 years for a new building that is 30% more efficient than an average-performing existing building to overcome, through efficient operations, the negative climate change impacts related to the construction process".[4] How many places that are built today will last for 80 years, given current construction practices? Far fewer than one might hope. In the same study, it was found that commercial office buildings that were built to a very high level of energy efficiency would not overcome emissions from the demolition of prior buildings, and their own construction, for 25 to 42 years. Many commercial offices built in the '80s are already nearing the end of their usable lives, without much hope of being converted into another use. Their deep floor plates don't lend themselves well to being broken up easily enough to justify the cost of redevelopment.

Buildings live many lives, for many lives, if we allow them. This means that we must build structures well enough such that they can either be adaptively reused into another asset class, or converted from the same asset class to a different degree of intensity (such as converting single-family homes to apartments and back again, should the market demand it). We used to build this way. There are a number of early-20th century parking garages that now serve as excellent offices, homes, and restaurants without their present-day occupants knowing anything about their past lives. It is inconceivable that the highly specialized buildings of today could ever be converted to something else tomorrow.

If the most sustainable building is one that's already been built, the second most sustainable is one that's built to last for a long time. As an aside, I won't entertain any arguments from neo-Malthusians or degrowthers who contest the need to accommodate our rising global population, or worse, think we must reduce civilization pursuant to a Procrustean bed of sustainability. Though more "sustainable" for the preservation of natural lands and resources, any philosophy which implies mass culling in order to obtain its goals is not worth spending any time on, other than to call out its villainy. Especially not when such a goal can easily be accomplished by other, less monstrous means.

According to the Intergovernmental Panel on Climate Change, the most sustainable thing cities can do is promote more infill development. From Chapter 8 of a very, very long report: "Established cities will achieve the largest GHG emissions savings by replacing, repurposing, or retrofitting the building stock, targeted infilling and densifying."[5] This should be intuitive. Building in places that have already been developed, with infrastructure and services already in place, is obviously superior to clearing forest lands and farms. Being a good steward of our built environment means not destroying our natural lands which support us.

We can reduce our footprint by employing more dense development patterns, infilling already built-up areas, and gradually moving away from environmentally cataclysmic exurban subdivisions. That they also require more money to operate than their revenues bring in, and drain a disproportionate amount of infrastructure spending to keep them operable, are further imperatives to stop propping up these sorts of communities. This isn't to say we should encourage people to abandon their homes tomorrow, but rather, that we should work towards creating an optimal structure that is eminently desirable such that they choose to move there of their own will, while gradually reducing the subsidies their towns and subdivisions currently receive. Pushing in one direction, pulling in the other.

For those communities that don't survive this transition, there are countless towns and cities with good bones that would not only be open to accommodating new residents, but ecstatic to have them. Youngstown, Gary, and St. Louis are just three of the many hundreds of places in the U.S. that have the infrastructure to support more people (these cities alone once housed more than 1.2 million far more than the 400,000 or so who live there today) and would benefit from their presence. Indeed, we'd all benefit from more people living in places like St. Louis from ecological and productivity perspectives, where they're closer to jobs, universities, shops, restaurants, and cultural institutions, rather than living in a tract home 30 miles outside of Phoenix. Understanding that this won't be palatable to broad swathes of the population, we must also pursue strategies that reinvest into agricultural communities and concentrate efforts in small- to medium-sized cities to serve as regional beacons. Where places like Hays, Kansas and Paducah, Kentucky are strengthened, but not metropolitanized.

In order to be proper stewards of our communities, we have to build infill housing, and it must last for a long time. But how do we go about that? It starts with materials, and being cognizant of the context we're building in. Framing a structure in two-by-fours might be a good way to build somewhere dry, but it doesn't make much sense in humid climates where wood rots when it absorbs too much moisture. Masonry would be more apt. Wood-framed buildings also have the distinct disadvantage of being easily seduced into going up in flames when a fire breaks out. Replacing structural elements that have been meaningfully compromised is far from simple, and so it often makes sense to tear down a structure

The Borough, a cottage court with eight foot-thick structural brick and mortar walled homes in Carlton Landing. Designed and built by Clay Chapman. Completed in 2018.

and build anew. This problem compounds when builders cheap out on certain materials in order to hit their returns. While this is an entirely rational approach in the short term, over time, if enough things are value engineered, upfront savings preclude any hope of longevity. This is the surest way for places to fall apart. Veneer trimming may be cheaper at the outset than using kiln-fired bricks, but it will result in a worse, less durable product. Same with vinyl over clapboard, single- versus double-glazed windows, sheetrock over concrete walls, thinner as opposed to thicker structural elements, or any number of a hundred other choices. Over the long term, it's more affordable to build well than it is to build cheaply.

Now, to shatter some hopes. Only for a moment, though. Promise. No matter how well one builds, or how high-quality the materials are, nothing lasts forever. That's not to say people aren't trying, Oklahoma builder Clay Chapman is working to build a "Thousand Year House" through his Hope for Architecture project, using the same construction techniques that have allowed millions of medieval and early industrial buildings around the world to last for hundreds of years. Chapman's pursuit isn't completely utopian.

Several places have managed to last for a thousand (and more) years, the Pantheon being only the most notable example. Santa Sabina in Rome, Aula Palatina in Germany, and the Brihadisvara Temple in Tamil Nadu are all likewise very old and still kicking.

Exceptions excepted, even the most well-constructed buildings rarely last. As writer and construction researcher Brian Potter notes, "Traditional design is unlikely to be sufficient to get you to 1000 years—Historic England lists just 225 houses built prior to 1400 AD, just 26 built prior to 1200 AD, and none built prior to 1000 AD".[6] Stuff happens. Water seeps into walls, trees fall onto roofs after storms, pipes corrode over time, someone breaks the side door by slamming it too hard after watching their team blow a lead in the last minute of the game. Ultimately everything decays and must either be replaced or restored. The goal, in my estimation, should not be for buildings to never deteriorate, but for there to be someone there to patch them back up again when they do. This is the core of stewardship: taking care of our communities so that future generations can enjoy them, just as we have.

Oftentimes, this takes the form of profoundly unsexy routine maintenance. Cutting a ribbon may well be more exciting than shoring up precarious foundations or replacing a burst pipe, but it's no more important. How can a landlord be compelled to take on this level of maintenance? At a transactional level, there's a profit incentive. Restoring and maintaining old buildings is a big business. Much profit can be gained from a tangible connection to the past, and indeed this forms the core of many tourism strategies. But this requires someone wanting to inhabit the space after it's been restored. There's no sense in renovating an old warehouse into offices if no one wants to rent them.

It seems there's something deeper at play here. The buildings that we maintain are those that we intrinsically value, so we find reasons to preserve their relevance in one form or another. Said another way, we're more likely to care for places that we love.

Lovable places may have some significant cultural or historical resonance, but for most buildings that have managed to survive until today (with no little intervention from fate), we love them because they're beautiful. We don't care particularly much for ugly things. Buildings that impel us to contort our faces, furrow our brows, or rush past them as fast as we can possibly manage because of their negative impact on us have little hope for longevity. No matter how much positive spin their benefactors put on their appearance, nor how assiduously architectural publications tell us that we ought to appreciate a given building, if it's not broadly loved, and regulations don't intervene, it won't last. Pieces of work they may well be, but beautiful they are not.

Living in a world where beauty is replaced by mundanity, or worse, brutality, deprives our souls of something fundamentally good. With good being a fleeting commodity in today's markets, we're pushed towards despair and down a vicious cycle. And so we cherish that which is good and beautiful, because we don't want to see it expire from our world. For those among us who have kids, there is a desire—no, an imperative—to give them the best life possible. Allowing beauty to be usurped by brutality is the opposite of this. It stands to reason, then, that if we want to build places that are sustainable and capable of lasting the arduous passage of time, we must make them as beautiful as possible so that future generations will want to continue to care for them, patch them up, and reuse them many times over.

Stewardship extends to the fabric of a community. If you would believe it, there's something even unsexier than maintaining our buildings: maintaining our streets, and keeping our cities clean. One can have the most beautiful collection of buildings in the world, capable of inspiring extraordinary amounts of affection, but if they're lining a trash-and-waste-strewn road where people feel unsafe walking in broad daylight (Market Street in San Francisco comes to mind), there's little reason to ever go to that place, much less care for its longevity. What is there to be proud of in somewhere so grim that pride has made itself an unattainable virtue? It takes a special sort of person to be willing to persevere in these conditions. Ultimately, if conditions deteriorate for long enough, there won't be many left who are willing to keep up the fight.

If a seven-year old can be relied upon to clean up after themselves, a city should be too. All it takes is a dedication to the basics: maintaining a labor force who sweep and power wash streets, and pick up any trash that's been left out from the night before or after a particularly windy day. This dedication applies to civil enforcement as well, where guardians of public safety protect the norms of society such that, say, young women walking home from work don't feel unsafe doing the most basic of things, or a crowd of tourists won't be berated by someone who may not be in the best psychological state. This is a win-win-win (and many more wins) scenario. By housing these roles within the city—and not pawning them off to nonprofits or consultancies beyond the reach of public accountability—governments can provide well-paying jobs, foster places where people will feel comfortable, and engender pride in neighborhoods that people can then carry into their own lives. The benefits of keeping a city clean and safe may well compound (as everything else in this book proves) into something ever greater. When trash piles up on streets and the proliferation of rodents, insects, and littering become accepted, it suddenly feels more okay to throw your soda can on the street because it doesn't seem like it matters. But it does matter. If we let our cities fall to squalor, destitution, crime, and filth, we stand to lose a critical part of our humanity.

The most noble people, in my estimation, are those who serve others. Those who clean, preserve, and maintain a high-quality of life for the rest of us. Janitors, mechanics, busboys, electricians, and bridge engineers. My heart is gripped by great appreciation whenever I pass someone power washing a dirty sidewalk, or replacing century-old utility pipes. These are honorable tasks worthy of celebration. Tasks, it must be noted, that aren't exclusive to wealthy areas. But because the best-maintained areas also tend to be the wealthiest, there is a false sense that care is expensive. It's true, of course, that caretaking requires real money. But there are more and less efficient ways of going about this.

Imagine that two towns each have a 10-million-dollar budget for repairs and maintenance. They have the same populations, too, of 20,000 people. The first town is a low-density suburb. Each home is on an acre-large lot, and has roughly 3 people living in it. The residential area sprawls across 10 square miles, with another 10 square miles dedicated to roads, office parks, strip malls, and municipal services. The other is a tight-knit community, with all 20,000 people living within one square mile. There's 1/20th of the land to support, fewer roads to maintain, fewer pipes to service, and fewer sidewalks to keep clean. $10 million worth of maintenance is concentrated in one square mile, while the other town allocates only $500,000 worth of maintenance per square mile. The sprawling town can't as easily afford to maintain itself, as money is always tight. This is true even in more fashionable, but perhaps not out-and-out wealthy areas. The mile-square town, on the other hand, may well have surpluses, which it can then reinvest back into itself, progressively making itself more and more attractive, which may well serve as an inducement for further investment.

A town that maintains itself effectively needn't be a particularly dense place. For an illustration of this, a bit of theoretical math is in order. To keep things simple, let's assume our base building block is a one-acre patch of land. This works out to roughly 200 by 218 feet. Eight buildings can front either side of such a block, extending 75 feet deep. The edge buildings would fully enclose the block, going 218 feet deep (as illustrated in the graphic on the next page). With these dimensions, a courtyard area of approximately 150 by 70 feet could be carved out in the middle of our standard acre-block. If the one square mile city were composed of two-story

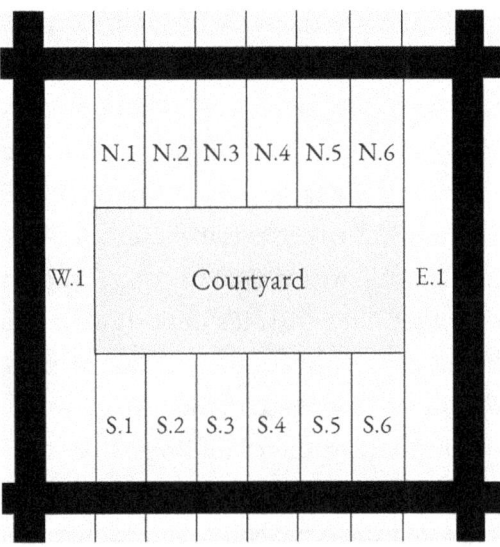

Example of a residential block (cardinally oriented) where apartment buildings comprising just two stories and four units could yield a city of 20,000 people per square mile, while reserving half of the land for open space in the city (not including courtyard space, which is counted towards the residential block).

buildings, with a front-and-back-facing unit on each floor for a total of 4 units in the building, only 310 acres would need to be developed to fit 20,000 people. The other 330 in our square mile could be left for streets, parks, civic buildings, hospitals, commercial strips, or anything else. If the city were composed of four-story buildings, allowing for some mixing of ground floor commercial space, less than 225 acres would be needed to house our 20,000 people. More than two-thirds of the city's land could be dedicated for open space or any other uses. Of course, how a city decides to actually split up its land is another matter, but this hypothetical exercise shows the power of gentle density.

Few would contest that better communities arise from using quality materials in service of creating attractive streetscapes and buildings where the public realm is well maintained. The corollary, necessarily, is that cheaper materials used to construct an unattractive built environment that is poorly cared for leads to worse communities. Sadly, as noted in Chapter 5, there exists a strong incentive to create these very sorts of places. Institutions need to secure high returns while mitigating risk wherever possible. This leads to building at a large scale, value engineering, and the rise of "anywhere USA", where everywhere looks like everywhere else. To these outcomes, we must add another: short-termism.

As with the other outcomes, it's important to note that short-termism is driven entirely by rational decisions, made by normal people. Rarely, if ever, are there malicious actors who set out to depress a community with their buildings. Even the worst places are the result of someone, somewhere, believing that the end result would be good. Or at the very least tolerable. Between architects, developers, lenders, subcontractors, and several dozen other people, thousands of cumulative hours are spent on the most basic of projects. It makes little sense to spend so much time and money, and incur no small amount of stress, on building something you believe will be bad. That projects turn out poorly is thus usually the result of something else, like too many compromises having to be made during the construction process, architectural experimentation gone awry, or the settling for "good enough" by people whose standards for good might leave the general public much wanting.

Let's illustrate this point with a hypothetical character named John, someone whose contrived existence requires little creative thinking. He started off his career in a rotational program at the Bank of Regional Interstate Novel Geography, spending countless hours honing his skills in the dull arts of crafting spreadsheets and formatting presentations, to which few people paid attention to despite the strict deadlines that were imposed on him, and the long nights he spent trying to complete them. After three years at BoRING, John jumped at the chance to work in private equity. All of his friends were making big bucks in the industry. The workdays weren't bad (12-hour shifts, of which six comprised sitting around pretending to be busy), dinner at one of the four passably edible fast casual chains within delivery distance which was paid for if he stayed past 8 (he always did, clocking out just after), and he could wear foam-bottomed shoes whenever he liked (they matched his business casual vest).

At the beginning, his time at Walnut Stream Capital Partners was exciting. He was in charge of underwriting new deals for acquiring laundromats, car washes, HVAC companies, and kitchen supply depots. On the phone for several hours a day, John got to talk to real people, running real businesses, far removed from the abstractions of whatever it was he did at BoRING. He couldn't quite remember what exactly the bank did, but was glad to not be doing it anymore. This was tangible, thrilling stuff. He got to dive into the P&L statements of these companies, identify inefficiencies, and then, once an acquisition was made, initiate a restructuring process (fire half the staff, lever up the firm with a lot of debt due to the high cash flow, low expense nature of the business, and strip the company of its assets). It was here that John learned about waterfalls for the first time, a complex form of financial modeling used to calculate the split of returns owed to investors (limited partners) and the sponsors who sourced and ran the deal (general partners).

John was taught that waterfalls work like this: in exchange for investing in an individual deal or fund, limited partners get the first position of non-debt returns up to a certain threshold. This seniority in the capital stack, or preferred return as it's known ("pref" for short), is meant to compensate investors for the risk they take when they could place their money elsewhere, in a more secure asset. No equity investor gets paid before the pref does. Once Walnut Stream delivers at least an 8% annualized return to its LPs (this is not $8 on a $100 investment paid out every year, but a time value of money adjusted measurement on cash distributed, which usually comes at the back of a deal), the waterfall hurdles, or flows, to another series of returns with investor splits. Here's where it gets interesting. Private equity firms limit their own equity contribution in deals, and use other people's money (via both debt and the equity of limited partners) in order to leverage their returns that much further. A given firm might invest 5% of a deal's equity needs (let's say $5 million), and raise $95 million from limited partners. After the 8% preferred return threshold is hit, another return hurdle is unlocked where ownership proportions change. In some cases, there may be one hurdle. In others, there may well be two or more.

Walnut Stream liked to have two hurdles. After the first is satisfied, their ownership share of the investment jumps from 5% to 20% of every dollar made above an 8% annualized return. They are now gaining a higher proportion of money than what they invested. If they take management fees on the money they're managing (as most firms do), they make even more. A 2% fee is standard. Combine the waterfall and the management fee, and you arrive at the exalted "2 and 20" structure that is the bedrock of high finance.

Walnut Stream is smart, though. They know their deals are going to yield way higher than an 8% annualized return, so they want to take more than 20% of the profits. In their operating agreement, they propose to give LPs an 80/20 split up to a 16% internal rate of return (a solid annualized return), and then take 30% of every dollar over a 16% return. Some firms even take 40 or 50%. It all depends on what investors agree to. If an investment goes very well, it's possible that limited partners can receive a 23% annualized return to choose a random but excellent number, while Walnut Stream gets a 5x multiple on their initial investment. This might not seem fair, but consider that if a limited partner only expected to receive 16%, and actually got 23%, they would be ecstatic, and not care how much the general partner made. It's a win-win. In fact, they'd want to invest in more deals in the future with Walnut Stream, as it's so rare to find returns so good. Walnut Stream could then use this success to command an even higher share of the waterfall. So long as they continue to find good deals, they can keep this money-printing machine going. Collecting $2 million a year in asset management fees on a $100-million fund (which is not particularly large), and a 5x return on $5 million is not a bad way to make a living. Even better if you double those numbers. Or triple. Or multiply them by 10. And then manage four of them.

John internalized all of this quickly while underwriting deals, and he got very excited. Though the intricacies of laundromats were not so exhilarating. If Walnut Stream could earn this sort of money on these boring businesses, could they not apply this model to other asset classes?

One day, the owner of one of the car washes that John was in charge of overseeing mentioned that his property had a lot of extra land. Surely something could be done with it all. After talking with his managing directors, who both thought the idea was compelling, John set about underwriting what could be done on the site. It was well-located on a busy stroad (just a five-minute drive to Whole Foods), and after a recent rezoning in the city, it would be the perfect place for apartments. Maybe even some mixed-use, too (a bank and a fast-casual chain). Walnut Stream weren't developers, though, so after some preliminary analysis they took their findings to a firm who specialized in this sort of stuff: Purple Cliff. Walnut Stream and Purple Cliff agreed to come together in a Joint Venture (JV) partnership.

In exchange for contributing the land, Walnut Stream got an ownership interest in the apartment building that the developers constructed. Just like Walnut Stream, Purple Cliff was institutionally backed. In fact, one of their LPs had invested in both firms separately. Interests were aligned, especially on the exit strategy. These funds typically have five- or seven-year life cycles, meaning sponsors have to identify, acquire, reposition/build, and sell all the assets before the fund's life is up. This immediately puts timing pressure on the sponsors. But pressure alone doesn't drive short-termism. Besides, the sponsors had options to extend the life of their funds by a few years if market conditions turned down, force majeures occurred (acts of God or other, more terrestrial extenuating circumstances), or they simply felt like collecting more management fees.

The real imperative for short-termism comes from something John figured out while he was playing around with the financial model. In the first iteration of the deal, the JV planned on entitling the land, building the project, and holding it for a few years to collect some cash flow, before selling in the fifth year of the investment. Curious how returns would look if they sold after they leased up the building immediately following construction, John ran an alternative scenario. His eyes widened in disbelief when he saw the returns. While the investor's net multiple on capital would be lower (a 1.6 multiple instead of closer to a 2), the IRR, the number most sophisticated investors really care about, was significantly higher. What was going on here? Well, on a time-adjusted return of money basis (what IRR calculates), it's far better to have a bit less money today, than a bit more a few years from now, because you can use the funds today to make other productive investments while the money tomorrow is illiquid. Would you rather have $1 million today, or $1.4 million in three years? At first blush, you might be tempted to take the $1.4 million. But consider the fact that if you can grow your money at 20% per year, $1 million after three years is worth more than $1.7 million. $1 million turns to $1.2 million after the first year, which then turns to $1.44 million after year two, and finally $1.73 million at the conclusion of the investment period. Rephrasing the original question, would you rather have $1m today with the possibility of turning it into $1.73 million in three years, or the possibility of having $1.4 million in three years. As John realized, the choice is clear.

With the IRR for the project much higher than before, Walnut Stream stood to make a higher profit split, boosting their returns from a 5x multiple to a 6.5 multiple. Talk about excitement! Here is the calculation in private equity language: if the JV could deliver a 20% IRR and a 2 multiple over five years (net management fees), or a 32% IRR and 1.6 multiple over two and a half, 10 times out of 10 they will choose to receive a higher annualized return over a shorter period of time, even though their multiple on investment would be lower. The quicker one can deliver a project, the better the IRR looks, and the more money they can take home.

Short-termism also means a firm can do more deals in a shorter amount of time, making more money on their promoted (waterfall) interests. After delivering high returns, many investors will want to throw money at Walnut Stream and Purple Cliff, allowing them to do yet more projects, and make management fees on higher sums of capital. 2% on $100 million can deliver a great lifestyle when shared among a few partners. 2% on $5 billion allows those same partners to live better than royalty. This is how the partners of private equity firms can ride in a different Bentley for every day of the week, and have homes in Manhattan, the Hamptons, Aspen, or wherever else they might want to spend time. One can make an unthinkable amount of money playing short-term games.

In case the above story was too technical, on the next page is a table John created showing the effect of the holding period on the returns for the development of a 20-unit apartment building. Though institutional builders normally operate at least an order of scale larger than this (200+ unit buildings), I instructed John to bring the unit count down as otherwise the numbers get a little too big to make sense of. As with any financial analysis, there are a lot of assumptions here. Let me qualify this exercise by noting these numbers will change materially depending on when the reader is referencing the chart. The figures will also be significantly different depending on what market one is familiar with. For our purposes, assume this is a Tier 2 coastal market, so not New York, but maybe Seattle. This schedule is not intended to be the final word on such analyses, as things change considerably over time. Real estate markets, I can say with conviction, will be markedly different in the

Equity Capital Schedule Analysis (Two Year Scenario)

Cash Flow Event	Date	Amount
Equity Required for Closing	1/1/2024	$ (300,000)
Equity Required for Interest Payments	1/1/2024	$ (250,000)
Soft Costs (First Tranche)	1/1/2024	$ (150,000)
Equity Required for Hard Costs	10/1/2024	$ (1,000,000)
Soft Cost (Second Tranche)	9/30/2025	$ (50,000)
Annual Distribution from Rent	12/31/2025	$ 8,750
Proceeds from Sale	12/31/2025	$ 2,800,000
Total Equity Invested		$ (1,750,000)
Total Cash Returned		$ 2,808,750
Net Profit		$ 1,058,750
XIRR		**35.74%**
Equity Multiple		**1.61**

future than they are today. Costs will rise, rents will differ, interest rates will fluctuate, and the amount of debt offered will be variable. Valuations will change. Where they will end up, I cannot say. But they will not be the same as today. With that cleared up, some assumptions to call out.

This hypothetical parcel of land costs $1,000,000, requiring a $300,000 equity down payment. The hard and soft costs will be $3.75 million, and the construction loan will be at a 68% loan to cost, meaning the sponsors will have to invest $1.2 million in cash equity. Interest payments will be $250,000 across the land and the construction loans over the initial term of the investment. In this scenario, it's assumed that after the land is acquired on January 1st of 2024, the team will spend 3 months working with architects, engineers, and contractors on feasibility, schematic, and construction drawings, before submitting plans to the city. After six months of review, building permits will be issued. Build out will take one year, completing in September 2025. Fully leased to boot. On an annualized basis, rent will be $500,000, or ~$2,085 per unit, per month. Operating expenses are projected to be 30%

of gross revenue, with net operating income, the most important number in real estate investment, being $350,000. At a 5% cap rate, the building would be valued at $7,000,000. After a new mortgage takes out the construction loan at 60% LTC ($4.2 million), at an interest rate of 7.5%, the property would generate $37,000 per year in net income, or a 2% cash on cash return.

One can easily gripe about any of these assumptions. I surely did as I wrote this, and thought John modeled the returns too aggressively. But hey, he works in private equity, that's what he does. Let's pretend it all works out this well. This book is about hoping for a better future, after all. If the joint venture sold this property at the end of 2025, for a total investment period of two years, the project level internal rate of return would be nearly 36%—a massive success. Beating the average S&P return by more than four times is a triumph. On a $1.75-million investment, profit would be just under $1.07 million, or a 1.6 times multiple on equity. If the JV didn't opt for the two-year scenario, they could also consider a five-, ten- or fifty-year scenario. For these models, John assumed that rents and expenses would grow rather conservatively at 2% per year. The results are jarring. The difference between selling in 2028 versus 2025 is a reduction in IRR of 1,600 basis points. That's not the difference between doing and not doing a deal. It's the difference between making average stock market returns over a year, or losing 8%. The IRR looks even worse for the ten-year scenario. The fifty-year is not even worth contemplating, according to John. Why would anyone hold for five years, much less 50, he wondered? There's no way his firm could ever hit their promotes, nor get their money out. Sure, the multiple would be far higher (13x at 50 years v, 1.6x at 2), but no investor would give them that amount of time. He did think it was interesting, however, that the longest-term owners yielded the highest cash on cash returns, while the newest ones didn't do all that well: a reminder that new development often doesn't bring in much cash flow.

Effect of Holding Period on Return

Category	Two Year Hold	Five Year Hold	Ten Year Hold	Fifty Year Hold
Date Acquired	Jan 1 2024	Jan 1 2024	Jan 1 2024	Jan 1 2024
Date Sold	Dec 31 2025	Dec 31 2028	Dec 31 2033	Dec 31 2073
Total Cost	$5,000,000	$5,000,000	$5,000,000	$5,000,000
Total Equity Basis	$1,750,000	$1,750,000	$1,750,000	$1,750,000
Annual Rent	$500,000	$538,445	$609,201	$1,635,745
Annual Expenses	$150,000	$161,534	$182,760	$490,723
Net Operating Income	$350,000	$376,912	$426,441	$1,145,021
Yield on Cost	7.00%	7.54%	8.53%	22.90%
Cap Rate	5.00%	5.00%	5.00%	5.00%
Valuation	$7,000,000	$7,538,234	$8,528,820	$22,900,427
Net Income after Debt	$35,000	$37,691	$42,644	$114,502
Cash on Cash Return	2.00%	2.15%	2.44%	6.54%
Years of Net Income	0.25	3.25	8.25	48.25
IRR	**35.74%**	**19.35%**	**12.21%**	**6.33%**

Of course, it's difficult to find many good deals in the historically risky and uncertain process of development. What's a private equity firm to do? Well, as John realized after a series of conversations with industry professionals, and a deep consultation with his financial models, they didn't actually have to build any new housing. They could simply add "value" to existing buildings without doing very much at all. Think buying a garden apartment complex in suburban Atlanta, painting the walls and replacing some fixtures, marking up the rents slightly, then selling the buildings at a compressed cap rate within a year, or maybe even less, to realize a super-powered IRR.

That's just what Purple Cliff did, only opting to do ground-up developments if they could be nearly certain of their success in a relatively short period of time. As we saw in Chapter 5, the best way to increase the likelihood of success would be to copy and paste the project they worked on with Walnut Stream in some other market. As soon as he internalized this, John wanted to play these games full-time in real estate, joining Purple Cliff with a beachfront villa in his mind's eye. *Once you figure it out,* John thought, *this real estate stuff is easy.*

There are thousands of Johns across America, following this exact trajectory. Over time, some of them have risen to take charge of the firms that are building the vast majority of housing in America. Rarely do they live near the sites they develop. They may say the right words, but their products tell a different story. There is little pride in the end result. For the renters who live in such a commodity, bereft of any charm or idiosyncrasy, they're more likely to dispose of it at the first opportunity of something newer, sleeker, and cheaper, like an iPhone but on a different scale. Cheap places breed cheaper lives, a sort of impermanence that's devastating to us. If unaddressed, this state of affairs will continue to spiral until there is a devolution of our world to such an extent that we lose our capacity to be optimistic entirely.

On the public markets front, the direct imperative of REITs is to deliver positive quarterly and annual results to shareholders. Long-term thinking is disincentivized by the sorts of dividend investors who look for consistent, stable quarterly cash flow—and these are the majority of investors in REITS. The safe projects they inevitably push for are antithetical to the more iterative, longer-gestating and potentially risky projects that positively impact communities. In my time working at a REIT after graduating college, I saw first-hand that many decisions were not based on optimizing quality of life or community, but what the market would view most favorably. After all, compensation at the company, and all others like it, is heavily skewed towards the performance of the stock. Maintaining its price, or increasing it, requires management to make decisions that are often in conflict with the sort of things discussed in this chapter. Again, this isn't to say those who work at these firms are malicious. Nearly everyone I interacted with was absolutely wonderful. You likely know people who work at these sorts of firms and would agree. The issue is that the imperatives tie people's hands behind their backs.

Homebuilders may be the worst offenders of this crime, as they throw up cheap tract homes, make money on the margins of value engineering at scale, sell off as soon as they can, and hold little to no responsibility for what happens after. This is known as merchant building. What's worse, it's actually in a homebuilder's best interest for their products to have a short life cycle, so that in a generation (or less), people will trade in their comparatively outdated home for the newest model. Planned obsolescence rules our built environment.

Traveling to places like Dallas, Phoenix, or Salt Lake City, one can read the consequences of this short-termism everywhere. Wealth, which has accumulated in great quantities in all of these cities, has seemingly not found its way into the public realm. Mega mansions with lavish pools and six-car garages? No shortage of them. Excellent public parks that more than a few privileged people can walk to? Inspiring civic architecture? Protected bike lanes—to say nothing of a viable public transportation system? Not so much. Sadly, this is the state of affairs in most cities that have seen the majority of their growth in the post-war period. In fairness, the basic foundation of these places doesn't make it easy for those who would like to improve them to do so, subsumed by highways, large subdivisions, and power centers as they are. While these places are doubtless desirable for the engineers and construction firms who take on large public contracts to build the roads and infrastructure that will always need repairing, they're failing on many other fronts.

Once laid down, it's very difficult to tear up an eight-lane highway, replat a subdivision of half acre lots and 50-foot right of ways, increase density around schools, services, and jobs, and build out a robust public transportation system. Sprawl cannot really be repaired. Especially not when so much of the land is owned by families and an alphabet soup of agencies who have an aversion to change. This guarantees these places will mostly remain as they are today, unless they decay to such an extent that they can be comprehensively redeveloped. Even then, it's not clear to me why we should redevelop one of many dozens of power centers to be a "walkable town center" in a low-density exurb of Nashville. Walkability will remain an elusive dream, because the entire infrastructure is entrenched in car dependency. Built to a finished state, these places cannot really be altered.

When communities are built to a finished state, there's no voice for future residents. When people don't feel they have any agency, they will leave, and go somewhere else they feel they can have some influence in shaping. This self-determination allows people to have a sense of ownership over where they live—a self-determination that is inhibited by our current planning environment and institutional development patterns.

What's the antidote to a loss of agency and short-termism? High volumes of local and community development. But not in the vetocratic form we have today. Whether it's on the Affordable, public or private side, it doesn't really matter. What's important is that the people who shape a community must have a vested interest in shepherding it, where one is not rewarded for rent seeking or speculation (this includes homeowners who campaign against zoning reforms in their neighborhoods), but stable and sustainable management. Accountability and incentives in equal parts are required here.

Maybe the primary motivation for stewardship is to ensure a safe place for one's kids to grow up. Maybe there's a deep, irrational love for an area that causes someone to do things that have no financial rewards, but offer significant interpersonal upside. Maybe there's a sense of obligation to take care of a given place so that others in the future, who the steward will never meet, will get to enjoy it just as they have. Transactionally, it may make sense to clean up trash in front of one's property (though it's surprising how few do this), but rarely does financial prudence deduce that planting flowers in beds around the block at great expense (including assiduous upkeep), just so that others can enjoy spring a little bit more is rational. But it is wonderful.

When one orients towards the long term, pride and beauty replace yield and return as principal values. Returns decay over time (as seen in the 50-year IRR calculation), but proud communities do not. This is a different game than the one John is playing, and that's alright. Thankfully, there are many developers, architects, and builders who are more than willing to do their part. Through hundreds of conversations, I've been deeply heartened by the many people who are desperate to do just this. Time after time, the people who are either doing the best work in the country, or aspire to do it, tell me *I just want to create something good. So long as I can make enough to keep the lights on, I'd prefer to reinvest as much as I can back into the community.*

Contrary to what many might think, we do not suffer from a shortage of enlightened community builders, but rather, the necessary ecosystem to support them does not exist. We have failed those who would like nothing more than to make our world just a little bit better, one project at a time. Shame on us. And yet, they still endeavor to do so, prevailing over the many obstacles set against them. In order to restore agency and prioritize long-termism, the rest of the ecosystem needs to step up. This requires reshaping the capital stack, and building a coalition of investors, lenders, and advocates who are able to think across decades, not months.

Instead of traditional lenders who have neglected small developers because their perceived risk is not worth the limited fees their projects generate, high net worth individuals who don't have an active need for capital and want to support the improvement of their community can provide debt at attractive rates. Philosophical alignment from parties that diverge meaningfully from the status quo is not so difficult as it might at first seem. There are countless individuals and institutions who, if presented the opportunity, would support the very sort of projects that have been referenced throughout this book. The trouble is there is a mismatch between where the people who are building enlightened projects are, and where those who might fund them via atypical means are. Introducing these groups to one another is critical. A database which takes very strong qualitative components into consideration with the purpose of matching the two would be phenomenally lucrative and impactful.

Even better than relying on individual beneficence, whose scalability is inherently limited, is if federal agencies like HUD or the FHA decided to provide and backstop favorable loans to small developers working on infill projects. For precedent on what our federal agencies might be able to do, we can look to our northern neighbors. The Canada Mortgage and Housing Corporation is a state-owned entity that operates like a private company, with a mix of public and commercial interests. CMHC offers an insurance program called MLI Select that functions similar to the FHA's single-family mortgage guarantee, but it applies to buildings with five units and more. Based on affordability, energy efficiency, and accessibility, projects are eligible for one of three financing tiers. The most generous tier offers a 50-year amortizing loan (longer amortization periods mean lower annual interest costs), up to 95% loan-to-value on construction costs, below private-market interest rates, and limited recourse.[7]

It's difficult to overstate how powerful MLI Select is as a financing mechanism. Its terms don't require very much capital at all. As such, small firms can enter the development ecosystem relatively easily and be unlocked to create the sorts of places larger institutional groups cannot, while making a meaningful impact on the housing crisis.

I'm not so naive to think these changes will arise exclusively out of promising precedent, positive nudges, the goodwill of people's hearts, or affection for their communities. Sometimes—perhaps most times—cudgels must be wielded to force actions beyond the better angels of an idealized reality. Our challenge is not that we do not possess the tools and means to rectify all that plagues our society, but whether the political will exists to use them. Strong leaders must prove their mettle.

Developers, for their part, have a sacred responsibility. As economist and former United States Secretary of the Treasury Lawrence Summers has astutely observed, "It has famously been said that we shape our built environment and then our built environment shapes us. If that is even close to true, developers are some of the most important people determining the destiny of our shared spaces, therefore the destiny of our cities, and therefore the destiny of all of us. What they do and how they do it is profoundly important. It is not just the stuff of abstract models or present value calculations, it is the stuff of dreams, persuasion, sales, motivation, and vision. These are as important as financial calculation or carpentry, or physical construction."[8] Quite true. Who better to entrust this responsibility to than those who will live in a neighborhood for decades, and whose interest in ensuring it will be a good place to live extends beyond quarterly earnings decisions and five-year fund cycles?

We are the product of all that has come before us. The bad, yes, which we must constantly labor to rectify, but also of the good. We would know nothing, and have even less, without the accumulated contributions from those who came before us. Our duty is to steward and add to that legacy so that humanity's sons and daughters can have a better life than we have enjoyed, which in turn was secured by our parents and ancestors. Our cities are never finished projects. They're living, breathing beings. So long as humans are alive, so too will our habitats be, continuously flexing to the needs and whims of those who occupy their environs. To allow our cities and towns to decay as they have is to guarantee the same fate for ourselves. We must work tirelessly to ensure this doesn't happen.

13.

A Call to All Who Occupy The Built Environment

Imagine a world where every city, town, and village was capable of inspiring joy, love, and wonder. A world full of places that are worth dreaming about, where the harsh embodied realities that cover so much of the globe today are the exceptions to how we live, not the rule.

Though we might have to imagine the pervasiveness of these places in the world, we don't have to imagine what they might look like. There's no shortage of inspiration to draw on: from Paris, London, Rome, Amsterdam, Brooklyn, Kyoto, Venice, Havana, Marrakesh, Edinburgh, Lisbon, and Copenhagen, to many smaller places, like Dubrovnik, Colmar, Bruges, Rothenburg, Lijiang, Bergen, Siena, San Miguel De Allende, St. Malo, Avignon, Zanzibar, Quebec City, and Bath. Thousands more exist. Layer in the great neighborhoods in cities that might not universally be viewed as beautiful, and one realizes the world is already full of enchanting places. They're just inequitably distributed.

As I've asked at various points throughout this book, why simply dream of visiting these places when we can live in them? Would it not be better to experience the built environments we love as our default ways of living, adjusted for local context, culture, and traditions?

Myths about why we don't exist in this reality are just that. Despite criticisms of cost being the prohibitive factor of living in or realizing great communities, price is an effect, not a root cause. If there were more lovable places, it stands to reason, they would be more affordable. This is why in Italy, a country with an embarrassment of places that have the characteristics we dream about, entire villages are listed cheaply for sale that would be among the most desirable in North America. Historic homes capable of making one's heart swell often sell for just a dollar.[1] Of course, these places require extensive renovations. Most of these renovations, depending on the ambition of the project, would likely end up costing more than the price of the median home in America, at $417,700 as of year end 2024.[2] And as we've seen, new developments of exceptional quality in North America can be built inexpensively in both absolute and relative terms when land costs are factored out. Price isn't the reason why we don't live in the world of our dreams

Neither can we blame deep-seated cultural preferences nor capabilities for why we don't have bountiful charming communities. North America isn't the only place where bad architecture and poor planning prevail. And we surely haven't forgotten how to build good places. As this book has attempted to prove, not only is this fatalism destructive, but it's also untrue. There are an extraordinary amount of fantastic places that are being created today. From single family homes, missing middle structures, and larger apartment buildings, all the way up to pocket neighborhoods and entire towns. These aren't luxury McMansions or Smart Cities that rely heavily on blustery marketing to sell a dream that fails to match reality, but fundamentally good places that do justice to the ways we used to build.

The reason why we don't build the kinds of lovable places we once did is more confusing—and less satisfying—than any of these theories. It's because, as a society, we've simply decided not to. Or rather, we've been inhibited from doing so via land use regulations and the attendant submission to the status quo.

While these codes and practices, in theory, are well-intentioned and not without some reasonable basis, their byzantine combination and mismanagement has fundamentally corrupted our built environment. Those who oversee these rules are seemingly unaware of the downstream consequences they effectuate. Our cities have been destroyed by a million cuts, and prevented from building themselves back up again by lines of municipal legalese. Though the consequences of this way of building are increasingly becoming known, it's worthwhile to hammer them home every chance one gets. It's not enough to hear, or even to understand at a surface level, why these development patterns are so insidious. They must be internalized to such an extent that their existence becomes unacceptable. And so, more hammering.

Instead of building for people first, as we always should have done, much of our last century of history has seen the destruction of cherished neighborhoods, and their replacement with development patterns to accommodate cars above all other modes of transportation. This way of growth has been harmful to both our environment and our humanity. Tens of millions of acres of farms and natural lands have been destroyed to accommodate this growth.[3] Greenhouse gas emissions have risen precipitously. Global temperatures have increased to dangerous levels. Air and water quality have been reduced significantly. Specific to America, but true of other places with similar development patterns, rates of obesity, depression and anxiety have increased, cognitive function has decreased, and respiratory diseases, cancers, and high blood pressure have become common. Of course, not all of these evils can be directly attributed to development patterns alone, but it is undeniable that they meaningfully exacerbate the problems.

These decisions have debased our cities and towns into highly segregated communities along racial, use, and class lines. Instead of unleashing the creativity of passionate residents, artists, architects, and designers to shape our cities, they have instead become monstrous creatures of inflexible code. Our world has been stretched out and deformed in the last century, while community connections have been severed.

We can no longer tolerate the consequences of this destructive, dangerous, and profligate way of building. We must move beyond a world ruled by codes, theory, and ideological fiat, to one of tested practice, common sense, and humanity.

In reading this book, I hope you have come to see, and even more importantly, believe, that not only can we dispatch with these harmful ways of building, but that in doing so we can improve any number of metrics relating to higher qualities of life. If dangerous, segregated, ugly, and unsustainable communities aren't the common-sense ways of building, as we've been told, then why have they persisted? You've learned from this book that land use regulations, car dependency, and financing are three major reasons for the paucity of good places, and the proliferation of bad ones. And the reason why we allow these things to continue existing when we know they're bad for us is because societally we have not adjusted our set of beliefs, nor coalesced around a coherent positive vision, to fix them. But change that, and we change everything. Internalize Optimism, and mountains can be moved (or at least the KFC parking lot can be infilled with some housing).

Cynicism is the enemy of Optimism. We must reject the belief that our best days are behind us. That all we have to look forward to is brutal division, partisanship, the fall of an empire, and, if we're lucky, a few "innovative" fast-casual buildings, replete with fast-casual chains. We must reject the notion that fighting for a better world by salvaging the one around us is futile. We must steer away from the division that naturally accompanies such a fight, and seek to sow unity between opposition forces.

Indeed, if certain media personalities and prognosticators had their way, our wildest fears would very well come to pass. Confident proclamations that the world is unsavable sound smart, as one surely must have done a lot of research to make such an audacious claim. I get it. In cynicism, a self-fulfilling set of beliefs are espoused, which further validates the observer who wishes to sound intelligent. *If it's not possible to build a better world, nor solve the problems of our day, then why even try?* asks the fatalist. *If no one is trying to build a better world, then it will doubtless get worse, or at best, stay the same in an unacceptable status quo,* responds the Optimist. We must guard ourselves against thoughts that on the surface might seem to hold some merit, but upon deeper review, are either excuses, malicious intentions masquerading as actions for the common good, or pure ignorance. Negativity may make one seem smarter, but it doesn't get anything done. Hope is critical in solving the challenges of our day. We're far past the time for caustic retorts as to why calls for building a better are simply the musings of idealists.

Progress doesn't find harmony with cynics, but rather cuts through them. If we want a better world, we must rise above petty partisan battles and fight *for* something, not *against* someone else. If we're too concerned with what's going on to the left and to the right of us, we can never move forward. It's time to adopt new beliefs: that a better world is possible. That we're capable of doing good things. Better yet, that we're capable of *magnificent* things. *Together.*

Urbanist and philosopher Michael Mehaffy's notion of "Quality In My Backyard" is as good of a framework for moving forward as I've seen.[4] In the interminable wars of YIMBYs and NIMBYs, where each side refuses to cede ground, resulting in a series of frustrating stalemates, a truce must find its beginnings on those areas, however small or seemingly inconsequential, that can be agreed on. We will fail in our goal of building a better world if we favor a coterie of the few instead of a coalition of the many. Where YIMBYs are right in campaigning for more housing as the solution to supply-demand imbalances that have delivered crippling crises, their total war ignores the more qualitative, sensitive community-based concerns opponents have. And though it's true many NIMBYs may not act in good faith in their opposition—often due to their vested economic interests and yes, sometimes, discriminatory beliefs—their concerns over a purely supply-driven solution are well merited as it can ignore the essential, but difficult to legislate, human element. We don't live at the intersection of supply and demand charts. We live in communities. Existing in a world where we have enough housing, but no one wants to live in it, is not a desirable situation. When we do get to an abundance of housing (which we will sooner, or more likely, later), those with the fewest choices will be relegated to the worst places. This is bad. We need to build as much as we can, as well as we can, so that even the cheapest housing still has a baseline of quality, and can stir pride in its residents.

With luck, and much work, Optimism can de-balkanize fighting among racial, class, religious, and other subcultural groups within cities, who are currently incentivized to wage war against one another in a zero-sum game encouraged by a zero-sum building paradigm. The best places are amalgams of those who live in them, and are at their best when these groups all come together. Perpetuating the segregation and stigmatization of any group, for any reason (no matter how righteous one may appear), is wrong. This is bigotry, and has no place in the future of city building. A good city has a diversity of housing forms, for a diversity of people, all intertwining with one another to create wonderful and unexpected outcomes. There are some who benefit from division, but for the sake of the greater good of us all, we must reject it.

We're all in this thing together, for better or worse, and we had better act like it. The warring schools of Modernist v. Traditionalist, YIMBY v. NIMBY, Capitalist v. Socialist, Wealthy v. Poor, Private v. Public, Developers v. Communities, Republican v. Democrat, etc. v etc., *Me Good, You Bad*, must be denied oxygen as they only serve to redirect it from where it's most needed.

Such divisions are counterproductive at best if our goal is to move forward with purpose to create communities as good as we possibly can. There is no one single person, no sole entity, who knows everything on their own. Each person brings something unique and valuable to the table. The good public official ensures that civic goals are kept in mind. The just activist understands the need for humanity and compassion for those who have been left out. The enlightened developer understands how something gets built well, bridging the gap between theory and reality to bring places into being. The capable architect designs these dreams. The excellent one dreams of them herself. The honest contractor actually builds them. The refined aesthete knows that what we build must be beautiful, or else the quality of people's lives will be diminished. The considerate urbanist understands that communities must be built around people in denser patterns for them to be more vibrant and sustainable. The studied urban economist knows that without building enough housing, supply will never meet demand, and we will never achieve true affordability. The common citizen gets to enjoy the fruits of these labors, and can push for ever better places. A dozen other critical roles are played by countless people up and down the chain of city building, bringing their indispensable piece of the puzzle to the fray. On their own, none of these individual actors have all of the answers. But when they come together, magic is made, and the Optimistic city can be realized.

The effects that some of the projects profiled in this book have had on their communities shows the outsized power that one good building can have on a city, especially in a context where nothing else is so hopeful. So don't lose hope. If your area doesn't have the kinds of places you want to live in or live near, go forth and build them yourself! Take inspiration from elsewhere, learn the lessons of those places, and it may well kick-start a virtuous cycle in your own community, too. The work will doubtless be hard at the beginning. It might seem like every code, neighbor, official, and contractor is conspiring against you. They may well. But if you're thoughtful in how you want to build, and determined in your resilience in the face of those challenges to common-sense's triumph, the rewards will stretch far beyond what you might expect.

Some nudging might be required to get the flywheel of Optimism started. Prescriptive processes like form-based codes or architectural boards of review might be needed, or simple templates like pattern books with pre-approved designs. In this latter way, cities can guide, but not prescribe, the kind of places they want built. Most builders will take the path of least resistance if offered to them, and cities can clear the brush by streamlining entitlements for their preferred typologies. This is optimal, in my opinion, as the diversity of 1,000 hands and 1,000 minds being allowed to make iterations on fundamentally good designs will almost always result in better places than the ideas of one, or the bureaucracy of a few. As mentioned in Chapter 7, community builders can then jump off of this foundation, only subconsciously referencing pattern books or pre-approved designs, taking the built environment in many beguiling, and hopefully unexpected, directions.

Positive affirmations at the front end of these efforts can have remarkable impacts. When a six-year-old first picks up a basketball wanting to learn the sport, chances are they won't be very good. But this doesn't mean you should tell them they have a weak jumper and to quit trying—even if their form is really bad. You give them encouragement, nurture their interest, and hope that over time, as they learn more, they'll get better. The same principle applies to city building. Not every place will be perfect at the beginning, and that's okay! It won't be perfect in the future either, but that's the beauty of it. We have to let people branch off to develop new vernaculars and typologies. To experiment with new ways of representing themselves. The goal of this endeavor should not be for the failure rate to be zero as much as for the ambition level to not be zero.

Once our regulatory challenges are solved—which I believe to be a fait accompli as the proposed reforms are too sensible to deny—the greatest limitation is that intersection of confidence and pragmatism. So to whomever may be reading this, I say this without the least bit of cynicism, nor the righteousness of a self help guru; go forth and build the world you want to inhabit. This will be difficult. There will be many challenges. But it is possible, and it is worth it! This call is not meant to sell you a bill of goods to send you ill-equipped into the world. Achieving your goal will require capital, resources, time, many competent partners you can trust, and no small degree of luck. Let me repeat—it will be difficult. Many days you'll wonder why you heeded the words of some overly excitable eccentric in some book you skimmed through. But look out to the world around you. Every single place you inhabit that's not an untouched patch of land was shaped by someone's hands. This is an incredibly empowering thing. Once you discover it and internalize it, you can unleash that force. Why can't those hands be yours for the future? Why can't you form your labors around creating the places people will one day come to orient their lives around?

In the last 30 years, there have been many thousands of excellent places built from the ground up. There may well be tens of thousands of merely good places that would have been considered great just a few decades ago. The Overton window of quality has shifted. I believe that it will continue to move until the places that aren't capable of inspiring love, at least in some small way, are left in the past. Who knows what another generation who believes in the power of creating better places will bring our built environment, especially now that they have so much inspiration to draw upon?

Our built environment is not an immutable reality, but the result of a series of very human decisions. Far from dispiriting, this, as I have emphasized, is empowering. We have the ability to create the world of our dreams. If we want better places, we need only make better choices.

The solution is to adopt a philosophy based on Optimism and abundance. We need to believe that we can create a better world, or else the status quo will never change. We will have to work tirelessly at this. But there are few things worth fighting so vigorously for. Once we achieve our dreams in select places, it's imperative that we scale this solution up to the greatest extent possible. An Optimism that limits itself to select neighborhoods or towns can never have the impact that's required to meaningfully effectuate change.

If neighborhoods like the West Village or Beacon Hill are so popular, and subsequently so expensive, because there are few other places like them, should we not simply build a hundred, or even a thousand areas just like them so that they are no longer so scarce? This is what both a rational market and an unapologetic romantic would do. This is an abundant romantic pragmatism.

If we were to follow this philosophy, in time, the market would demand that places compete not exclusively on price, or even primarily, but on quality, improving outcomes for people of all walks of life. The few major cities where one can reasonably afford a home in a beautiful, walkable neighborhood—Philadelphia, Baltimore, Chicago, New Orleans—are validation of this. There is such an abundance of excellent places in these cities that there's less competition over them, which leads to relative affordability. This isn't to say there aren't other community- and city-level problems that need to be addressed in these places—there certainly are—but the urbanism and architecture are undeniable. Demand might not be solved in the order of millions of people, but tens of millions. We must build until it's satisfied.

The creation of better cities won't happen overnight, or spontaneously. But this process can be supercharged via a prioritization of federal funding and private allocation of resources. Just as we have subsidized trillions of dollars' worth of roads and exurban planned communities, we can subsidize a better world. One that is more sustainable, walkable, integrated, and attractive. It all comes down to priorities. If allocations could be found for urban highways to tear through the hearts of our communities, surely we should be able to muster at least as much for their redevelopment. There's no reason why a similar mass federal- and state-level funding effort cannot be directed towards places that bring us together. Imagine how significant the positive reverberations world would be?

This is a call—a formal call—to anyone reading this book to go out and imbue beauty and joy into your neighborhoods. Be bold. Create the world of your own dreams! There are thousands of us around North America trying to do our small part, but this is a big tent movement that requires millions more to come together. We can hardly bring about real change without you all.

Everyone reading this has the capacity to be a built environment advocate. Whether you have the title of architect, planner, developer, or citizen (which is arguably the most important; places can't be successful without people), this includes you. We must be unafraid in the pursuit of a better future, undaunted by the uncertainty this path presents. We must adopt a practice of Optimism, so that, through sheer desire and brute force, we can create a new paradigm that delivers worthwhile places for all. Places people can enjoy, where they may reap many quotidian benefits, too. We need as robust and broad a coalition of Optimists as possible to turn around the state of our world. We are a growing movement who recognize the need to bring this about. Join us. Reject the cynics and fatalists who tell you it's not possible, or that we're little better than utopians.

Let's build the next Amsterdam, the next Lijiang. The next Marrakesh or Cusco. Let's build the next Rome. Though it won't be built in a day, that's alright. It all starts with each of us doing our own small part, kick-starting a virtuous cycle that can hopefully last for centuries. The best places aren't created through master developers or top-down imposition, but by thousands upon millions of hands shaping the environment around them in wonderful, sustainable, idiosyncratic, and prudent ways. The world is in desperate need of some beautiful Optimism. Go forth, Optimists, and build it.

Acknowledgements

Though there may be one name on the cover, no book is the work of a single person. That's particularly true of this one. This book would not have been possible without the support, guidance and wisdom I've received throughout the course of writing it from family, friends, and colleagues. In a similar vein, as Mark Twain so astutely observed, there is no such thing as a new idea. Indeed, this book is a physical representation of my own mental kaleidoscope, confirming that no idea can trace its lineage to a single creator. This is not some strained attempt at humility in order to gain the sympathies of the reader. The premise of this book is that a series of decisions, when properly strung together, have the power to compound on one another to form a virtuous cycle which can improve the quality of our world in many profound and salutary ways. I did not kick start this cycle, and can claim no responsibility for certain key decisions that have positively influenced cities and towns around the country. My role has been that of a simple documentarian, to gather some of the good which has arisen in the last few decades in the hopes of providing a useful guide for others who want to effectuate positive change in their own communities.

Our modern strain of Optimism can trace its roots to Jane Jacobs, the New Urbanists, and scores of planners, architects, and developers worldwide who have labored admirably to correct the many ills that have beleaguered our built environment for much of the last century. But in truth, this legacy stretches much further back than the 1960s. Contemporary Optimists are doing nothing so much as reapplying and refashioning centuries old lessons back into their practices after being absent for too long. In this spirit, the work that is done today is but the latest link in a millennia long chain. We owe just as much gratitude to Christopher Wren and Vitruvius as the humble 19th-century mason.

More tangibly, I owe specific gratitude to several people who made me believe that I could be an author. And moreover, an author of a book like this. When I first began writing about the built environment, I never imagined I would have much of an audience. Again, this is not faux humility. The great benefit of online writing is that readership data is readily available. Perhaps too available. Though dozens of friends and colleagues would lavish praise over some essay I wrote, the data told me only 2, maybe even 3 people actually read the piece. And they were rather close to home. Mom, Dad, thank you for being my greatest supporters from the very beginning, helping me navigate all of the twists and turns that life has presented, and importantly, facing them with optimism, resilience, and a smile on my face. You have enabled me to pursue my many idealisms fully and freely. Parents may well instill an undue confidence in their children, and I thank you for mine. Without your belief, I wouldn't have progressed much further than a few lines of unintelligible ravings on the soulless state of our world. To this acknowledgement, I must append my gratitude for my siblings, who are likely laughing at my usage of "soulless", as they have been on the receiving end of many an unsolicited stream of consciousness rant where the word makes frequent appearance. Your continued advocacy of my work touches me deeply, as have your tangible efforts in furthering it. Though I'm sure singling out Jenna will do me no favors with Trent, Kyle, Brady, and Kendall, it is well deserved, for your indispensable editing has made sense of the earliest manuscript. Your efforts have made this book far better than it would otherwise have been, and I cannot thank you enough for the time, care, and consideration you have exerted on it.

To Uncle Dave, another of my earliest and most steadfast supporters. Though there are many things I could dedicate this acknowledgement towards, perhaps the most meaningful are the lenses of wonder and curiosity with which you see the world through, and that I am most grateful to have inherited. My perspective on cities has been informed by nothing so much as deep observation, one that I relish cultivating on our walks around New York City and beyond.

Every writer with hopes of achieving any level of success needs their first break. Mine came from Gloria Oh, a Senior Editor at Medium who provided me with my first opportunity to write for a broader audience. Gloria, you may not know how impactful your first email to me was, but without your support, I can't be sure that much of anything would have come after. My many thanks to you.

To my friends, who via their actions, embodied the true meaning of that word. Holding me to account, pushing me forward, and walking beside me on every step of the journey. Though I won't be able to name all of you here, know that my appreciation for you is profound. To Thomas Slipsager, Joseph Kim, Matthew Baker, Roee Gold, Gabriel Freifeld, Enrico Bueno Leite, Evan Ferraro, Jack Saunders, Josh Farazhad, Lyn Stoler and Cam Wiese, Devon Zuegel, Luis-Miguel Aste-Herrera, Andrew Gillen, Mike Guimond, Marc and Clare Bielas, and dozens of others.

And to Optimists everywhere, who provided me with the inspiration to write this book, and give me much to look forward to in the future.

Image Credits

Without photographic materials, this book would not be able to adequately convey its intended messages. As such, the author would like to extend a profound gratification to the individuals and institutions who have kindly provided materials for this book. For each photograph, every effort has been made to contact the owner to offer appropriate acknowledgement. In some cases, the author was not able to reach the owner, and offers sincere apologies for anyone who may not have been properly recognized. Should there be any omissions or errors, the author would be happy to rectify the mistakes in any subsequent edition of this book.

Chapter 1: On Building Optimism: A Brief History of How We Got Here
Page 29: clerkenwellboyec1. Fall at The Boundary Estate.
Page 29: Michelle Mason. Rochelle School at The Boundary Estate.
Page 34: Joey Haddon. Alfred Tredway White's Warren Place Mews in Cobble Hill, designed by William Field & Son.
Page 47: Wikimedia Commons. (2016, October 31). Model of the Plan Voisin for Paris by Le Corbusier displayed at the Nouveau Esprit Pavilion (1925). Wikimedia Commons. https://commons.wikimedia.org/w/index.php?title=File:Plan_Voisin_model.jpg&oldid=714535305
Page 50: Wikimedia Commons, from the United States Geological Survey. An aerial view of The Wendell O. Pruitt Homes and William Igoe Apartments complex in St Louis. Completed in 1955. Demolished in 1972. The contrast between the traditional fabric of St. Louis and that of the housing project's is stark. https://commons.wikimedia.org/w/index.php?title=File:Pruitt-igoeUSGS02.jpg&oldid=765814764

486 IMAGE CREDITS

Page 54: Levittown Public Library, Levittown History Collection. An aerial of one of the early phases of Levittown, Long Island.

Chapter 2: The Need For Optimism

Page 66: AevanStock / Shutterstock. A streetcar along St. Charles Avenue in New Orleans. June 18, 2019 [Photograph].

Page 67: University City District. Men gathering around tables in Clark Park. www.universitycity.org/publicspace/clarkpark

Page 72: Reprinted (adapted) with permission from Vesilind, P.A., & Tedford, L.A. *Environmental Science & Technology*, Vol. 48, No. 4, 2203–2210. https://pubs.acs.org/doi/abs/10.1021/es4034364. Copyright 2013 American Chemical Society.

Page 83: Colburn & Aldern (2022). Rental vacancy rate versus PIT count (per capita). Homelessness is a Housing Problem. University of California Press.

Page 83: Colburn & Aldern (2022). Rental vacancy rate versus PIT count (per capita). Homelessness is a Housing Problem. University of California Press.

Chapter 3: The Pendulum of Development

Page 100: From the Manchester School of Art slide library and Manchester Metropolitan University Special Collections Museum. The George Street facade of the Manchester Athenaeum covered in soot, photographed in the late 1960s.

Page 100: Wikimedia Commons, user Beep boop beep. The Manchester Athenaeum as it exists today, with its soot removed.

Chapter 4: Theory Has to Meet Reality—A Common Sense Way of Building

Page 138: Coby Lefkowitz. Table illustrating a market rate v. Affordable development return analysis.

Page 140: Coby Lefkowitz. Table illustrating an Operating & Sale Analysis for a market rate building v. an Affordable building.

Page 146: NYU Furman Center. (2023). Map showing subsidized housing units in New York City. CoreData.nyc

Page 146: NYU Furman Center. (2023). Map showing the poverty rate by neighborhood in New York City. CoreData.nyc

Page 147: NYU Furman Center. (2023). Map showing neighborhoods broken down by racial composition in New York City, filtered by percent Black. CoreData.nyc

Page 147: NYU Furman Center. (2023). Map showing neighborhoods broken down by racial composition in New York City, filtered by percent Hispanic. CoreData.nyc

IMAGE CREDITS 487

Page 160: Google Earth. Aerial view of a Walmart in rural Pauls Valley, Oklahoma [Satellite image] https://earth.google.com/web/@0,-0.494,0a,22251752.7737565 5d,35y,0h,0t,0r.

Page 164: Photos © Carol M. Highsmith Archive, Library of Congress, Prints and Photographs Division (left), Alexandre Fagundes De Fagundes / Dreamstime (right). Americans' preferred architecture for federal buildings: National Civic Art Society Harris Poll survey—Hubert H. Humphrey Building (HHS HQ) v. National Archives Building. National Civic Art Society.

Page 164: Photos © Carol M. Highsmith Archive, Library of Congress, Prints and Photographs Division. Americans' preferred architecture for federal buildings: National Civic Art Society Harris Poll survey—William Jefferson Clinton Federal Building (EPA HQ) v. Robert C. Weaver Federal Building (HUD HQ). National Civic Art Society.

Page 173: Machado Silvetti. (n.d.). *Shady Hill School* project. Machado Silvetti. www.machado-silvetti.com/posts/shady-hill-school

Chapter 5: Why Does Everywhere Look The Same?

Page 181: Windsor Communities. Windsor by the Galleria, Dallas, TX apartment exterior.

Page 187: Coby Lefkowitz. (2023). *Units Started by Top 25 Developers.* Data sourced from the National Multifamily Housing Council and the U.S. Census Bureau.

Page 193: Coby Lefkowitz. (2023). *New Apartment Buildings Developed In US By Unit Count.* Data sourced from the U.S. Census Bureau.

Page 193: Coby Lefkowitz (2023). Number of new multifamily buildings with 50 or more units.

Page 195: Steve Hall ©. Chevy Chase Lake project exterior view, designed by DMSAS. Completed in 2023.

Page 208: Coby Lefkowitz. (2023). *Building Valuation Variance between High & Low Credit Tenants.*

Page 212: Barbara Lombardi. Merchant's Square in Williamsburg, Virginia, an extraordinary recent commercial development. Completed in 2002. Quinlan Terry Architects.

Chapter 6: An Optimistic Foundation

Page 240: Coby Lefkowitz. (2023, May). *Entrances to apartment buildings in Paris.*

Page 241: Coby Lefkowitz. (2023, May). *A covered entryway to the Cour du Commerce Saint-André, and a shopfront in Paris.*

Chapter 7: How To Create Better Communities

Page 253: Hana Borodina. Exterior view of the Brutalist Robarts Library at the University of Toronto. Courtesy of the University of Toronto Libraries

488 IMAGE CREDITS

Page 253: Robert Watson Photography. Race Residence II exterior view in Toronto's South Riverdale neighborhood. Craig Race Architecture.

Page 255: The Brooklyn Daily Eagle / New York State Historic Newspapers. An 1899 Brooklyn Daily Eagle ad for homes developed by William H. Reynolds in Borough Park, Brooklyn.

Page 257: Nathan Jackson / NextSTL. Rowhomes in St. Louis, built between 1860 and 1864 by the St. Louis Mutual House Building Company.

Page 261: Urban Design Associates. Historic North Wheeling Affordable Housing in Wheeling, WV.

Page 261: Urban Design Associates. Historic North Wheeling Affordable Housing in Wheeling, WV.

Page 263: Guerrilla Development. Street view of Jolene's First Cousin in Portland, OR. Designed by Brett Schulz, developed by Guerrilla Development.

Page 263: Guerrilla Development. Aerial view of Jolene's First Cousin in Portland, OR. Designed by Brett Schulz, developed by Guerrilla Development.

Page 265: Fairfax & Sammons. Newly built townhomes on State Street in Downtown Brooklyn. Designed by Fairfax & Sammons.

Page 269: Ryan DiRaimo. Diagram illustrating how building more homes on a lot reduces a unit's relative land cost.

Chapter 8: What Better Communities Look Like (And What They Do Not Look Like)

Page 281: Lever Architecture. The lovely infill office building Albina Yard in Portland designed by Lever Architecture.

Page 281: Leonid Furmansky. Spoke Street Townhomes, a mixed-use project in Wheeler District, Oklahoma City, designed & developed by Sam Day of Dryline Architecture.

Page 283: Ammodramus / Wikimedia Commons. Loup City Township Carnegie Library, Loup City, Nebraska.

Page 284: Ngoc Doan. Pulaski Park in Northampton, Massachusetts, designed by Stimson Studio. Completed in 2016.

Page 286: City of Lancaster. Before and after view of a road diet with many new trees planted on Lancaster Boulevard in Lancaster, California.

Page 293: Mississippi State Athletics. Crowds outside in the Cotton District during a street fair.

Page 293: The Cotton District. Buildings and streets in Starkville's Cotton District, the anti-town center.

Chapter 9: Why Are Some Places More Optimistic Than Others?

Page 302: Preservation Society of Charleston. 42 South Street, a Carolopolis winner from the 68th annual Awards in 2022.

IMAGE CREDITS 489

Page 305: New World Byzantine. The Byzantine House, built in 1996 by George Holt.
Page 308: New World Byzantine. The Moorish House (1 Tully Alley), built in 2001 by George Holt.
Page 308: New World Byzantine. The Roman Villa House (6 Charles Street), built in 2002 by George Holt.
Page 310: New World Byzantine. Homes along St. Philip Street, built in the late 90s to early 2000s, with entrances to Tully Alley (left), and Charles Alley (right).
Page 314: Loci South. Homes overlooking East Lake (top) and a canal at I'On (bottom). Construction began in 1997, with homes delivering throughout the early 2000s.
Page 317: Loci South. Homes on a tree lined street in I'On.
Page 318: New World Byzantine. "The Blue House" at 23 Catfiddle Street, designed and built by Andrew Gould and George Holt. Completed in 2008.
Page 320: New World Byzantine. Andrew's house at 21 Catfiddle Street (left), completed in 2009, with a 2018 addition. 25 Catfiddle (right), the small mixed-use office building Andrew designed next to his parent's home. Completed in 2013.
Page 321: New World Byzantine. Villa Witold, designed by George Holt, Andrew Gould, and owner Reid Burgess at 24 Catfiddle (right). Completed 2011. 26 Catfiddle (left), designed by George Holt and Andrew Gould. Completed in 2012.
Page 323: Urban Ergonomics. Reid Burgess and Sally Eisenberg's courtyard house, Highcourt. Completed in 2017.
Page 325: Liberatos Architects. Liberatos Architects' counterproposal to the WestEdge apartment complex in Charleston. Isometric view.
Page 327: Google Maps. Street view image of the northeast corner of Columbus and Meeting in Charleston's East Side.
Page 327: RAMSA. The northeast corner of Columbus and Meeting in Charleston's East Side after redevelopment showing the Guild and Courier Square.
Page 328: RAMSA. The Guild, designed by RAMSA, developed by Greystar. Completed in 2019.
Page 330: Google Maps. The northwest corner of Marion Square along King street
Page 330: Modus Photography. Hotel Bennett. Designed by Fairfax & Sammons, developed by Bennett Hospitality. Completed in 2019.
Page 334: Steve Hall ©. Gaillard Center, a 2,700-seat auditorium and office building designed by DMSAS. Completed in 2015.
Page 344: Jim Bartsch. Ablitt Tower, a single family home designed by Jeff Shelton in downtown Santa Barbara. Completed 2006.
Page 346: Alex Nye. El Andaluz, designed by Jeff Shelton Architects. Completed in 2009.

490 IMAGE CREDITS

Page 347: Nancy L Kogevinas. The interior court of El Andaluz.

Page 349: Jason Rick. El Jardin, designed by Jeff Shelton. Completed 2014.

Page 351: Jim Bartsch. Oak Tree House, designed by Jeff Shelton.

Page 353: Cearnal Collective. The Santa Barbara Public Market, designed by The Cearnal Collective, and developed by Victoria Street Partners. Completed in 2014.

Page 354: Cearnal Collective. Alma Del Pueblo apartment complex, designed by The Cearnal Collective, developed by Victoria Street Partners. Completed 2014.

Page 355: Cearnal Collective. Paseo Bonito (top), designed by Cearnal Collective. Completed in 2007.

Page 355: RRM Design Group. Arlington Village (middle left), designed by Cearnal and RRM, developed by Bruce Corwin and Urban Developments. Completed in 2018.

Page 355: designARC. Chapala One, (middle right) designed by designARC, developed by Don Hughes. Completed in 2008.

Page 355: Cearnal Collective. Mayee Plaza, (bottom), designed by Cearnal, developed by Kibo Group, completed in 2021.

Page 356: Christine Pierron. Artisan Court (top) designed by Christine Pierron for HACSB. Completed in 2011.

Page 356: HACSB. Artisan Court (top) designed by Christine Pierron for HACSB. Completed in 2011.

Page 356: RRM Design. Casa De Las Fuentes (bottom) designed by RRM for HACSB. Completed in 2002.

Page 358: Cearnal Collective. The Santa Barbara Bank & Trust (top) designed by Cearnal. Completed in 2001.

Page 358: Cearnal Collective. Santa Barbara County District Attorney's Office (bottom left), designed by Cearnal.

Page 358: Granada Garage & Office Building (bottom right) designed by Watry Design and Henry Lenny Design. Completed in 2006.

Page 360: Erik Spike Thiesmeyer. Entrada de Santa Barbara, including Hotel Californian. Designed by designARC, developed by Next Century Associates. Completed in 2017.

Page 364: Dan Bertolet. The Urbana Apartments in Seattle's Ballard Neighborhood, a project deemed worthy enough to have successfully made its way through the city's Byzantine Design Review Process.

Page 370: Caitlin Murray. Retirement home ADU for homeowner's parents, designed by Webster Wilson Architect. Completed in 2018.

Page 372: The Cottage Company. Greenwood Avenue Cottages, an early example of the new generation of cottage courts. Designed by Ross Chapin in Shoreline, WA. Completed in 2001.

IMAGE CREDITS **491**

Page 375: The Cottage Company. Third Street Cottages, the pioneering cottage court in Langley, WA which started a cozy, communal revolution. Designed and developed by The Cottage Company. Completed in 1998.

Page 376: Communitecture. Homes at Cully Grove. Designed by Communitecture, developed by Orange Splot. Completed in 2013.

Page 379: Alfred Twu / Sightline Institute. A sketch created by Alfred Twu depicting the housing options legalized by Portland's Residential Infill Project.

Page 380: Coby Lefkowitz. *Permits Issued by Building Size in Portland 2000–2022 (Proportion of Total Permits),* Data Sourced from U.S. Census Bureau.

Page 382: Polyphon. The Village Co-housing, designed by Polyphon, and developed by Owen Gabbert. Completed in 2019.

Page 382: Open Door. Aerial of The Village.

Page 384: Polyphone. Berkeley 6, a six-plex built by Ethan Beck Homes, and designed by Polyphon. Completed in 2019.

Page 388: PARCEL. Kite Lofts, a 3-unit infill development in Northeast Portland designed and developed by PARCEL. Completed in 2020.

Page 389: Jeremy Bittermann. Origami, a 12-unit townhome development designed by Waechter Architecture and developed by Project^. Completed in 2019.

Page 390: Waechter Architecture. Claybourne Commons, a 20-unit townhouse development designed by Waechter Architecture and developed by Anlon Construction. Completed in 2017.

Page 391: Lara Swimmer. Milwaukie Way with Claybourne Commons in the background, designed by Waechter Architecture and developed by Jim Morton & Drew Prell. Completed in 2016.

Page 393: Guerrilla Development. The 2/3rds Project, designed by Brett Schulz Architect and developed by Guerrilla Development. Completed in 2015.

Page 393: Emerick Architects. 1930 Alberta, a 33-unit mixed-use building designed in an Art Deco inspired style by Emerick Architects. Completed in 2018.

Page 395: Lara Swimmer. The Mississippi Building, a mass timber mixed-use office building designed and developed by Waechter Architecture. Completed in 2022.

Page 396: ZGF Architects. The PAE Living Building, a mass timber mixed-use office building designed by ZGF Architects, and developed by a consortium of Downtown Development Group, Edlen & Co, Walsh Construction Co, Apex Real Estate Partners, PAE, and ZGF. Completed in 2022.

Chapter 10: The Optimism of Universities

Page 401: Yale University. Branford College, originally a part of Memorial Quadrangle. Designed by James Gamble Rogers in 1921, expanded in 1933.

Page 403: Yale University. Harkness Tower, designed by James Gamble Rogers. Completed in 1921.

Page 404: RAMSA. Exterior photographs of Pauli Murray College and Benjamin Franklin College at Yale University. Completed in 2017.

Page 404: RAMSA. Exterior and interior photographs of Pauli Murray College and Benjamin Franklin College at Yale University. Completed in 2017.

Page 408: Steve Hall ©. E. Bronson Ingram Residential College at Vanderbilt, a 350-bed, 205,000 square foot community designed by DMSAS. Completed in 2018.

Page 410: Steve Hall ©. Nicholas S. Zeppos College, Designed by DMSAS. Completed in 2020.

Pages 411: Steve Hall ©. Rothschild College, designed by DMSAS. Completed in 2022.

Page 413: Goody Clancy. Dunne and Flaherty Halls, designed by Goody Clancy. Completed in 2016

Page 415: The University of Notre Dame Class of 1969 Blog. Old McKenna Hall (top).

Page 415: HBRA Architecture. The new McKenna Hall (bottom) designed by HBRA. Completed in 2021.

Chapter 11: Moving Beyond Utilitarianism: In Defense of Beautiful, Aspirational Places

Page 420: Leon Krier. Leon Krier's Res Publica Res Economica Civitas diagram.

Page 426: BearFotos / Shutterstock. Guggenheim Museum Bilbao. July 4th, 2015.

Page 429: Francois Roux / Shutterstock. The High Line, with Zaha Hadid's 520 W 28th Street (completed in 2017) in the background.

Page 431: cktravels.com / Shutterstock. One of London's latest vanity projects, Marble Arch Mount, has failed because its existence adds neither beauty nor utility to its surroundings.

Page 437: Ashok Sinha for Bloomberg Pursuits. Aerial of Little Island overlooking Chelsea and Midtown Manhattan. Completed in 2021.

Chapter 12: On Stewardship

Page 445: SBJ Group. Love Lane Mews, a 38-unit condominium property realized through the conversion of 5 prewar parking garages in Brooklyn Heights. Designed by SBJGroup, developed by Donald Zucker Real Estate Company. Completed in 2013.

IMAGE CREDITS

Page 448: Clay Chapman. The Borough, a cottage court with eight structural foot-thick brick and mortar walled homes in Carlton Landing, Designed and built by Clay Chapman. Completed in 2018.

Page 453: Coby Lefkowitz. Example of a residential block (cardinally oriented) where apartment buildings comprising just two stories and four units could yield a city of 20,000 people per square mile, while reserving half of the land for open space in the city (not including courtyard space, which is counted towards the residential block).

Page 460: Coby Lefkowitz. Equity Capital Schedule Analysis (Two Year Scenario).

Page 462: Coby Lefkowitz. Effect of Holding Period on Returns Scenarios

References

Chapter 1: On Building Optimism: A Brief History of How We Got Here

1. Henry C. Binford. (n.d.). *Tenements.* Chicago Historical Society, Encyclopedia of Chicago. http://www.encyclopedia.chicagohistory.org/pages/1240.html
2. Jacob A. Riis, Otto H. Bacher, Kenyon Cox, W.H. Drake, W.C. Fitler, & Victor Semon Pérard, Jacob A. Riis, photographer. (1890). *How the other half lives: studies among the tenements of New York.* New York: Charles Scribner's Sons, 104.
3. Peter Higginbotham. (n.d.). *Model Dwellings and Modern Lodging Houses.* The Workhouse: The Story of an Institution. www.workhouses.org.uk/model.
4. A. S. Wohl. (1971). *Octavia Hill and the Homes of the London Poor.* Journal of British Studies, Vol. 10, no. 2, 105–131.
5. Charity Organisation Review. (1885). *The Kyrle Society.* Charity Organisation Review, Vol. 1, No. 12, 505–507.
6. Charles Welch, revised by H. C. G. Matthew for the Oxford University Press. (September 2004). *Sir Sydney Hedley Waterlow, first baronet.* Oxford Dictionary of National Biography. www.oxforddnb.com/display/10.1093/ref:odnb/9780198614128.001.0001/odnb-9780198614128-e-36761
7. J.A. Mays. (1863). *Improved dwellings for the industrial classes: ground plan and elevation of Langbourn Buildings, Mark Street, Paul Street, Finsbury Square, designed and erected for Alderman Waterlow by Mr. Matthew Allen, with descriptive notes, and an appendix by J.A Mays.* London: Conway Hall Library and Archives Digital Collections, Robert Hardwicke.
8. Judith Lever. (1976). *Home sweet home : housing designed by the London County Council and Greater London Council architects 1888-1975.* Academy Editions [for] the Greater London Council.
9. Social Welfare History Project. (2011). *Stanton Coit—Founder of Neighborhood Guild, the first settlement house in the U.S. in 1886 and founder*

of the South Place Ethical Society in London in 1887. Social Welfare History Project. https://socialwelfare.library.vcu.edu/people/coit-stanton/
10. Anne E. Krulikowski. (2020). *Octavia Hill Association.* The Encyclopedia of Greater Philadelphia. https://philadelphiaencyclopedia.org/essays/octavia-hill-association/
11. Alfred Treadway White. (1879). *Improved Dwellings for the Laboring Classes.* New York: G.P. Putnam's Sons, 2.
12. Alfred Treadway White. (1885, November). *Better Homes for Workingmen,* National Conference on Social Welfare, vol. 12, no. 1, 5, 365–382.
13. Ibid.
14. Ibid, 370.
15. Joseph Lee, Jacob A. Riis. (1906). *Constructive and Preventive Philanthropy.* New York: The Macmillan company, 71–72.
16. Olive and Ari Hoogenboom. (1989, Fall). *Alfred T. White: Settlement Worker and Housing Reformer.* Hayes Historical Journal, vol. 9, no. 1. www.rbhayes.org/research/hayes-historical-journal-alfred-t.-white/
17. Kathy A. Kolnick. (2008). *Order Before Zoning : Land Use Regulation in Los Angeles 1880–1915.* University of Southern California. https://search.worldcat.org/title/309352342
18. Erin Stone. (2023, January 24). *L.A. County to phase out oil drilling.* LAist. https://laist.com/news/climate-environment/l-a-county-to-phase-out-oil-drilling
19. Roger L. Rice. (1968). *Residential Segregation by Law, 1910–1917.* The Journal of Southern History vol. 34, no. 2, 179–99. https://doi.org/10.2307/2204656
20. Jesse Barber. (2019, March 12). *Berkeley zoning has served for many decades to separate the poor from the rich, and whites from people of color.* Berkeleyside. www.berkeleyside.org/2019/03/12/berkeley-zoning-has-served-for-many-decades-to-separate-the-poor-from-the-rich-and-whites-from-people-of-color
21. Detroit Historical Society. (n.d.). *Model T.* Encyclopedia of Detroit. https://detroithistorical.org/learn/encyclopedia-of-detroit/model-t#:~:text=The%20Model%20T%20was%20the,four%20months%27%20pay%20in%201914
22. U.S. Department of Transportation, Federal Highway Administration and Federal Transit Administration. (n.d.). *STATE MOTOR VEHICLE REGISTRATIONS, BY YEARS, 1900–1995.*
23. National Safety Council. (2024, April 25). *Historical car crash deaths and rates.* Injury Facts. https://injuryfacts.nsc.org/motor-vehicle/historical-fatality-trends/deaths-and-rates/
24. Bill Loomis. (2015, April 26). *1900–1930: The years of driving dangerously.*

The Detroit News. www.detroitnews.com/story/news/local/michigan-history/2015/04/26/auto-traffic-history-detroit/26312107/
25. Detroit Historical Society. (n.d.). *Davison Freeway*. Encyclopedia of Detroit. https://detroithistorical.org/learn/encyclopedia-of-detroit/davison-freeway#:~:text=On%20November%2025%2C%201942%2C%20the,around%20three%20to%20four%20minutes
26. Laura Hale. (2016, June 29). *Happy birthday, Interstate Highway System! The History of the Interstate Highway System*. Infrastructure Report Card https://infrastructurereportcard.org/happy-60th-birthday-interstate-highway-system/#:~:text=Today%20that%20drive%20could%20be,investment%20has%20paid%20off,%20literally
27. Wendell Cox. (n.d.). *USA Interstate Highway System: Miles opened by Year*. Public Purpose. http://www.publicpurpose.com/hwy-intmiles.htm
28. U.S. Department of Transportation, Federal Highway Administration and Federal Transit Administration. (2021, October 8). *Status of the Nation's Highways, Bridges, and Transit: Conditions & Performance Report to Congress, 24th Edition*. https://doi.org/10.21949/1521794.
29. Camillo, Sitte. (1945). *The Art of Building Cities : City Building According to Its Artistic Fundamentals*. New York: Reinhold Pub. Corp.
30. Le Corbusier. (1929). *The City of To-Morrow and Its Planning*. London: J. Rodker.
31. Le Corbusier. (1986). *Towards a New Architecture*. New York: Dover Publications.
32. Adolf Loos. (2019). *Ornament and Crime*. United Kingdom: Penguin Books Limited.
33. Alain De Botton. (2006). *The Architecture of Happiness*, 62. 1st McClelland & Stewart hardcover edition. Toronto: McClelland & Stewart.
34. United States Holocaust Memorial Museum. (n.d.). *United States Immigration and Refugee Law, 1921–1980*. https://encyclopedia.ushmm.org/content/en/article/united-states-immigration-and-refugee-law-1921–1980
35. United States Department of Homeland Security, Office of Immigration Statistics. (November 2022). *2021 Yearbook of Immigration Statistics*. Washington, D.C.: U.S. Department of Homeland Security. www.dhs.gov/sites/default/files/2023-03/2022_1114_plcy_yearbook_immigration_statistics_fy2021_v2_1.pdf
36. L.B. Wheildon. (1946). *National Housing Emergency, 1946–1947*. CQ Researcher. Thousand Oaks, California: CQ Press. https://doi.org/10.4135/cqresrre1946121700.
37. United States Census Bureau. (n.d.). *Incorporated place*. www.census.gov/glossary/?term=Incorporated%2Bplace

38. Richard Rothstein. (2017). *The Color of Law: A Forgotten History of How Our Government Segregated America*. First ed. New York: Liveright Publishing Corporation a division of W.W. Norton & Company.
39. Witold Rybczynski. (n.d.). *The Pioneering "Levittowner*. Zell/Lurie Real Estate Center Working Paper No. 556. https://realestate.wharton.upenn.edu/wp-content/uploads/2017/03/556.pdf
40. CBS Interactive. (2020, July 13). *Deeds to land in Levittown, nation's first suburb, rooted in systemic racism*. CBS News. www.cbsnews.com/newyork/news/deeds-to-land-in-levittown-nations-first-suburb-rooted-in-systemic-racism/
41. Congress for the New Urbanism. (n.d.). *Charter of the New Urbanism*. CNU. www.cnu.org/chapter/florida/charter_of_the_new_urbanism#:~:text=The%20Congress%20for%20the%20New%20Urbanism%20views%20disinvestment%20in%20central,one%20interrelated%20community%2Dbuilding%20challenge

Chapter 2: The Need For Optimism

1. Todd Litman. (2015), *Analysis of Public Policies That Unintentionally Encourage and Subsidize Urban Sprawl, Victoria Transport Policy Institute*, Supporting paper commissioned by LSE Cities at the London School of Economics and Political Science, on behalf of the Global Commission on the Economy and Climate for the New Climate Economy Cities Program.
2. U.S. Department of Agriculture. (2020). *Summary Report: 2017 National Resources Inventory, Natural Resources Conservation Service*, Washington, DC, and Center for Survey Statistics and Methodology, Iowa State University, Ames, Iowa. www.nrcs.usda.gov/wps/portal/nrcs/main/national/technical/nra/nri/results/
3. Thomas R. Plaut. (1980, August). *Urban Expansion and the Loss of Farmland in the United States: Implications for the Future*. American Journal of Agricultural Economics, Vol. 62, No. 3, 537–542. https://doi.org/10.2307/1240211
4. David L. Ames, Linda Flint McClelland. (2002, September). *Historic Residential Suburbs. Guidelines For Evaluation And Documentation For The National Register Of Historic Places*. U.S. Department of the Interior, National Park Service, National Register of Historic Places. https://shpo.nv.gov/uploads/documents/NR_Bulletin_Suburbs-compressed.pdf
5. United States Census Bureau. (n.d.). *Census data for ZCTA5 70115*. https://data.census.gov/profile/70115?g=860XX00US70115.
6. United States Census Bureau. (n.d.). *Census data for ZCTA5 02135*. https://data.census.gov/all?q=ZCTA5%2002135,%20Massachusetts.

7. United States Census Bureau. (n.d.). *Census data for various cities and zip codes.* https://data.census.gov/
8. EPA. (2024). *Inventory of U.S. Greenhouse Gas Emissions and Sinks: 1990–2022.* U.S. Environmental Protection Agency, EPA 430-R-24-004. www.epa.gov/system/files/documents/2024-04/us-ghg-inventory-2024-main-text_04-18-2024.pdf
9. Ibid.
10. Christopher Jones and Daniel M. Kammen. (2014). *Spatial Distribution of U.S. Household Carbon Footprints Reveals Suburbanization Undermines Greenhouse Gas Benefits of Urban Population Density.* Environmental Science & Technology, Vol. 48, No. 2, 895–902. DOI: 10.1021/es4034364
11. Sumil K. Thakrar, Srinidhi Balasubramanian, Peter J. Adams, Inês M. L. Azevedo, Nicholas Z. Muller, Spyros N. Pandis, Stephen Polasky, C. Arden Pope III, Allen L. Robinson, Joshua S. Apte, Christopher W. Tessum, Julian D. Marshall, and Jason D. Hill. (2020). *Reducing Mortality from Air Pollution in the United States by Targeting Specific Emission Sources.* Environmental Science & Technology Letters, Vol. 7, No. 9, 639–645. DOI: 10.1021/acs.estlett.0c00424
12. National Center for Statistics and Analysis. (2022, May). *Early estimates of motor vehicle traffic fatalities and fatality rate by sub-categories in 2021 (Crash Stats Brief Statistical Summary. Report No. DOT HS 813 298).* National Highway Traffic Safety Administration.
13. Brittany Moye. (2023, April 20). *Annual cost of new car ownership crosses $10K Mark.* AAA. https://newsroom.aaa.com/2022/08/annual-cost-of-new-car-ownership-crosses-10k-mark/#:~:text=According%20to%20the%20latest%20research,%249%2C666%20or%20%24805.50%20per%20month
14. Keegan Ramsden (2020, November 3). *Cement and concrete: The environmental impact.* PSCI, Princeton University. https://psci.princeton.edu/tips/2020/11/3/cement-and-concrete-the-environmental-impact
15. EPA. (2022, December). *The 2022 EPA Automotive Trends Report. Greenhouse Gas Emissions, Fuel Economy, and Technology since 1975.* U.S. Environmental Protection Agency, EPA 420-S-22-001. www.epa.gov/system/files/documents/2022-12/420s22001.pdf
16. Charlie Gardner. (2011, December 12). *We are the 25%: Looking at street area percentages and surface parking.* Old Urbanist. https://oldurbanist.blogspot.com/2011/12/we-are-25-looking-at-street-area.html
17. Marissa Hauptman, Jonathan M. Gaffin, Carter R. Petty, William J. Sheehan, Peggy S. Lai, Brent Coull, Diane R. Gold, & Wanda Phipatanakul. (2020). *Proximity to major roadways and asthma symptoms in the School Inner-City Asthma Study.* The Journal of Allergy and Clinical Immunology, Vol. 145, No. 1, 119–126.e4. https://doi.org/10.1016/j.jaci.2019.08.038

18. Peeyush Khare et al. (2020). *Asphalt-related emissions are a major missing nontraditional source of secondary organic aerosol precursors.* Science Advances, Vol. 6, No. 36. DOI:10.1126/sciadv.abb9785
19. Environmental Protection Agency. (n.d.). Heat Island Effect. U.S. Environmental Protection Agency. www.epa.gov/heatislands#:~:text=Structures%20such%20as%20buildings%2C%20roads,temperatures%20relative%20to%20outlying%20areas
20. Ambarish Vaidyanathan, Josephine Malilay, Paul Schramm, Shubhayu Saha. (2020, June 19). *Heat-Related Deaths—United States, 2004-2018.* CDC Morbidity and Mortality Weekly Report 2020;69:729–734. DOI: http://dx.doi.org/10.15585/mmwr.mm6924a1
21. Sheldon H. Jacobson, Douglas M. King, Rong Yuan. (2011, September). *A note on the relationship between obesity and driving.* Transport Policy, Vol. 18, No. 5, Pages 772-776, ISSN 0967-070X. https://doi.org/10.1016/j.tranpol.2011.03.008.
22. Bryan Stierman, Joseph Afful, Margaret D. Carroll, Te-Ching Chen, Orlando Davy, Steven Fink, Cheryl D. Fryar, Qiuping Gu, Craig M. Hales, Jeffrey P. Hughes, Yechiam Ostchega, Renee J. Storandt, Lara J. Akinbami. (2021, June 14). *National Health and Nutrition Examination Survey 2017—March 2020 Prepandemic Data Files—Development of Files and Prevalence Estimates for Selected Health Outcomes.* NCHS National Health Statistics Reports. https://stacks.cdc.gov/view/cdc/106273
    a. Zachary J. Ward, Sara N. Bleich, Michael W. Long, Steven L. Gortmaker. (2021, March 24) *Association of body mass index with health care expenditures in the United States by age and sex.* PLoS One Vol. 16. No. 3, e0247307. https://doi.org/10.1371/journal.pone.0247307
23. Michael Antoun, Kate M. Edwards, Joanna Sweeting, & Ding Ding. (2017). *The acute physiological stress response to driving:* A systematic review. PLoS One, Vol. 12, No. 10, e0185517. https://doi.org/10.1371/journal.pone.0185517
24. Kathleen Ries Merikangas, Joel Swendsen, Ian B. Hickie, Lihong Cui, Haochang Shou, Alison K. Merikangas, Jihui Zhang, Femke Lamers, Ciprian Crainiceanu, Nora D. Volkow, Vadim Zipunnikov. (2019, February 1). *Monitoring of the Dynamic Associations Among Motor Activity, Energy, Mood, and Sleep in Adults With Bipolar Disorder.* JAMA Psychiatry, Vol. 76, No. 2,190–198. DOI: 10.1001/jamapsychiatry.2018.3546. PMID: 30540352; PMCID: PMC6439734.
25. Nicole K. Valtorta, Mona Kanaan, Simon Gilbody, et al. (2016). *Loneliness and social isolation as risk factors for coronary heart disease and stroke: systematic review and meta-analysis of longitudinal observational studies.* Heart, Vol 102, 1009–1016. DOI:10.1136/heartjnl-2015-308790

26. Julianne Holt-Lunstad, Timothy B. Smith, J. Bradley Layton. (2010, July 27). *Social Relationships and Mortality Risk: A Meta-analytic Review.* PLoS Medicine, Vol. 7, No. 7: e1000316. https://doi.org/10.1371/journal.pmed.1000316
27. Joint Center For Housing Studies of Harvard University. (2024). *America's Rental Housing 2024.* www.jchs.harvard.edu/americas-rental-housing-2024
28. Alexander Hermann, Peyton Whitney. (2024, January 22). *Home price-to-income ratio reaches record high.* Joint Center for Housing Studies of Harvard University. www.jchs.harvard.edu/blog/home-price-income-ratio-reaches-record-high-0
29. U.S. Census Bureau. (n.d.). *Quickfacts: San Francisco City, California.* www.census.gov/quickfacts/fact/table/sanfranciscocitycalifornia/PST045223
30. Hans Johnson, Eric McGhee. (2024, February 7). *Who's Leaving California-and Who's Moving In?* Public Policy Institute of California. www.ppic.org/blog/whos-leaving-california-and-whos-moving-in/
31. Veera Korhonen. (2024, July 5). *Resident population in California from 1960 to 2022.* Statista. www.statista.com/statistics/206097/resident-population-in-california/
32. March of Dimes. (2024, January). *Fertility Rate: California, 2012–2022.* www.marchofdimes.org/peristats/data?top=2&lev=1&stop=1&reg=99&sreg=06&obj=8&slev=4
33. Marisol Cuellar Mejia, Cesar Alesi Perez, Hans Johnson. (2024, January). *Immigrants in California.* Public Policy Institute of California. www.ppic.org/publication/immigrants-in-california/
34. State of California, Department of Finance, E-6. *Population Estimates and Components of Change by County—July 1, 2020–2023.* Sacramento, California, December 2023.
35. Mark Baldassare, Dean Bonner, Rachel Lawler, Deja Thomas. (2023, February). *PPIC Statewide Survey: Californians and their Government.* Public Policy Institute of California. www.ppic.org/publication/ppic-statewide-survey-californians-and-their-government-february-2023/
36. Benjamin Oreskes. (2023, June 23). *4 in 10 California residents are considering packing up and leaving, new poll finds.* Los Angeles Times. www.latimes.com/california/story/2023-06-23/california-residents-considering-leaving-cost-new-poll
37. Mike Kingsella, Anjali Kolachalam, Leah MacArthur. (2023). *Housing Underproduction in the U.S. 2023.* Up For Growth. https://upforgrowth.org/apply-the-vision/2023-housing-underproduction/
    a. Sam Khater, Len Kiefer, Venkataramana Yanamandra. (2021, May 7). *Housing Supply: A Growing Deficit.* The Economic & Housing

Research Group at Feddie Mac www.freddiemac.com/research/insight/20210507-housing-supply
  b. Realtor Magazine. (2021, September 17). *Report: America is Short 5.24m Homes*. National Association of Realtors. www.nar.realtor/magazine/real-estate-news/sales-marketing/report-america-is-short-524m-homes
38. Jordyn Lee. (2017, December 14). *Share of Adults Living with Roommates Higher than Ever Before*. Zillow MediaRoom https://zillow.mediaroom.com/2017-12-14-Share-of-Adults-Living-with-Roommates-Higher-than-Ever-Before
39. Prudential Newsroom. (2022, July 12). *58% of young adults are still living at home, impacting their parents' path to retirement*. Prudential Financial, Inc.. https://news.prudential.com/latest-news/prudential-news/prudential-news-details/2022/58-of-young-adults-are-still-living-at-home-impacting-their-parents-path-to-retirement-07-12-2022/default.aspx
40. HUD Public Affairs. (2023, December 15). *HUD Releases January 2023 Point-In-Time Count Report*. U.S. Department of Housing and Urban Development (HUD). www.hud.gov/press/press_releases_media_advisories/hud_no_23_278#:~:text=The%20report%20found%20more%20than,a%2012%25%20increase%20from%202022
41. Tanya de Sousa, Alyssa Andrichik, Ed Prestera, Katherine Rush, Colette Tano, Micaiah .Wheeler. (2023, December). *The 2023 Annual Homelessness Assessment Report (AHAR) to Congress*. The U.S. Department of Housing and Urban Development (HUD) Office of Community Planning and Development. www.huduser.gov/portal/sites/default/files/pdf/2023-AHAR-Part-1.pdf
42. Gregg Colburn, Clayton Page Aldern. (2022). *Homelessness is a Housing Problem: How Structural Factors Explain U.S. Patterns*. University of California Press.
43. National Association of REALTORS®. (n.d.). *Q3 2022 Metro Area Ranked [Metro Area by Vacancy Rate]*. National Association of REALTORS®. https://cdn.nar.realtor/sites/default/files/documents/2022-q3-multifamily-metro-area-vacancy-rates-ranked-and-precovid-08-02-2022.pdf
44. U.S. Census Bureau. (n.d.). *Quickfacts: Detroit City, Michigan*. www.census.gov/quickfacts/fact/table/detroitcitymichigan/PST045223
45. Chris Glynn, Thomas H. Byrne, Dennis P. Culhane. (June 2021). *Inflection points in community-level homeless rates*. Ann. Appl. Stat. Vol. 15, No. 2, 1037— 1053. https://doi.org/10.1214/20-AOAS1414
46. Los Angeles City & County spending on homelessness
  a. BOS Liaison Team 2021. (2021). *Homeless Spending Los Angeles County, Los Angeles City 2010–2021*. Los Angeles County Sheriff's

Department. https://lasd.org/wp-content/uploads/2021/06/Homeless-Spending-2.pdf

    b. City News Service | Los Angeles. (2021, June 2). *Garcetti signs $11 billion budget, with nearly $1 billion for homeless crisis.* Spectrum News 1. https://spectrumnews1.com/ca/la-west/homelessness/2021/06/02/garcetti-signs--11-billion-budget--with-nearly--1-billion-for-homeless-crisis

    c. City News Service. (2023, February 7). *LA County Approves Record Budget, Over $600 Million for Homeless Initiatives.* NBC Los Angeles. www.nbclosangeles.com/news/local/la-county-approves-record-budget-over-600-million-for-homeless-initiatives/3091281/

47. Los Angeles Mission. (n.d.). *Measure H Marks a Big Change for Homelessness in LA.* Los Angeles Mission. https://losangelesmission.org/measure-h-marks-a-big-change-for-homelessness-in-la/

48. County of Los Angeles Homeless Initiative. (n.d.). *FY 2023–24 Spending Plan.* County of Los Angeles. https://homeless.lacounty.gov/fy-2023–24-budget/

49. County of Los Angeles Homeless Initiative. (n.d.). *The Homeless Initiative Team.* County of Los Angeles. https://homeless.lacounty.gov/our-staff/

50. County of Los Angeles Homeless Initiative. (n.d.). *FY 2022–23 Budget.* County of Los Angeles. https://homeless.lacounty.gov/2022–2023-budget/

51. The Associated Press. (2024, April 9). *Audit finds California spent $24B on homelessness in 5 years, didn't consistently track outcomes.* CBS News. www.cbsnews.com/sanfrancisco/news/california-homelessness-spending-audit-24b-five-years-didnt-consistently-track-outcomes/

52. Nolan Hicks. (2019, February 10). *Shelter deemed unsafe for children—yet organizers have over $100M in public funds.* New York Post. https://nypost.com/2019/02/10/shelter-deemed-unsafe-for-children-yet-organizers-have-over-100m-in-public-funds/

53. Nolan Hicks. (2020, February 2020). *Kids endangered at non-profit's homeless housing: city records.* New York Post. https://nypost.com/2018/11/19/kids-endangered-at-non-profits-homeless-housing-city-records/

54. Expedia. (n.d.). *Find 5 Star Hotels in New York, NY.* Expedia. www.expedia.com/5Star-New-York-Hotels.s50-0-d178293.Travel-Guide-Filter-Hotels

55. Jennifer Friedenbach et. al. (2020, September). *Stop The Revolving Door.* Coalition On Homelessness. www.cohsf.org/wp-content/uploads/2020/11/Stop-the-Revolving-1.pdf

56. Doug Smith. (2023, September 14). *Can licensed tent villages ease California's homelessness epidemic? This nonprofit thinks so.* Los

Angeles Times. www.latimes.com/california/story/2023-09-14/california-homelessness-epidemic-licensed-tent-villages
57. Anna Scott. (2021, May 25). *High Cost Of Los Angeles Homeless Camp Raises Eyebrows And Questions*. NPR. www.npr.org/2021/05/25/999969718/high-cost-of-los-angeles-homeless-camp-raises-eyebrows-and-questions
58. Zillow Rental Manager. (n.d.). *Los Angeles, CA Rental Market [studios and one bedrooms]*. Zillow. www.zillow.com/rental-manager/market-trends/los-angeles-ca/?bedrooms=0
59. Liam Dillon, Ben Poston. (2022, June 20). *Affordable housing in California now routinely tops $1 million per apartment to build*. Los Angeles Times. www.latimes.com/homeless-housing/story/2022-06-20/california-affordable-housing-cost-1-million-apartment
60. Sarah Saadian, Steve Berg. (2023, February 13). *The Case For Housing First*. National Low Income Housing Coalition, National Alliance To End Homelessness. https://nlihc.org/sites/default/files/Housing-First-Research.pdf
61. Jennifer Perlman, John Parvensky. (2006, December 11). *Denver Housing First Collaborative Cost Benefit Analysis And Program Outcomes Report*. Colorado Coalition For the Homeless. https://housingis.org/sites/default/files/Supportive_Housing_in_Denver%20-%20Cost%20Benefit.pdf
62. Kelly McEvers. (2015, December 10). *Utah Reduced Chronic Homelessness By 91 Percent; Here's How*. NPR. www.npr.org/2015/12/10/459100751/utah-reduced-chronic-homelessness-by-91-percent-heres-how
63. Ryan Dwyer, Anita Palepu, Claire Williams, Daniel Daly-Grafstrin, Jiaying Zhao. (2023, August 29). *Unconditional cash transfers reduce homelessness*. PNAS Vol. 120, No. 36: e2222103120. https://doi.org/10.1073/pnas.2222103120

Chapter 3: The Pendulum of Development

1. Digital Scholar Lab. (n.d.). *Renewing Inequality. Family Displacements through Urban Renewal, 1960–1966*. University of Richmond. https://dsl.richmond.edu/panorama/renewal/#view=0/0/1&viz=cartogram&city=newyorkNY&loc=13/40.7065/-73.9706&cityview=pr&project=536
2. William J. Collins, Katharine L. Chester. (2011, September). *Slum Clearance and Urban Renewal in the United States*. National Bureau of Economic Research. Working Paper No. 17458. DOI: 10.3386/w17458. http://www.nber.org/papers/w17458
3. Robert A. Caro. (1974). *The power broker: Robert Moses and the fall of New York*. New York: Knopf.
4. Hilary Ballon, (2007). *Robert Moses And Urban Renewal. The Title I Program*. Robert Moses and the Modern City: The Transformation of New York. United Kingdom, WW Norton. 94–115

5. William J. Collins, Katharine L. Chester. (2011, September). *Slum Clearance and Urban Renewal in the United States*. National Bureau of Economic Research. Working Paper No. 17458. DOI: 10.3386/w17458. http://www.nber.org/papers/w17458
6. William J. Collins, Katharine L. Chester. (2011, September). *Slum Clearance and Urban Renewal in the United States*. National Bureau of Economic Research. Working Paper No. 17458. DOI: 10.3386/w17458. http://www.nber.org/papers/w17458
7. United States. National Commission on Urban Problems. (1969). *Building the American city : report of the National Commission on Urban Problems to the Congress and to the President of the United States*. United States: U.S. Government Printing Office.
8. Dumpson, J. R. (1960, February). *A changing city, new issues and new relationships*. Crisis Magazine, Vol. 67, No. 2, 72.
9. Robert A. Caro. (1974). *The power broker: Robert Moses and the fall of New York*. New York: Knopf. 890.
10. Digital Scholar Lab. (n.d.). *Renewing Inequality. Family Displacements through Urban Renewal, 1960-1966*. University of Richmond. https://dsl.richmond.edu/panorama/renewal/#view=0/0/1&viz=cartogram&city=newyorkNY&loc=13/40.7065/-73.9706&cityview=pr&project=536
11. Keith Williams. (2017, December 21). *How Lincoln Center Was Built (It Wasn't Pretty)*. The New York Times. www.nytimes.com/2017/12/21/nyregion/how-lincoln-center-was-built-it-wasnt-pretty.html
12. Emily Klein. (2017, December 27). *The Hill District, a community holding on through displacement and development*. Public Source. www.publicsource.org/hill-district-displacement-development/
13. Bureau Of The Census. (1953, July). *1950 Census of Population. Racial Composition Of The Population, For The United States By States: 1950*. U.S. Department Of Commerce. www2.census.gov/library/publications/decennial/1950/pc-14/pc-14-13.pdf
14. Andreas Georgoulias, Ali Khawaja. (2010, December). *Lower Manhattan Expressway*. Lower Manhattan Expressway
15. Rebecca Tuhus-Dubrow. (2017, February 3). *An Ad Hoc Affair. Jane Jacobs's clear-eyed vision of humanity*. The Nation. www.thenation.com/article/archive/jane-jacobss-radical-vision-of-/
16. Walter Carlson. (1964, May 9). *MOSES BELABORS CRITICS ON ROADS; 'Miserable Scribbler' and 'Candid Snapshot Taker' Attacked With Scorn; BUREAUCRATS ASSAILED; Message at Fair Calls for 50% Gasoline Tax Rise—Speech Read by Aide*. The New York Times. www.nytimes.com/1964/05/09/archives/moses-belabors-critics-on-roads-miserable-scribbler-and-candid.html

17. Jerusalem Demsas. (2022, April 22). *Community Input Is Bad, Actually.* The Atlantic. www.theatlantic.com/ideas/archive/2022/04/local-government-community-input-housing-public-transportation/629625/
18. Zumper. (2023, December). *Rent comparables in West Village, New York, NY.* Zumper. www.zumper.com/rent-research/new-york-ny/west-village
19. Property Shark. (2023, December). *West Village Real Estate Market Trends.* Property Shark, www.propertyshark.com/mason/market-trends/residential/nyc/manhattan/west-village
20. Jacob Anbinder. (2022, May 2). *What Historic Preservation Is Doing to American Cities.* The Atlantic. www.theatlantic.com/ideas/archive/2022/05/historic-preservation-has-tenuous-relationship-history/629731/
21. Gil Duran. (2022, June 16). *'Absurdity': San Francisco leaders stall SOMA housing project to preserve parking lot.* San Francisco Examiner. www.sfexaminer.com/archives/absurdity-san-francisco-leaders-stall-soma-housing-project-to-preserve-parking-lot/article_404ef58e-f31d-5961-815c-585645fc30ad.html
22. Greg Kamiya. (2021, July 9). *How S.F. neighborhood sprouted where horses once raced.* San Francisco Chronicle. www.sfchronicle.com/vault/article/How-S-F-neighborhood-sprouted-where-horses-once-16302613.php
23. San Francisco Planning Commission. (2000, June). *Ordinance designating 90 Cedro Avenue, the Joseph Leonard/Cecil F. Poole House, as Landmark No. 213 pursuant to Article 10 of the Planning Code.* City and County of San Francisco. File Number 000528. http://ec2-50-17-237-182.compute-1.amazonaws.com/docs/landmarks_and_districts/LM213.pdf
24. United States Census Bureau. (n.d.). Black Or African American Alone Or In Combination With One Or More Other Races. https://data.census.gov/table/ACSDT1Y2019.B02009?q=Black%20or%20African%20American&g=050XX00US06075_010XX00US&hidePreview=false&tid=ACSDT1Y2019.B02009
25. Census Reporter. (n.d.). Census Tract 309, San Francisco, CA. https://censusreporter.org/profiles/14000US06075030900-census-tract-309-san-francisco-ca/
26. Joan Ganau. (2008, July). *Reinventing Memories: The Origin and Development of Barcelona's Barri Gotic, 1880–1950.* Journal of Urban History, Vol. 34, No. 5: 795–832. 34(5):795–832. DOI:10.1177/0096144208315681
27. Daniel Herriges. (2019, June 12). *A City Shaped by Many Hands.* Strong Towns. www.strongtowns.org/journal/2019/6/11/a-city-shaped-by-many-hands

Chapter 4: Theory Has To Meet Reality—A Common Sense Way of Building

1. Joint Center For Housing Studies of Harvard University. (2024). *America's Rental Housing 2024*. www.jchs.harvard.edu/americas-rental-housing-2024.
2. Robert J. Shiller. (n.d.). *US Stock Price, Earnings and Dividends as well as Interest Rates and Cyclically Adjusted Price Earnings Ratio (CAPE) since 1871.* Shiller Data. https://shillerdata.com/
3. Loop Net. (2024, March). *Los Angeles Apartment Buildings for Sale*. www.loopnet.com/search/apartment-buildings/los-angeles-ca/for-sale/20/?sk=78b8a2c3f63df2ee763efbf9036467f7
4. Y Charts. (2023, December). *10 Year Treasury Rate (I:10YTCMR)* https://ycharts.com/indicators/10_year_treasury_rate
5. www.nmhc.org/globalassets/research--insight/quick-facts/apartment-investment/capitalization-and-treasury-rates.xlsx
6. Real Capital Analytics (2021). [Apartment cap rate data]. MSCI. Mwww.nar.realtor/blogs/economists-outlook/commercial-cap-rates-likely-to-keep-compressing-in-2022-despite-higher-interest-rates
7. Avalon Bay Statistics
    a. National Multifamily Housing Council. (2023). *2022 Rankings. NMHC 50 Largest Apartment Owners.* National Multifamily Housing Council. www.nmhc.org/research-insight/the-nmhc-50/top-50-lists/2022-top-owners-list/
    b. Companies Market Cap. (2023). *Market capitalization of AvalonBay Communities (AVB)*. https://companiesmarketcap.com/avalonbay-communities/marketcap/
8. AvalonBay Communities. (2022). *2021 Annual Report*. https://s1.q4cdn.com/777653952/files/doc_financials/2021/ar/2021-annual.pdf
9. Irina Lupa. (2019, December 16). *The Decade in Housing Trends: High-Earning Renters, High-End Apartments and Thriving Construction.* RentCafe. www.rentcafe.com/blog/rental-market/market-snapshots/renting-america-housing-changed-past-decade/
10. Laurie Goodman, Amalie Zinn, Kathryn Reynolds, Owen Noble. (2023, April). *A Profile of Institutional Investor—Owned Single-Family Rental Properties.* Urban Institute.
11. Michael Langemeier, Elizabeth Yeager. (2020, October 6). *Operating Profit Margin Benchmarks.* Purdue University Center For Commercial Agriculture. https://ag.purdue.edu/commercialag/home/resource/2020/10/operating-profit-margin-benchmarks/#:~:text=For%20farms%20that%20were%20in,profit%20margin%20was%2024.4%20percent.
12. Mahboubeh Jahantab, Babak Abbasi, Pierre Le Bodic. (2023). Farmland

allocation in the conversion from conventional to organic farming. European Journal of Operational Research, Vol. 311, No. 3, 1103–1119.ISSN 0377-2217, https://doi.org/10.1016/j.ejor.2023.05.019.
13. Ted Nordhaus, Saloni Shah.(2022, March 5). *In Sri Lanka, Organic Farming Went Catastrophically Wrong.* Foreign Policy. https://foreignpolicy.com/2022/03/05/sri-lanka-organic-farming-crisis/
14. Associated General Contractors of America. (n.d.). *Construction Data.* www.agc.org/learn/construction-data#:~:text=Construction%20is%20a%20major%20contributor,worth%20of%20structures%20each%20year.
15. Steve Sharp.(2023, September 20). *L.A. City Council approves $53M in funding for affordable housing near MacArthur Park.* Urbanize LA. https://la.urbanize.city/post/la-city-council-approves-53m-funding-affordable-housing-near-macarthur-park
16. Liam Dillon, Ben Poston. (2022, June 20). Affordable housing in California now routinely tops $1 million per apartment to build. Los Angeles Times. www.latimes.com/homeless-housing/story/2022-06-20/california-affordable-housing-cost-1-million-apartment
17. Jason M. Ward. (2021, August 2). *The Effects of Project Labor Agreements on the Production of Affordable Housing. Evidence from Proposition HHH.* RAND Corporation. www.rand.org/pubs/research_reports/RRA1362-1.html
18. Steve Lopez. (2022, March 5). *Spending $800,000 for a single unit of homeless housing is a red flag for L.A.* Los Angeles Times. www.latimes.com/california/story/2022-03-05/lopez-column-hhh-homeless-housing-costs
19. Sarah Stefanski. (2016, February). *The Impact of Prevailing Wage Requirements on Affordable Housing Construction in New York City.* New York City Independent Budget Office. www.ibo.nyc.ny.us/iboreports/the-impact-of-prevailing-wage-requirement-on-affordable-housing-construction-in-new-york-city.pdf
20. Rafael E. Cestero. (2020). *Prevailing Wage: A Price We Can't Afford.* Community Preservation Corporation. https://communityp.com/blog/housing-policy-legislation/prevailing-wage-a-price-we-cant-afford/
21. Turner Construction. (n.d.). *Cost Index.* www.turnerconstruction.com/cost-index
22. Erik Sherman. (2022, April 14). *Never Mind the CPI, the Construction Producer Price Index Is Really Soaring.* Globe Street. www.globest.com/2022/04/14/never-mind-the-cpi-the-construction-producer-price-index-is-really-soaring/?slreturn=20240226224310
23. Jenny Schuetz. (2021, January 14). *Four reasons why more public housing isn't the solution to affordability concerns.* Brookings. www.brookings.edu/articles/four-reasons-why-more-public-housing-isnt-the-solution-

to-affordability-concerns/#:~:text=Public%20agencies%20aren%27t%20 designed%20to%20be%20real%20estate%20developers&text=Public%20 agencies%20operate%20under%20more,more%20difficult%20and%20 more%20expensive.
24. U.S. Department of Housing and Urban Development. (n.d.). *HUD's Public Housing Program*. www.hud.gov/topics/rental_assistance/phprog
25. Michael Kimmelman. (2022, June 15). *How Houston Moved 25,000 People From the Streets Into Homes of Their Own*. The New York Times. www.nytimes.com/2022/06/14/headway/houston-homeless-people.html
26. Corianne Payton Scally, Amanda Gold, Carl Hedman. Matt Gerken, Nicole DuBois. (July 2018). *The Low-Income Housing Tax Credit Past Achievements, Future Challenges*. Urban Institute. www.urban.org/sites/default/files/publication/98761/lithc_past_achievements_future_challenges_final_0.pdf
27. Brian Balkus. (2022, June 9). *Why America Can't Build*. Palladium Magazine. www.palladiummag.com/2022/06/09/why-america-cant-build/
28. Pamela Blumenthal, Ethan Handelman, Alexandra Tilsley. (2016, July 26). *How affordable housing gets built*. Urban Institute. www.urban.org/urban-wire/how-affordable-housing-gets-built
29. U.S. Department of Housing and Urban Development. (2023). *2024 Budget in Brief*. www.hud.gov/sites/dfiles/CFO/documents/2024-Budget-in-Brief-Final.pdf
30. Statista Research Department. (2023, October 17). *Number of housing units and annual percentage increase in the United States from 1975 to 2022*. Statista. www.statista.com/statistics/240267/number-of-housing-units-in-the-united-states/
31. U.S. Census Bureau and U.S. Department of Housing and Urban Development. (2023). *Median Sales Price of Houses Sold for the United States [MSPUS]*, retrieved from FRED, Federal Reserve Bank of St. Louis; https://fred.stlouisfed.org/series/MSPUS.
32. Mark P. Keightley . (2023, April 26). *An Introduction to the Low-Income Housing Tax Credit. Congressional Research Service*. RS22389. https://sgp.fas.org/crs/misc/RS22389.pdf
33. Office of Policy Development and Research. (2024, April 12). *Low Income Housing Tax Credit (LIHTC): Property Level Data*. U.S. Department of Housing and Urban Development. www.huduser.gov/portal/datasets/lihtc/property.html
34. New York City Housing Authority. (2023, April). *NYCHA 2023 Fact Sheet*. www.nyc.gov/assets/nycha/downloads/pdf/NYCHA-Fact-Sheet-2023.pdf
35. Kathryn Brenzel. (2020, January 14). *NYCHA head: Agency now needs $40B in repairs*. The Real Deal. https://therealdeal.com/new-york/2020/01/14/nycha-head-agency-now-needs-40b-in-repairs/

36. Tatyana Turner. (2023, September 26). *NYCHA Faces Scrutiny For $78.3B Repairs Price Tag.* City Limits. https://citylimits.org/2023/09/26/nycha-faces-scrutiny-for-78-3b-repairs-price-tag/
37. Ashley James. (2021, October 7). *Opinion: It's Time to Finally Address the Health Risks of NYC Public Housing.* City Limits. https://citylimits.org/2021/10/07/opinion-its-time-to-finally-address-the-health-risks-of-nyc-public-housing/
38. New York State Department of Health. (2018, March). *Assessment of New York City Housing Authority (NYCHA) Properties.* www.governor.ny.gov/sites/default/files/atoms/files/FINAL_Assessment_of_NYCHA_Report.pdf
39. Nolan Hicks, Olivia Bensimon. (2019, July 19). *Elderly NYCHA tenants trapped in their homes for 13 days because of elevator.* New York Post. https://nypost.com/2019/07/19/elderly-nycha-tenants-trapped-in-their-homes-for-13-days-because-of-elevator/
40. Sam Raskin. (2021, December 19). *NYC tops own naughty lessor list for the 4th year in a row.* New York Post. https://nypost.com/2021/12/16/nycha-tops-own-worst-landlord-list-for-fourth-year-in-a-row/
41. Office of New York City Public Advocate. (2023). *Top 100 Worst Landlords Watchlist Overview.* Landlord Watchlist. www.landlordwatchlist.com/landlords
42. Office of New York City Public Advocate. (2023). *New York City Housing Authority.* Landlord Watchlist. www.landlordwatchlist.com/nycha
43. New York City Rent Guidelines Board. (2023, March 30). *2023 Income and Expense Study.* https://rentguidelinesboard.cityofnewyork.us/wp-content/uploads/2023/03/2023-IE-Study.pdf
44. U.S. Attorney's Office, Southern District of New York. (2024, February 6). *70 Current And Former NYCHA Employees Charged With Bribery And Extortion Offenses.* www.justice.gov/usao-sdny/pr/70-current-and-former-nycha-employees-charged-bribery-and-extortion-offenses
45. Greg B. Smith. (2024, February 26). *How Much Does It Cost NYCHA to Replace a Lightbulb? $708 in One Case.* The City. www.thecity.nyc/2024/02/26/lightbulbs-bribery-corruption-nycha/
46. Louise Hunt, Mary Schulhof, Stephen Holmquist. (1998, December). *Summary of Title V, Public Housing and Tenant-Based Assistance, of the Quality Housing and Work Responsibility Act of 1998.* Office of Policy, Program and Legislative Initiatives Office of Public and Indian Housing. www.hud.gov/sites/documents/DOC_8927.PDF
47. U.S. Census Bureau. (n.d.). *Quickfacts: New York City, New York.* www.census.gov/quickfacts/fact/table/newyorkcitynewyork/PST045222
48. CoreData.Nyc. (2023). *Belmont/East Tremont BX06 Neighborhood Indicators.*

NYU Furman Center. https://furmancenter.org/neighborhoods/view/belmont-east-tremont
49. NYU Furman Center. (2023). *State of New York City's Housing and Neighborhoods in 2023.*
50. Julie Satow. (2019, January 11). *Better Than the Powerball.* The New York Times. www.nytimes.com/2019/01/11/realestate/better-than-the-powerball.html
51. Richard Fry, Paul Taylor. (2012, August 1). *The Rise of Residential Segregation by Income.* Pew Research Center. www.pewresearch.org/social-trends/2012/08/01/the-rise-of-residential-segregation-by-income/
52. Patrick Sharkey. (2013). *Stuck in Place: Urban Neighborhoods and the End of Progress toward Racial Equality.* The University of Chicago Press.
53. George Galster, Patrick Sharkey. (2017). *Spatial Foundations of Inequality: A Conceptual Model and Empirical Overview.* RSF: The Russell Sage Foundation Journal of the Social Sciences, Vol. 3, No. 2, 1–33. https://doi.org/10.7758/rsf.2017.3.2.01
54. Opportunity Insights. (n.d.). *Neighborhoods Matter. Children's lives are shaped by the neighborhood they grow up in.* https://opportunityinsights.org/neighborhoods/
55. Brian J. Asquith, Evan Mast, Davin Reed. (2019). *Supply Shock Versus Demand Shock: The Local Effects of New Housing in Low-Income Areas.* Upjohn Institute Working Paper 19–316. Kalamazoo, MI: W.E. Upjohn Institute for Employment Research. https://doi.org/10.17848/wp19-316
56. Jonathan Jones. (2024). *Construction Coverage analysis of U.S. Census Bureau's Building Permit Survey and Population and Housing Unit Estimates data.* Construction Coverage. https://constructioncoverage.com/research/cities-investing-most-in-new-housing
57. Anthony Gardner. (2024, January 23). *The Rent Report January 2024.* Rent. www.rent.com/research/january-2024-rent-report/
58. Evan Mast. (2023). *The effect of new market-rate housing construction on the low-income housing market.* Journal of Urban Economics, Vol 133. https://doi.org/10.1016/j.jue.2021.103383
59. Karen Chapple, Jackelyn Hwang, Jae Sik Jeon, Iris Zhang, Julia Greenberg, Vasudha Kumar. (2022, March). *New Development for Whom? How New Housing Production Affects Displacement and Replacement in the San Francisco Bay Area.* Institute of Governmental Studies, University of California, Berkeley. www.urbandisplacement.org/wp-content/uploads/2022/03/IGS_1_New-Production_Brief_03.01.22.pdf
60. New York City Department of City Planning. (2019, November 7). Greenpoint-Williamsburg Community Update. www.nyc.gov/assets/planning/download/pdf/planning-level/housing-economy/greenpoint-williamsburg_19.11.07.pdf

61. Vicki Been, Ingrid Gould Ellen, Katherine O'Regan. (2018, August 20). *Supply Skepticism: Housing Supply and Affordability.* NYU Furman Center https://furmancenter.org/files/Supply_Skepticism_-_Final.pdf
62. Seairra Jones. (2022, September 13). *Main Street vs. Big Box Stores: A Western North Carolina Analysis.* Strong Towns. www.strongtowns.org/journal/2022/9/13/mainstreet-vs-chain-stores-a-western-north-carolina-analysis
63. Tischler & Associates. (2002, July). *Fiscal Impact Analysis of Residential and Nonresidential Land Use Prototypes*
64. Philip Mattera. (2011, February). *Shifting the Burden for Vital Public Services: Walmart's Tax Avoidance Schemes.* Good Jobs First. https://fitsnews.com/wp-content/uploads/2011/05/2011-Walmart-Shifting-The-Burden.pdf
65. David Halpern. (1995). *Mental health and the built environment: More than bricks and mortar?* Taylor & Francis.
66. Francisco Contreras Chávez, David Milner. (2019). *Architecture For Architects? Is There A 'Design Disconnect' Between Most Architects And The Rest Of The Non-Specialist Population?* New Design Ideas, Vol. 3, No. 1, 32–43. www.createstreets.com/wp-content/uploads/2019/09/Architecture-for-Architects-Milner-Salingaros.pdf
67. National Civic Art Society. (October 2020). Americans' Preferred Architecture for Federal Buildings A National Civic Art Survey Conducted by The Harris Poll.
68. Steven W. Semes. (2019, July 26). *Teaching Historic Preservation at Notre Dame.* Traditional Building. www.traditionalbuilding.com/features/teaching-historic-preservation-notre-dame
69. Pierluigi Nicolin. (1983). THE DEBATE "Contrasting Concepts of Harmony in Architecture". Lotus International 40.
70. Sarah Williams Goldhagen. (2017). *Welcome to your world: how the built environment shapes our lives.* New York, NY: Harper, an imprint of HarperCollins Publishers
71. Colin Ellard. (2015). *Places of the Heart: The Psychogeography of Everyday Life.* New York: Perseus Books, LLC.
72. Colleen Merrifield, James Danckert. (2014). *Characterizing the psychophysiological signature of boredom.* Experimental Brain Research, Vol. 232, 481–491. https://doi.org/10.1007/s00221-013-3755-2
73. Jan Gehl, Birgitte Svarre. (2013). *How to study public life.* Washington, D.C.: Island Press.
74. Peter Barrett, Yufan Zhang, Joanne Moffat, Khairy Kobbacy. (2013). *A holistic, multi-level analysis identifying the impact of classroom design on pupils' learning.* Building and Environment, Vol. 59, 678–689, ISSN

0360–1323, https://doi.org/10.1016/j.buildenv.2012.09.016.
75. Aenne A. Brielmann, Nir H. Buras, Nikos A. Salingaros, Richard P. Taylor. (2022). *What Happens in Your Brain When You Walk Down the Street? Implications of Architectural Proportions, Biophilia, and Fractal Geometry for Urban Science.* Urban Science Vol. 6, No. 1. https://doi.org/10.3390/urbansci6010003

Chapter 5: Why Does Everywhere Look The Same?
1. Justin Fox. (2019, February 13). *Why America's New Apartment Buildings All Look the Same.* Bloomberg. www.bloomberg.com/news/features/2019-02-13/why-america-s-new-apartment-buildings-all-look-the-same?embedded-checkout=true
2. Brett Christophers. (2023). *How and Why U.S. Single-Family Housing Became an Investor Asset Class.* Journal of Urban History, Vol. 49, No. 2, 430–449. https://doi.org/10.1177/00961442211029601
3. Brent W. Ambrose, Peter Linneman. (1998, March). *Old REITs and New REITs.* Zell/Lurie Center Working Papers 300, Wharton School Samuel Zell and Robert Lurie Real Estate Center, University of Pennsylvania.
4. Gregory H. Chun, J. Sa-Aadu, James D. Shilling. (2004). *The Role of Real Estate in an Institutional Investor's Portfolio Revisited.* The Journal of Real Estate Finance and Economics Vol. 29, 295–320. https://doi.org/10.1023/B:REAL.0000036675.46796.21
5. Orest Mandzy. (2020, December 18). *Institutional Investors Increased Allocation to Real Estate This Year, Remain Under-Allocated.* Trepp. www.trepp.com/trepptalk/institutional-investors-increased-allocation-to-commercial-real-estate-this-year-remain-under-allocated
6. U.S. Census Bureau. (2023). *Total Private Construction Spending: Total Construction in the United States [TLPRVCONS]*, retrieved from FRED, Federal Reserve Bank of St. Louis; https://fred.stlouisfed.org/series/TLPRVCONS
7. Jim Boyle. (2019, July 16). *Multifamily: From a Second-Tier Asset Class to King of the Hill.* Trepp. www.trepp.com/trepptalk/the-history-of-multifamily-from-a-second-tier-asset-class-to-king-of-the-hill
8. Philippa Maister. (2023, August 30). *Private Equity Investors Raised CRE Allocations in H1.* Globe Street. www.globest.com/2023/08/30/private-equity-investors-raised-cre-allocations-in-h1/#:~:text=Once%20again%2C%20public%20pension%20funds,to%209.52%25%20in%20H2%202022.
9. The Asset. (2022, May 20). *Global real estate AuM hits record US$4.7 trillion.* www.theasset.com/article/46778/global-real-estate-aum-hits-record-us47 trillion

10. Multiple Sources on estimate of institutionally managed real estate
    a. Alexander Carlo, Piet Eichholtz, Nils Kok. (March 1, 2021). *Three Decades of Global Institutional Investment in Real Estate*. Available at SSRN: https://ssrn.com/abstract=3802518 or http://dx.doi.org/10.2139/ssrn.3802518
    b. Property Funds Research, Institutional Real Estate, Inc. (2022). *Global Investment Managers 2022*. https://propertyfundsresearch.com/wp-content/uploads/2022/08/2022_PFR-IREI-REPORT-USDOLLARS.pdf
    c. Market Size Research Team. (2023, July). *The size of the professionally managed global real estate investment market in 2022*. MSCI. https://info.msci.com/l/36252/2023-07-25/xzrdbm/36252/1690294261EkCqzb02/Research___MSCI_2022_Real_Estate_Market_Size__2_.pdf
11. California State Board of Equalization. *(2024). Assessed Property Values, by City*. www.boe.ca.gov/dataportal/dataset.htm?url=PropTaxAssessedValueStateCountyIncorp
12. Property Tax Division. (2024, March). *2024 Property Values and Assessment Practices Report Assessment Year 2023*. Minnesota Department of Revenue. www.revenue.state.mn.us/sites/default/files/2024-03/2024-property-values-and-assessment-practices-report.pdf
13. Sources on the total value of West Coast Real Estate
    a. Oregon Department of Revenue Research Section. (2021). *Oregon Property Tax Statistics: Fiscal Year 2020–21*. Salem, OR: Oregon Department of Revenue.
    b. Department of Revenue Washington State. (2021). *Property Tax Statistics 2021*
14. Data sources for finding that 25% of multifamily starts are conducted by 25 builders.
    a. U.S. Census Bureau. (2024). *New Privately Owned Housing Units Started in the United States by Purpose and Design*. www.census.gov/construction/nrc/pdf/quarterly_starts_completions.pdf
    b. National Multifamily Housing Council. (2024). *2023 Rankings. NMHC 25 Largest Apartment Developers*. www.nmhc.org/research-insight/the-nmhc-50/top-50-lists/2023-top-developers-list/
15. Ibis World. (2024, July). *Housing Developers in the US—Number of Businesses*. www.ibisworld.com/industry-statistics/number-of-businesses/housing-developers-united-states/#:~:text=There%20are%2063%2C175%20Housing%20Developers,over%20the%20past%205%20years%3F

16. Eric Lynch. (2023, June 21). *Top 10 Builder Share Jumps in 2022*. National Association of Home Builders, Eye on Housing. https://eyeonhousing.org/2023/06/top-10-builder-share-jumps-in-2022/#:~:text=In%201989%2C%20the%20top%2010,2021%20and%2043.2%25%20in%202022
17. American Express. (2018, November). Small Business Economic Impact Study.
18. National Retail Federation. (n.d.). *Small Business Insights*. https://nrf.com/topics/small-business#:~:text=The%20overwhelming%20majority%20of%20retailers,employing%20fewer%20than%2050%20people
19. Philip Smith. (2023, July 13). *Number of retail establishments in the United States from 2015 to 2022*. Statista. www.statista.com/statistics/1079239/brick-and-mortar-retail-store-count-us/
20. Chain Store Guide. (2024). *Full Industry Location Datasets*.
21. Statista Chain Store stats (really should come from their 10k)
    a. Statista Research Department. (2024). *Number of Subway restaurants in the U.S. 2015–2022*. Statista. www.statista.com/statistics/469341/number-of-subway-restaurants-us/
    b. Philip Smith. (2024). *Dollar General: number of stores in the U.S. 2022, by state*. Statista. www.statista.com/statistics/1121086/number-of-dollar-general-stores-in-the-united-states-by-state/
    c. Statista Research Department. (2024). *Number of Starbucks stores in the U.S. 2005–2023, by type*. Statista. www.statista.com/statistics/218360/number-of-starbucks-stores-in-the-us/
    d. Statista Research Department. (2024). *Number of McDonald's restaurants in North America 2012–2023, by country*. Statista. www.statista.com/statistics/256040/mcdonalds-restaurants-in-north-america/
22. Godfrey M. Lebhar. (1952). *Chain Stores in America 1859–1950*. New York: Chain Store Publishing Corporation. https://ia904709.us.archive.org/26/items/chainstoresinameoolebhrich/chainstoresinameoolebhrich.pdf
23. Frank Hobbs, Nichole Stoops. (2002, November). Demographic Trends in the 20th Century. Census 2000 Special Reports. U.S. Census Bureau.
24. Economic Indicators Division, Retail Indicator Branch. (2024, January 17). *Advance Monthly Sales For Retail And Food Services, December 2023*. U.S. Census Bureau.
25. Economic Indicators Division, Retail Indicator Branch. (2023, February 17). *Quarterly Retail E-Commerce Sales. 4th Quarter 2022*. U.S. Census Bureau.
26. Technomic. (2023). *Top 500 Chain Restaurant Report*.
27. Kantar. (2023). *Top 100 Retailers 2023 List*. National Retail Federation. https://nrf.com/research-insights/top-retailers/top-100-retailers/top-100-retailers-2023-list

28. U.S. Census Bureau.(2023). *E-Commerce Retail Sales as a Percent of Total Sales [ECOMPCTSA]*, retrieved from FRED, Federal Reserve Bank of St. Louis; https://fred.stlouisfed.org/series/ECOMPCTSA
29. Tugba Sabanoglu. (2024). *Number of retail store openings and closures in the United States from 2017 to 2019*. Statista. www.statista.com/statistics/757160/retail-store-opening-closing/
30. Statista Research Department. (2022). *Retail space per capita in selected countries worldwide in 2018*. Statista. www.statista.com/statistics/1058852/retail-space-per-capita-selected-countries-worldwide/#:~:text=Retail%20space%20per%20capita%20in%20selected%20countries%20worldwide%202018&text=In%202018%2C%20the%20United%20States,and%2011.2%20square%20feet%2C%20respectively
31. Ibis World. (2023, November 27). *Small Specialty Retail Stores in the US—Number of Businesses*. www.ibisworld.com/industry-statistics/number-of-businesses/small-specialty-retail-stores-united-states/
32. Brendan Duke. (2024, March 18). *Entrepreneurship, Startups, and Business Formation Are Booming Across the U.S.* The Center for American Progress. www.americanprogress.org/article/entrepreneurship-startups-and-business-formation-are-booming-across-the-u-s/#:~:text=Nationally%2C%20the%20total%20number%20of,the%20pandemic%2C%202017%20to%202019.

Chapter 6: An Optimistic Foundation

1. Alain Bertaud. (2018). *Order without design : how markets shape cities*. MIT Press.
2. Bureau of Policy and Research. (2022, August). *BRINGING BASEMENT APARTMENTS INTO THE LIGHT: Establishing a NYC Basement Board to Provide Basic Rights, Responsibilities, and Protections for Basement Apartment Residents and Owners*. Office of the New York City Comptroller Brad Lander.
3. Hikari Hida. (2022, October). *A 95-Square-Foot Tokyo Apartment: 'I Wouldn't Live Anywhere Else'*. The New York Times. www.nytimes.com/2022/10/03/business/tiny-apartments-tokyo.html
4. Paul Emrath, Caitlin Sugrue Walter. (2022). *Regulation: 40.6 Percent of the Cost of Multifamily Development*. National Association of Home Builders, National Multifamily Housing Council.
5. Additional studies on costs of regulation on housing
    a. Paul Emrath, Caitlin Sugrue Walter. (2018). *Multifamily Cost of Regulation*. National Association of Home Builders, National Multifamily Housing Council.
    b. Joseph Gyourko, Raven Molloy. (2015). *Regulation and Housing*

Supply. Handbook of Regional and Urban Economics, Vol. 5: 1289–1337, Elsevier.

6. 2019. *Housing Constraints and Spatial Misallocation*. American Economic Journal: Macroeconomics, Vol. 11, No. 2. 1–39. DOI: 10.1257/mac.20170388.
7. Marcia Kaplan. (2015, December 2). *Sales Report: 2015 Thanksgiving Day, Black Friday, Cyber Monday*. Practical Ecommerce. www.practicalecommerce.com/Sales-Report-2015-Thanksgiving-Day-Black-Friday-Cyber-Monday#:~:text=Black%20Friday%20sales%20in%20physical,were%20open%20on%20Thanksgiving%20Day
8. Adobe Digital Insights. (2024, January). *Unboxing the 2023 Holiday Shopping Results*. Adobe.
9. Quoctrung Bui, Matt A.V. Chaban, Jeremy White. (2016, May 20). *40 Percent of the Buildings in Manhattan Could Not Be Built Today*. The New York Times. www.nytimes.com/interactive/2016/05/19/upshot/forty-percent-of-manhattans-buildings-could-not-be-built-today.html
10. Luisa Godinez-Puig, Sharon Cornelissen. (2023, May 8). *The Incorporation of New Cities Has Increased Racial Segregation in Metro Atlanta*. Joint Center For Housing Studies of Harvard University. www.jchs.harvard.edu/blog/incorporation-new-cities-has-increased-racial-segregation-metro-atlanta
11. Urban Kchoze. (2014, April 6). *Japanese zoning*. Blogspot. https://urbankchoze.blogspot.com/2014/04/japanese-zoning.html
12. Office of Planning & Community Development. (2024). *Seattle Municipal Code, § 23.30.010*. City of Seattle.
13. City of Seattle ArcGIS Online. (2024). Current Land Use Zoning Detail. Seattle GeoData. https://data-seattlecitygis.opendata.arcgis.com/datasets/SeattleCityGIS::current-land-use-zoning-detail/explore?location=47.613682%2C-122.329567%2C14.50&showTable=true
14. Mike Eliason. (2018, June 1). *What Is the Correct Percentage of Single-Family Zoning in Seattle?* The Urbanist. www.theurbanist.org/2018/06/01/correct-percentage-single-family-zoning-seattle/
15. Patrice de Moncan, Claude Heurteux. (2002). *Le Paris d'Haussmann*. Ed. du Mécène.
16. Georges-Eugène baron Haussmann. (1890). *Mémoires du baron Haussmann*. France: Victor-Havard.
17. Russell Kelley. (2021). The Making of Paris: *The Story of How Paris Evolved from a Fishing Village Into the World's Most Beautiful City*. United States: Lyons Press.
18. Peter G. Hall. (1998). *Cities in civilization* (1st American ed). Pantheon Books.
19. Donald J. Olsen. (1986). *The City as a Work of Art: London, Paris, Vienna*. United Kingdom: Yale University Press.

20. Lluís Permanyer Lladós. (2011). *L'Eixample: 150 anys d'història*. Spain: Viena.

Chapter 7: How To Create Better Communities

1. The Aesthetic City. (2022, March 25). *Mieke Bosse, Scala Architecten: The fundamentals of building*. Spotify Podcasts. https://open.spotify.com/episode/4wWyDJMyuGEBCDt4RBN9RQ?si=016893b6fa6245de
2. U.S. Census Bureau. (1902). *1900 Census: Volume II. Population, Part 2, Statistics of Population, Table 32, 334*.
3. Suzanne Spellen. (2010, April 29). *Walkabout: William H. Reynolds*. Brownstoner www.brownstoner.com/brooklyn-life/walkabout-trump/
4. Cynthia Danza, Doron Taleporos, Donald G. Presa. (2009, June 23). *Prospect Heights Historic District Designation Report*. New York City Landmarks Preservation Commission.
5. William H. Reynolds. (1899, April 16). *Why Can I Sell Houses at These Prices?* Brooklyn Daily Eagle.
6. Suzanne Spellen. (2015, April 10). *Building of the Day: 645 Carlton Avenue, Upscale Flats in Prospect Heights*. Brownstoner. www.brownstoner.com/architecture/building-of-the-day-645-carlton-avenue-upscale-flats-in-prospect-heights/
7. N.A. (1941, December 7). *Flatbush—Priced for quick sale*. Brooklyn Eagle, 40.
8. Multiple Texts
    a. Asher Benjamin. (1806). *The American Builder's Companion*. Boston: Etheridge and Bliss.
    b. Minard Lafever. (1841). *The Modern Builders' Guide*. United States: W.D. Smith.
    c. Andrew Jackson Downing, Alexander Jackson Davis. (1842). Cottage Residences. New York: Wiley & Putnam.
9. RIBA. (2018, February 7). Pattern books: *Creating the Georgian ideal*. Architecture.com www.architecture.com/knowledge-and-resources/knowledge-landing-page/pattern-books-creating-the-georgian-ideal
10. Joni Floyd. (2023). *Kit Houses*. University of Maryland University Libraries. https://lib.guides.umd.edu/kithouses
11. Vitruvius. (1914). *Ten Books on Architecture*. (; M. H. Morgan, Translator.). Dover Publications.
12. Library of Congress. (n.d.). *Thomas Jefferson's Library. The Architecture of A. Palladio* www.loc.gov/exhibits/thomas-jeffersons-library/interactives/palladio-architecture/
13. James Gibbs. (1728). A Book of Architecture: Containing Designs of Buildings and Ornaments. United Kingdom: William Bowyer.
14. Zillow property sales
    a. Zillow. (2023). *2622 S 12th St, Saint Louis,*

MO 63118 [Listing]. www.zillow.com/homedetails/2622-S-12th-St-Saint-Louis-MO-63118/2935388_zpid/
   b. Zillow. (2023). *13 Westmoreland Pl, Saint Louis, MO 63108 [Listing].* www.zillow.com/homedetails/13-Westmoreland-Pl-Saint-Louis-MO-63108/2989558_zpid/
15. Richard Walker. (1995, January). *Landscape and City Life: Four Ecologies of Residence in the San Francisco Bay Area.* Ecumene, 1995, Vol. 2, No. 1.
16. Urban Development Associates. (n.d.). Wheeling Heights Affordable Housing. www.urbandesignassociates.com/wheelingheights
17. U.S. Department of Housing and Urban Development. (1999, August 31). *CUOMO ANNOUNCES $17.1 MILLION HOPE VI GRANT TO WHEELING, WV TO TRANSFORM PUBLIC HOUSING AND HELP RESIDENTS.* HUD Archives: News Releases.
18. Leah Sottile. (2016, September 21). *Maverick Portland Developer Kevin Cavenaugh Builds Diamonds of Design in the Urban Rough.* Portland Monthly. www.pdxmonthly.com/home-and-real-estate/2016/09/maverick-portland-developer-kevin-cavenaugh-builds-diamonds-of-design-in-the-urban-rough
19. ULI Case Studies. (n.d.). *Deal Profile: Jolene's First Cousin.* Urban Land Institute. https://casestudies.uli.org/deal-profile-jolenes-first-cousin/
20. Zillow. (2023). *353 State St, Brooklyn, NY 11217 [Listing].* www.zillow.com/homedetails/353-State-St-Brooklyn-NY-11217/109171599_zpid/
21. Nancy A. Ruhling. (2018, July 11). *Fairfax & Sammons Architects' Traditional-Style Townhouses.* Period Homes. www.period-homes.com/palladio-awards/traditional-style-townhouses
22. Office of the City Register. (n.d.). *ACRIS Property Records.* New York City Department of Finance.
23. Le Corbusier. (1929). *The City of To-morrow and Its Planning,* 154–156. United Kingdom: J. Rodker.
24. Georges-Eugène baron Haussmann. (1888). *Confession d'un lion devenu vieux.* Published anonymously by Haussmann in Paris.

Chapter 8: What Better Communities Look Like (And What They Do Not Look Like)

1. Fitch Wire. (2023, December 21). *US Commercial Real Estate Deterioration to Increase in 2024, Led by Office.* Fitch Ratings. www.fitchratings.com/research/insurance/us-commercial-real-estate-deterioration-to-increase-in-2024-led-by-office-21-12-2023#:~:text=Note%3A%20YTD%20data%20through%20Dec,up%20from%2012.2%25%20at%20YE19
2. Thomas Brosy. (2023, August 22). *The Future Of Commercial Real Estate*

And Big City Budgets. Tax Policy Center www.taxpolicycenter.org/taxvox/
future-commercial-real-estate-and-big-city-budgets#:~:text=Of%20
the%2012%20major%20cities,reliance%20on%20commercial%20
property%20taxes.

3. Lynn Pollack. (2022, June 23). *For the First Time CBD and Suburban Office Vacancies are the Same*. Globe Street www.globest.com/2022/06/23/for-the-first-time-cbd-and-suburban-office-vacancies-are-the-same/?slreturn=20240528-12657

4. Office of the Surgeon General. (2023). *Our Epidemic of Loneliness and Isolation. The U.S. Surgeon General's Advisory on the Healing Effects of Social Connection and Community.* Department of Health and Human Services.

5. Teaching with Historic Places program. (n.d.). *Carnegie Libraries: The Future Made Bright.* National Park Service. www.nps.gov/articles/carnegie-libraries-the-future-made-bright-teaching-with-historic-places.htm#:~:text=One%20of%2019th%2Dcentury%20industrialist,large%20and%20small%20across%20America

6. Roger S. Ulrich. (1984). *View through a window may influence recovery from surgery.* Science, Vol. 224, No. 4647:420–1. doi: 10.1126/science.6143402. PMID: 6143402.

7. Steven Malanga. (2015). *Boardwalk Vampire.* City Journal. www.city-journal.org/article/boardwalk-vampire#:~:text=Atlantic%20City%20wasn%27t%20the,areas%2C%20and%20blew%20the%20chance

8. Atlantic City Public Schools expenditures per student, sources:
    a. Christopher Doyle. (2023, March 19). With a boat in state aid Atlantic City Board of Education unveils $287 million budget. The Press of Atlantic City https://pressofatlanticcity.com/news/local/with-a-boost-in-state-aid-atlantic-city-board-of-education-unveils-287-million-budget/article_d13b95c8-c6a7-11ed-aa42-cf80ef9d08c0.html
    b. Melanie Hanson.(2024, July 14). *U.S. Public Education Spending Statistics.* Education Data Interactive. https://educationdata.org/public-education-spending-statistics

9. New Jersey Business Magazine. (2023, February 28). *Atlantic City Convention Center Improving Customer Experience in 2023.* https://njbmagazine.com/njb-news-now/atlantic-city-convention-center-improving-customer-experience-in-2023/

10. Wayne Parry. (2018, January 8). *Former Revel casino in Atlantic City is sold.* 6 ABC. https://6abc.com/new-jersey-news-bruce-deifik-atlantic-city-casino-revel/2912522/

11. Chris Fry. (2023, May 15). *Stockton University Opens New*

Residence Hall in Atlantic City. Jersey Digs. https://jerseydigs.com/stockton-university-residence-hall-atlantic-city/

Chapter 9. Why Are Some Places More Optimistic Than Others?
Charleston

1. Preservation Society of Charleston. (n.d). About. www.preservationsociety.org/about/
2. The New York Preservation Archive Project. (n.d.). *The Old and Historic Charleston District.* www.nypap.org/preservation-history/the-old-and-historic-charleston-district/
3. Preservation Administration. (2022, February 3). *68th Carolopolis Award Winners Announced.* Preservation Society of Charleston. www.preservationsociety.org/68th-carolopolis-award-winners-announced/
4. Clement Bellet, Jan-Emmanuel De Neve, George Ward. (October 14, 2019). *Does Employee Happiness have an Impact on Productivity?* Saïd Business School WP 2019-13, http://dx.doi.org/10.2139/ssrn.3470734
5. Witold Rybczynski. (2019). *Charleston Fancy: Little Houses and Big Dreams in the Holy City.* Yale University Press.
6. Vince Graham. (2009, January). Comment on *Density, Walkability, Objectivism, and Orthodoxy.* Things I Think About. https://rub-a-dub.blogspot.com/2009/01/density-walkability-objectivism-and.html?showComment=1232246340000#c2208872509160128093
7. Zillow. (2024). *Listings of Homes for Sale in I'On, Mount Pleasant, South Carolina.* www.zillow.com/mount-pleasant-sc/ion_att/
8. Bevan & Liberatos. (n.d). *Guiding Growth in Charleston's Historic District.* Civic Conservation. www.civicconservation.org/casestudy
9. RAMSA. (2019). Courier Square. www.ramsa.com/projects/project/courier-square
10. Hotel Bennett. (2024, September). Booking Rates as of September, 2024. www.hotelbennett.com/offers/?nck=8447945977&gclid=CjoKCQiAhc-sBhCEARIsAOVwHuRuD1b37qIonDeL2nSExmW-4u5hLI-DeSvUdc-aVAUeKMfOXuAZPl4aAlC7EALw_wcB&gclsrc=aw.ds
11. Robert Behre. (2015, April 30). *Mayor Riley honored for national design leadership.* The Post and Courier. www.postandcourier.com/archives/mayor-riley-honored-for-national-design-leadership/article_a55206db-7860-5354-b339-f1170db49afc.html
12. Witold Rybczynski. (2019). *Charleston Fancy: Little Houses and Big Dreams in the Holy City.* Yale University Press, 39.
13. American College Of The Building Arts. (n.d). *Degree Programs.* https://acba.edu/arts-and-sciences

14. Witold Rybczynski. (2019). *Charleston Fancy: Little Houses and Big Dreams in the Holy City*. Yale University Press.

Santa Barbara

1. Michael Redmon. (2014, May 1). Bernhard Hoffmann. The Father of Architectural Planning in Santa Barbara. Santa Barbara Independent. www.independent.com/2014/05/01/bernhard-hoffmann/
2. Ellen K. Knowles. (2011). A Unifying Vision: Improvement, Imagination and Bernhard Hoffmann in Stockbridge (New England) and Santa Barbara (New Spain). ProQuest Dissertations & Theses
3. Roxanne M. Barker. (1997, Spring). *Small Town Progressivism: Pearl Chase and Female Activism in Santa Barbara, California, 1911–1918*. Southern California Quarterly Vol. 79, No. 1, 49.
4. Lee Michelle August Simpson. (1996). *Selling the City: Women and the California City Growth Game*. University of California, Riverside.
5. Ray Lyman Wilbur. (1931). *The Better Homes Manual, Preface*. Better Homes In America. Chicago: The University of Chicago Press.
6. Florence Christman. (1969). *The Romance of Balboa Park*, 43. United States: Neyenesch Printers, 43.
7. *Carleton Winslow, Sr. Papers*. ((1910–1946 (bulk 1935–1945)). Processed by Ken Kenyon and Nancy E. Loe, 2009; encoded by Byte Managers, 2009, Special Collections Department California Polytechnic State University.
8. Carleton Monroe Winslow, Clarence S. Stein. (1916). *The Architecture and the Gardens of the San Diego Exposition: A Pictorial Survey of the Aesthetic Features of the Panama California International Exposition*. United States: P. Elder.
9. Austin Whittlesey. (1917). *The Minor Ecclesiastical, Domestic, and Garden Architecture of Southern Spain*. United States: Architectural Book Publishing Company.
10. Hilda Blanco. (2000). *Style Matters: The Case of Santa Barbara*. Places, Vol. 13, No. 2.
11. Chesterton, G. K. (1908). *Orthodoxy*, 123. United Kingdom: Dodd, Mead,.
12. Michael Seabaugh.(2009, June 25). Jeff Shelton, *Santa Barbara's Architectural Wizard*. Santa Barbara Independent. www.independent.com/2009/06/25/jeff-shelton-santa-barbaras-architectural-wizard/
13. Rebecca L. Rhoades. (2019, April 8). *Dream Weaver*. Phoenix Home + Garden. www.phgmag.com/dream-weaver/
14. Michael Seabaugh.(2009, June 25). Jeff Shelton, *Santa Barbara's Architectural Wizard*. Santa Barbara Independent. www.independent.com/2009/06/25/jeff-shelton-santa-barbaras-architectural-wizard/
15. Charlotte Beach. (2022, August 25). *Architect Jeff Shelton Brings His Wildest*

Dreams to Life on the Streets of Santa Barbara. Print Magazine. www. printmag.com/designer-interviews/jeff-shelton/

16. Charlotte Beach. (2022, August 25). *Architect Jeff Shelton Brings His Wildest Dreams to Life on the Streets of Santa Barbara*. Print Magazine. www. printmag.com/designer-interviews/jeff-shelton/
17. Zillow Home Value Index. (2023, December). *Santa Barbara, CA Housing Market*. Zillow. www.zillow.com/home-values/13712/santa-barbara-ca/
18. Rents for selected HACSB properties
    a. Housing Authority of The City of Santa Barbara. (n.d.). *Casa de Las Fuentes*. https://hacsb.org/properties/casa-de-las-fuentes/
    b. Housing Authority of The City of Santa Barbara. (n.d.). *Artisan Court*. https://hacsb.org/properties/artisan-court/
    c. Housing Authority of The City of Santa Barbara. (n.d.). *El Carrillo*. https://hacsb.org/properties/el-carillo/
19. Housing Authority of the City of Santa Barbara. (2022). *2022 Annual Report*.
20. Zillow Rental Manager. (2023, December). *Santa Barbara, CA Rental Market*. Zillow. www.zillow.com/rental-manager/market-trends/santa-barbara-ca/?bedrooms=1
21. Housing Authority of the City of Santa Barbara. (n.d.). *An Applicant's Guide To The Waiting Lists*, where 5,000 households are waiting for assistance.
22. Matt Construction. (2017, November 7). *Grand Opening: Lavish Hotel Californian Anchors Santa Barbara's El Pueblo Viejo*. www.mattconstruction.com/blog/restoration-reuse/hotel-californian/
23. Hilda Blanco. (2000). *Style Matters: The Case of Santa Barbara*. Places, Vol. 13, No. 2.
24. Craig Nakano. (2006, January 19). *Pushing the city's limits*. Los Angeles Times. www.latimes.com/archives/la-xpm-2006-jan-19-hm-shelton19-story.html
25. Seattle For Everyone. (n.d.). Seattle Design Review: Public Statement & Program Recommendations. https://seattleforeveryone.org/2021/09/20/design-review-statement-and-reform-recommendations-from-s4e-workgroup/#:~:text=Design%20Review%20is%20a%20locally,specific%20guidelines%20by%20volunteer%20boards
26. Andrew Engelson. (2022, May 3). *Is It Time for Seattle to Do Away With Design Review?* Publicola. https://publicola.com/2022/05/03/is-it-time-for-seattle-to-do-away-with-design-review/

Portland

1. Planning and development. (2023, August 3). *Urban growth boundary*. Metro. www.oregonmetro.gov/urban-growth-boundary
2. Timothy Kea, Senior Financial Analyst Budget & Grants Department. (2022,

August 1). *June 2022 Monthly Performance Report (Includes FY22 Summary)*. TriMet. https://trimet.org/about/pdf/2022/June%202022%20MPR.pdf
3. Nick Christensen. (2015, May 21). *Urban growth review: A Q&A on the region's urban growth boundary.* Metro. www.oregonmetro.gov/news/urban-growth-review-qa-regions-urban-growth-boundary
4. Rolf Pendall, Jonathan Martin. (2002, August). *Holding The Line: Urban Containment In The United States.* The Brookings Institution Center on Urban and Metropolitan Policy.
5. U.S. Census Bureau. (n.d.). *Quickfacts: Multnomah County, Oregon; United States; Portland city, Oregon.* www.census.gov/quickfacts/fact/table/multnomahcountyoregon,US,portlandcityoregon/PST045223
    a. Data for calculating price to income ratios for various cities.
    b. Statista Research Department. (2024, April 17). *Median price of existing homes in the United States from 3rd quarter 2017 to 4th quarter 2023 with forecast until 2025.* Statista www.statista.com/statistics/272776/median-price-of-existing-homes-in-the-united-states-from-2011/
6. Gloria Guzman, Melissa Kollar. (2023, September 12). *Income in the United States: 2022, Report No. P60–279.* U.S. Census Bureau.
7. Alan Durning. (2013, March 12). *Nothing ADU-ing.* Sightline Institute. www.sightline.org/2013/03/12/nothing-adu-ing/
8. Lina Menard. (2016, March 4). *How Portland Became ADU-Friendly (And How Your City Can, Too).* AccessoryDwellings.org https://accessorydwellings.org/2016/03/04/how-portland-became-adu-friendly/
9. U.S. Census Bureau. (2018). *New Privately Owned Housing Units Authorized Unadjusted Units by Metropolitan Area.* www.census.gov/construction/bps/txt/tb3u2018.txt
10. Emily Badger, Quoctrung Bui. (2019, June 18). *Cities Start to Question an American Ideal: A House With a Yard on Every Lot.* The New York Times. www.nytimes.com/interactive/2019/06/18/upshot/cities-across-america-question-single-family-zoning.html
11. Eli Spevak. (2014, February 14). *Letter to Portland Bureau of Planning and Sustainability Director Susan Anderson.* Sightline Institute. www.sightline.org/wp-content/uploads/2020/08/Code-Updates-to-Meet-Portlands-Future-Housing-Needs.pdf
12. Orange Splot. (n.d.). *Staff.* www.orangesplot.net/staff/
13. Planning and Community Development Department. (n.d.). *Bungalow Courts in Pasadena.* City of Pasadena. www.cityofpasadena.net/planning/planning-division/design-and-historic-preservation/historic-preservation/projects-studies/bungalow-courts-in-pasadena/

14. Ross Chapin. (n.d.). *Codes for Courtyards*. PocketNeighborhoods.net www.pocket-neighborhoods.net/blog/codes-for-courtyards/
15. PocketNeighborhoods.net. (n.d.). *About. Beginnings*. https://pocket-neighborhoods.net/beginnings.html
16. Orange Splot. (n.d.). Ruth's Garden Cottages www.orangesplot.net/ruths-garden-cottages/
17. Sarah Mirk. (2008, October 2). *Hot Houses*. Portland Mercury. https://web.archive.org/web/20200925235343/www.portlandmercury.com/portland/hot-houses/Content?oid=910298
18. Michael Andersen. (2020, August 11). *Portland just passed the best low-density zoning reform in US history*. Sightline Institute. www.sightline.org/2020/08/11/on-wednesday-portland-will-pass-the-best-low-density-zoning-reform-in-us-history/
19. Michael Andersen. (2019, June 30). *Oregon Just Voted to Legalize Duplexes on Almost Every City Lot*. Sightline Institute. www.sightline.org/2019/06/30/oregon-just-voted-to-legalize-duplexes-on-almost-every-city-lot/
20. Bureau of Planning and Sustainability. (n.d.). *Residential Infill Project*. City of Portland. www.portland.gov/bps/planning/rip
21. U.S. Census Bureau. (2023). *Permits by CBSA (formerly Permits by MSA)*. www.census.gov/construction/bps/msamonthly.html
22. U.S. Census Bureau. (2001). *Table 26. Home Value: 2000. Summary Social, Economic, and Housing Characteristics*, Census 2000, 174.
23. U.S. Census Bureau. (n.d.). *Quickfacts:Portland city, Oregon*. www.census.gov/quickfacts/fact/table/portlandcityoregon/PST045222
24. Zumper. (2023). *Zumper National Rent Report*. www.zumper.com/blog/rental-price-data/
25. Wendell Cox. (2023, March 14). *2022 Residential Building Permits by Housing Market*. www.newgeography.com/content/007766-2022-residential-building-permits-housing-market
26. Owen Gabbert LLC. (n.d.). *The Village*. https://owengabbertllc.com/work#/the-village-21/
27. Open Door. (n.d.). *The Village*. https://opendoor.io/properties/village/
28. Zillow. (n.d.). *7579 N Berkeley Ave, Portland, OR 97203 [Listing]*. www.zillow.com/homedetails/7579-N-Berkeley-Ave-Portland-OR-97203/2083583056_zpid/
29. Portland Housing Bureau. (2023). *Median Income Percentages 2023 (effective 5/15/2023)*. City of Portland, Oregon. www.portland.gov/phb/documents/2023-income-and-rent-limits-phb/download
30. Portland Housing Bureau. (2023, February). *2022 State of Housing in Portland*. City of Portland, Oregon.

526 REFERENCES

31. ECONorthwest. (2021, March). *Implementing a Regional Housing Needs Analysis Methodology in Oregon: Approach, Results, and Initial Recommendations*. Oregon Housing and Community Services.
32. Parcel Development & Architecture, LLC. (n.d.). *About*. www.parceldevelopment.com/about
33. Zillow. (n.d.). *1732 NE 79th Ave, Portland, OR 97213 [Listing history]*. www.zillow.com/homedetails/1732-NE-79th-Ave-Portland-OR-97213/248434384_zpid/
34. Waechter Architecture. (n.d.). *Origami*. https://waechterarchitecture.com/Origami
35. Lever Architecture. (n.d.). *Albina Yard*. https://leverarchitecture.com/projects/albina_yard

Chapter 10. The Optimism of Universities

1. RAMSA. (n.d.). *Greenberg Conference Center*. www.ramsa.com/projects/project/greenberg-conference-center
2. James Gamble Rogers. (1921). *The Harkness Memorial Quadrangle, Yale University*. United States: Charles Scribner's Sons.
3. Office of Institutional Research. (2020, October). *Yale University Student Enrollment 1875–2020*. Yale University.
4. David Leonhardt. (November 1994). *On, or Off?* Yale Alumni Magazine.
5. Zainab Hamid, Ishaan Srivastava. (2017, September 13). *New colleges get more funds*. Yale Daily News. https://yaledailynews.com/blog/2017/09/13/new-colleges-get-more-funds/
6. Mikhail Zinshteyn. (2022, July 8). *How much student housing does $1.4 billion buy?* Cal Matters. https://calmatters.org/education/higher-education/2022/07/student-housing-affordable-dorms/
7. Fernando de Querol Cumbrera. (2024, August). *Average construction costs of educational buildings in the United States in 1st quarter of 2024, by city*. Statista. www.statista.com/statistics/830447/construction-costs-of-educational-buildings-in-us-cities/
8. Gordon H. Bock. (2020, November 12). *Robert A.M. Stern Designs New Colleges at Yale*. Traditional Building. www.traditionalbuilding.com/palladio-awards/new-colleges-yale
9. Jennifer Plant Johnston. (2018, February 26). *On the City's Western Border: $600 million living—learning initiative to transform campus along West End Avenue*. Vanderbilt Magazine. https://news.vanderbilt.edu/2018/02/26/on-the-citys-western-border-600-million-living-learning-initiative-to-transform-campus-along-west-end/
10. Simmons Studio. (n.d.). *Vanderbilt Martha Rivers Ingram Commons*.

11. Goody Clancy. (n.d.). *Vanderbilt University Warren & Moore Residential Colleges*. www.goodyclancy.com/project/warren-moore-residential-colleges/
12. Christopher Alexander, Sara Ishikawa, Murray Silverstein, Max Jacobson, Ingrid Fiksdahl-King, Angel Shlomo. (1977). *A pattern language : towns, buildings, construction,* 1108–1111. Oxford University Press.
13. Charles Linn. (2019, November 11). *Vanderbilt University E. Bronson Ingram College.* Architect Magazine. www.architectmagazine.com/project-gallery/vanderbilt-university-e-bronson-ingram-college_o
14. Vanderbilt University. (n.d.). *The Evolution of Carmichael Towers West.* www.vanderbilt.edu/futurevu/towers-implosion/
15. u/BaronRiker. (2019, May). Reddit. www.reddit.com/r/nashville/comments/br1eyl/it_looks_like_carmichael_towers_west_are_about_to/
16. Jennifer Plant Johnston. (2018, February 26). *On the City's Western Border: $600 million living—learning initiative to transform campus along West End Avenue.* Vanderbilt Magazine. https://news.vanderbilt.edu/2018/02/26/on-the-citys-western-border-600-million-living-learning-initiative-to-transform-campus-along-west-end/
17. Jason Gonzales. (2018, January 22). *Vanderbilt's $600 million capital project to change the face of West End Avenue.* The Tennessean. www.tennessean.com/story/news/education/2018/01/22/vanderbilts-600-million-capital-project-change-face-west-end-avenue/1044469001/
18. Edward Gunts. (2021, July 1). *Notre Dame's Thomas Gordon Smith, who led a revival in classical architecture, dies at 73.* The Architect's Newspaper. www.archpaper.com/2021/07/thomas-gordon-smith-dies-at-73/#:~:text=Serving%20as%20chair%20from%201989,like%2Dminded%20educators%20to%20campus
19. School of Architecture. (n.d.). *About.* University of Notre Dame. https://architecture.nd.edu/about/
20. Mackey Mitchell Architects. (n.d.). *Duncan Residence Hall.* www.mackeymitchell.com/projects/duncan-hall/
21. Facilities Design & Operations. (2016, May 17). *Dunne & Flaherty Halls Undergraduate Residence Halls.* University of Notre Dame. https://web.archive.org/web/20160720064641/http://architect.nd.edu/construction-information/undergraduate-residence-halls/
22. Allie Kirkman. (2019, October 14). *Five major Notre Dame construction projects you should know about.* South Bend Tribune. www.southbendtribune.com/story/news/education/2019/10/14/five-major-notre-dame-construction-projects-you-should-know-abou/46365817/

Chapter 11: Moving Beyond Utilitarianism: In Defense of Beautiful, Aspirational Places

1. Sarah Williams Goldhagen. (2014, July 17). *Let there be light: The forgotten genius of Louis Kahn*. Prospect Magazine. www.prospectmagazine.co.uk/culture/46528/let-there-be-light-the-forgotten-genius-of-louis-kahn
2. Alain De Botton. (2006). *The Architecture of Happiness*, 13. 1st McClelland & Stewart hardcover edition. Toronto: McClelland & Stewart.
3. TED. (2022, July 6). *The Case for Radically Human Buildings | Thomas Heatherwick | TED*. Youtube. www.youtube.com/watch?v=bhb0P5GGpys&t=31s
4. William Berry, LMHC., CAP.. (2019, July 21). *You Aren't Built to be Happy*. Psychology Today. www.psychologytoday.com/us/blog/the-second-noble-truth/201907/you-arent-built-be-happy
5. Lea Marie Reisch, Martin Wegrzyn, Friedrich G. Woermann, Christian G. Bien, Johanna Kissler. (2020). *Negative content enhances stimulus-specific cerebral activity during free viewing of pictures, faces, and words*. Human brain mapping, Vol. 41, No. 15, 4332–4354. https://doi.org/10.1002/hbm.25128.
6. Sources which informed estimates for annual visitors to the High Line.
7. Karen Matthews. (2019, June 9). *New York's High Line park marks 10 years of transformation*. Associated Press. https://apnews.com/general-news-home-and-garden-travel-and-tourism-5b372bcbbec24b5dbfb54bb766b23efe
    a. Michael Levere. (2014, December). *The High Line Park and Timing of Capitalization of Public Goods*. https://api.semanticscholar.org/CorpusID:130043418.
    b. Steven Heller. (2013, February 21). *Duplitectural Marvels: Exploring China's Replica Western Cities*. The Atlantic. www.theatlantic.com/entertainment/archive/2013/02/duplitectural-marvels-exploring-chinas-replica-western-cities/273366/
8. Rowan Moore. (2017, October 1). *The Bilbao effect: how Frank Gehry's Guggenheim started a global craze*. The Guardian. www.theguardian.com/artanddesign/2017/oct/01/bilbao-effect-frank-gehry-guggenheim-global-craze
9. Henry Grabar. (2021, June 7). *The Big Problem With Little Island*. Slate. https://slate.com/business/2021/06/little-island-new-york-city-barry-diller-thomas-heatherwick.html
10. Hudson River Park. (n.d.). *About Us*. https://hudsonriverpark.org/
11. Barry Diller. (2015, June 19). *Barry Diller and Diane von Furstenberg Pledge Letter*. Giving Pledge. https://givingpledge.org/pledger?pledgerId=189
12. The B1M. (2021, June 23). *The Battle to Build the Big Apple's Little Island*.

Youtube. www.youtube.com/watch?v=3bUMJxbpfJg&t=2s
13. Paul Goldberger. (2016, November 9). *How Thomas Heatherwick Became the Pied Piper of Architecture.* Vanity Fair. www.vanityfair.com/culture/2016/11/how-thomas-heatherwick-became-the-pied-piper-of-architecture#:~:text=He%20does%20not%20design%20the,of%20a%20new%20type%20of
14. Edwin Heathcote. (2017, January 26). *Age of the 'starchitect'.* Financial Times. www.ft.com/content/d064d57c-df01-11e6-86ac-f253db7791c6

Chapter 12. On Stewardship

1. Hannah Ritchie, Pablo Rosado, Max Roser. (2020). *Breakdown of carbon dioxide, methane and nitrous oxide emissions by sector.* OurWorldInData.org. https://ourworldindata.org/emissions-by-sector.
2. Franklin Associates. (1998, June). *Characterization of Building-Related Construction And Demolition In The United States.* The U.S. Environmental Protection Agency, Municipal and Industrial Solid Waste Division.
3. Arthur C. Nelson. (2004, December). *Toward a New Metropolis: The Opportunity to Rebuild America.* The Brookings Institution Metropolitan Policy Program.
4. Preservation Green Lab. (2011). *The Greenest Building: Quantifying the Environmental Value of Building Reuse.* National Trust For Historic Preservation.
5. Xuemei Bai, Hilda Blanco, Kevin R. Gurney, Şiir Kılkış, Oswaldo Lucon, Jin Murakami, Jiahua Pan, Ayyoob Sharifi, Yoshiki Yamagata. *Urban systems and other settlements.* In IPCC, 2022: Climate Change 2022: Mitigation of Climate Change. Contribution of Working Group III to the Sixth Assessment Report of the Intergovernmental Panel on Climate Change [P.R. Shukla, J. Skea, R. Slade, A. Al Khourdajie, R. van Diemen, D. McCollum, M. Pathak, S. Some, P. Vyas, R. Fradera, M. Belkacemi, A. Hasija, G. Lisboa, S. Luz, J. Malley, (eds.)]. Cambridge University Press, Cambridge, UK and New York, NY, USA. doi: 10.1017/9781009157926.010.
6. Brian Potter. (2021, December 17). *How to design a house to last 1000 years (Part I).* Construction Physics. www.construction-physics.com/p/how-to-design-a-house-to-last-1000
7. CMHC SCHL. (n.d.). *MLI Select.* www.cmhc-schl.gc.ca/professionals/project-funding-and-mortgage-financing/mortgage-loan-insurance/multi-unit-insurance/mliselect
8. Lawrence H. Summers. (2021). *Prologue: Symposium—Built Up: An Historical Perspective on the Contemporary Principles and Practices of Real Estate Development.* London: Routledge

Chapter 13. A Call to All Who Occupy the Built Environment

1. Janna Brancolini. (2021, October 7). *Buck the system: In Italy, old towns eager for new blood sell homes for about $1*. Los Angeles Times. www.latimes.com/world-nation/story/2021-10-27/italy-super-cheap-homes-one-euro
2. U.S. Census Bureau and U.S. Department of Housing and Urban Development. (2023). *Median Sales Price of Houses Sold for the United States [MSPUS]*, retrieved from FRED, Federal Reserve Bank of St. Louis; https://fred.stlouisfed.org/series/MSPUS.
3. Jonathan Knutson. (2018, May 9). *31 million acres lost: Development cuts into U.S. farmland*. Agweek. www.agweek.com/business/31-million-acres-lost-development-cuts-into-u-s-farmland
4. Michael Mehaffy. (2021, July 13). *Never mind NIMBY and YIMBY—it's time for 'QUIMBY' urbanism*. CNU Public Square. www.cnu.org/publicsquare/2021/07/13/never-mind-nimby-and-yimby%E2%80%93it%E2%80%99s-time-%E2%80%98quimby%E2%80%99-urbanism

www.ingramcontent.com/pod-product-compliance
Lightning Source LLC
Chambersburg PA
CBHW060447030426
42337CB00015B/1514